The Varieties of Spiritual Experience

The Varieties of Spiritual Experience

21st Century Research and Perspectives

DAVID B. YADEN
ANDREW B. NEWBERG

OXFORD
UNIVERSITY PRESS

OXFORD
UNIVERSITY PRESS

Oxford University Press is a department of the University of Oxford. It furthers the University's objective of excellence in research, scholarship, and education by publishing worldwide. Oxford is a registered trade mark of Oxford University Press in the UK and certain other countries.

Published in the United States of America by Oxford University Press
198 Madison Avenue, New York, NY 10016, United States of America.

Library of Congress Cataloging-in-Publication Data
Names: Yaden, David B., editor. | Newberg, Andrew B., editor.
Title: The varieties of spiritual experience : 21st century research and perspectives /
David B. Yaden, Andrew B. Newberg.
Description: New York, NY, United States of America : Oxford University Press, 2022. |
Includes bibliographical references and index.
Identifiers: LCCN 2021057775 (print) | LCCN 2021057776 (ebook) |
ISBN 9780190665678 (hardback) | ISBN 9780190665692 (epub) | ISBN 9780197627525
Subjects: LCSH: Experience (Religion) | Spirituality.
Classification: LCC BL53 .Y334 2022 (print) |
LCC BL53 (ebook) | DDC 204/.2—dc23/eng20220301
LC record available at https://lccn.loc.gov/2021057775
LC ebook record available at https://lccn.loc.gov/2021057776

DOI: 10.1093/oso/9780190665678.001.0001

Printed by Integrated Books International, United States of America

To my wife, Bit, whose love has been a transformative experience.
David B. Yaden

To my wife, Stephanie, who has always been a spiritual inspiration.
Andrew B. Newberg

Dedicated to Roland R. Griffiths for his seminal work on the science
of spiritual experience.
Andrew B. Newberg and David B. Yaden

Contents

Acknowledgments

The idea for this book is almost exactly a decade old and it took a little over five years to write. The scientific progress over this time has been so astounding that it has been difficult to keep up with the evolving research, scholarship, and standards. What we once considered a fairly fringe sub-field is now becoming mainstream. This development is cause for celebration for us and we suspect it would be for William James as well, were he alive to see it. While this progress has been impressive, we believe the need for William James's balanced and nuanced approach is more important than ever. As the field has become more visible, it has seemed to attract ever more extreme statements that often go well beyond the available data. We hope that James's insights in his original works and as we have tried to describe them in this book will help to temper statements from the super-enthusiasts and the super-cynics alike. In short, we are as grateful for James's foundational work as ever.

We want to acknowledge our families' patience for all the events on nights and weekends that we have missed while needing to write and for their essential love and support. For DBY, special thanks to parents David and Elizabeth, sister Heather, aunts/uncles, cousins, in-laws, and granny. For ABN, special thanks to parents Fred and Joan and daughter Amanda.

There are several people who have made the writing of this book possible through their understanding of certain deadlines along the way and their institutional support. These include Martin E. P. Seligman at the University of Pennsylvania (for DBY), Roland R. Griffiths at Johns Hopkins University School of Medicine (for DBY) and Daniel A. Monti at the Marcus Institute of Integrative Health at Jefferson University Hospital (for ABN).

Thank you to our literary agent, Jim Levine, for guidance and support, and editors Abby Gross, Nadina Persaud, and Reyman Joseph at Oxford University Press.

We are grateful to those who reviewed the text and provided feedback such as catching errors, suggesting missing citations, and contributing thoughts. These include: Roland R. Griffiths, Johannes Eichstaedt, Marianna Graziosi, Andrea Berghella, Jer Clifton, Eitan Scher, Vera Ludwig, Jonathan Iwry, Justin Barrett, William Richards, Wes Skolits, Michiel Van Elk, Bruce

Hood, George Vaillant, and Bit Yaden. We appreciate these contributions but of course any remaining errors in the text are ours.

Many people provided crucial insights during informal conversations. These include: Roland Griffiths, Fred Barrett, Albert Garcia-Romeu, Sandeep Nayak, Mary Cosimano, Matt Johnson, Manoj Doss, David Mathai, Chis Letheby, Brian Earp, Ryan Niemic, Martin Seligman, Tim Beck, James Pawelski, Bit Yaden, Jer Clifton, Kristopher Smith, Daniel Yudkin, Jessie Sun, Dan Haybron, Peggy Kern, Daniel Monti, Johannes Eichstaedt, Alejandro Adler, Derek Anderson, Melissa Kibbe, Emlen Metz, Dan Greene, Steve Marion, Doug O'Neil, Matthew Dermond, Matt Jakl, Jon Mecca, Dan Ledder, Chris Brodhecker, Ted Kinni, Kurt Spellmeyer, Heddy, Simon Burger, David Morgan and Sigma, Jonathan Haidt, Marianna Graziosi, Crystal Park, Ralph Hood, Lyle Ungar, Andy Schwartz, Spencer Greenberg, Justin McDaniel, Charles Stang, Dave Vago, George Vaillant, Josh Knobe, Kevin Rudd, Molly Crockett, Brenda Curtis, Paul Bloom, Laurie Paul, Laurie Santos, Miguel Farias, Peter Hendricks, Brian Muraresku, Susan Cain, Dacher Keltner, Scott Barry Kaufman, Tanya Luhrmann, Ann Taves, Michael Barlev, Phillip Corlett, John Medaglia, Roy Hamilton, Dean Zimmerman, David Chalmers, Julien Musolino, Michael Ferguson, Robert Wright, Tenzin Gyatso, Eugene d'Aquili (in years past). We deeply appreciate these discussions.

Lastly, we thank the scientists and scholars who have advanced, are advancing, and will advance our understanding of the experiences described in this book through careful, creative, and rigorous work.

PART I

THE SCIENCE
OF ALTERED STATES

1

Introduction

Toward a Science of Spiritual Experience for the 21st Century

In the midst of life's many ordinary moments, some experiences feel extraordinary. They can mark inflection points in one's life, after which one is never quite the same. Most brief experiences capable of making a long-lasting impact involve obvious changes in one's outward circumstances, like a birth, a death, a marriage, or an illness. Yet some life-changing moments seem to come wholly from another source, appearing as mental states or altered states of consciousness from either deep within a person's mind or, perhaps, a source beyond the self. These experiences have been called by different names over time: spiritual, religious, mystical, peak, or self-transcendent, and people around the world and throughout history have experienced them, up to and including the present day. The sacred texts of every major religion describe these moments, philosophers since the ancient Greeks have pondered them, and according to recent Gallup polls (2003), well over 30% of contemporary Americans have experienced them.

Consider the following accounts:

I felt myself one with the grass, the trees, birds, insects, everything in Nature. I exalted in the mere fact of existence, of being part of it all. I knew so well the satisfaction of losing self in a perception of supreme power and love. (quoted in James, 1902/2009, p. 299)

I lost the boundary to my physical body. I had my skin, of course, but I felt I was standing in the center of the cosmos. I spoke, but my words had lost their meaning. (quoted in Watts, 1957, p. 121)

I could no longer clearly discern the physical boundaries of where I began and where I ended. I sensed the composition of my being as that of a fluid rather than that of a solid. I no longer perceived myself as a whole object separate from everything. (Taylor, 2008, p. 42)

The Varieties of Spiritual Experience. David B. Yaden and Andrew B. Newberg, Oxford University Press. © David Yaden and Andrew Newberg 2022. DOI: 10.1093/oso/9780190665678.003.0001

People who have had experiences like these—whether they're a Christian experiencing God's presence, a Buddhist experiencing enlightenment, or a secular neuroscientist having a stroke (as respectively given in the just mentioned three examples)—often count them among the most meaningful moments in life (Yaden et al., 2017). Yet peoples' interpretations of these experiences widely diverge. Here William James (1902/2009, p. 292) was describing the experiences that are our subject:

> Our normal waking consciousness, rational consciousness as we call it, is but one special type of consciousness, whilst all about it, parted from it by the flimsiest of screens, there lie potential forms of consciousness entirely different. We may go through life without suspecting their existence; but apply the requisite stimulus, and at a touch they are there in all their completeness, definite types of mentality which probably somewhere have their field of application and adaptation. No account of the universe in its totality can be final which leaves these other forms of consciousness quite disregarded. How to regard them is the question—for they are so discontinuous with ordinary consciousness.

How *should* we regard these experiences? The author of the above quote—psychologist, physician, and philosopher William James—pondered this question in *The Varieties of Religious Experience: A Study in Human Nature* (1902). We are still searching for the answer. Yet, the specifics of the answer have certainly changed in the 122 years or so since he wrote those words. Given our advances in the sciences of brain, mind, and behavior over the past century and the diminished reliance on entirely religious explanations, how can contemporary people make sense of these experiences? Do such experiences still have validity and worth in an increasingly secular world? What has modern science revealed about these experiences? And how might we categorize these experiences in terms of their content and intensity? These are the questions that drive this book.

To answer these questions, we begin by returning to the foundational insights contained in James's *The Varieties of Religious Experience* (*The Varieties*, hereafter) (1902), an undisputed, if somewhat controversial, classic on the scientific study of these experiences. The book grew out of James's Gifford lectures, *The Varieties of Religious Experience: A Study in Human Nature*, which he delivered at the University of Edinburgh, Scotland in 1901–1902. The lectures attracted one of the largest audiences in the 14-year history of the Gifford lectures to that point, which included academics as well as the public. In the 19th century equivalent of a standing ovation at a TED talk, the audience sang, "For He's a Jolly Good Fellow" after James finished his last lecture.

The many written accounts of extraordinary religious and spiritual experiences that James included in *The Varieties* likely accounts for much of the continued fascination surrounding the book; it can feel like a voyeuristic journey into the psyche of people in the midst of some of their most meaningful moments. But its true brilliance comes from James's method. James approached spiritual experiences from the standpoint of empirical science, while putting aside metaphysical and theological questions surrounding these experiences. This is to say, he recorded and cataloged religious/spiritual experiences and described their psychological and physiological aspects largely *without speculating about whether or not they actually pointed to some religious/spiritual reality.*

The Varieties can be read in several different ways. For scientists, it provides a sensible rationale for conducting research on spiritual experiences. For religious scholars, it provides a contentious account of the origin and perpetuation of religions. For readers who have not had a spiritual experience, it provides vivid descriptions of some strange and spectacular mental states. For readers who *have* had a spiritual experience, it can be a source of great consolation, as these readers often come to realize that they are not alone or "crazy," which is unfortunately a common reaction caused, in part, by the social taboo around discussing these experiences. For us, *The Varieties* is not only a perennial classic but also a source of continual inspiration for future work in this area.

James largely succeeded in bringing out the many layers of personal meaning and scientific potential in studying spiritual experiences without making it clear whether he endorsed a supernatural or nonsupernatural worldview. In *The Varieties*, James maintains an essentially agnostic and even-handed approach throughout. Readers tend to feel that they are along for the ride of engaging in scientific and philosophical inquiry about a fascinating subject, rather than being sold a particular worldview (which is a more typical approach to this topic).

However, the epigraph to the book may provide some clues to James's ultimate sympathies: James dedicated *The Varieties* to his mother-in-law, Eliza Putnam Gibbens (E. P. G.). He did this, according to one biographer, out of an admiration and maybe even envy of her, "whose simplicity of faith, whose unquestioning belief in human immortality, psychical phenomena, and a vital world 'behind the veil' he so desperately wished he could share" (Simon, 1998, p. 297). Questions about James's personal beliefs regarding a spiritual side of reality is a topic that we will withhold, as James himself did in *The Varieties*, until revealing them toward the end of this book.

Notably, James opened *The Varieties* with a note of humility directed toward the eminent audience in attendance when giving his lectures in Edinburgh (though a professor at Harvard, the University of Edinburgh then carried more academic cachet). James (1902/2009, p 6). addressed his audience:

> It is with no small amount of trepidation that I take my place behind this desk, and face this learned audience. . . . Such juvenile emotions of reverence never get outgrown.

We wholeheartedly echo this sentiment of humility and direct it first back toward James himself, whose monumental reputation towers over our attempt to examine *The Varieties* and provide an update on relevant scientific findings and contemporary scholarly work. It is no small task to approach the work of a nearly universally acknowledged genius. According to philosopher John McDermott, "James's thought is the vestibule to the thought and values of the twentieth century" (2007, p. 146). For contemporary psychologist Steven Pinker, James was "one of the greatest writers in the history of modern English" (Toor, 2016).

We also direct a note of humility toward those scholars who have devoted their careers to the finer points of James's philosophy. While we conduct scientific research on the experiences described in James's *Varieties*, we are not scholars of James's life or his philosophical writings.

Additionally, we express humility toward those among our readers who may have had a spiritual experience. We know such moments are often so meaningful that they are can be held close to the core of one's identity. While some readers may feel uncomfortable with examining such intimate experiences in the light of scientific inquiry, our intention is to illuminate these experiences for the purpose of further understanding, not to diminish their value, a sentiment with which James would have wholeheartedly agreed.

In *The Varieties of Religious Experience*, James hoped to inspire future scientific work on "religious" experiences—an initiative he called the "science of religion." Due to the broad and nondogmatic way James handled these experiences, modern scholars have suggested that if James were to rewrite the *Varieties* today, he would opt for the more expansive title, *The Varieties of Spiritual Experience* (Miller & Thoresen, 1999, p. 7; found in Hood& Chen, 2005). We agree and have named the present work accordingly.

Religious experiences generally refer only to those experiences that involve content explicitly derived from a particular religious tradition. However, for our purposes, we would like to use "spiritual" to refer to not only religious experiences, such as a Christian seeing Christ, but also experiences that are not specifically religious in nature, such as feeling at one with all things. We are aware that some people and scholars may not agree with this usage, but we feel that "spiritual experience" can include all religious experiences as well as the large variety of other experiences that may be referred to in religious, spiritual, or even secular terms. We will see that a number of agnostics and atheists, such as Bertrand Russell, Sam Harris, and Barbara Ehrenreich, have had experiences that they refer to as "spiritual" or "mystical" despite their lack of supernatural beliefs. We will address the many meanings of spirituality, spiritual belief, and spiritual experience throughout this book.

We expand on James's work by including a diverse set of historical and contemporary accounts across traditions and cultures, rather than the more limited accounts that fill the pages of *The Varieties*. Several researchers have conducted surveys of spiritual experiences (James himself drew on the survey work of one of his students, Edwin Starbuck). We have conducted a number of surveys on spiritual experiences, and we include the results throughout this book. We have found this approach to be a valuable way to educate about the research process when it has been similarly described in books by other leading researchers on this subject, such as anthropologist Tanya Luhrmann (e.g., Luhrmann, 2012). In one survey that we conducted for this book, called the Varieties Survey, we gathered data on around 500 individuals; the data include their demographic information, religious and spiritual history, religious practices, well-being, mental illness, and, most importantly, questions about their most intense spiritual experience(s). The sample was generally representative of the U.S. population and will provide additional empirical data to complement some of our comments throughout the book. (Note: The sample consisted of 461 subjects who provided complete data. This U.S. sample had more females than males [62.5% to 36.7%]; ranged from 18 to 71 years old, with an average age of 36; and was 81% White [6% Black, 5% Hispanic, 4% Asian]. The sample had all graduated from high school, and 66% had a college degree of some kind.) We also posted a website called The Varieties Corpus (https:www.VarietiesCorpus.com), where you can share your experience and read about other contemporary experiences.

In our data, we find that "spiritual experience" is the label that the largest percentage of participants prefer when describing the sorts of experiences James set out to study. Thus, the advice of contemporary scholars and our data converge on the term "spiritual." Going forward, we use the term spiritual experience when referring to all such experiences in general, although we introduce more specific terms as we progress.

Many other aspects of James's approach require updates or alterations after over 100 years of scholarship and scientific developments. However, we believe the core insights of *The Varieties* remain valuable, specifically those aspects of James's analysis that are phenomenologically sensitive, philosophically sensible, and scientifically oriented. We also intend to build our work on these foundations.

First, by *phenomenologically sensitive*, we mean the respectful curiosity James shows his subjects, those people who provided the written descriptions of experiences that he analyzes throughout *The Varieties*. James holds up the dignity of each individual report, never falling into condescension or detached objectification. James's approach would later inspire Edmund Husserl (Smith, 2013), who explicitly acknowledged James as an influence when he articulated "phenomenology" as a formal philosophical school that prioritizes subjective experience.

We follow in this approach by appreciating individuals' subjective experiences, regardless of whether we agree with their particular interpretations of their experience. We commend the bravery of every person who shared an experience that we include in this book, not only because these experiences are deeply personal and meaningful, but also because many people still reflexively view these experiences as indicative of mental illness—a view we intend to challenge throughout this book (while also acknowledging the nuanced relationship between some spiritual experiences and some mental disorders). For over 100 years, many physicians and psychologists dismissed spiritual experiences as merely symptoms of epilepsy or mental illness, but we think it is high time to change this perspective. James's work, as well as our own, is made possible by people who are willing to share some of their most meaningful and personal moments.

Second, by *philosophically sensible* we mean the way in which James "bracketed," or put to the side, the question of the ultimate metaphysical reality of spiritual experiences in order to examine them scientifically. Again and again James resisted the temptation to allow his own particular metaphysical beliefs to enter into his psychological and physiological investigations of spiritual experiences. James was less concerned with the *origins* of spiritual experiences—whether they come exclusively from changes in the brain or ultimately from a supernatural source—and was far more interested in their *outcomes*. That is, he focused on how such experiences impact people's everyday lives. Put more poetically, James advocated focusing on the "fruits" (outcomes) rather than the "roots" (origins) of spiritual experiences. This approach is in line with his philosophy of "pragmatism," which emphasized considering the effects of an action or belief when seeking to determine its value.

We follow this approach by attempting to take a metaphysically agnostic stance toward the question of whether spiritual experiences ultimately spring from a supernatural source. While we find this question fascinating from the standpoints of philosophy and theology, as we will discuss, there are few if any testable claims for science to address. Whether it is possible to ever find incontrovertible evidence that such experiences either are or are not supernatural in their origin is a question for the future that must be carefully evaluated and considered. Unfortunately, we find that some of our colleagues who have a metaphysical axe to grind can allow obvious biases to enter into their discussion of spiritual experiences. For example, religious researchers will sometimes claim that certain experiences "prove" the reality of a religious or spiritual doctrine, while atheist researchers will sometimes attempt to "prove" that spiritual experiences are mere delusions. Both of these biases can result in faulty reasoning and unsound science, as such conclusions are drawn from beyond what the data allow.

Third, by *scientifically oriented*, we mean that James brought his training in physiology and medicine as well as his foundational work in psychology to bear in his study of spiritual experiences. James repeatedly called for future research on the physiology and psychology of spiritual experience. James also anticipated a number of scientific findings related to spiritual experiences, such as some of their triggers, as well as the fact that spiritual experiences can exert positive, pathological, or mixed effects on the lives of those who report them.

Our aim in this book is to carry forward James's insights and fill in some of the empirical gaps of his speculations with decades of scientific work on spiritual experiences. In James's interdisciplinary spirit, we include findings from a number of fields, but as psychology, psychiatry, pharmacology, and neuroscience are our primary domains of expertise, we feature findings related to the brain, mental processes, and behavior.

In neuroscience, neuroimaging scanners now allow researchers to measure changes in the brain and body of people who are having spiritual experiences. This approach has been called "neurotheology," and Andrew Newberg is among the pioneers of this field (Newberg, 2010, 2018). This field studies the relationship between brain states and mental phenomena related to religion and spirituality, including spiritual experience. We feel that neurotheology can play an important role in the development and understanding of the varieties of spiritual experience. Thus, we hope to show not only the psychological nature of these experiences, but also their associated biological correlates. This multidisciplinary approach, we hope, provides a rich and comprehensive analysis of such experiences.

In psychology, an entire subfield is dedicated to the study of religious and spiritual beliefs, practices, rituals, and experiences (Division 36 of the American Psychological Association). We draw on findings from this field throughout this book. Yet another subfield in psychology, called positive psychology, founded by Martin Seligman and others is the scientific study of well-being and may be particularly relevant to the study of how spiritual experiences affect people's lives. Positive psychology includes, among a number of subjects, the study of mental states related to well-being, such as awe, love, and joy (Seligman, 2002). Previously, the dominant approach in psychology in terms of spiritual experiences was to study them as forms or manifestations of mental illness. Pathological aspects of spiritual experiences also exist, and have been described in the *Diagnostic and Statistical Manual of Mental Disorders* (*DSM*; American Psychiatric Association, 2013), and we discuss these connections in detail. But the positive aspects of such experiences are just beginning to be studied systematically. We consider both positive and pathological aspects of spiritual experience throughout this book. As we argue, the data show that spiritual experiences are surprisingly common and are usually not related to mental illness. On the contrary, spiritual experiences are often potent sources of well-being. Emerging research on psychedelic substances is testing whether such experiences can be harnessed for therapeutic purposes.

This book provides a tour through the contemporary science of spiritual experience and an overview of what James dubbed the "Science of Religions" as it appears in the 21st century. This tour takes us to the heights and depths of individual subjective experience as we investigate some of the most profoundly meaningful moments of some people's lives. Along the way, we peer into the inner life of a diverse group of people, as spiritual experiences occur in people from all belief systems—religious, spiritual, agnostic, and atheistic alike—from all over the world (Yaden et al., 2021).

This book is broken into three parts. Part I opens with the story of William James and the unique perspective that he brought to the study of spiritual experience. We then turn to his book, *The Varieties of Religious Experience*, to summarize its primary points and especially its emphasis on the study of experience over beliefs. Next, we explore the ways in which spiritual experiences are currently studied using modern scientific methods, looking at methods from psychology, psychiatry, psychopharmacology, and neuroscience. We then discuss common triggers, like spiritual practices, rituals, and, especially, psychedelic substances, each of which have been shown to increase the likelihood of having a spiritual experience. This part concludes with a preliminary consideration of the evidence about whether spiritual experiences exert a mostly positive, negative, or neutral effect on people's lives.

Part II focuses on the different types, or "varieties," of spiritual experiences. Here, we provide an evidence-based classification of spiritual experiences complete with historical and contemporary examples. First, we examine "numinous" experiences of divinity, or God, which involve a sense of communion with a greater kind of mind or spirit. Next, we cover "revelatory" experiences, visions, and voices that seem to come from beyond one's self and often relate to one's life purpose. We then examine "synchronicity," the sense that events and seeming coincidences have a hidden message. Next, we examine feelings of unity or oneness, which James broadly referred to as "mystical" experiences. We then explore "aesthetic" experiences, like awe and wonder, which almost everyone has felt to some degree with art, nature, or seeing someone exhibit excellence or moral courage. Last, we investigate "paranormal" experiences, moments when individuals seem to perceive a nonphysical entity (e.g., a seeming visitation from a deceased family member). Each type of experience is described in terms of its prevalence, triggers, and outcomes, as well as examples from people who report having had them. This part of the book functions as something like a field guide for identifying the various types of spiritual experiences one might spot in the wild—in one's family, friends, acquaintances, or oneself.

In Part III, we focus on interpreting and integrating these experiences. We begin by examining how people tend to treat their spiritual experiences as real (even somehow "realer than real"). We then turn to philosophical considerations around spiritual experience, such as whether we can determine if these experiences are real or illusory, and how some beliefs may change as a result of these experiences (as well as how some beliefs may change the nature of the experiences themselves). Next, we consider how such experiences are sometimes "transformative" and how such brief moments can exert lasting impacts on one's behavior and beliefs. We follow this with a chapter on the question of whether the positive impact of some of these experiences can somehow be harnessed for the purpose of therapeutic applications, with a special emphasis on emerging research on psychedelics. In the penultimate chapter, we consider whether the study of spiritual experiences has any relevance for the study of consciousness given that these experiences can temporarily change one's sense of time, space, and self. Finally, we offer some visions about the potential future of the scientific study of spiritual experience.

The aim of this book is to provide a contemporary, scientific guide to spiritual experiences. We aim to convey William James's insights while describing the state of the art of scientific research on meaningful, inner "spiritual experiences"—substantially altered states of consciousness involving a perception of, and connection to, an unseen order of some kind. We think that James would have been pleased to see this study taken up by other thinkers and scientists over the years. In fact, in the closing chapter of *The Varieties* James (1902/2009, p. 398) wrote: "But all these statements are unsatisfactory from their brevity, and I can only say that I hope to return to the same questions in another book." Unfortunately, James was not able to return to the topic in another book before his death. This book, we hope, picks up where James left off with the benefit of over a century's worth of scholarly and scientific work on the subject.

References

American Psychiatric Association. (2013). *Diagnostic and statistical manual of mental disorders* (5th ed.; *DSM-5*). American Psychiatric Association.

Gallup, G. H. (2003). *Religious awakenings bolster Americans' faith*. https://news.gallup.com/poll/7582/religious-awakenings-bolster-americans-faith.aspx

Hood, R. W., & Chen, Z. (2005). Mystical, spiritual, and religious experiences. In R. F. Paloutzian & C. L. Park (Eds.), Handbook of the psychology of religion and spirituality (pp. 348–364). Guilford Press.

James, W. (1902/2009). The varieties of religious experience: A study in human nature. *eBooks@Adelaide*. https://csrs.nd.edu/assets/59930/williams_1902.pdf

Luhrmann, T. M. (2012). *When God talks back: Understanding the American evangelical relationship with God*. Knopf.

McDermott, J. J. (2007). *The drama of possibility: Experience as philosophy of culture.* Fordham University Press.

Miller, W. R., & Thoresen, L. E. (1999). Spirituality and health. In W. R. Miller (Ed.), *Integrating spirituality into treatment* (pp. 3–18). American Psychological Association.

Newberg, A. B. (2010). *Principles of neurotheology*. Ashgate.

Newberg, A. B. (2018). *Neurotheology: How science can enlighten us about spirituality.* Columbia University Press.

Seligman, M. E. (2002). Positive psychology, positive prevention, and positive therapy. In C. R. Snyder & S. J. Lopez (Eds.), Handbook of positive psychology (pp. 3–12). Oxford University Press.

Simon, L. (1998). *Genuine Reality: A Life of William James*. University of Chicago Press.

Smith, D. W. (2013). Phenomenology. In E. N. Zalta (Ed.), *Stanford encyclopedia of philosophy*. Stanford University. https://plato.stanford.edu/entries/phenomenology/

Taylor, J. B. (2008). *My stroke of insight: A brain scientist's personal journey.* Viking Penguin.

Toor, R. (2016, August 1). Scientists talk writing: Steven Pinker. *Chronicle of Higher Education*. https://www.chronicle.com/article/Scholars-Talk-Writing-Steven/237315

Watts, A. (1957). *The way of Zen*. Pantheon.

Yaden, D. B., Giorgi, S., Kern, M. L., Adler, A., Ungar, L. H., Seligman, M. E., & Eichstaedt, J. C. (2021). Beyond beliefs: Multidimensional aspects of religion and spirituality in language. *Psychology of Religion and Spirituality*.

2

William James: A Study in Human Nature

> I am going to try to stick to the study of the nervous system and
> psychology.
>
> —William James

According to James, if you want to understand a person's beliefs, then
you should seek to learn more about that person's temperament and life
circumstances. In other words, to understand an individual's philosophy,
look to her or his psychology (Yaden & Anderson, 2021). Thus, we begin
with the story of William James's life and his influences to understand how
he developed the worldview and approach that he brought to *The Varieties of
Religious Experience: A Study in Human Nature* (*The Varieties*).

Becoming "Jamesian"

James's life was a study in contrasts. He became a scientist, but trained first as
an artist; he was a skeptic, but was fascinated by spiritual feelings; he hoped
to understand mental states in terms of physiology, but he defended the inherent value of individual subjectivity; he taught physiology for years, but
always argued *against* simplistic biological reductionism of mental events.
In the words of biographer Linda Simon: "He was a scientist with the disposition of a philosopher and a philosopher with the disposition of an artist"
(Simon, 1998, p. xvi).

   His career was slow to start. Yes, James would eventually become president of both the American Philosophical Association *and* the American
Psychological Association due to his monumental contributions to both
fields. But at 34 years old he was bedridden, unemployed, and living in his
parent's home. It took him 10 years or so to finish the manuscript of a book,
The Principles of Psychology, which provided the foundations of the new field

The Varieties of Spiritual Experience. David B. Yaden and Andrew B. Newberg, Oxford University Press. © David Yaden
and Andrew Newberg 2022. DOI: 10.1093/oso/9780190665678.003.0002

of psychology. In the note to his editor accompanying the final manuscript, he called himself "an incapable" (Richardson, 2006, p. 298). This could hardly be further from the truth.

James's thought is, like his life, not easy to summarize. Scholars of James point to numerous contradictions in his philosophical work—and the reconciliation of those ideas remains a major part of contemporary scholarship on James. Despite the kaleidoscopic perspective James brought to his work, he did eventually form a coherent and distinct scientific and philosophical approach that is frequently referred to as "Jamesian." This Jamesian approach—rigorously scientific yet humanistic, ever striving for scientific progress yet rejecting of certainty—has left a lasting influence on the modern fields of physiology, psychiatry, philosophy, religious studies, neuroscience, and psychology. According to scholar Cheryl Misak: "James was the most famous academic of his time, both at home and abroad" (Misak, 2018, p. 52). While his name is less known today, the impact of his thought is ubiquitous in these fields.

Many of James's early life influences can be traced throughout his later work. Thus, illuminating some aspects of his childhood may help us understand his motivation to write *The Varieties* and the scientific and philosophical perspectives he brought to the study of spiritual experience.

A Remarkable Family

To say James had an unusual childhood would be an understatement. His family has been described as "perhaps the most remarkable family the country has ever known in terms of its literary and intellectual accomplishments" (Lewis, 1991, p. 1).

The family's typical way of telling its mythology begins with William James's grandfather, "Old Billy," who came to the United States as a penniless Irish immigrant in 1789. In a quintessentially American rags-to-riches tale (this case being one of the rare occasions in which it is actually true), he became one of the richest men in New England. He bought real estate throughout New York State, including nearly the entire city of Syracuse, and helped finance large infrastructure projects like the Erie Canal. Old Billy had an intimidating personality (Simon, 1998, p. 3) and was influential in New England high society (Richardson, 2006, p. 25). In contrast, William's grandmother, Catharine, was shy and introverted, preferring the company of the household's gardeners, cooks, and maids (Simon, 1998, p. 3).

William James's father, who would become known as "Henry Sr.," openly rebelled against Old Billy. By 8 years old Henry Sr. had the habit of stopping by the local cobbler's shop to have a drink of brandy on the way to school—if he made it to school at all (Simon, 1998, p. 4). He enrolled in college and quickly became known as a drunk who squandered his father's money on cigars and oysters. Old Billy called his son a "swindler" (Simon, 1998, p. 10) and tried (but failed) to cut him out of his will.

Religion was the only subject that caught Henry Sr.'s interest, eventually becoming his scholarly and personal obsession. After hitting rock bottom with his drinking and mental health in college and then recovering with the help of his minister brother, he pursued studies in theology. He worked at a Unitarian newspaper in New England before following his brother's example by enrolling at Princeton Theological Seminary in New Jersey. As his studies progressed, his thinking became increasingly heretical and anti-institutional. After a trip to Ireland, Henry Sr. decided to leave the seminary and become a freethinker and author. Shortly thereafter he met Mary Walsh, who showed genuine interest in his ideas, and they were married in an unorthodox wedding ceremony outside of the church (officiated by the mayor of New York City; Simon, 1998, p. 15).

Henry Sr.'s writing was dense and narrow in focus. Nearly all of his publications argue for the inherent goodness of human beings, blame society for humanity's failings, and promote the "negation of the self and the exaltation of God" (Simon, 1998, p. 188). His dismissal of academic (and all other) institutions meant that his writing was difficult for both academics and laypeople to understand—and this later motivated his son William James to strive to be clear and accessible in his own work. A passage from one of Henry Sr.'s books, *Substance and Shadow* (which received some rare praise) addresses the problem of evil in his labyrinthine prose:

> It is no doubt very tolerable finite or creaturely love to love one's own in another, to love another for his conformity to one's own self: but nothing can be in more flagrant contrast with the creative love, all whose tenderness ex vi termini [to the farthest limit of one's strength] must be reserved only for what intrinsically is most bitterly hostile and negative to itself. (as cited in Richardson, 2006, p. 33)

Henry Sr. wrote a number of articles and essays (which his son William James would later edit into a volume of his writings) despite his lack of commercial success. Henry Sr. was far better known for his gifts as a conversationalist than as an author. His intellectual interests and outgoing personality brought him into close contact with many of the era's most important thinkers, artists, and scientists, including, to mention just a few of many illustrious names: Michael Faraday, Nathaniel Hawthorne, Henry Longfellow, Oliver Wendell Holmes, Henry David Thoreau, and Ralph Waldo Emerson.

Of these, Emerson was the closest to the James family. When Emerson and Henry Sr. first met, Emerson was already famous for his advocacy of individualism and Transcendentalism. Transcendentalism was a syncretic blending of Judeo-Christianity with mostly Hindu-based traditions such as Vedanta, which became popular among New England intellectuals for a time. According to one Emerson historian, his emphasis in Transcendentalism could be summarized as: "The purpose of life was spiritual transformation and direct experience of divine power, here and now on earth" (Gordon, 2007, p. 16).

Emerson's writing also contained frequent descriptions of spiritual raptures:

> Standing on the bare ground,—my head bathed by the blithe air, and uplifted into infinite spaces,—all mean egotism vanishes. I become a transparent eye-ball; I am nothing; I see all; the currents of the Universal Being circulate through me; I am part or parcel of God. (Emerson, 1836, p. 3)

Emerson enjoyed Henry Sr.'s company, describing him as "wise, gentle, polished, with heroic manners, and a serenity like the sun" (Simon, 1998, p. 19). These sentiments were opposite to Henry Sr.'s own father's harsh judgments of him, so Emerson became a kind of spiritual father to Henry Sr. The James family often hosted Emerson at their home, even setting aside a room for the purpose, nicknamed the "Emerson room." When Henry Sr. and Mary's first child, William James, was born in New York City on January 11, 1842, Emerson stopped by to give his blessing. Emerson thus became godfather (Simon, 1998, p. 19) to the child who, 60 years later, would publish *The Varieties*.

A Bewildering Forest

Religious experience was a common topic of discussion in the James household. Besides dinner table conversations with Transcendentalists like

Emerson and Thoreau, Henry Sr. himself had an experience that he came to believe had profound religious implications. His experience came when his son William was about 2 years old (making Henry Sr. about 33 years old). Henry Sr. wrote the following of that moment:

> One day . . . towards the close of May [1844], having eaten a comfortable dinner, I remained sitting at the table after the family had dispersed, idly gazing at the embers in the grate, thinking of nothing, when suddenly—in a lightning flash as it were—"fear came upon me, and trembling, which made all my bones shake." To all appearance it was a perfectly insane and abject terror, without ostensible cause, and only to be accounted for, to my perplexed imagination, by some damned shape squatting invisible to me within the precincts of the room, and raying out from his fetid personality influences fatal to life. The thing had not lasted ten seconds before I felt myself a wreck. (Richardson, 2006, p. 18)

This experience initially prompted a nervous breakdown. Eventually, though, Henry Sr. came to see it as a spiritual second birth. His attempts to understand his experience led him to the work of Emanuel Swedenborg, an 18th-century Christian mystic who was influential with a number of 19th-century European intellectuals. According to Swedenborg, Henry Sr.'s experience was a "vastation," or a kind of awakening to the spiritual side of life. This interpretation intensified Henry Sr.'s already obsessive interest in religious topics. William later quoted his father's experience in *The Varieties*, and William himself would later report a similar experience of his own, though William's understanding of it would be far more scientific and broader than his father's fixation on the purely spiritualist, Swedenborgian interpretation.

In addition to religion, Henry Sr. was preoccupied with educating his children. His spiritual aspirations, guilt about his misspent youth, and friendships with prominent intellectuals made for some unorthodox views on education—to put it mildly. He moved the family throughout Europe and New England in order to find a school that fit his educational ideals, which prioritized authenticity, individualism, and virtue. At various points, the family lived in New York, Boston, London, Paris, Geneva, Boulogne, and Rhode Island. This transcontinental and multilingual educational quest required the James children—now (from oldest to youngest) William, Henry (the famous novelist), Garth ("Wilky"), Robertson ("Bob"), and Alice (the influential feminist diarist)—to spend their childhoods in at least *18* different households (Richardson, 2006, p. 19). As biographer Linda Simon put it, the James family "wandered through a bewildering forest of cultural experiences. (Simon, 1998, p. 47)

A picture of life in the James home and its compelling cast of characters is captured well by E. L. Godkin, the founding editor of the *Nation* magazine, who was a close family friend:

> There could not be a more entertaining treat than a dinner at the James house, when all the young people were at home. They were full of stories of the oddest kind, and discussed questions of morals or taste or literature with a vociferous vigor so great as sometimes to lead the young men to leave their seats and gesticulate on the floor. (Richardson, 2006, p. 26)

A Constructive Passion

William James (James hereafter) emerged from his childhood having seen much of Europe and, through his father, having met many of the leading intellectuals of his time. He had also briefly studied painting with artist William Morris Hunt before dropping his artistic training in favor of science. Despite this cultural richness, in his late teens and 20s he felt lost and was in desperate search of his calling. The search took many years and was stalled at times by health troubles. He frequently experienced pains in his back, his stomach, and his eyes—ailments for which no medical diagnosis could be reached. He sought out "cures," which today might be considered "alternative medicine," across New England and Europe, some involving alterations to diet and exercise while others consisted of various "water cures," essentially spending time in baths, a popular medical treatment at that time. He would struggle with periodic episodes of depression throughout his life, though none as severe as in his adolescence. He would also continue to explore alternative therapies, for both his own benefit and in his scientific work.

When the Civil War broke out, James enlisted as a volunteer in a local group supporting the Union army. While he worked briefly for the war effort, he did not go to battle like his brothers Wilky and Bob (Richardson, 2006, p. 55). Though James hoped to join the Union cause, Henry Sr. did not want any more of his sons at war. James used this as a bargaining chip to force his father to allow him to go to college—which the anti-institutional Henry Sr. thought was worse than worthless. But Henry Sr. did not want to lose his eldest son to the military, so he relented and allowed his son to enroll at Harvard.

James first studied chemistry under Charles Eliot, a young professor who later became the school's president and a pivotal figure in the history of higher education. Eliot wrote that James was a "very interesting and agreeable pupil, but . . . not wholly devoted to the study of chemistry" (Menand, 2001, p. 23). Eliot was right. James was fascinated by the explosion of scientific developments in chemistry at that time, but he was even more swept away with enthusiasm for Charles Darwin's recent theory of natural selection. After reading *On the Origin of Species* (Darwin, 1859/2004), James switched his studies from chemistry to biology in order to study evolution. Darwin's book would become a guiding light for much of James's later work.

At this point, James aimed to become a naturalist to follow in Darwin's footsteps. In this era, many naturalists and biologists began their careers by first studying medicine. This, too, had briefly been Darwin's path. Likewise, for James, medicine was a means to becoming a naturalist, though he also thought of it as a backup profession if he failed to realize his intellectual ambitions. James enrolled in Harvard's medical school. Medicine was then just at the cusp of becoming scientific. James learned human anatomy through the dissection of human cadavers, an exercise he continued to consider valuable scientific training throughout his life. At this time, he also took a trip to Brazil with famous naturalist Louis Agassiz in order to train in collecting specimens. On finding himself seasick on the journey and then often bored during the systematic collection of specimens, James decided the life of a naturalist was not for him.

James graduated with a medical degree in 1869, but never practiced medicine. Instead, he spent long periods of time alone reading, eventually absorbing most of the Western canon in philosophy and literature. He then fell into another depression. He traveled to Germany, where a number of renowned medical doctors were working on mental illness. James was, again, actively searching for a calling, writing in a letter, "much would I give for a constructive passion of some kind" (Richardson, p. 93). He would later say that his first philosophical statement came in the context of trying to find a vocation, writing that he believed the ultimate aim of life was to be of "as much use as possible" (Myers, 1986/2001, p. 3).

While in Germany, he visited several scientific laboratories focused on psychological research. In James's view, Germany was home to excellent scientists and some well-known, but ultimately misguided, philosophers.

Much of his later work advocated the application of the scientific method to psychology in controlled laboratory settings (as German scientists were doing), while attempting to rid psychology of the quasi-theological strain of German philosophy (best exemplified by Hegel). German scientists Hermann von Helmholtz and Wilhelm Wundt were then conducting their pioneering work in psychology grounded in physiology. In Germany, after attending many lectures in physiology and meeting some of Germany's leading psychological scientists, James was inspired by the prospect of a truly scientific psychology.

This trip cemented James's decision to become a scientist. At the time, he wrote to his father: "As a central point of study I imagine that the border ground of physiology and psychology, overlapping both, would be as fruitful as any, and I am now working on to it" (Richardson, 2006, p. 87). Elsewhere, he wrote: "My only ideal of life is a scientific life" (Richardson, 2006, p. 94). By the time he returned to New England, James held a thoroughly scientific and purely physical view of the universe, writing: "I feel that we are Nature through and through, that we are wholly conditioned, that not a wiggle of our will happens save as a result of physical laws" (Richardson, 2006, p. 101). His ideas in this regard would shift throughout his life.

An Adventurer in the Realm of Ideas

James was a restless and unfocused student but he nonetheless made a good impression on a few teachers. After returning from Germany, he was offered a teaching position in physiology at Harvard in 1872. The job offer was approved by Eliot, James's former chemistry professor, who had since become Harvard's president. Despite this unexpected and prestigious offer, James hesitated. He was unsure if he was mentally and physically up to the task of teaching. The depression that had hampered him throughout his adult life—and may have required institutional care at McLean hospital in Boston at least once—had again become crippling. What kept James going was reading broadly, deeply, and constantly while trying to exist on, as he put it, the " 'little spoonful' of energy that gave out, generally, by ten o'clock in the morning" (Simon, 1998, p. xiii). After a bout of his typical indecisiveness, he accepted the teaching offer.

Agreeing to teach changed James's life. Teaching was, he wrote to his brother Henry, "a perfect godsend to me just now. An external motive to work, which yet does not strain me—a dealing with men instead of my own mind, and a diversion from those introspective studies which had bred a sort of philosophical hypochondria in me of late" (Richardson, 2006, p. 144). The flood of mental and physical ailments that had threatened to drown him for most of his young adulthood began to dissipate.

Many of his students loved him. Despite his personal insecurities about his ability to teach, he strived to convey to his students how to think philosophically, scientifically, and above all, clearly. Some of his best-known students included

- Theodore Roosevelt, U.S. president
- Gertrude Stein, poet and novelist
- Walter Cannon, physiologist and discoverer of the "fight-or-flight" response
- Mary Calkins, the first female president of both the American Psychological Association and the American Philosophical Association
- W. E. B. DuBois, philosopher and cofounder of the NAACP (National Association for the Advancement of Colored People)

Many of James's students acknowledged his effect on them. Stein, for example, wrote: "He said 'never reject anything. Nothing has been proved. If you reject anything, it is the beginning of the end as an intellectual.' He was my big influence." DuBois wrote: "I was repeatedly a guest in the house of William James; he was my friend and guide to clear thinking" (Myers, 1986/2001, p. 13). If their testimony regarding his efforts on their behalf is any evidence, William James loved his students right back.

The adult James was described in very different terms than the adolescent James. Now, he was seen as energetic, "with an afterglow of Bohemia about him" (Richardson, 2006, p. 13). His personality, however, remained multifaceted and as contradictory as ever. One colleague wrote: "There was, in spite of his playfulness, a deep sadness about James. You felt that he had just stepped out of this sadness in order to meet you and was to go back into it the moment you left him" (Richardson, 2006, p. 236). Many remarked on his kindness. Philosopher George Santayana said: "William James was the soul of courtesy. . . . Nobody ever recognized more heartily the chance that others had of being right, and the right they had to be different" (Simon, 1998, p. 317).

James was enthralled by all mental phenomena. In his physiology classes and public lectures, he seemed to move effortlessly from mainstream topics to those on the fringes of the field. Another colleague wrote: "There was no aspect of human activity that did not interest him. . . . He was always responsive to something that might open a new door of knowledge"; the colleague added, "He appealed to me as a romantic adventurer in the realm of ideas" (Simon, 1998, p. 273). This openness was no doubt essential to his later decision to work on spiritual experience.

Beyond physiology, James would become increasingly drawn to psychology (and, eventually, philosophy). He viewed these two fields as more interesting and more fertile for pioneering work. He spent many years focusing on psychology, creating the first psychology lab in North America (Note: Although the first official psychology laboratory in North America was at Johns Hopkins, James had been conducting small studies by himself and with students for many years prior) and producing the foundational textbook for the field (discussed in the next section).

After about a decade in psychology, though, James's calling shifted yet again. He wrote, "I decide today to stick to biology for a profession in case I am not called to a chair of philosophy. . . . Philosophy I will nevertheless regard as my vocation" (Richardson, 2006, p. 148). Some years after, he did indeed become a professor of philosophy at Harvard, a post he would keep for the rest of his working life. Nevertheless, his subsequent writings in philosophy and psychology show the continued influence of his earlier studies in medicine, biology, and physiology.

Several years into teaching, he met Alice Gibbens, the woman who would become his wife in 1878. Alice had a "gift of vivacious and humorous talk," a "vigorous affirmative temperament," and an "experiencing nature" (Richardson, 2006, p. 168). Due to her personal interests, Alice heavily influenced James's interest in religious and spiritual phenomena (Note: As did his brother Henry, who wrote several stories involving spiritualist phenomena and ghosts). James welcomed this shared interest, as he found it absent in his academic colleagues. After his father's death, and while editing his father's religious writings for a posthumous collection, James wrote to his wife, Alice: "Dear you have one new function hereafter. . . . You must not leave me till I understand a little more of the value and meaning of religion in father's sense. . . . My friends leave it altogether out" (Richardson, 2006, p. 238). James would certainly return to the topic later in his life.

An American Masterpiece

When James began publishing his writings around 1878, there was some pressure to make up for the time he had lost searching for his calling. By the time William James wrote his first book in 1890, his brother Henry James was already an internationally acclaimed novelist. Many biographers have attempted to understand the influence the two brothers had on one another's work. Journalist Rebecca West observed: "One of the James brothers grew up to write fiction as though it were philosophy, and the other to write philosophy as if it were fiction" (Richardson, 2006, p. 305).

There is an obvious literary quality within much of James's scientific writing. James's *Principles of Psychology* (1890), for example, which was meant to be a technical academic textbook of psychology, was reviewed as being "an American masterpiece which, quite like *Moby Dick*, ought to be read from beginning to end at least once by every person professing to be educated" (Richardson, 2006, p. 302). James aimed to make his ideas intelligible to anyone, not only to fellow academics. His writing, unlike his father's and many of his academic colleagues, was clear and accessible. It was also inventive. He coined several still-used phrases, including "stream of consciousness," "dissociation," "multiverse," and "time-line," among others (Richardson, 2006, p. 306).

The gist of many of James's academic publications was to take abstract mental phenomena and ground them firmly in human nature. He had little patience for Platonic ideals or the philosophical abstractions common to German philosophy at the time. Instead, he preferred a Darwinian approach and British Empiricism combined, whenever possible, with concrete facts from biology. In an article, "The Sentiment of Rationality," James argued that reason itself could be understood as a psychological adaptation, advocating a psychological and biological approach to rationality itself (Richardson, 2006, p. 183), a kind of psychology of philosophy (e.g., Yaden & Anderson, 2021). In an article, "The Spatial Quale," James argued that the sense of space comprises sensory data and is not merely an abstract, purely intellectual concept, which was the prevailing view at that time.

His writing often incorporated sensual descriptions to illustrate the view that mental states have their basis in the body. For example, to explain the role that sensory perception plays in people's sense of the space around them, he wrote: "The sound of the brook near which I write, the odor of the cedars, the feeling of satisfaction with which my breakfast has filled me, and my interest in writing this article all simultaneously coexist in my consciousness" (Richardson, 2006, p. 197). In his writing and his thought, James attempted to ground abstract ideas in the sights, sounds, and experiences of daily life.

James's other academic articles take a similar approach to increasingly abstract mental phenomena, such as willpower (in "The Feeling of Effort"), belief (in "The Psychology of Belief"), and time (in "The Perception of Time"). In each, James took the role of a scientist equipped with physical facts entering into a philosophical debate comprising of mostly rationalistic abstractions. Often drawing on his training in medicine and biology, James understood subjective experience as depending on physiology:

> Mental states occasion also changes in the caliber of blood-vessels, or al-
> teration in the heart-beats, or processes still more subtle, in the glands and
> viscera. . . . It will be safe to lay down the general law that no mental mod-
> ification ever occurs which is not accompanied or followed by a bodily
> change. (James, 1890, p. 18, as cited in Pawelski, 2007, p. 111)

At the same time that he advocated for a physiological study of mental states, James disliked *overly* reductive approaches and often defended the inherent value and complexity of individual subjectivity. In one of his first popular articles, James criticized English biologist and philosopher Herbert Spencer's popular but, to his mind, too simplistic account of consciousness. Spencer regarded consciousness as arising from nervous activity solely in order to respond to one's environment in a strictly stimulus–response manner (a view largely anticipating behaviorism). James's critique rested on two points. First, he argued that Spencer's view of the mind is too limited, as it leaves out "all sentiments, all aesthetic impulses, all religious emotions and personal affections." Second, James argued that Spencer leaves out the influence of other people, writing "to the individual man, as a social being, the interests of his fellows are a part of his environment." James consistently argued that *any* account of consciousness must be large enough to include *all* of one's mental and social life. One's body and one's society, in other words, inevitably influence one's ideas and subjectivity itself.

Thus, James's psychological work advanced a scientific approach that, at the same time, did *not* deny the richness of individual subjectivity. He observed that too many psychological perspectives fall into one of two extremes. On the one hand, he thought that some scientists were overly reductive, writing: "Naturalists and physiologists are publishing extremely crude and pretentious psychological speculations under the name of 'science'" (Richardson, 2006, p. 167). On the other hand, he thought some scholars were too ignorant of known scientific facts, writing: "Professors whose educations has been exclusively literary or philosophical, are too apt to show a real ineptitude for estimating the nature of man" (Richardson, 2006, p. 167). In other words, James thought that some scientists were attempting to reduce human beings to overly simplistic, mechanistic explanations, while some humanities scholars were ignorant of known facts of biology and behavior. To move past this dichotomy, James proposed "a union of the two disciplines" (Richardson, 2006, p. 167), that is, a synthesis of the best of what the sciences and the humanities have to offer. (Note: Philosopher and William James scholar James Pawelski is currently carrying out such a Jamesian project at the University of Pennsylvania.)

James's psychological contributions reached a culmination in his *Principles of Psychology* (1890), a 2,970-page textbook that advocated for a scientific and biologically informed approach to psychology that also considers the subjective complexity of mental life. The book remains a historic achievement in psychology. It provides a foundation for several fundamental topics in the field, including chapters on the self, habit, attention, memory, imagination, perception, movement, and emotion. For decades, all students of psychology read this book, or a shorter version published soon after, as the field's primary textbook (students called the longer version "the James" and the shorter version "the Jimmy"). James's place in the history of psychology thus assured, he moved on to scientifically explore further frontiers of mental life.

A White Crow

Because of his scientific approach to psychology, some scholars have been puzzled by James's interest in what are now considered "fringe" topics. His research included investigations into psychics, alternative medicine, hypnosis, and relaxation techniques. For James, these investigations were simply a continuation of his attempts to provide scientific inquiries into *all* mental phenomena. While the following lines from James refer to hypnosis, they could describe his approach to each of these topics at the fringe, so to speak, he wrote that it was "high time that a . . . phenomenon which had played a prominent part in human history from time immemorial should be rescued from the hands of uncritical enthusiasm and charlatanry and conquered for science" (Richardson, 2006, p. 270). James's curiosity as a scientist and a scholar extended to topics that many had considered outside of science's reach.

James invested a fair portion of his energy to investigating claims related to "spiritualism," an ideology that was the seed of what is now called "New Age spirituality." The movement included various cures and therapies involving various unseen, and sometimes explicitly supernatural, forces. James was also initially interested in testing the possible existence of psychic phenomenon. He was critical of both the overeager and blind faith of some enthusiasts as well as the unexamined dismissal by other scientists. As part of this research, James attended séances (in which a person would attempt to contact dead persons) and several sessions by people claiming to be psychic. He believed that if a genuine example of psychic phenomenon could be proved, it would represent an enormous scientific discovery.

> A universal proposition can be me made untrue by a particular instance. If you wish to upset a rule that all crows are black, you mustn't seek to show that no crows are; it is enough if you prove one single crow to be white. (as cited in Richardson, 2006, p. 261)

His interest in psychic phenomena can be seen as a search for this "white crow." He was looking for even just a singular instance of demonstrable psychic phenomena. But instead of finding exceptions to general physical laws, James found himself again and again in the role of debunker of charlatans (Richardson, 2006, p. 259). Eventually, the many frauds he encountered diminished his interest in the subject. In the words of one of his biographers:

> In the end, even with his extravagant investment of time and energy in psychic research—his habitual holding open the door, his insistent defense of one's right to believe—when it came down to it, he simply couldn't cross the line. His skeptical and scrupulous approach had become his conclusion. (Richardson, 2006, p. 510)

Following many other psychologists of the day, James also studied hypnosis (Richardson, 2006, p. 269). Hypnosis was first known as "mesmerism" after Franz Mesmer, a French physician who speculated that trances were caused by an invisible fluid-like energy. This is where the term "mesmerize" comes from. (Note: Interestingly, Benjamin Franklin took part in scientifically testing and refuting this claim while serving as a diplomat in France.) Interest in hypnosis as a subjective phenomenon (stripped of the "fluid-like energy" interpretation) was later revived by the English physician James Braid, who described it as an aspect of imagination that could be used as an anesthetic. For a while, hypnosis was used during surgery to reduce or in some cases eliminate pain before the invention of ether and other anesthetics (Dormandy, 2006).

The possible application of hypnosis as a psychological therapy for hysteria made it again a subject of interest to French physician Jean-Martin Charcot and his not-yet-famous student, Sigmund Freud. James, who also briefly studied with Charcot, later hypnotized Harvard students in class to demonstrate it as a mental phenomenon of interest (Richardson, 2006, p. 263). James also believed hypnosis had untapped therapeutic potential. He suggested hypnosis to his sister Alice to help ease her pain as she was dying, as she was unable to tolerate morphine (Simon, 1998, p. 240).

In addition to hypnosis and psychic phenomena, James took an interest in relaxation practices more generally. He was convinced of their value by Annie Call, the author of a book called *Power Through Repose* (Richardson, 2006, p. 311). In this book, Call argued that many people are in a state of chronic stress for which deliberate relaxation can provide relief. James made it a habit to practice such relaxation techniques regularly. One acquaintance wrote this about James: "What he recommended to all intellectuals was the relaxation of the rather strained surface tensions" (Richardson, 2006, p. 318). Many decades later, American Physician Herbert Benson wrote *The Relaxation Response*, which vindicated many of these ideas about relaxation through scientific research on observable changes in autonomic nervous system activity during relaxation techniques and some health benefits to regular practice. Incidentally, Benson's research on the relaxation response was carried out in the same Harvard laboratory in which James's student Walter Cannon discovered the stress response, better known as the "fight-or-flight" response.

Thus, the results of James's investigations into these fringe topics were mixed. To summarize: (1) he found no evidence of psychic phenomena; (2) he thought some benefit could potentially come from some but not most alternative therapies; and (3) he seemed convinced of the therapeutic effects of hypnosis and relaxation (though he rejected supernatural explanations for their effectiveness). He would apply his experiences investigating these subjects when he turned his attention to the study of religious experience.

Taking the Visions on Trust

Given his early exposure to religious and spiritual concepts from the Transcendentalists sitting around the dinner table of his childhood, in addition to his career-long habit of scientifically studying anomalous mental states, when James was invited to speak at the prestigious Gifford Lectures in Edinburgh, Scotland, his decision to address spiritual experience makes sense. Religious and spiritual experiences are yet another poorly understood, yet important feature of human psychology that James hoped to understand scientifically. While we revisit James's nuanced views on supernatural beliefs in a further chapter—James himself withheld his own views on religion until the end of this lecture series—suffice it to say that the topic of spiritual experience was of great scientific interest to James.

James was interested in spiritual experience despite his claims that he never had such an experience. He wrote regarding spiritual experience: "My own constitution shuts me out from their enjoyment almost entirely, and I can speak of them only at the second hand" (as cited in Pawelski, 2007, p. 105). However, as biographer Richard Perry and philosopher James Pawelski point out, the "almost" in this statement is a little misleading. While James may never have had an intense "mystical" type of experience of the kind he described in *The Varieties*, he seemed to have had a number of experiences that came close (Pawelski, 2007).

First, there was an experience similar to his father's "vastation", which he experienced around the same age that his father had (Richardson, 2006, p. 119). James included in *The Varieties* his own experience (though he kept his identity anonymous) that occurred during his medical training:

> I went one evening into a dressing room in the twilight to procure some article that was there: when suddenly there fell upon me without any warning, just as if it came out of the darkness, a horrible fear of my own existence. (Richardson, 2006, p. 117)

While this was a frightening experience, James later felt that it enhanced his empathy toward the psychological sufferings of others. He later wrote, "It was like a revelation," and then went on to explain, "and although the immediate feelings passed away, the experience has made me sympathetic with the morbid feeling of others ever since" (Richardson, 2006, p. 118). James did seem to maintain a sincere sympathy for those suffering from mental illness in his writings, refusing to dehumanize or objectify these people, as was unfortunately more common at that time.

Second, James described in a letter to his wife, Alice, an experience that he had while traveling through Switzerland. He felt overcome by an aesthetic appreciation of nature, mixed with love for his family, and tinged with a moral aspect:

A sort of moral revolution poured through me. . . . This dear sacred Switzerland, whose mountains, trees and grass and waters are so pure, so good, and as it seemed to me so honest, so absolutely honest, all got mixed up in my mood, and in one torrent of adoration for them, for you, and for virtue. I rose toward the window to look out at the scene. . . . I am not crazy dear at all, only that I had one of those moral thunderstorms that go all through you and give you such relief. (Richardson, 2006, p. 210)

His third experience was triggered by a drug. James experimented with several psychoactive and psychedelic substances over the course of his life. He tried mescaline, but there seems to have been a problem with his dose, because while mescaline usually causes an intensely altered state, it only gave him a headache (though it is also possible that he did not take the mescaline). James reported the disappointing lack of effects to the friend who had given him the drug (a neurologist) and had enthusiastically described its intense subjective effects. James told him that, unfortunately, he would need to "take the visions on trust" (Richardson, 2006, p. 467).

James had also read about another psychoactive substance, written about in pamphlets by Benjamin Blood, "The Anaesthetic Revelation," describing the psychological effects of breathing nitrous oxide. When James tried the substance, he was so impressed by his experience that he claimed it caused the "the strongest emotion" of his life. In *The Varieties*, he wrote:

Looking back on my own experiences [with nitrous oxide] . . . the keynote of it is invariably a reconciliation. It is as if the opposites of the world, whose contradictoriness and conflict make all our difficulties and troubles, were melted into unity. (James, 1902/2009, p. 293)

We follow James in discussing the connection between psychoactive substances—especially so-called classic psychedelics—and spiritual experiences. The scientific study of psychedelics is among the most exciting topics in the science of spiritual experience, and we refer to findings from psychedelic research throughout this book.

James's fourth experience occurred while James was wandering outside of a cabin at night in New York State. This experience also seems like it was spurred on by a deep appreciation for natural beauty:

> The moon rose and hung above the scene before midnight, leaving only a few of the larger stars visible, and I got into a state of spiritual alertness of the most vital description. . . . Its everlasting freshness and its immemorial antiquity and decay . . . all whirled inexplicably together. . . . It was one of the happiest lonesome nights of my existence. (Richardson, 2006, p. 374)

This final experience may have convinced James to choose religious experience as his topic for the prestigious Gifford Lectures in Edinburgh. He even wrote of his experience: "Doubtless in more ways than one though, things in the Edinburgh lectures will be traceable to it" (Richardson, 2006, p. 375), and it is these Gifford Lectures in Edinburgh that were published as *The Varieties*.

Conclusion

While James's use of written descriptions of religious experiences throughout *The Varieties* demanded that he trust the self-reports of other people, he seems to have had enough experiences of the kind himself to convince him of their genuine subjective reality. James had also investigated a number of topics tangentially related to religious and spiritual experience throughout his career.

Of the many vocations that James pursued through his life, he began *The Varieties* by introducing himself as a psychologist:

> As regards the manner in which I shall have to administer this lectureship, I am neither a theologian, nor a scholar learned in the history of religions, nor an anthropologist. Psychology is the only branch of learning in which I am particularly versed. To the psychologist the religious propensities of man must be at least as interesting as any other of the facts pertaining to his mental constitution. It would seem, therefore, that, as a psychologist, the natural thing for me would be to invite you to a descriptive survey of those religious propensities. (James, 1902/2009, p. 7)

In *The Varieties,* as with many of James's earlier psychological writings, he sought to find a way to ground abstract mental states in evidence from psychology and physiology. His childhood influences and perhaps his personality, too, may have helped him to integrate the many complexities and seeming contradictions involved with approaching religious or spiritual experiences from a scientific perspective.

References

Darwin, C. (2004). *On the origin of species.* Routledge. (Original work published 1859)

Dormandy, T. (2006). *The worst of evils: The fight against pain.* Yale University Press.

Emerson, R. W. (1836). *Nature.* http://www.emersoncentral.com/nature.htm

Gordon, R. C. (2007). *Emerson and the light of India: An intellectual history.* NBT India.

James, W. (1890). *The principles of psychology* (Vol. 1, No. 2). Macmillan.

James, W. (1902/2009). The varieties of religious experience: A study in human nature. *eBooks@Adelaide.* https://csrs.nd.edu/assets/59930/williams_1902.pdf

Lewis, R. W. B. (1991). *The Jameses: A family narrative.* Farar, Straus and Giroux.

Menand, L. (2001). *The metaphysical club.* Macmillan.

Misak, C. (2018). *Cambridge pragmatism: From Peirce and James to Ramsey and Wittgenstein.* Oxford University Press.

Myers, G. E. (2001). *William James: His life and thought.* Yale University Press. (Original work published 1986)

Pawelski, J. O. (2007). *The dynamic individualism of William James.* SUNY Press.

Richardson, R. D. (2006). *William James: In the maelstrom of American modernism.* Houghton Mifflin.

Simon, L. (1998). *Genuine reality: A life of William James.* University of Chicago Press.

Yaden, D. B., & Anderson, D. E. (2021). The psychology of philosophy: Associating philosophical views with psychological traits in professional philosophers. *Philosophical Psychology, 34*(5), 721–755.

3

The Varieties: The Classic Text and Its Impact

Religion is the great interest of my life.

—William James

The Varieties of Religious Experience (*The Varieties* hereafter) is a special book (James, 1902/2009). Over the years, it has become James's most well-known work and has quietly cemented itself into the Western canon. Continuously in print since it was first published over 100 years ago, it is among the most successful books in psychology (Hood et al., 2009, p. 22). Furthermore, "The Varieties of X" has become a template for the titles of other books and articles, such as, "The Varieties of Scientific Experience" (Sagan, 2006), "The Varieties of Psychedelic Experience" (Masters & Houston, 1966), and even scientific articles "Varieties of Visual Working Memory Representation in Infancy and Beyond" (Kibbe, 2015)—as well as our own article, "The Varieties of Self-Transcendent Experience" (Yaden et al., 2017).

In James's *The Varieties*, one of the first chapters is "Circumscription of the Topic," in which James outlines and defines the topics under discussions. In the present chapter, we attempt to do the same, as these concepts appear in both *The Varieties* and contemporary research. In particular, we build toward working definitions of religion/spirituality and spiritual experience.

Aspects of Religion

James's initial plan for the Gifford Lecture series was that the first half would be called "The Varieties of Religious Experience," which would describe experiences and consider them scientifically, and the second part would be more philosophical, "The Tasks of Religious Philosophy." This second half

The Varieties of Spiritual Experience. David B. Yaden and Andrew B. Newberg, Oxford University Press. © David Yaden and Andrew Newberg 2022. DOI: 10.1093/oso/9780190665678.003.0003

would comprise, as he wrote, "my own last will and testament, setting forth the philosophy best adapted to normal religious needs" (Richardson, 2006, p. 391). That is, James intended to provide a philosophical view for why these experiences provide psychological consolation and how this could be leveraged to improve mental health. These are high hopes. Instead, though, James became so swept up with the prospect of a scientific study of the experiences (the subject of the first half) that he spent the vast majority of the 20 lectures on psychological analysis and devoted only a small portion at the end to philosophical considerations.

James had an overriding aim for his lectures, which was to shift the focus away from the study of religious beliefs and theological doctrines, and to instead devote the lectures to religious *experience*. James thought that almost all of the scholarly discussion around religion at the time was engaged with the topic of religious beliefs and doctrines. He wanted *The Varieties* to serve as a corrective, emphasizing the importance of personal inner subjective experiences. James recognized the importance of this shift as well as the deep complexity that arises from attempting to focus on experiences rather than beliefs:

> The problem I have set myself is a hard one; 1st to defend . . . "experience" against "philosophy" as being the real backbone of the world's religious life . . . and second, to make the hearer or reader believe what I myself invincibly do believe, that although all the special manifestations of religion may have been absurd (I mean its creeds and theories) yet the life of it as a whole is mankind's most important function. (Richardson, 2006, p. 391)

This is an exquisitely contradictory comment! In the same sentence, James manages to claim that religion may be both "absurd" and yet also "mankind's most important function." One way out of this seeming paradox, already hinted at in this quotation, is to identify and differentiate various *aspects* of religion.

Bringing Empirical Data to Bear

Given James's unique family life and his intellectual development, it's not surprising that he would choose to focus on the study of spiritual experience for these lectures. There is, however, another crucial influence that must be acknowledged. James gave his Gifford Lectures in 1901–1902, but a few years earlier, in 1899, James had read the book *The Psychology of Religion: An Empirical Study of the Growth of Religious Consciousness* (1899) by psychologist Edwin Starbuck, a former student of James's at Harvard, who went on to become a professor of psychology at Stanford University. James wrote the preface to the book and indeed owed a giant intellectual debt to it. He made explicit reference to it in several places throughout *The Varieties*.

Starbuck's book describes the results from a survey that he administered across New England, asking people whether they had a "conversion experience," and if so, to answer a number of questions about it. In his preface to Starbuck's book, James related his embarrassment at initially doubting Starbuck's plan to scientifically study religious experiences using survey data. While still a student at Harvard, Starbuck had proposed mailing surveys out to people asking for them to describe their religious "conversion" experiences and to answer several questions about them, a project he eventually accomplished, providing a rudimentary statistical analysis of the survey responses. James described his initial doubt regarding the project:

> I think I said to Dr. Starbuck that I expected the chief result of his circulars would be a certain number of individual answers relating peculiar experiences and ideas in a way that might be held as typical. The sorting and extracting of percentages and reducing to averages, I thought, would give results of comparatively little significance. (James in preface to Starbuck, 1899, p. viii)

In other words, James thought that subjecting spiritual experience to quantitative measurement would provide little of value. But James was wrong. He openly admitted his mistake in the preface:

> I must say that the results amply justify his own confidence in his methods, and that I feel somewhat ashamed at present of the littleness of my own faith. (James in preface to Starbuck, 1899, p. viii)

James then went on to advocate for future studies of a similar kind on individuals from the world's other faith traditions (e.g., Judaism, Islam, Buddhism, and Hinduism) because Starbuck's survey was limited to Christians. We report a number of results from contemporary quantitative survey studies of this kind, including our own, throughout this book.

Starbuck's book contains the seeds of a number of ideas that James developed further in *The Varieties*. First and foremost, Starbuck advocated generally for the psychological study of religion, stating: "The business of the psychology of religion is to bring together a systemized body of evidence" (Starbuck, 1899, p. 6). Second, Starbuck pointed to the value of physiological research: "We shall find that the data of religious experience are being illuminated at every point by the results of physiological psychology" (Starbuck, 1899, p. 5). Third, Starbuck, like James, believed that science could add a great deal to our understanding about religious experience, but could not offer answers to the kinds of metaphysical questions pondered by philosophers and theologians (e.g., it cannot determine whether or not there is a supernatural dimension of existence). In his book, Starbuck wrote: "The end of our study is not to resolve the mystery of religion, but to bring enough of it into orderliness that its facts may appeal to our understanding" (Starbuck, 1899, p. ii).

James echoed these sentiments throughout *The Varieties*—as do we. Last, but not least, a line in Starbuck's book provided James with his title:

> These conclusions in regard to the close connection between temperament and the nature of religious experience will stand us in good stead as we proceed, in helping us to understand the causes that underlie certain *varieties of religious experience*. (emphasis added; Starbuck, 1899, p. 75)

Accounts

The Varieties consists of dozens of personal descriptions of spiritual experiences from contemporary and historical sources. The way James used these accounts drew on his training in naturalism and biology. He documented and referred to these personal accounts in much the same way as his former professor of biology might have illustrated biological concepts with specimens (as James himself collected on expeditions during his brief phase studying to be a naturalist in the style of Darwin). James justified his method thus:

> In my belief that a large acquaintance with particulars often makes us wiser than the possession of abstract formulas, however deep, I have loaded the lectures with concrete examples, and I have chosen these among the extremer expressions of religious temperament. (James, 1902/2009, p. 5)

Here, James also described his method of selection. He chose the most extreme examples of spiritual experience because, he argued, one can often learn about a general phenomenon from studying its more extreme manifestations. But this means that his sample of personal accounts is therefore biased toward intense and potentially transformative experiences instead of subtle, daily kinds of experiences—though he did include a few more subtle experiences as well.

This argument may have also come from his background in physiology. In order to learn about an organ's normal functions, it is often useful to study it when it has been damaged or is operating under otherwise unusual conditions. We agree with this method of selection, especially since it is generally easier to observe and measure phenomena that produce a stronger effect using scientific instruments. For example, with brain imaging, it is easier to observe more intense changes in the brain compared to more mild ones. Simple amplification is often helpful when making scientific measurements.

Many psychological processes are so subtle and intertwined with other processes that it is difficult to isolate particular causes and effects. For example, to measure the physiological underpinnings of anger, one would usually be better off studying someone who is in a fit of rage rather than someone who is merely mildly annoyed. This general rule holds with other mental processes, whether it is sadness, joy, pain—or spiritual experience. In other words, James picked extreme examples to analyze the more general properties of spiritual experience (as will we). However, while we focus on these more intense experiences, we also hope to uncover the wide-ranging continuum of such experiences from the mild to the most mystical.

As mentioned, the personal accounts that fill *The Varieties* came from both classic and contemporary sources. James used personal accounts to illustrate various psychological points from the likes of Saint Teresa, Saint Augustine, Martin Luther, Sophocles, Goethe, Spinoza, Plato, Kant, Marcus Aurelius, George Fox, Hindu Vedantist Vivekananda, the Sufi al-Ghazali, Saint John of the Cross, and Ignatius Loyola. In terms of accounts from James's contemporaries, some were taken from Starbuck's study while others were taken from published books and articles. These include personal accounts from Leo Tolstoy, Emerson, Henry James Sr., Mary Baker Eddy, Walt Whitman, Henry David Thoreau, Richard Bucke, and Margaret Fuller. While these names may seem historical to modern readers, James knew many of these people personally. Defending this approach, James wrote:

I may take my citations, my sentences and paragraphs of personal confes-
sion, from books that most of you at some time will have already in your
hands, and yet this will be of no detriment to the value of my conclusions.
(James, 1902/2009, p. 7)

We draw on historical as well as contemporary accounts in much the same
manner.

James's Definitions

Among the first major points of *The Varieties* is to distinguish experiences,
which are James's subject, from religious/spiritual beliefs, doctrines, and
institutions. In limiting his discussion to experiences, his intention was not
to dismiss the value of these other aspects of religion/spirituality, but rather
to direct attention to a topic that he believed had been neglected. James considered religious beliefs to be the typical topic of scholarly inquiry. By instead
choosing to focus on experiences, he wrote, "I may succeed in discussing
religious experiences in a wider context than has been usual in university
courses" (James, 1902/2009, p. 23). Scholars have made it a habit of critiquing
James's selective attention to experiences, but if this can be called an over-
sight, then it was intentional.

Further in this book, as we turn to more contemporary research (including our own), we, too, focus on experiences. With that said, we also include some discussion about the influence of beliefs, culture, and various
rituals/practices. Thus, we recognize a significant reciprocal relationship
between religious beliefs, practices, social groups, culture, and experiences.
In addition, we hope to bring to light the implications of this research on
the more "everyday" religious and spiritual experiences. These can occur
going to church or gazing at a beautiful sunset. Some of these more minor
experiences, including beliefs themselves, may contain subjective elements
and utilize brain structures and functions that are associated with the more
intense religious and spiritual experiences cited by James.

One of James's early tasks in *The Varieties* was defining religion. Religion
is a classically difficult concept to define—and spirituality is perhaps more
difficult still. Of course, religion has been defined in enumerable ways over
time. Sociologist Durkheim (1912) discussed religion in terms of its group-
related aspects, as a set of beliefs shared by a community. Theologian Paul

Tillich (1965) described religion as referring to that which is one's "ultimate concern." Another theologian, Friedrich Schleiermacher (1893), associated religion with a "feeling of absolute dependence." Many, many more examples could be given.

At first, James claimed that an abstract definition of religion would be more misleading than informative. He cited "government" as another concept that is common and intuitive but difficult to encapsulate in a sentence or two. Later, the philosopher Wittgenstein (1953) would similarly describe his failed attempt to define the word "game" to make the point that definitions of the sort that require a necessary and sufficient set of conditions can sometimes add more confusion than clarity. But James did ultimately provide some working definitions.

First, though, he cited with disapproval a few examples of scholars who attempt to define religion in terms of something else:

> In the psychologies and in the philosophies of religion, we find the authors attempting to specify just what entity it is. One man allies it to the feeling of dependence; one makes it a derivative from fear; others connect it with the sexual life; others still identify it with the feeling of the infinite; and so on. (James, 1902/2009, p. 25)

But James did *not* want to define religion in terms of some other, seemingly related concept. Instead, he first identified what he did *not* mean by religion, to bring the reader closer to his intended subject.

> One way to mark it out easily is to say what aspects of the subject we leave out. At the outset we are struck by one great partition which divides the religious field. On the one side of it lies institutional, on the other personal religion. (James, 1902/2009, p. 26)

James's distinction between "institutional" religion and "personal" religion hints at the distinction between beliefs and experiences. He reiterated his intention to focus on *experience* here. To say that James insisted on this point would not be an overstatement. He made the point in several different other places:

> In critically judging the value of religious phenomena, it is very important to insist on the distinction between religion as an individual personal

function, and religion as an institutional, corporate, or tribal product. (James, 1902/2009, p. 255)

While James firmly established his intention to focus on what he termed "personal religion" rather than institutions or doctrine, James provided several further definitions related to religion throughout *The Varieties*. One definition of religion supplied by James has a belief-based component.

> [Religion] consists of the belief that there is an unseen order, and that our supreme good lies in harmoniously adjusting ourselves thereto. (James, 1902/2009, p. 43)

However, this belief-based definition is undercut by how loosely one can interpret the phrase "unseen order." In Robert Wright's (2010) book *Evolution of God*, he argued that other concepts, such as morality (or even entropy), could constitute this unseen order. James himself further undermined this belief-based definition by arguing elsewhere that religion could be considered a much broader concept, without the need even of the "unseen order." James wrote: "Religion, whatever it is, is a man's total reaction upon life, so why not say that any total reaction upon life is a religion?" (James, 1902, p. 30). James noted that while this may be an accurate way of characterizing religion in terms of how people sometimes use the word (he similarly noted that atheists can be "devout" in their disbelief of God), it would be impractical. This definition would include too much and make it too difficult to hone in on the topic he hoped to discuss.

Ultimately, James arrived at a definition that emphasized the role of experience:

> Religion, therefore, as I now ask you arbitrarily to take it, shall mean for us the feelings, acts, and experiences of individual men in their solitude, so far as they apprehend themselves to stand in relation to whatever they may consider the divine. (James, 1902, p. 27)

In this definition, James considered a fundamental element of religion is the "relation" to what an individual deems "divine." This statement contains two important points. The first is the notion of a relationship—a connection between one's self and something else. Second, that relationship can be between the self and any number of referents as long as the individual considers that other as divine in some way. That could include, for example, God, spirits, an all-pervading mind, or perhaps, existence itself or even humanity. It is not clear whether James intended to stipulate whether or not supernatural concepts were necessary to a definition of religion, but given the looseness of his other definitions, it's reasonable to assume that he would rather be permissive in his characterization of what can be considered religious here, too.

Contemporary Approaches to Definition

Importantly, we believe that James would have been fine with our relabeling of his "religious" experiences as "spiritual" experiences. He basically said as much, writing "I am willing to accept almost any name for the personal religion of which I propose to treat" (James, 1902, p. 39). As mentioned in our introduction, other modern scholars have noted this as well, as psychologists Miller and Thorenson (1999, p. 7) wrote that "When William James (1902/1985) wrote the book, *The Varieties of Religious Experience*, a century ago, he was clearly describing the broader domain that is now called spirituality." "Spirituality" as a term is broader and incorporates more types of experiences than just religious ones.

In the survey that we conducted for this book, the Varieties Survey, we asked participants what they preferred to call their experience. We asked them whether they have had an experience that could be described using any of the following terms, and then listed: religious, spiritual, mystical, peak, transcendent, numinous, ecstatic, paranormal, self-transcendent experience, or an experience of intense awe. We then asked what word that they most preferred to use when referring to their experience. As shown in Figure 3.1, we found that "spiritual experience" was the most commonly endorsed term.

We follow James's approach in *The Varieties* by focusing on experiences that are broadly considered spiritual, but what is spirituality? Spirituality is not only frequently linked with religion, but is also viewed as somewhat distinct. For many, spirituality relates more to individual conceptions and less to institutionally stipulated understandings. There is an important relationship between religion and spirituality, and it is difficult to define either religion or spirituality without some reference to the other. Interestingly, their word origins are markedly different. "Spirituality" is derived from Middle English and the Latin word *spiritus*, which means "breath," suggesting it represents an essential component of life. The word *religion* is generally thought to derive

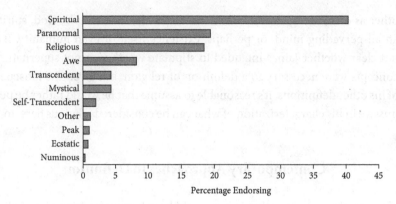

Figure 3.1 Preferred terms for experiences. Drawn by David B. Yaden.

from Latin influences from words meaning "to bind." These definitions suggest that religion is a way to bind people together (and ultimately with God), which could point to a more institutional or at least community-based quality. Spirituality could refer to something closer to one's inner life, or subjective experience. Whether these differences spring from the etymologies or not, this is how they are typically construed in contemporary contexts (Hill et al., 2000).

There was an early iteration during James's time of what is commonly considered New Age spirituality today, called the "mind-cure" movement. The mind-cure movement was based on the belief that adopting a healthy attitude toward life could be beneficial to one's overall health. It also included a number of beliefs about unseen "forces" and "energies" that could be tapped into for one's personal benefit. James included quotations of some proponents of the central tenants of this movement in *The Varieties* neither approvingly nor disparagingly, but simply descriptively. Here, James cited a proponent of the movement in *The Varieties,* who described it in a way that has clear resonances with contemporary New Age spirituality:

The great central fact of the universe is that spirit of infinite life and power that is back of all, that manifests itself in and through all. This spirit of infinite life and power that is back of all is what I call God. I care not what term you may use, be it Kindly Light, Providence, the Over-Soul, Omnipotence, or whatever term may be most convenient, so long as we are agreed in regard to the great central fact itself. . . . The great central fact in human life is the coming into a conscious vital realization of our oneness with this

Infinite Life and the opening of ourselves fully to this divine inflow. (cited in James, 1902/2009, p. 79)

Then as now, the distinctions between religiousness and spirituality are often unclear. For example, many spiritual people meditate or engage in spirituality as a group. Additionally, many religions require people to pray at home or work as individuals rather than in groups. Religions tend to be more doctrinal with specific rituals, prayers, ceremonies, and holidays that follow more particular and institutionally codified patterns. However, spiritual pursuits have also become more codified, such that many people do meditation in particular ways, almost in a ritualistic manner. Also, even noninstitutional spiritual traditions will frequently turn to ancient sacred texts in much the same way more traditional religions do.

While psychologist Carl Gustav Jung is more often cited as the psychologist most anticipating contemporary spirituality, James was also aware of broad emerging forms of spirituality (i.e., the mind-cure movement) and seemed to have recognized the psychological needs that it was appealing to in people. In contemporary parlance, this is associated with those who consider themselves "spiritual but not religious."

According to a large study conducted by Pew, about one fifth of the U.S. population, and almost one third for individuals under 30, consider themselves spiritual but not religious (Funk & Smith, 2012). Notably, the same study showed that the vast majority of religious people consider themselves religious *and* spiritual. In the United States, only a small percentage of the population considers themselves neither religious nor spiritual, although this number is growing and is much more prevalent in Europe.

There are also individuals who define spirituality in a way that does not include supernatural beliefs. Some individuals, like Sam Harris (2014) in his book *Waking Up: A Guide to Spirituality Without Religion*, use the term in such a way that it does not refer to anything supernatural whatsoever. He wrote: "Spirituality must be distinguished from religion—because people of every faith, and of none, have had the same sorts of spiritual experiences" (Harris, 2014, p. 8). Unusual uses like this underscore the importance of defining one's terms, at least to some degree, when referring to religion and spirituality.

Religiosity and spirituality are typically understood by psychologists to be matters of degree. However, while there is a continuum, it should be emphasized that people also seem to know the difference between a spiritual experience and what might be regarded as an "everyday" experience. Psychologists tend not to measure these constructs as simple yes/no binaries, but rather measure the *degree* to which one feels that they are a religious or spiritual person. Measures of religion and spirituality correlate very highly with one another, demonstrating that most (but not all) religious individuals are spiritual and, likewise, most (but not all) spiritual people are religious (though with the exceptions noted previously). Here are a couple of typical survey questions, or what psychologists call "items," to measure religiosity and spirituality:

- To what extent do you consider yourself to be a religious person?
  Not at all religious—Slightly religious—Somewhat religious—Very religious
- To what extent do you consider yourself to be a spiritual person?
  Not at all spiritual—Slightly spiritual—Somewhat spiritual—Very spiritual

There have been several recent attempts to arrive at commonly accepted definitions of both religion and spirituality. One way forward on this front is to abandon the notion of a propositional definition of religion or spirituality, or a set of necessary and sufficient conditions, and to attempt a *substantive* definition, which attempts to gather the elements often associated with the concepts. This is the approach that we take and describe in the next section.

Beyond Beliefs—Religion and Spirituality as Multidimensional Constructs

James made some headway in *The Varieties* by providing definitions of religion and religious experience that are more abstract, and therefore at least slightly more universal and amenable to scientific inquiry, than those that had been typically offered by philosophers and theologians. He also made substantial progress in differentiating elements of religion and spirituality from one another. For example, James insisted on breaking what some viewed as a necessary connection between beliefs and experiences.

Contemporary attempts to define religion or spirituality have tended to follow in James's footsteps by distinguishing religious beliefs from experiences and providing conceptualizations that treat beliefs, experiences, and affiliations as distinct and differentiable elements. Psychologists call concepts like this, which have a number of different aspects, "multidimensional" (Graham & Haidt, 2010; Yaden et al., 2021). Entire academic conferences have been convened specifically for the purpose of arriving at shared definitions of religion and spirituality (Fetzer, 1999). The general consensus of several of these conferences has been to propose aspects, or dimensions, of religiousness and spirituality as opposed to propositional definitions.

We often work with a specific multidimensional understanding of religion and spirituality that we developed in collaboration with Justin McDaniel, chair of the University of Pennsylvania's Department of Religious Studies. The definition describes the elements that tend to co-occur in spirituality and religion, with the soft distinction that religion is more explicitly institutionally codified and has more widely accepted details for each element than spirituality. Here are the various major elements involved in the study of religion and spirituality:

- Practices
- Rituals
- Affiliation
- Institutions
- Scripture
- Experiences
- Beliefs

This list forms an acronym—PRAISE-Be—and while this acronym was an accident (fortunate or unfortunate, we're still not sure), it does make the model rather memorable. Practices refer to activities that individuals can and often (though not always) perform alone, such as prayer or meditation. Rituals refer to activities that people tend to perform in group settings, such as attending mass or other services held in places of worship. Affiliation relates to identity, the degree to which one considers themselves as being religious or spiritual and the particular religion or sect to which one belongs. Institution describes the community to which one belongs, the specific individuals and the particular place that form one's actual religious or spiritual community. Scripture includes the sacred texts, stories, and symbols of one's religion or spiritual tradition and how one engages with them (e.g., reading passages or wearing religious garb). Experiences refer to transient mental states or altered states of consciousness to which one attributes religious or spiritual significance or that *involve the perception of and connection to an unseen order of some kind* (following one of James's definitions, which forms our rough working definition of spiritual experience, as will be discussed).

Last, beliefs refer to what one thinks is true about the nature or meaning of existence. We return to the issue of belief further in this book, as it is the most difficult aspect to isolate and address. In general, though, *a belief will be considered religious or spiritual if it involves or entails a nonphysical mind of some kind.* This mind could be God's mind, some other nonphysical entity, or one's own mind if it could exist beyond a physical body (i.e., a soul).

The takeaway here is that religion and spirituality contain many components, which may or may not necessarily coappear with one another in a given individual or group. This model surprises some people because religions are typically associated solely with beliefs, yet here beliefs constitute only one of seven other elements. Readers might compare their own relationship with aspects of religion/spirituality other than religion using this list:

- Do you pray or meditate?
- Do you attend religious services?
- Do you identify with a particular belief system (Christian, Buddhist, atheist, agnostic)?
- Do you belong to a particular, local religious or spiritual group?
- Do you read religious texts?
- Do you have specific religious/spiritual beliefs?

Each of these elements undoubtedly influences, but is not reducible to, the one element that constitutes our primary focus in this book—*experience*. There are a number of cultural examples that include apparent contradictions that this model helps make sense of. For example, philosopher Alain de Botton's (2012) book *Religion for Atheists* promotes the use of religious rituals (like spending time with family on the Sabbath) without endorsing religious beliefs. As previously mentioned, atheist Sam Harris (2014) described the value of meditation in *Waking Up: A Guide to Spirituality Without Religion*, but disparaged religious and spiritual beliefs. Journalist Barbara Ehrenreich (2014) described several spiritual experiences in her autobiography, *Living With a Wild God*, but did not use religious or spiritual beliefs to interpret her experiences. Mindfulness meditation, an originally Buddhist practice, is now one of the fastest growing psychological interventions in healthcare and has been made widely available to people of all belief systems. Similarly, there may be many individuals who practice prayer, participate in rituals, affiliate as religious, attend a specific church/temple/mosque, read scripture regularly, and believe in God—but who have not had an intense spiritual experience.

This discussion of the continuum of spiritual experiences also brings forth one other important topic—consciousness. Consciousness (or more precisely phenomenal consciousness) refers to the subjective sensations, "what it's like" to be a particular organism. We are generally conscious of ourselves, our feelings, thoughts, and experiences. Thus, spiritual experiences occur *within* our consciousness. Furthermore, spiritual experiences often result in changed beliefs about the nature of consciousness. We explore these issues in more depth in Chapter 19, which focuses on consciousness. Last, the spiritual experiences that we focus on are "altered states of consciousness," meaning that they are substantial deviations from one's normal waking state of awareness.

One final point to emphasize regarding definitions has to do with their origins. For example, we have considered many accounts of religiousness and spirituality as derived from psychological perspectives. However, theologians and philosophers might have a completely different conception of these and other related terms. Other scientists, sociologists, anthropologists, and clergy might have still other definitions. And, of course, the general population holds a diverse array of definitions of religion, spirituality, soul, God, and others. We treat the definitions and categories in a way similar to James—as rough proxies to move closer to our intended topic. While our rough working definition of spiritual experience is a substantially altered state of consciousness involving a perception of, and connection to, an unseen order of some kind, we continue to characterize and define spiritual experience(s) in increasingly specific terms throughout this book.

Conclusion

In *The Varieties*, James argued that many types of people have had what he called "religious experiences," which we call "spiritual experiences." In contemporary psychological research, it is now taken for granted that religion and spiritualty can be broken down into different aspects, as multidimensional constructs. We have also seen that spiritual experience can be studied with some degree of independence from beliefs—which is important, as atheists, agnostics, the spiritual but not religious, Christians, Jews, Hindus,

Buddhists, and Muslims (and many others) all report spiritual experiences. We continue to characterize spiritual experiences and investigate their causes and effects using data from fields such as psychology, neuroscience, and statistics in the coming chapters.

References

De Botton, A. (2012). *Religion for atheists: A non-believer's guide to the uses of religion.* Vintage.

Durkheim, E. (1912). *The elementary forms of religious life.* Free.

Ehrenreich, B. (2014). *Living with a wild God: A nonbeliever's search for the truth about everything.* Grand Central.

Fetzer Institute/National Institute on Aging Working Group. (1999). *Multidimensional measurement of religiousness/spirituality for use in health research.* John E. Fetzer Institute.

Funk, C., & Smith, G. (2012). *"Nones" on the rise: One-in-five adults have no religious affiliation.* Pew Research Center.

Graham, J., & Haidt, J. (2010). Beyond beliefs: Religions bind individuals into moral communities. *Personality and Social Psychology Review, 14*(1), 140–150.

Harris, S. (2014). *Waking up: A guide to spirituality without religion.* Simon & Schuster.

Hill, P. C., Pargament, K. I., Hood, R. W., McCullough, J. M. E., Swyers, J. P., Larson, D. B., & Zinnbauer, B. J. (2000). Conceptualizing religion and spirituality: Points of commonality, points of departure. *Journal for the Theory of Social Behaviour, 30*(1), 51–77.

Hood, R. W., Hill, P. C., & Spilka, B. (2009). *The psychology of religion: An empirical approach.* New York, NY: Guilford.

James, W. (1902/2009). *The varieties of religious experience: A study in human nature. eBooks@Adelaide.* https://csrs.nd.edu/assets/59930/williams_1902.pdf

Kibbe, M. M. (2015). Varieties of visual working memory representation in infancy and beyond. *Current Directions in Psychological Science, 24*(6), 433–439.

Masters, R. E., & Houston, J. (1966). *The varieties of psychedelic experience* (Vol. 9289). Holt, Rinehart and Winston.

Miller, W. R., & Thoresen, L. E. (1999). Spirituality and health. In W. R. Miller (Ed.), *Integrating spirituality into treatment* (pp. 3–18). American Psychological Association.

Richardson, R. D. (2006). *William James: In the maelstrom of American modernism.* Houghton Mifflin.

Sagan, C. (2006). *The varieties of scientific experience: A personal view of the search for God.* Penguin.

Schleiermacher, F. (1893). *On religion: Speeches to its cultured despisers.* K. Paul, Trench, Trübner & Company.

Starbuck, E. D. (1899). *The psychology of religion: An empirical study of the growth of religious consciousness* (Vol. 38). Walter Scott.

Tillich, P. (1965). *Ultimate concern.* Harper & Row.

Wittgenstein, L. (2009). *Philosophical investigations.* Wiley. (Original work published 1953)

Wright, R. (2010). *The evolution of God: The origins of our beliefs.* Hachette UK.

Yaden, D. B., Giorgi, S., Kern, M. L., Adler, A., Ungar, L. H., Seligman, M. E., & Eichstaedt, J. C. (2021). Beyond beliefs: Multidimensional aspects of religion and spirituality in language. *Psychology of Religion and Spirituality.* https://doi.org/10.1037/rel0000408

Yaden, D. B., Haidt, J., Hood, R. W., Jr., Vago, D. R., & Newberg, A. B. (2017). The varieties of self-transcendent experience. *Review of General Psychology, 21*(2), 143–160.

4

The Psychology of Spiritual Experiences

> It seems to me that here the statistical method has held its own, and
> that its percentages and averages have proved to possess genuine
> significance.
>
> —James in the preface of Starbuck, 1899, p. ix.

William James is well known among scientists and scholars, but his work
is little known among the general population. This became apparent
when one of us (D. B. Y.) was taking a taxi to Harvard's Countway Library,
which holds the only copy of a deleted chapter from C. G. Jung's autobiography where he describes his relationship with James. Driving through
the streets of Cambridge, Massachusetts, on the way to read the manuscript, D. B. Y. struck up a conversation with the driver about his visit to
the library. Of the three historical psychologists that were discussed—
William James, Carl Gustav Jung, and Sigmund Freud—the cab driver
definitely knew of Freud, had maybe heard of Jung, but did not know
anything about William James. This experience is pretty representative
of the general population. In our Varieties Survey, we found that 90% of
our sample had not heard of William James or *The Varieties of Religious
Experience: A Study in Human Nature* (hereafter *The Varieties*; James,
1902) (Figure 4.1).

This is unfortunate. While psychological theories from the better known
Freud and Jung are now studied more in English Departments than in
Psychology Departments, James's ideas remain part of the foundation of
contemporary scientific psychological research. Unlike the other two early
psychologists, James's support of quantitatively measuring beliefs, behaviors,
and experiences and grounding our understanding of psychology in terms of
physiology and experimental research are all consistent with contemporary
psychology.

The Varieties of Spiritual Experience. David B. Yaden and Andrew B. Newberg, Oxford University Press. © David Yaden
and Andrew Newberg 2022. DOI: 10.1093/oso/9780190665678.003.0004

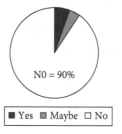

Figure 4.1 Percentage of sample who had ever heard of William James or *The Varieties of Religious Experience*. Drawn by David B. Yaden.

James, though world famous in his day (note: philosopher Bertrand Russell described him as one of the most famous academics in the world; Russell, 1945), his legacy was eclipsed for several decades by figures in psychoanalysis, behaviorism, and humanistic psychology. The scientific study of spiritual experience followed a similar pattern, resurfacing only recently as a viable topic of psychological research. This chapter describes several false starts in the field of psychology on the study of spiritual experience since *The Varieties* was published (James, 1902/2009). We then describe the conceptual and statistical advances that have made the contemporary scientific study of spiritual experiences possible. We argue that the field of psychology has only recently become capable of fully pursuing James's scientific vision as described in *The Varieties*.

Science of Religions

In *The Varieties*, James (1902/2009) largely succeeded in examining spiritual experiences from an empirical perspective, as he focused his discussion on those aspects of spiritual experience that are observable or reportable. While he did dive into philosophical discussions at the end of *The Varieties*, he resisted the temptation for most of the book. This may have been done in the service of first convincing his audience that such experiences can be studied scientifically before engaging in philosophical speculation. Again, it is important to remember that for almost the entirety of *The Varieties* James avoided addressing the question of whether spiritual experiences could be considered "real" in the supernatural sense. We similarly postpone this question, citing James's own words in our defense:

But I shall keep myself as far as possible at present to the more "scientific" view; and only as the plot thickens in subsequent lectures shall I consider the question of its absolute sufficiency as an explanation of all the facts. (James, 1902/2009, p. 180)

James was especially insistent on focusing on what can be observed empirically when describing his vision for a "science of religions." James recommended that scientific inquiries into spiritual experience "abandon metaphysics and deduction" and instead engage in "criticism and induction" (James, 1902/2009, p. 344). In other words, James advocated for scientific studies on the subject. This empirical approach would depend in part on people's self-reports—that is, from accounts provided by individuals who have had spiritual experiences. Here, James described the importance of self-report in psychological research on spiritual experience:

Yet as the science of optics has to be fed in the first instance, and continually verified later, by facts experienced by seeing persons; so the science of religions would depend for its original material on facts of personal experience, and would have to square itself with personal experience through all its critical reconstructions. (James, 1902/2009, p. 345)

James was drawing a comparison between the study of vision, which requires careful observations of what someone is seeing, and the surrounding conditions of light, shape, and motion. A science of religions, just like the study of vision, would still depend on people reporting their experience, although rather than light, shape, and motion, issues such as culture, beliefs, and physiological conditions would play more of a role.

James (1902/2009) confined most of his writing about the science of religions to the last few chapters of *The Varieties*. But while this topic was raised last, it would be a mistake to consider it the least among his concerns. Indeed, it may have been a chief motivation for *The Varieties*, a goal traceable to his preface in Starbuck's (1899) book years earlier. The present book, we hope, will show that James would have reason to be happy were he able to witness the state of the art in scientific progress on the topic of spiritual experience. This progress was hard won, however, and required a number of conceptual and methodological advances in psychology, which we review in the following sections.

PSYCHOLOGICAL APPROACHES 53

The Margins of Consciousness

In *The Varieties* (1902/2009), James discussed some potential psychological processes that make spiritual experiences possible. One such psychological process is what James called the "transmarginal" or "subliminal" aspects of the mind, which sounds close to the conception of the "unconscious" in psychoanalysis. James explicitly acknowledged Freud's early work in this area, citing Freud in a footnote in *The Varieties*, but his discussions of this idea are brief. Furthermore, James's conception of the unconscious is much less definite than Freud's speculations. For instance, James did not grant the same kind of sexual and malevolent agency as Freud did to this region of the psyche. Instead, James seemed to use the notion of the subliminal as a placeholder for whatever mental process related to the imagination from which dreams and creative epiphanies come:

> In religion we have a department of human nature with unusually close relations to the transmarginal or subliminal region. If the word "subliminal" is offensive to any of you . . . call it by any name you please, to distinguish it from the level of full sunlit consciousness. Call this latter the A-region of personality, if you care to, and call the other the B-region. (James, 1902/2009, p. 365)

At the same time, James was sensitive to how some people might take such an explanation as deflating the value of spiritual experience. That is, James reiterated his agnostic method. He specifically addressed those individuals who might wonder if he was being overly reductionistic:

> But if you, being orthodox Christians, ask me as a psychologist whether the reference to a phenomenon to a subliminal self does not exclude the notion of a direct presence of the Deity altogether, I have to say that as a psychologist I do not see why it necessarily should. (James, 1902/2009, p. 184)

James was, yet again, being explicit about setting aside the question of whether or not spiritual experiences have anything to say about supernatural beliefs. James's approach was, in our opinion, balanced, integrating a number of seeming contradictions and ever open to possibilities. Even when James suggested that there may be a nonconscious region of the mind involved in spiritual experience, he was unwilling to rush to any sweeping conclusions. That is, he remained firmly agnostic in his method.

Psychoanalysis

James's empirical and nuanced take on spiritual experience was temporarily eclipsed by Freud's more simplistic psychoanalytic view. Freud and James shared some similarities in their training and influences. Like James, Freud was also interested in hypnosis, and he dedicated several years of his life to its study. Both had backgrounds in physiology and medicine and shared an affinity for Darwin. Freud's psychoanalytic perspective, however, differed dramatically from James's vision of empirical psychology.

Psychoanalysis depends largely on the interpretation of symbols and unconscious content, while largely eschewing scientific research methods. These differences are especially visible in their different takes on spiritual experience, which can be illustrated by Freud's response to a question about spiritual experience posed by Nobel Prize–winning author Romain Rolland. In the first chapter of *Civilization and Its Discontents* (1930/1989), Freud described his correspondence with Rolland, a scholar who was instrumental in relating Vedantic philosophy from India to European audiences. (Note: In acknowledgment of his cross-cultural scholarly work, Hermann Hesse's novel *Siddhartha* was dedicated to Rolland.) Rolland wrote to Freud saying that he largely agreed with Freud's assessment of many religious beliefs (i.e., that they are illusory projections onto the universe of one's yearnings for parental comfort)—but he asked Freud's opinion regarding spiritual experiences. After considering Rolland's account of what Freud referred to as "oceanic feelings of oneness," Freud wrote:

> The idea of men's receiving an intimation of their connection with the world around them . . . sounds so strange and fits so badly with the fabric of our psychology that one is justified in attempting to discover a psycho-analytic . . . explanation of such a feeling. (Freud, 1930/1989, p. 12)

To Freud, spiritual experiences involving feelings of unity are "strange" and do not fit his assumption of normal psychological health. Freud did admit that when one is in romantic love the boundary between one's self and another can melt away, and that people can behave in a selfless way toward their partners. However, Freud did *not* admit the possibility of this mental state in other contexts, such as in spiritual experience, as anything other than pathological.

In other words, where James was curious, Freud was judgmental. Where James was careful and complex, Freud was reductive. These tendencies went beyond his views of spiritual experiences—it was also James's personal impression of Freud's character. In a special moment in the history of psychology, James met Freud and Freud's student, Carl Gustav Jung, at Clark University in 1909, seven years after the publication of *The Varieties* (James, 1902/1902). According to one biographer, James was unimpressed by Freud but liked Jung.

> James was favorably impressed by Jung, but less admiring of the fifty-three year old Freud, who lectured on dreams, a talk that James found troubling because of its sexual references. Freud, he said, seemed to him "a man obsessed by fixed ideas. I make nothing in my own case with his dream theories, and obviously symbolism is a most dangerous method." (Simon, 1998, p. 363)

James seemed to have made little impact on Freud, but Jung later came to agree with many of James's ideas (Richardson, 2006, p. 515). In fact, there is good evidence that Jung's later career was more influenced by James than by Freud. Jung went on to cite James in his writings, referred explicitly to his ideas, and by some accounts after he returned to Europe became something of an evangelist for reading James's work on religion.

Even more convincing evidence for this argument comes from a chapter on William James that was posthumously removed from Jung's (1963) autobiography, *Memories, Dreams, Reflections*. This missing chapter about James in Jung's autobiography was excluded by the book's editor, Aniela Jaffe, who some have charged with intentionally perpetuating a Freud-centric narrative of Jung's life. When one reads this excluded chapter from Jung's autobiography (which can only be read by physically going to the basement of Harvard's Countway Library), there appears to be some merit to this critique. Here again is Jung from the deleted chapter of his autobiography:

> I was most stimulated by James's ideas about religious psychology. His effort to give some objective picture of what is felt to be religious experience served to some extent as a model for me. I was profoundly stirred by his

presentation of the religious experience as a direct occurrence, a fact whose nature is what it is. In other words, he did not attempt to fit any such experience into a theoretical formula. . . . He approached these phenomena with an unbiased pragmatic attitude, and thus showed me a path which subsequently led me to gratifying results. (Jung & Jaffe, unpublished Manuscript)

Jung's appreciation of James went well beyond his character. Jung was also impressed, one might almost say "converted," by James's views on spiritual experience.

While Freud had never had a spiritual experience, Jung certainly did. Jung underwent an extended period of time during which he was nearly overwhelmed by frequent and intense spiritual experiences. He recorded some of his experiences in *The Red Book* (Jung et al., 2009), his personal spiritual autobiography. Jung kept this book locked away in a Swiss vault and insisted in his will that it should not be made public until 60 years after his death. The alleged reason for this secrecy was that he "dreaded the reaction of the public for one thing because of the candor with which he had revealed his religious experiences" (Jaffe in introduction to Jung, 1963, p. xii). The taboo around spiritual experience was such that it compelled Jung to lock away his accounts of his own experiences for decades after his death—a taboo that has only partially lifted over the years.

In general, while psychoanalysis provides a number of speculative perspectives on spiritual experience, these views do not generally persist in their influence on contemporary research. In some clinical settings, however, Freud's negative views on spiritual experience have had a significant influence. On the other hand, Jung's positive views have continued to affect some contemporary subcultures of spirituality and a few clinical groups, but remain largely irrelevant to the research literature. In our view, James provided a more balanced and evidence-based account of spiritual experience than either Freud's pathologizing perspective or Jung's almost wholly enthusiastic assessment.

Behaviorism

Behaviorism was in some ways the methodological opposite of psychoanalysis. Rather than adopting psychoanalysis's quasi-literary style of analyzing dreams and therapy sessions, behaviorism attempted to ban all talk of mental states from psychological research. Famously promoted by Ivan Pavlov, John Watson, and B. F. Skinner, behaviorism attempted to study *only* observable actions. Instead of memories, dreams, and reflections (note: the title of Jung's autobiography)—stimulus and response became the primary subject of psychological study.

This view also has discernible roots in James's thought. James was famous for being the codiscoverer of the "James–Lange" theory of emotion. According to this view, behaviors are primary and one's feelings and sensations related to them come secondarily and hold little causal power. That is, in the domain of emotions, it is our actions that determine our feelings—not the other way around. To illustrate this idea, James described the experience of being startled by a bear in the forest. Most people would think that one *first* sees the bear, then feels fear, and *then* runs. James, however, considered another possibility: What if, rather than feeling fear and then running away, one feels fear *because* one is already running away from the bear? That is, behavior may play a primary role, and the emotions that we feel are the result of our mind making sense of that behavior. Put yet another way: "we feel sorry because we cry, angry because we strike, afraid because we tremble . . . " (James, 1890, p. 499; note that the expression commonly attributed to James: "We don't laugh because we're happy, we're happy because we laugh" is a misattribution). The paradigm of behaviorism would study the laugh, but not attempt to investigate the feeling of happiness or how the mind processed the humor.

Behaviorism, as the name suggests, focuses on studying behavior alone. James's ideas on this topic were acknowledged as early influences, but behaviorists often claimed that only observable demonstrations of all claims could aspire to be considered valuable. Behaviorism, while empirical and based on laboratory science, ignored spiritual experiences. This is understandable, since although spiritual experiences are intense, they remain almost entirely subjective. Therefore, behaviorism did not have the scientific or conceptual tools necessary to study spiritual experiences (Belzen & Hood, 2006) and so passed over them in silence.

Humanistic and Transpersonal Psychology

Humanistic psychology was an attempt to find a way forward that went beyond the then-entrenched views of psychoanalysis and behaviorism. For this reason, it was nicknamed the "third force" in psychology. Transpersonal psychology, yet another subfield that took spirituality and spiritual experience as a primary subject of interest, emerged as a branch of humanistic psychology.

In broad strokes, humanistic and transpersonal psychology drew on existentialist philosophy. Rather than the deterministic theories of psychoanalysis and behaviorism, these paradigms in psychology advocated a faith in free will and the seeking of personal authenticity. For example, Victor Frankl, a Jewish psychiatrist from Vienna and Holocaust survivor, was an early inspiration for this movement. In *Man's Search for Meaning* (1946/1985), Frankl wrote that one could create or find *meaning* in any circumstance, no matter how terrible, and he claimed that this ability is an essential component of mental health. Notably, Frankl also described a spiritual experience that he had while he was in the concentration camp:

> A thought transfixed me: for the first time in my life I saw the truth as it is set into song by so many poets, proclaimed as the final wisdom by so many thinkers. The truth—that love is the ultimate and the highest goal to which man can aspire. Then I grasped the meaning of the greatest secret that human poetry and human thought and belief have to impart: The salvation of man is through love and in love. . . . For the first time in my life I was able to understand the meaning of the words, "The angels are lost in perpetual contemplation of an infinite glory." (Frankl, 1946/1989, p. 37)

Abraham Maslow, an American psychologist, was the person most responsible for founding humanistic and transpersonal psychology. Maslow had a deep interest in spiritual experiences (he referred to them as "peak experiences"). Through the course of interviewing highly successful, creative, and emotionally balanced individuals, who he called "self-actualized," he found that a large portion of them described peak experiences to him. Maslow, like James, emphasized that these experiences could occur to individuals of any belief (or nonbelief) system.

Maslow considered peak experiences conducive to psychological growth and maturity and something like the opposite of traumas. According to Maslow, those who have a peak experience temporarily take on the characteristics of a self-actualized individual. In *Religion, Values, and Peak Experiences* (1964), written about 60 years after *The Varieties* (James, 1902/2009), Maslow articulated a number of features of peak experiences that square well with how James described religious experience—here are just a few:

- "The whole universe is perceived as an integrated and unified whole." (Maslow, 1964, p. 59)
- "To say this in a different way, perception in the peak-experiences can be relatively ego-transcending, self-forgetful, egoless, unselfish." (Maslow, 1964, p. 62)
- "In the peak-experience there is a very characteristic disorientation in time and space, or even the lack of consciousness of time and space. Phrased positively, this is like experiencing universality and eternity." (Maslow, 1964, p. 63)
- The world seen in the peak-experiences is seen only as beautiful, good, desirable, worthwhile, etc. and is never experienced as evil or undesirable. The world is accepted. (Maslow, 1964, p. 59)
- In the peak-experiences, there tends to be a loss, even though transient, of fear, anxiety, inhibition, of defense and control, of perplexity, confusion, conflict, of delay and restraint. (Maslow, 1964, p. 66)
- "The peak-experiencer becomes more loving and more accepting . . . " (Maslow, 1964, p. 67)

These and Maslow's other observations comport well with James's analysis and have the added virtue of being phrased in somewhat more universal language (i.e., he does not make sense of them in explicitly religious terms). Maslow commented that these observations are "testable" but did not endeavor to do so. Humanistic psychology and transpersonal psychology generally engaged in conceptual writing rather than experimental research.

This is starting to change, though. Some contemporary researchers, led by psychologist Scott Barry Kaufman, are conducting quantitative research on concepts from humanistic psychology, such as self-actualization (Kaufman, 2018). For an in-depth look at insights from Maslow and how they relate to contemporary psychology research, see his book *Transcend* (Kaufman, 2021). Historically, however, humanistic and transpersonal psychology generally did not conduct empirical research on spiritual experience.

Early Psychedelic Research

Research using psychedelic substances came, for a brief time in the 1960s, to dominate the study of spiritual experiences. This work was conducted by a number of different scientists at major research universities. While James had discussed the possibility of using mescaline and nitrous oxide to study spiritual experience, a growing awareness of other psychedelic substances in the 20th century made this kind of research more accessible.

Maslow also commented on this controversial way of potentiating spiritual experiences:

> I may add a new possibility for scientific investigation of transcendence. In the last few years it has become quite clear that certain drugs called "psychedelic," especially LSD and psilocybin, give us some possibility of control in this realm of peak-experiences. It looks as if these drugs often produce peak-experiences in the right people under the right circumstances, so that perhaps we needn't wait for them to occur by good fortune. (Maslow, 1964, p. 27)

Timothy Leary is the most famous—or rather infamous—researcher who studied the use of psychedelic substances to induce spiritual experiences. Leary first came into contact with psychedelic substances through Gordon Wasson, an amateur mycologist who brought psychedelic mushrooms (*Psilocybe*) back with him from Mexico after trying them with Maria Sabina, a Mazatec healer. Sabina received little to no compensation for this, and the flood of tourists from the United States and Europe would severely damage her community in the ensuing years. Psychedelic mushrooms (containing psilocybin) had been used for centuries in Mexico and elsewhere in the world in religious contexts (Muraresku, 2020), a fact that is sometimes not acknowledged in histories of psychedelic use and research. Leary also later tried LSD, first synthesized by Swiss chemist Albert Hoffman in 1938.

After using each of these psychedelic substances himself, Leary was possessed by a revolutionary fervor regarding their potential to transform society and was indirectly involved in distributing some of these substances to college students. He is often (rightly, we think) cited as a poster child for irresponsible and overreaching advocacy of psychedelic use.

Leary and colleagues did, however, conduct several experimental studies on psychedelic substances as they pertain to spiritual experiences. The most famous of these was "the Good Friday experiment" conducted by one of Leary's collaborators, Walter Pahnke (1963). During a church service at Boston University's Marsh Chapel, seminary students were given either psilocybin (the active ingredient in psychedelic mushrooms) or niacin, a mostly inert vitamin. Researchers observed differences between these two groups, and found that the psychedelic group indicated that they felt the experience was far more meaningful and beneficial than the placebo group.

Of historical interest, comparative religion scholar Huston Smith was a subject in this study who received an active psychedelic dose. Huston said this about his experience in an interview (Jesse, 1997, p. 100):

> For as long as I can remember I have believed in God. . . . But until the Good Friday Experiment, I had had no direct personal encounter with God of the sort that bhakti yogis, Pentecostals, and born-again Christians describe.

Huston Smith would go on to write a number of books about his religious experience, as well as religions in general. A number of books by thinkers like Aldous Huxley (*The Doors of Perception*, 1954/2010) and Alan Watts (*The Joyous Cosmology*, 1962/2013) also describe the connection between psychedelic substances and spiritual experiences. These books typically went well beyond scientific interest and could in some cases be better described as examples of contemporary spirituality. Richard Alpert, another Harvard psychologist, was fired for distributing psychedelics to students and later went to India to study with a guru. As a result of his experiences there, he changed his name to Ram Dass and became a spiritual teacher, which he described in his book *Be Here Now* (Dass, 1971/2010). Together, these popular books raised public awareness about spiritual experiences, but they were written amid a rising tide of social and legal taboo around psychedelics due to their connection with the counterculture.

Psychedelic substances quickly expanded beyond controlled laboratory settings and into the culture at large. As a result of political forces, and in no small part due to Leary's irresponsible statements and behaviors, psychedelic substances were made illegal, and for all practical purposes were banned from research for many decades (Baumeister & Placidi, 1983). As we discuss further in this book, responsible psychedelic research is making a comeback in several leading research institutions, such as the work by Roland Griffiths and the team at Johns Hopkins (Yaden, Yaden, & Griffiths, 2021), which is providing breakthrough evidence-based insights into spiritual experience.

The Cognitive Revolution

The cognitive revolution in psychology largely took precedence over the paradigms of psychoanalysis, behaviorism, and humanistic/transpersonal psychology. It advocated for the potential to rigorously and systematically study mental processes. The cognitive revolution was in part inspired by advances in computer science and applying the metaphor of the computer to the human brain. According to this perspective, the mind can be understood (in crude terms) as like the "software" that operates through the "hardware" of the brain. Features of this software (i.e., mental processes) could thus be understood quantitatively. The proponents of this revolution believed that it was possible to study thoughts, beliefs, and mental states in a rigorously scientific way. The revolution effectively opened a new avenue for scientific research of mental processes, beyond introspection and speculation, as in psychoanalysis and humanistic psychology, and beyond observable behaviors alone, as in behaviorism. The cognitive revolution was the conceptual innovation that allowed the contemporary scientific study of spiritual experiences to truly begin.

The cognitive revolution dethroned behaviorism as the dominant paradigm of psychological research in large part due to three publications. The first was Noam Chomsky's critique (1959) of B. F. Skinner's explanation of language learning. Chomsky argued convincingly that language learning could not occur through a stimulus–response pattern alone—children learned language too quickly. Therefore, certain innate (or "prewired") cognitive capacities must make children prepared to learn certain aspects of the structure of language at birth. Second, George Miller (1956) showed that short-term memory operates under certain rules regardless of reward or punishment. He demonstrated that seven (plus or minus two) is approximately the number of objects that can be held simultaneously in short-term memory. This demonstrated that distinct mental processes have a specificity that can be reliably measured. Third, later and in the clinical domain, Martin Seligman (1972) showed that animals and humans are capable of transferring representational-like learning across contexts. Specifically, if a subject learns that nothing that they do matters in one situation, they will tend to carry that "learned helplessness" into other situations where they actually could have some control. This research showed that mental representations, not just behavior, need to be invoked to explain some phenomena.

These and other studies convinced the field of psychology that the mind should no longer be considered a "black box" about which nothing worthwhile (or reproducible) can be learned, as behaviorists had believed. This also opened the possibility of scientifically studying subjective experiences.

The cognitive approach, which remains the dominant paradigm, is more in line with James's views than those of psychoanalysis, behaviorism, or humanistic psychology (though none of these fields are alien to James's thinking, either). Specifically, James would have been sympathetic to the experimental rigor and quantitative approach in behaviorism, yet he would have wanted to study the kinds of topics that interested those in psychoanalysis and humanistic psychology. Contemporary psychology, under a broadly cognitive framework, allows for this application of rigorous methods to subjective experiences.

Gordon Allport, himself an important figure in the psychology of religion, described how James's thought was obscured for decades by the rise and fall of various perspectives in psychology, such as psychoanalysis and behaviorism. But James's views are broadly consistent with postcognitive revolution, contemporary approaches. Allport wrote:

> But now that we have recovered from the irreverent shocks administered by Freud, Pavlov, Watson, we begin to perceive that the psychological insights of James have the steadiness of a polar star. (Strandberg, 1981, p. 279)

Indeed, James anticipated a number of methods used in contemporary psychological research, and the field remains saturated with James's thinking across a number of topics.

Statistics and Psychometrics

The contemporary psychological study of spiritual experience has moved well beyond the limited paradigms of interpreting interviews of individuals (as in psychoanalysis and humanistic psychology) or reducing the scope of inquiry to observable behavior alone (as in behaviorism). New findings from psychological research often involve the measurement of mental processes using methods such as psychometrics.

Psychometrics is predicated on the idea that individuals can answer questions that reveal aspects of mental processes. That is, researchers can simply ask people what they are thinking or feeling, albeit in a systematic and quantifiable way. The conceptual advance of the cognitive revolution, that the measurement of mental processes is possible and worthwhile, was married to a methodology that has deep roots in the history of psychology—the measure of individual differences. This combination produced modern self-report survey research in psychology, itself an essential tool in the study of spiritual experience.

Darwin's *On the Origin of Species* (1859/2004) is largely a study of individual differences in various animal species. Inspired by Darwin's work, British scientist (and Darwin's half-cousin) Francis Galton began to apply the study of individual differences to humans.[1] His work and that of others resulted in the standardization of self-report measures—as well as commonly used statistical concepts like the standard deviation, regression, and correlation.

Historically, the rapid rise in popularity of self-report scales can be attributed, at least in part, to the success of French psychologist Alfred Binet's intelligence test, the forerunner of the modern IQ test. Binet conducted pioneering quantitative research on intelligence and personality (and was yet another influential psychologist who, like James and Freud, studied with French neurologist Jean-Martin Charcot and participated in his hypnosis research). In *The Varieties* (James, 1902/2009), James mentions Binet in the context of personality types that may be particularly susceptible to spiritual experience. Binet's work, in addition to other intelligence and personality inventories, resulted in the psychometric method that is now a common tool in contemporary psychological research.

The acknowledgment of the predictive value of these psychometric instruments has steadily taken over psychology and turned the field into a data-oriented field of research. There have been a number of pivotal demonstrations of the value of these psychometric methods, but Meehl's (1954) *Clinical Versus Statistical Prediction: A Theoretical Analysis and Review of the Evidence* is a major turning point. In this book, Meehl demonstrated the superiority of quantitative methods of prediction over interviews. Meehl showed that analyzing quantitative data in a systematic way produces more reliable predictions of outcomes like grades in school, parole violations, and even success in pilot training than clinical interviews with therapists (see Kahneman, 2011; Kahneman et al., 2021). Most psychology studies, including those on spiritual experience, now collect data from self-report questionnaires.

Starbuck's Classic Survey of Spiritual Experience

In *The Varieties* (1902), James drew many of his accounts of spiritual experiences from the surveys distributed by Starbuck (who, recall, was James's former student and the first to use the phrase "varieties of religious experience" in a book for which James provided a praise-filled preface). Besides written accounts, Starbuck collected quantitative data—a method that James was initially resistant to, but later embraced (Pawelski & Yaden, 2021). The method that Starbuck used in his survey is an early example of psychometric survey research.

How did Starbuck distribute his spiritual experience surveys? Here is Starbuck (humorously) explaining to James one method of incentivizing subjects to answer his spiritual experience surveys:

> Starbuck later related how at one particular meeting James pulled a copy of the questionnaire from his coat pocket and waived it in front of him. "But this is New England," James reminded Starbuck, "and people here will not reply to an inquisitional document of that sort." . . . James asked how he managed to do so. "I wheedle them," replied Starbuck, "I explain that this is the beginning of a new science in the world—the psychology of religion, and we must have the facts. Failing in this approach, my favorite technique, since I am a husky, is to throw the victim flat on the floor or lawn, sit on his chest, and exhort a solemn promise to confess everything." (Bridgers, 2005, p. 49)

Many studies have been carried out over the years using survey methods (without the need to sit on top of participants and demand that they respond!). Typically, researchers gather responses to surveys from participants who respond out of a civic sense of duty to assist the efforts of researchers, to learn something about themselves from the results, or to receive a small monetary incentive. In Starbuck's case, he asked a number of questions in his survey (psychologists refer to questions in a survey instrument as "items").

While spiritual experiences in adolescence (what he called conversion experiences; Figure 4.2) were his primary subject, Starbuck also asked more general questions, such as the following:

THAT IN WHICH CONVERSION CONSISTS.	Female.	Male.	Total.
Spontaneous Awakening	24	23	24
Forgiveness	15	19	16
Public Confession	17	13	16
Sense of Oneness (with God, friends, etc.)	13	16	14
Self-Surrender	14	11	13
Determination	10	8	9
Divine Aid	7	10	8

TABLE XI. — *Showing the relative frequency of certain things regarded as central in conversion.*

Figure 4.2 The psychology of religion: an empirical study of the growth of religious consciousness. By Edwin Diller Starbuck; with a preface by William James. Wellcome Collection. Public Domain Mark.

What changes did you find that your conversion had worked out in your life?

How did relief come? Was it attended by unnatural sights, sounds, or feelings? (Starbuck, 1899, p. 23)

Contemporary Psychometric Study of Spiritual Experience

Psychometric survey research relies on people responding to individual items as well as combinations of items called "scales." These results are then summarized using *descriptive statistics*. For example, how many people of a given sample agree that they have had a spiritual experience? The answer, given as a percentage of those who responded "yes" out of the whole sample, is the kind of answer descriptive statistics can provide. Throughout this book we include several figures showing descriptive data from our Varieties Survey.

Once a number of responses to different items have been gathered in a sample, researchers can also use *inferential statistics*. Inferential statistics are used to infer, or estimate, from a sample what the relationship between variables might be in a whole population. We include correlations with significance tests, especially in Part II of this book, that represent the relationship between certain kinds of spiritual experiences and measures of well-being.

A number of psychometric measures of spiritual experience have been administered in large self-report surveys. Psychologist Ralph Hood, a contemporary expert in the study of mystical experience, has summarized a number of single-item questions that have been asked over the years. He referred to these according to the researcher who first posed them, such as the "Laski question" and the "Hardy question," as well as several others.

The Laski question was posed by Margharita Laski, who was interested in gathering accounts similar to those collected by James from her contemporaries. She wished to study the prevalence of these kinds of experiences. Though not a professional scientist, Laski's inquiry was an example of a study on spiritual experience that relied on psychometric surveys. As described in her book *Ecstasy in Secular and Religious Experiences* (1961), she asked her friends and colleagues the following question:

"Do you know a sensation of transcendent ecstasy?"

If her respondents indicated that they had such an experience, then they were asked to answer additional questions. These further questions included: How many times have you had this experience? What were the subjective qualities of the experience? and What effects did the experience have on your life? She also included some questions about creativity, as the relationship between spiritual experience and creativity was of interest to her. The results from her study are reviewed in the chapter on aesthetic experience (Chapter 13).

Alister Hardy was another researcher who collected a number of accounts of spiritual experiences. Hardy was a professor of zoology at Oxford with a lifelong interest in religion and spirituality. Like James, he also gave a Gifford Lecture (later, in 1963), which focused on religion and evolution. Several years after his Gifford lecture, he founded the Religious Experience Research Center, which collected written descriptions of religious experience from people living in the United Kingdom. This laboratory's mission statement explicitly mentioned its desire to continue the Starbuck–James legacy:

An extension and development of those pioneer studies of Professor E. D. Starbuck (*The Psychology of Religion: An Empirical Study of the Growth of Religious Consciousness*, 1899) and by William James (*The Varieties of Religious Experience: A Study in Human Nature*, 1902). These classics have never been added to in the same spirit in which they were undertaken. (Hay, 1990, p. 27)

The surveys sent out to collect this information contained the following item (Hardy, 1979; Hay, 1990):

Have you ever been aware of or influenced by a presence or power, whether you call it God or not, which is different from your everyday self?

In a U.K. sample of 1,865 people, 36% of the sample responded in the affirmative to this question (Hay & Morisy, 1978). A decade later, in a U.K. survey using the same question, a 985-person Gallup survey found a 48% affirmative response rate (Hay & Heald, 1987).

This approach was taken up by large-scale polling companies and other researchers using slightly different variations of these questions. Another item was used in several large-scale surveys in the United States administered by the General Social Survey (GSS) in 1984, 1988, and 1989. This item was the following:

Have you ever felt as though you were close to a powerful spiritual force that seemed to lift you out of yourself?

In the years surveyed, the rates of affirmative responses in samples of around 1,000 people per survey were 41%, 32%, and 30%, respectively (Fox, 1992, p. 422).

Another item administered by Gallup (1978) explicitly mentions mystical experience:

Would you say that you have ever had a "religious or mystical experience"— that is, a sudden religious insight or awakening?

In a 1976 Gallup study, 31% of the respondents answered in the affirmative in a nationally representative survey (Gallup, 1978). This question has been asked in a series of surveys by Gallup (see Figure 4.3).

These findings demonstrate that spiritual experiences are surprisingly prevalent and *support a generally accepted estimate that about 35% of a given*

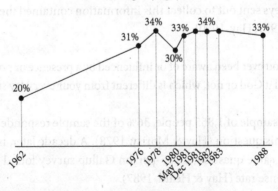

"Would you say that you have ever had a 'religious or mystical experience' – that is, a moment of sudden religious insight or awakening?"*

Figure 4.3 Gallup survey results (Gallup, 2002). Copyright © 2003 Gallup, Inc. Source: https://news.gallup.com/poll/7582/religious-awakenings-bolster-americans-faith.aspx

sample will likely report a spiritual experience (for a discussion of this estimate and a review of these surveys and findings, see Hood et al., 2018). We continue to discuss findings from these and other similar surveys throughout this book. We also explain in detail how psychometric self-report measures can help us to understand the triggers, types, and common outcomes of various types of spiritual experiences, especially in Part II of this book.

That is not to say that there are not problems with this approach. Self-report survey items are highly impacted by the particular terms used. While they benefit from standardization (the same question is posed to everyone in the same way), some people may misunderstand the question. Also, people are not given an opportunity to explain what they mean by their answers. Many of these issues are at least partly addressed by gathering large samples of participants, so that these random differences between people cancel out and the true nature of the relationship can be therefore be estimated. Also, these items work best when they are combined together to form scales. Lastly, these kinds of self-report items typically work best when they are used in conjunction with qualitative analyses and other kinds of data collection methods. Multiple research methods allow scientists to triangulate by using different ways of trying to understand the same phenomenon. Ideally, a mix of quantitative and qualitative methods should be used to understand the psychology of spiritual experiences.

Conclusion

The psychological study of spiritual experiences has undergone a number of conceptual, methodological, and statistical advances since James's call for a science of religions. Many parts of James's general approach to psychology have prevailed through the developments of psychoanalysis, behaviorism, humanistic psychology, early psychedelic research, and the cognitive revolution—and much of James's thought is in line with contemporary psychology. Contemporary psychology, among many other behavioral and physiological measures, also often uses psychometric self-report items and scales to learn more about a vast array of mental phenomena, including spiritual experiences. These items, phrased in many different ways over the years, have been distributed to a large number of people through surveys, and researchers have found that spiritual experiences are surprisingly prevalent today.

Note

1. Galton's views on race were deplorable and are deservedly widely reviled.

References

Back, K. W., & Bourque, L. B. (1970). Can feelings be enumerated? *Behavioral Science*, 15(6), 487–496.

Baumeister, R. F., & Placidi, K. S. (1983). A social history and analysis of the LSD controversy. *Journal of Humanistic Psychology*, 23(4), 25–58.

Belzen, J. A., & Hood, R. W. (2006). Methodological issues in the psychology of religion: Toward another paradigm? *Journal of Psychology*, 140(1), 5–28.

Bridgers, L. (2005). *Contemporary varieties of religious experience: James's classic study in light of resiliency, temperament, and trauma*. Rowman & Littlefield.

Chomsky, N. (1959). A review of BF Skinner's verbal behavior. *Language*, 35(1), 26–58.

Darwin, C. (2004). *On the origin of species*. Routledge. (Original work published 1859)

Dass, R. (2010). *Be here now*. Harmony. (Original work published 1971)

Fox, J. W. (1992). The structure, stability, and social antecedents of reported paranormal experiences. *Sociological Analysis*, 53(4), 417–431.

Frankl, V. F. (1985). *Man's search for meaning*. Simon & Schuster. (Original published 1946)

Freud, S. (1989). *Civilization and its discontents*. Norton. (Original work published 1930)

Gallup, G., Jr. (1978). *The Gallup Poll: Public opinion 1972–1977*. Washington, DC: Scholarly Resources.

Gallup, G. H. (2002). *Religious awakenings bolster Americans' faith*. https://news.gallup.com/poll/7582/religious-awakenings-bolster-americans-faith.aspx

Hardy, A (1979) *The spiritual nature of man*. Oxford University Press.

Hay, D. (1990). *Religious experience today: Studying the facts*. Mowbray.

Hay, D., & Morisy, A. (1978). Reports of ecstatic, paranormal, or religious experience in Great Britain and the United States: A comparison of trends. *Journal for the Scientific Study of Religion*, 17(3), 255–268.

Hay, D., & Heald, G. (1987). Religion is good for you. *New Society*, 80(1268), 20–22.

Hood, R. W., Jr., Hill, P. C., & Spilka, B. (2018). *The psychology of religion: An empirical approach*. Guilford.

Huxley, A. (1954/2010). *The doors of perception: And heaven and hell*. Random House.

James, W. (1890). *The principles of psychology* (Vol. 1, No. 2). Macmillan.

James, W. (1890). *The principles of psychology, Volume Two*, H. Holt, New York.

James, W. (1902/2009). *The varieties of religious experience: A study in human nature*. *eBooks@Adelaide*. https://csrs.nd.edu/assets/59930/williams_1902.pdf

Jesse, R. N. (1997). Recollections of the Good Friday experiment: An interview with Huston Smith. *The Journal*, 29(2), 99.

Jung, C. G. (1963). *Memories, dreams, reflections* (Vol. 268). Vintage.

Jung, C. G., & Jaffe, A. (unpublished manuscript). *Memories, Dreams, Reflections, editorial manuscript*. Countway Library of Medicine, Harvard Medical School, Boston.

Jung, C. G., Shamdasani, S. E., Kyburz, M. T., & Peck, J. T. (2009). *The red book: Liber novus*. Norton.

Kahneman, D. (2011). *Thinking, fast and slow*. Macmillan.

Kahneman, D., Sibony, O., & Sunstein, C. R. (2021). *Noise: A flaw in human judgment*. Little Brown.

Kaufman, S. B. (2018). Self-actualizing people in the 21st century: Integration with contemporary theory and research on personality and well-being. *Journal of Humanistic Psychology*. https://doi.org/10.1177%2F0022167818809187

Kaufman, S. B. (2021). *Transcend: The new science of self-actualization*. Penguin.

Laski, M. (1961). *Ecstasy in secular and religious experiences*. Tarcher.

Maslow, A. H. (1964). *Religions, values, and peak-experiences* (Vol. 35). Ohio State University Press.

Meehl, P. E. (1954). *Clinical versus statistical prediction: A theoretical analysis and a review of the evidence*. University of Minnesota Press.

Miller, G. A. (1956). The magical number seven, plus or minus two: Some limits on our capacity for processing information. *Psychological Review, 63*(2), 81.

Muraresku, B. C. (2020). *The immortality key: The secret history of the religion with no name*. St. Martin's Press.

Pahnke, W. N. (1963). *Drugs and mysticism: An analysis of the relationship between psychedelic drugs and the mystical consciousness* [Unpublished doctoral thesis]. Harvard University.

Pawelski, J., & Yaden, D. B. (2021). William James and the quest for meaningful measurement. In S. Marchetti (Ed.), *The Jamesian mind* (pp. 475–481). Macmillan.

Richardson, R. D. (2006). *William James: In the maelstrom of American modernism*. Houghton Mifflin.

Russell, B. (1945). *History of Western philosophy*. Routledge.

Seligman, M. E. (1972). Learned helplessness. *Annual Review of Medicine, 23*(1), 407–412.

Simon, L. (1998). *Genuine reality: A life of William James*. University of Chicago Press.

Starbuck, E. D. (1899). *The psychology of religion: An empirical study of the growth of religious consciousness* (Vol. 38). Walter Scott.

Strandberg, V. H. (1981). *Religious psychology in American literature: a study of the relevance of William James*. Studia Humanitatis.

Watts, A. (1962/2013). *The joyous cosmology: Adventures in the chemistry of consciousness*. New World Library.

Yaden, D. B., Yaden, M. E., & Griffiths, R. R. (2021). Psychedelics in psychiatry—Keeping the renaissance from going off the rails. *JAMA Psychiatry, 78*(5), 469–470.

5

The Brain on Spiritual Experiences

The Brain—is wider than the Sky—
For—put them side by side—
The one the other will contain
With ease—and you—beside . . .

The Brain is just the weight of God—
For—Heft them—Pound for Pound—
And they will differ—if they do—
As Syllable from Sound—

—Emily Dickinson (1924)

Several years ago, one of us (A. B. N.) brought both Tibetan meditators and Franciscan nuns into his laboratory to study the effects that spiritual experiences have on the brain (Newberg et al., 2001). These contemplatives had practiced daily meditation or prayer for several hours a day for many years, to the point that they were able to voluntarily put themselves into a mental state of deep unity. To conduct this research, we used an imaging technique called single-photon emission computed tomography (SPECT) imaging. While in the laboratory, subjects meditated or prayed until they were in that deep state of unity. Subjects then gently pulled on a string to indicate it was time for researchers to inject a small amount of a radioactive tracer that would go wherever blood flow went in their brain. The subjects continued to perform their practice while the tracer circulated in their brain.

After the scan, the meditators and nuns were asked about how they felt at their moment of peak unity. There were similarities and differences in the subjective reports of the contemplatives from these two religious traditions. The Tibetan meditators reported that their mental state involved a sense of connection to everything, while the nuns reported a sense of connection with God—but both groups agreed regarding their feelings of unity.

The Varieties of Spiritual Experience. David B. Yaden and Andrew B. Newberg, Oxford University Press. © David Yaden and Andrew Newberg 2022. DOI: 10.1093/oso/9780190665678.003.0005

Interestingly, for both groups, the same region of the brain was less active, or what researchers call "inhibited." This region, the posterior superior parietal lobe, appears to be partly responsible for representing the boundaries between one's body and its surroundings. We revisit the findings of this study in Chapter 12 on mystical experiences.

Neuroscience has undergone a revolution in the last several decades that allows studies like this to be possible. Nearly all of what we now know about brain processes was not known during James's time. Today we can further contribute to James's "science of religions" by measuring the underlying physiological and brain processes associated with spiritual experience. To do this, neuroscientists use sophisticated neuroimaging equipment capable of revealing brain activity before, during, and after spiritual experiences. Our Varieties Survey found that the *average spiritual experience lasts about 18.5 minutes.* What has neuroscience told us about what goes on in the brain during that period of time?

Neuroscience in *The Varieties of Religious Experience*

William James was a Harvard professor in physiology for many years, but he could probably not have imagined the technological advances made by modern neuroscience. He did, however, anticipate the study of spiritual experience from a neurological perspective—after all, he called the first chapter of *The Varieties of Religious Experience: A Study in Human Nature* (hereafter *The Varieties*) "Religion and Neurology" (James, 1902/2009, p. 6). James, ever influenced by his training and teaching in physiology, was a proponent of understanding the biological mechanisms of mental states whenever possible. The following famous, though often misunderstood, passage in *The Varieties* is about understanding spiritual experiences at the level of physiology:

> Medical materialism finishes up Saint Paul by calling his vision on the road to Damascus a discharging lesion of the occipital cortex, he being an epileptic. It snuffs out Saint Teresa as an hysteric, Saint Francis of Assisi as an hereditary degenerate. . . . All such mental over-tensions, it says, are, when come to the bottom of the matter, mere affairs of diathesis (auto-intoxifications most probably), due to the perverted action of various glands which physiology will yet discover. (James, 1902/2009, p. 14)

Some scholars quote this passage to support the idea that James was against studying the physiological and neurological aspects of spiritual experience, but this is mistaken. James was indeed criticizing something here, but he was *not* arguing against the value of understanding the physiology of spiritual experiences. He was instead criticizing the tendency to assume that such experiences are inherently pathological or psychologically meaningless merely because they are associated with physiological changes. To be clear, James was against the "medical materialism" described in this quotation because it is reflexively pathologizing. Also, it is worth reiterating James's claim that just because an experience has a physiological basis does not *necessarily* mean that it precludes other kinds of religious, spiritual, or otherwise nonphysical causes—though we continue to delay a full discussion of this point until further chapters on philosophy.

James was well aware of what was at stake when considering whether an experience comes exclusively from one's own brain. One of the accounts featured in *The Varieties* explicitly raised the concern that spiritual experiences are entirely (i.e., merely) neurological:

> These highest experiences that I have had of God's presence have been rare and brief—flashes of consciousness which have compelled me to exclaim with surprise—God is here!—or conditions of exaltation and insight, less intense, and only gradually passing away. I have severely questioned the worth of these moments. To no soul have I named them, lest I should be building my life and work on mere phantasies of the brain. (James, 1902/ 2009, p. 301)

James would have likely been sympathetic to this person's questioning of their own experience. Indeed, James would probably have joined her or him in the questioning! However, James would also have bracketed the question of how to interpret one's experience as an issue separate from the work of scientifically studying the outcomes and underlying physiology of spiritual experience. After all, brain activity underlies *all* activity—including lofty moments like falling in love or even reading these very words. Understanding the link between mental states and physiological states is *not* the same as reducing the meaning of an experience.

James spoke to this distinction directly. He assumed that the mental and the physical are related, and perhaps identical in a sense, yet he did *not* believe that understanding the physiological changes associated with a mental state decided its value. For example, understanding the physiological changes associated with falling in love does not determine whether or not that relationship is worthwhile.

> Modern psychology, finding definite psycho-physical connections to hold good, assumes as a convenient hypothesis that the dependence of mental states upon bodily conditions must be thoroughgoing and complete. If we adopt the assumption, then of course what medical materialism insists on must be true in a general way, if not in every detail. . . . But now, I ask you, how can such an existential account of facts of mental history decide in one way or another upon their spiritual significance? According to the general postulate of psychology just referred to, there is not a single one of our states of mind, high or low, healthy or morbid, that has not some organic process as its condition. (James, 1902, p. 15)

In other words, physiological findings regarding mental states cannot determine the psychological value or spiritual significance of that mental state. With these qualifications in place, James made the case that valuable physiological research can be done on mental states like spiritual experiences.

Historical Notes on the Brain and Spiritual Experience

The connection between bodily states and spiritual experiences has been observed in a number of religious and philosophical traditions throughout history. This is particularly obvious in Buddhism and Hinduism. Both of these traditions have a number of texts discussing the relationship between bodily conditions, mental processes, and spiritual states. This connection between the brain and spiritual states is also mentioned in the Vedas, an ancient Hindu text. This verse from about the sixth century B.C. specifically mentions the parietal bones in the skull:

> The Lord of Love dwells in the hearts of all.
> To realize him is to go beyond death.
> Between the parietal bones of the skull
> Swings the sagittal door as the lobe swings
>
> (cited in Baird, 2017, p. 32)

There are other historical examples in which a brain or bodily occurrence was associated with a spiritual experience. In ancient Greece, for example, epilepsy was referred to as "the divine disease" due to the spiritual experiences sometimes reported after seizures. Hippocrates, the father of modern medicine, was called on to determine whether epilepsy was indeed more divine then other ailments. He determined that seizures were no more "divine" than any other disease (Devinsky & Schachter, 2009). But he may have been at least partially wrong about that because about 1%–5% of epileptics *do* in fact experience spiritual experiences during their seizures (Ogata & Miyakawa, 1998).

Or consider, from the Christian religion, St. Paul's previously mentioned experience on the road to Damascus. In this moment, the Bible describes him falling to the ground and being temporarily blinded. Similar symptoms have been reported in patients with epilepsy, particularly epilepsy involving the visual cortex. Paul's conversion on the road to Damascus, along with other famous examples, have led some neuropsychologists to develop theories about the genesis of spiritual experiences. In an article from 1997, Saver and Rabin provided a table of the great religious figures of history along with possible neurological diagnoses (see Table 5.1).

While an interesting exercise in speculative neurology, the most obvious problem with this approach is that there is no way to prove or disprove whether these individuals truly had neurological disorders. Still, it makes for a compelling point to consider. It is no doubt important to think about the relationship between certain kinds of brain states and spiritual experiences. But like James, we must emphasize that any analysis of this type would not necessarily diminish the meaning of the spiritual experience itself, and it does not necessarily preclude the possibility of supernatural origins.

Introductory Tour of the Brain

Much of what we now know about brain processes was not available in any substantive way when James wrote *The Varieties*. Most accurate knowledge of the brain developed in the 20th century. Though the history of neuroscience is far too complicated to detail here, we will provide some highlights to help understand the tools that contemporary neuroscientists use and the kinds of questions that they ask, with a focus on how neuroscientists can investigate spiritual experiences, which a number of scholars have addressed including the exciting work of Patrick McNamara (2009) and Uffe Schoedt (2009).

Table 5.1 Historical–Religious Figures Suggested in the Medical Literature to Have Had Epilepsy

Person	Description of Spells	Frequency	Likelihood of Epilepsy	Differential Diagnosis[a]	Religious Aspects
Saint Paul (?–65)	Conversion on road to Damascus; sudden bright light, falling to the ground, hearing the voice of Jesus, blindness for 3 days with inability to eat or drink Ecstatic visions	Unknown	+	CPS with generalization[52,133,134] Psychogenic blindness Burns of cornea/retina Vertebrobasilar ischemia Occipital contusion Lightning stroke Digitalis poisoning Vitreous hemorrhage Migraine equivalent	Father of Catholic Church Possible ecstatic aura, interictal hypernoralism, hyperreligiosity, hypergraphia
Muhammad (570–632)	Pallor, appearance of intoxication, falling, profuse sweating, visual and auditory hallucinations	At least several	+	Complex partial seizures[135,136]	Islamic prophet
Margery Kempe (ca. 1373–1438)	A cry, falling with convulsive movements, turning blue, nausea, psychotic behavior	Recurrent	+	Epilepsy[137] Hysteria Postpartum psychosis Migraine	14th-century Christian mystic and autobiographer
Joan of Arc (1412–1431)	"I heard this Voice [of an angel] . . . accompanied also by a . . . great light. . . . There is never a day when I do not hear this Voice; and I have much need of it."	At least daily by the time of her execution in 1431	+	Ecstatic partial seizure and musicogenic epilepsy[138] Intracranial tuberculoma	Extraordinary, deeply held, idiosyncratic religious beliefs motivating martial prowess in the defense of Oriléans

Continued

Table 5.1 *Continued*

Person	Description of Spells	Frequency	Likelihood of Epilepsy	Differential Diagnosis[a]	Religious Aspects
St. Catherine of Genoa (1447–1510)	Extreme sense of heat or cold, whole-body tremor, transient aphasia, automatisms, sense of passivity, hyperesthesia, regression to childhood, dissociation, sleepwalking, transient weakness, transient suggestibility, inability to open eyes	Unknown	+	Complex partial seizure[52] Hysteria	Christian mystic
St. Teresa of Avila (1515–1582)	Visions, chronic headaches, transient LOC,[a] tongue biting	1 major LOC spell; frequent headaches	++	Complex partial seizure[52]	Catholic saint
St. Catherine dei Ricci (1522–1590)	LOC, visual hallucinations, mystical states	Every Thursday at noon with recovery by Friday at 4:00 P.M.	+	Complex partial seizure[52]	Catholic saint
Emanuel Swedenborg (1688–1772)	Acute psychosis; foaming at the mouth; olfactory, gustatory, and somatic hallucinations; hallucinations; postictal trance states	Recurrent	++	Complex partial seizure[139,140]	Founder of the New Jerusalem Church
Anne Lee (1736–1784)	Visual, auditory hallucinations; postictal trance states		Mania Schizophrenia		Church
Ann Lee (1736–1784)	Visual, auditory hallucinations	From childhood until at least 1774	+	Epilepsy[22]	Founder of the Shaker movement

[a]LOC, loss of consciousness.

Reprinted with permission from the Journal of Neuropsychiatry and Clinical Neurosciences, (Copyright © 1997). American Psychiatric Association. All Rights Reserved.

One of the major advances in neuroscience occurred just a few years after *The Varieties* was published. In the early 1900s, the German neurologist Korbinian Brodmann (1909/2007) published his work on the functional neuroanatomy of the brain, *Localisation in the Cerebral Cortex*. In the book, he laid out evidence for his theories that specific structures of the brain could be better understood in terms of their major functions. Brain regions are still referenced in modern cognitive neuroscience research as "Brodmann areas."

In the years after Brodmann's discovery, other scientists studied the brain anatomically and identified regions of the brain that were associated with various mental and behavioral functions. But it was not until 50 years later that major revolutions again occurred in neuroscience. In the 1970s and 1980s, several major technological advances made neuroimaging possible. Magnetic resonance imaging (MRI) and computed tomography (CT) were developed, resulting in Nobel Prizes for the scientists involved (Seeram, 2006). These imaging technologies allow physicians to see structural features or functional changes in the brain or body noninvasively (without breaking the skin). This meant researchers could peer into the brain to see the structure and functioning of the brain while people remained alive and not having to remove the scalp and skull or wait to do an autopsy after death.

The so-called decade of the brain then followed in the 1990s. During those years, there was increasingly rapid expansion of knowledge in how different parts of the brain function. Suddenly, scientists were able to understand which brain regions are associated with many of our perceptions, thoughts, feelings, and behaviors. This led to a detailed delineation of how specific anatomical brain structures, and more recently brain networks, are related to mental processes, such as language, memory, and emotions. However, despite these advances, this area of research is still in its infancy due to the complexity of these subjects.

The next sections provide a brief overview of how the brain is structured and how it functions, emphasizing the features that are most relevant to spiritual experiences. There are, of course, many more details regarding the various processes and structures of the brain than could possibly be included here (for a more thorough summary, see Bear et al., 2020). Furthermore, it's important to remember that as much as neuroscience has developed in the past decades, neuroscientists are still just scratching the surface of our overall knowledge of the brain and its functions.

The Nervous System

To begin, the brain is part of the nervous system. Most multicellular organisms, including human beings, have nervous systems. For humans and other mammals, the nervous system has two major parts: the central and peripheral nervous systems. The brain and spinal cord are part of the *central nervous system*, which directs movement, information processing, and all manner of sensory input and control. The *peripheral nervous system*, which primarily executes motor functions and obtains sensory information, also includes the autonomic nervous system, which controls many processes, like heart rate, digestion, respiration, and other functions.

We focus this overview on the brain, but it's worth first taking a closer look into the *autonomic nervous system*. The autonomic nervous system is further broken down into the sympathetic branch and the parasympathetic branch. The *sympathetic branch*—sometimes referred to as the arousal system—enables the body to react to various important stimuli in the environment. The sympathetic nervous system is well known for eliciting the "fight-or-flight" response. The *parasympathetic branch*, on the other hand—sometimes referred to as the quiescent system—prepares the body to store energy and relax, or the "rest-and-digest" response. The parasympathetic nervous system is primarily involved in reducing heart rate and blood pressure, increasing digestion, and decreasing energy utilization.

A number of spiritual practices and rituals seem designed to specifically manipulate either the sympathetic or parasympathetic branches of the nervous system. In one study, the physician Herbert Benson, at the urging of a group of meditators, studied the impact of meditation practice on the nervous system. He found that sitting quietly and focusing one's attention could effectively elicit what he called a "relaxation response" in the parasympathetic nervous system: The heart rate, oxygen use, and muscular tension of subjects decreased during meditation (Benson & Klipper, 1975). Recall that Benson conducted his research in the same Harvard laboratory as Walter Cannon, who discovered the "fight-or-flight" response (and Cannon was one of William James's students).

The sympathetic and parasympathetic branches are ordinarily inversely correlated (that is, when one is on the other tends to be off). Peaceful practices such as most Buddhist meditations and Catholic prayers seem to activate the parasympathetic branch, whereas more active, devotional practices such as rhythmic dancing or the whirling of dervishes in Sufism seem to activate the sympathetic branch. But during some activities, such as sex, both branches can become active in what is sometimes called a "paradoxical response." This paradoxical response of the nervous system may also occur during spiritual experiences (Newberg & d'Aquili, 2008). The possibility that there is a paradoxical response in the autonomic nervous system during spiritual experiences may be one of the keys to understanding spiritual experiences, though more research is needed to explore this speculation.

The Brain

Returning to the central nervous system, at the top of the spinal cord, cradled in the skull, is the brain. Once thought by the Greeks to be nothing more than an organ to cool blood, scientists now understand that the brain is one of the most complex objects in the known universe (note: this phrase has been used by many scientists, though it is unclear where it originates).

This section provides some basic details regarding the 3-pound organ currently resting behind your eyes. For some initial orientation, imagine the structure of the brain as similar to planet Earth. The Earth's crust, or the outer layer of the planet, is like the brain's *cortex*. The cortex is thin (~3 millimeters), which is surprising given how much of what makes us human—functions like reason and language—appear to depend on this region. The cortex can then be divided into parts, or *lobes*, which are like the continents and oceans that cover the surface of the globe.

All kinds of mental processes depend on various regions of the cortex, and it is impossible to provide simple accounts of everything each lobe does (it would be as impossible as trying to describe the geographic and cultural complexities of entire continents). Here, we focus on just a few key functions of the frontal, temporal, parietal, and occipital lobes (see Figure 5.1).

The *frontal lobe* contains many of the executive functions of the brain, including the capacity to self-regulate, or control behavior and attention. With respect to spiritual practices, the frontal lobes are most noted for being able to help focus attention in general, for example, on a particular object of meditation or piece of scripture in prayer. The *temporal lobes* are associated with language and associative memory. The *occipital lobes* process visual information. The *parietal lobes* are responsible for spatial awareness, including of one's own body. It was a region within the parietal lobes that was inhibited, or less active, during the unity experiences in the

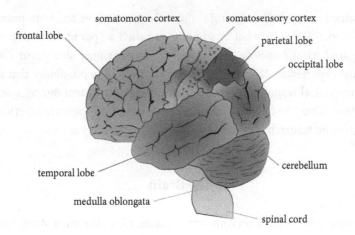

Figure 5.1 Lobes of the brain. From https://commons.wikimedia.org/wiki/
File:Cerebrum_lobes.svg.

neuroimaging study that opens this chapter. Again, this is an incredibly
simplistic description, but these general functions suffice for much of what
is discussed in this book.

The Earth analogy works well for the next regions of the brain we
consider—the *left hemisphere* and the *right hemisphere*. (Note that notions
about being a "left hemisphere type" that is more creative or a "right hemisphere type" that is more analytical are popular myths that are not based in
scientific findings). These two brain regions share many similar structures
and functions, with substantial redundancy across hemispheres. The two
hemispheres, which comprise the whole brain, are connected by the *corpus
callosum*. When the corpus collosum is severed, which was for a time a necessary procedure to treat some kinds of severe epilepsy, the two hemispheres
can vie for control of the body. In a series of Nobel Prize–winning studies on
the corpus collosum, Roger Sperry and colleagues demonstrated that the left
and right hemispheres of the brain act with some degree of independence
from one another (Gazzaniga, 2005).

In fact, these split-brain researchers found that in patients with a severed
corpus callosum there is a dominant hemisphere that the person feels is "really" them and a nondominant hemisphere, which feels almost like an alien
intelligence in their body. In one striking case, researchers asked a participant whether they believed in God and, incredibly, one hand (controlled by

one hemisphere) wrote "yes," while the other hand (controlled by the other hemisphere) simultaneously wrote "no" (Ramachandran, 2003)!

All areas that are underneath the thin layer of cortex are called *subcortical structures* (as in "below the cortex"). In terms of our Earth analogy, these organs would reside beneath the crust—in the mantle and core. There are more subcortical structures than we can describe here, but several noteworthy ones play a role in spiritual experiences: the amygdala, the hippocampus, and the hypothalamus. While each of these brain regions is associated with a number of functions (far too many to list here), taken together, these regions are often referred to (simplistically) as the *limbic system*. The limbic system is associated with emotional responses. Spiritual experiences can sometimes prompt dramatic emotional responses—and the so-called limbic system would play a central role in such cases.

Some subcortical structures associated with the limbic system are closely involved with *hormones* and *neuropeptides*. The hormone *cortisol*, for example, is released in response to stress. Religious and spiritual practices that effectively reduce stress, such as meditation and prayer, would also reduce levels of cortisol (note: via the hypothalamic–pituitary–adrenal pathway).

The neuropeptides *oxytocin* and *vasopressin* have been implicated in a number of social behaviors related to bonding and are released during activities like hugging, breastfeeding, or sex (oxytocin has been referred to as the "cuddle hormone"). Some evidence suggests that these neuropeptides are also released during spiritual experiences (Grigorenko et al., 2011). These neuropeptides are not always associated with universal forms of love, however. While they are related to bonding, some studies have shown that this bonding is limited to one's in-group (e.g., family or religious community; De Dreu et al., 2011). The oxytocin response could therefore be more constrained than the universal love that some religious and spiritual traditions advocate.

The cells that comprise the brain are called *neurons*. There are very roughly the same number of stars in the Milky Way as neurons in the brain (~86 billion). Neurons "communicate" with one another through a chemical and electrical process in which a neuron receives "messages" from other neurons until a threshold is reached (called an *action potential*), and at that point, the neuron then sends a message to other neurons. These messages between neurons consist of chemicals called *neurotransmitters*. Most psychoactive substances, such as alcohol, caffeine, or psychedelics, involve changes to neurotransmitter systems. The brain is awash with neurotransmitters, making the specific neurological effects of psychoactive substances difficult to trace. As we will see, this poses a problem for understanding how psychoactive substances like psychedelics induce spiritual experiences.

Neurotransmitters are involved in nearly every complex mental process. Here again, we are wading into a very complicated topic for which generalizations almost do more harm than good. However, for the purpose of this book, there are a few neurotransmitters worth knowing by name and understanding at least one of their main functions. *Glutamate* is present in nearly half of all of the brain's synapses (synapses are the gaps between neurons), making it the most abundant neurotransmitter. It is known as an excitatory neurotransmitter, in that it tends to prompt more brain activation. *GABA* (gamma-aminobutyric acid) is the second most abundant neurotransmitter, and it usually prompts inhibition of brain activity. *Acetylcholine* is often associated with physical movement of the body due to its importance in muscle contraction. *Norepinephrine* and *epinephrine* (more commonly known as noradrenaline and adrenaline) are an important part of the fight-or-flight response. *Dopamine* might be the best known neurotransmitter due to its role in pleasure, motivation, and reward. *Serotonin* is involved in a number of important psychological functions, such as sleep and mood, and it plays some role in depression—though it is not yet fully understood. Serotonin is also the neurotransmitter most involved with psychedelics (e.g., psychedelics bond to serotonin 5-H$_{2A}$ receptors) and appears to be involved in promoting prosocial behavior (Crockett et al., 2010), as well as in triggering spiritual experience.

Importantly, *there is no single area of the brain that is exclusively involved in spiritual experiences.* Hence, there is no "God spot" or "spiritual part" of the brain. Spiritual experiences frequently involve multiple domains of brain function. In addition, the various means and mechanisms by which people enter into spiritual experiences, including rituals, prayers, near-death experiences, and many others, would have varying effects on different parts of the brain. However, even some basic understanding of the brain can help in understanding the role that the nervous system plays in spiritual (and all) experiences.

This brief, vastly simplified (really simplistic) tour of the brain should give some sense of why the brain has been called the most complex object in the known universe. Even the basic information presented here has been hard won. Thousands of scientists working over decades of time have provided our current understanding of the brain. James would have marveled.

Networks and the Brain

A more recent development in neuroscience has been the recognition of specific networks in the brain. These networks comprise different structures and perform global functions such as focusing attention (attentional network), daydreaming (default mode network), determining the importance of things (salience network), and many others. Brain networks represent complicated sets of interactions and are just beginning to be reliably specified by neuroscience research.

These networks may be activated in complex ways during spiritual experiences. For example, the areas involved in the attentional network, such as the prefrontal cortex, are involved in attention-focusing tasks such as during prayer or ritual practices. When an individual focuses on a particular object or prescribed set of behaviors, there is intense focus of attention on this task. Research by psychedelic researcher Carhart-Harris suggested that the default mode network is suppressed during psychedelic-triggered spiritual experiences (Carhart-Harris, 2018), although others have pointed out that this suppression is not unique to psychedelics. Again, the science on this topic is still at an early and largely exploratory phase.

The emotional aspects of spiritual experiences are likely tied to the limbic system, which helps elicit emotional responses and also identifies the extreme importance of the spiritual content of the experience. The sense of connection or oneness is likely associated with inhibiting regions of the parietal lobe that generally help with representing one's body in relation to the surrounding environment. Thus, depending on the type of spiritual experience and its specific elements, we would expect a variety of brain structures and networks to become involved.

Modern Neuroimaging

Neuroimaging is a relatively recent technology for neuroscience research. A few decades ago, journalist Tom Wolfe wrote, "It is called brain imaging, and anyone who cares to get up early and catch a truly blinding twenty-first-century dawn will want to keep an eye on it" (1996, p. 210).

The last century saw several major advances in neuroscience that directly relate to the scientific study of spiritual experience. These advances include brain surgery and the systematic evaluation of neurological and psychiatric disorders. But the technology most relevant to the scientific study of spiritual experience was neuroimaging, which only became widespread in the 1990s. Neuroimaging technology allows scientists to measure brain structure and function in living subjects. While the conclusions that can be drawn from neuroimaging are sometimes limited, and there are trade-offs for each of these techniques, these technologies make possible insights about the role of the brain during spiritual experience that James could have scarcely imagined.

Early neuroimaging modalities like CT and MRI focused on *structural imaging* of the brain, which enabled scientists and physicians to evaluate patients with disorders that create lasting physical changes in the brain, like tumors or hemorrhages. However, structural imaging is unable to assess how different parts of the brain are actually working in a given moment. But these structural findings could also reflect long-term effects. For example, the practice of meditation can change the structure of the brain over time. The brain is changed as the result of doing these practices over long periods of time, a little bit like how a muscle can become thicker and stronger by exercising. Studies by neuropsychologist Sara Lazar (e.g., Lazar et al., 2005) demonstrated that people who perform meditation practices daily for many years tend to have thicker areas of the brain's cortex, particularly in the frontal lobe.

Functional brain imaging is far more important to our discussion of spiritual experiences, as this method can show how brain activity changes in response to engaging in various mental processes. These imaging techniques take advantage of the physiological processes in the brain that occur at higher rates, in particular brain regions, while particular kinds of thoughts, feelings, and experiences are occurring. When certain parts of the brain are being used, that specific region will generally require more oxygen and hence more blood flow. Several brain imaging techniques show regions of the brain that have momentary increases in blood flow, and researchers infer from this that the mental process that the person is engaging in is related to that brain region. Functional brain scans can also show how different parts of the brain interact with one other.

Despite this advance, it is important not to draw too much from these findings, as it is possible that the brain regions that show the biggest changes are only a small part of a given mental process. Concluding on the basis of observed brain changes that a particular brain area is responsible for a particular mental process is called reverse inference and should be avoided when possible and done only with caution. However, these brain associations can provide important clues about which major systems may be involved in particular mental processes.

There are a few major types of brain imaging technologies worth briefly discussing. These are: *functional magnetic resonance imaging* (fMRI), *positron emission tomography* (PET), and *single-photon emission computed tomography* (SPECT). Each of these technologies has been used to study spiritual experience in the laboratory setting.

Functional magnetic resonance imaging uses strong magnets to assess changes in blood flow and blood oxygenation levels in particular regions of brain tissue. Scans can be performed while people are engaged in various tasks to determine which areas of the brain are activated or inhibited (activation decreased) during the task.

A major advantage of fMRI is that it has relatively good spatial and temporal resolution, meaning that the technique can distinguish differences within 3–4 millimeters and can take an image every 2–3 seconds. For example, if a subject in the scanner were, say, solving math problems and first did addition questions for 5 seconds and then subtraction problems for another 5 seconds, an fMRI brain scan could show differences in brain activity between those two tasks. Similarly, different parts of the process of meditation can be tracked through brain scans over time. The main downside of fMRI is that the subject needs to be in the scanner at the time that the scan is acquired. This is a serious issue with studying spiritual experiences as the scanner environment is not particularly conducive to these moments due to the claustrophobic space and loud banging noises that are made by the scanner (see Andersen et al., 2014). However, fMRI can be used to assess the effects of such practices on other brain processes, such as cognitive or emotional functions.

The PET technique is a nuclear medicine technique in which a person is injected with a small, safe amount of radioactive tracer. There are thousands of tracers that have been developed over the years that can explore all types of physiological processes, and one of the most common ones is called fluorodeoxyglucose (FDG). This radioactive glucose enters the brain and will tend to go to more highly activated regions, allowing researchers to observe where cerebral metabolism is occurring. In general, cerebral glucose metabolism is correlated with cerebral blood flow. Again, this is a way to measure activation or inhibition of particular regions of the brain while a participant is engaged in a particular task (i.e., meditation) compared to when that subject is not engaging in that task.

The related nuclear medicine technique called SPECT also involves the injection of radioactive tracers into the brain, allowing researchers to similarly observe specific physiological processes in the brain. The most commonly used tracers evaluate changes in blood flow, similar to what is observed on fMRI. SPECT was the technology used for the Tibetan meditator and Franciscan Nun prayer study described previously.

The primary downside of PET and SPECT imaging is their poor temporal resolution. It typically takes anywhere from several minutes to a half hour for these radioactive tracers to enter the brain. Whatever the person is doing during that period of time is what will be captured on the brain scan. If a person is injected and is then given an addition task for 5 seconds and a subtraction task for 5 seconds, the PET brain scan would show what is happening during both of those tasks averaged together. If a research subject were praying for 30 minutes, the brain scan would show what was happening throughout that entire 30-minute period. The problem with this is obvious: A person's brain activity will be different during the first minute of a prayer session compared to the last minute, but the PET scan will observe the entire period of time.

The advantage of PET and SPECT imaging is that the patient can be injected outside of the scanner. During that time, the person can, for example, say a prayer, chant, or meditate in relative peace and quiet—rather than inside a noisy scanner. After the practice is completed, the person can then be brought into the scanner, and the resulting image will show what was happening throughout the time following injection—during the spiritual practice in this example. Our research team has made extensive use of this approach since it has allowed us to explore spiritual practices beyond the Tibetan meditators and Franciscan nuns. We have also conducted neuroimaging studies on practices such as speaking in tongues and Islamic prayer that involves a variety of movements of the body and hands (Newberg et al., 2006, 2015). We describe the results of these studies throughout Part II.

Another important aspect of the brain's function is changes in neurotransmitter levels. Currently, the most effective way of evaluating neurotransmitters is to inject small, safe amounts of radioactive tracers that have molecular structures that are similar to specific neurotransmitters and then to use PET or SPECT imaging. Thus, researchers might use a dopamine analogue that is radioactively labeled in order to determine how dopamine is processed in the brain during a particular activity. One of the few studies that has explored the effects of spiritual practices on neurotransmitters used PET imaging to show a release of dopamine when an individual performed a yoga nidra meditation (Kjaer et al., 2002). We also conducted a study on neuro-transmitter changes in the brain after attending an intensive retreat based on the spiritual exercises of St. Ignatius, involving silence, contemplation, and prayer (Newberg et al., 2018).

Consciousness and the Brain

The nature of the relationship between consciousness and the brain remains a mystery. Philosophers refer to the question of how the physical brain gives rise to the mind (consciousness) as the "explanatory gap" (Chalmers, 1995). Philosophers also distinguish between the "easy problem" and the "hard problem" of consciousness (Chalmers, 1995). Studies that show associations between brain activities and subjective sensations would all be part of the easy problem. Therefore, all of the findings related to spiritual experience that we have discussed in this chapter would be examples of the easy problem of consciousness (though nothing about conducting these studies is easy!). The hard problem, on the other hand, refers to the question of how the brain produces subjective experience (consciousness) itself. At present, the hard problem has not been resolved by any scientific findings. We return to these issues related to consciousness in Chapter 19.

Spiritual experiences are frequently referred to as involving an "altered state of consciousness." This term refers to change in the contents of con-sciousness rather than referring to the nature of consciousness itself. In other words, an altered state of consciousness is more like an emotion—it is some-thing one can experience *within* consciousness. This term does not refer to an alteration to the nature of consciousness itself, but rather a change in the contents of consciousness. The changes in subjectivity in an altered state of consciousness are associated with patterns of activity throughout the brain. Thus, investigations involving altered states of consciousness would fall under the easy problem of consciousness.

As we describe the varieties of spiritual experiences using 21st-century science, we can continue to reflect on their relationship with the brain. Our focus is on the various elements of these experiences and how such elements may be related to brain processes. However, we cannot ignore the underlying problem of how consciousness is involved. We take this up in Part III, but it's worthwhile to consider these issues in this chapter to introduce a fundamental theme that must be held in the background as we discuss the variety of spiritual experiences.

Conclusion

As mentioned in the introductory material of the chapter, the use of neuroimaging and neuroscience in general is also part of an emerging field called *neurotheology* that specifically seeks to delineate the link between the brain and our religious and spiritual selves, of which one of us (A. B. N.) is a founder and proponent (Newberg, 2018). We feel that it is essential to bring the biological dimension to bear on the varieties of spiritual experiences. In this way, we not only can determine the various types and elements of these experiences, but also better understand how these experiences intersect with the function of the brain and body. Such biological information has implications for understanding the nature of these experiences.

The technological advances in neuroscience that have been made in the past century would have been unimaginable for James, but there is little doubt that James would have advocated for their use in the scientific project of understanding spiritual experience. Neuroscience now routinely makes use of neuroimaging technologies to examine the parts of the brain that are involved in the varieties of spiritual experience. Throughout the rest of the book, we explore a number of studies that draw on these brain regions and neuroimaging technologies to examine the neuroscience of spiritual experience.

References

Andersen, M. N., Schjødt, U., Nielbo, K. L., Sørensen, J. (2014). Mystical experience in the lab. In: *Method and Theory in the Study of Religion, 26*, 217–245.

Baird, F. (2017). *Philosophic classics: Asian philosophy* (Vol. 6). Routledge.

Bear, M., Connors, B., & Paradiso, M. A. (2020). *Neuroscience: Exploring the brain*. Jones & Bartlett Learning.

Benson, H., & Klipper, M. Z. (1975). *The relaxation response* (pp. 1–158). Morrow.

Brodmann, K. (2007). *Brodmann's: Localisation in the cerebral cortex*. Springer Science & Business Media. (Original work published 1909)

Carhart-Harris, R. L. (2018). The entropic brain-revisited. *Neuropharmacology, 142*, 167–178.

Chalmers, D. J. (1995). Facing up to the problem of consciousness. *Journal of Consciousness Studies, 2*(3), 200–219.

Crockett, M. J., Clark, L., Hauser, M. D., & Robbins, T. W. (2010). Serotonin selectively influences moral judgment and behavior through effects on harm aversion. *Proceedings of the National Academy of Sciences of the United States of America, 107*(40), 17433–17438.

De Dreu, C. K., Greer, L. L., Van Kleef, G. A., Shalvi, S., & Handgraaf, M. J. (2011). Oxytocin promotes human ethnocentrism. *Proceedings of the National Academy of Sciences of the United States of America, 108*(4), 1262–1266.

Devinsky, J., & Schachter, S. (2009). Norman Geschwind's contribution to the understanding of behavioral changes in temporal lobe epilepsy: The February 1974 lecture. *Epilepsy & Behavior, 15*(4), 417–424.

Dickinson, E. (1924). The brain is wider than the sky. In The *complete poems* of Emily Dickinson (p. 312). Little, Brown.

Gazzaniga, M. S. (2005). Forty-five years of split-brain research and still going strong. *Nature Reviews Neuroscience, 6*(8), 653–659.

Grigorenko, E. L., Warren, A. E. A., Lerner, R. M., & Phelps, E. (2011). Closeness of all kinds: The role of oxytocin and vasopressin in the physiology of spiritual and religious behavior. In A. E. A. Warren, R. M. Lerner, & E. Phelps (Eds.), *Thriving and spirituality among youth: Research perspectives and future possibilities* (pp. 33–60). Wiley.

James, W. (1902/2009). The varieties of religious experience: A study in human nature. *eBooks@Adelaide.* https://csrs.nd.edu/assets/59930/williams_1902.pdf

Kjaer, T. W., Bertelsen, C., Piccini, P., Brooks, D., Alving, J., & Lou, H. C. (2002). Increased dopamine tone during meditation-induced change of consciousness. *Cognitive Brain Research, 13*(2), 255–259.

Lazar, S. W., Kerr, C. E., Wasserman, R. H., Gray, J. R., Greve, D. N., Treadway, M. T., . . . & Rauch, S. L. (2005). Meditation experience is associated with increased cortical thickness. *Neuroreport, 16*(17), 1893.

McNamara, P. (2009). *The Neuroscience of Religious Experience.* New York: Cambridge University Press.

Newberg, A. (2018). *Neurotheology: How science can enlighten us about spirituality.* Columbia University Press.

Newberg, A., Alavi, A., Baime, M., Pourdehnad, M., Santanna, J., & d'Aquili, E. (2001). The measurement of regional cerebral blood flow during the complex cognitive task of meditation: a preliminary SPECT study. *Psychiatry Research: Neuroimaging, 106*(2), 113–122.

Newberg, A., & d'Aquili, E. G. (2008). *Why God won't go away: Brain science and the biology of belief.* Ballantine Books.

Newberg, A. B., Wintering, N. A., Morgan, D., & Waldman, M. R. (2006). The measurement of regional cerebral blood flow during glossolalia: A preliminary SPECT study. *Psychiatry Research: Neuroimaging, 148*(1), 67–71.

Newberg, A. B., Wintering, N. A., Yaden, D. B., Waldman, M. R., Reddin, J., & Alavi, A. (2015). A case series study of the neurophysiological effects of altered states of mind during intense Islamic prayer. *Journal of Physiology–Paris, 109*(4–6), 214–220.

Newberg, A. B., Wintering, N., Yaden, D. B., Zhong, L., Bowen, B., Averick, N., & Monti, D. A. (2018). Effect of a one-week spiritual retreat on dopamine and serotonin transporter binding: A preliminary study. *Religion, Brain & Behavior, 8*(3), 265–278.

Ogata, A., & Miyakawa, T. (1998). Religious experiences in epileptic patients with a focus on ictus-related episodes. *Psychiatry and clinical neurosciences, 52*(3), 321–325.

Ramachandran, V. S. (2003). *The emerging mind: The Reith Lectures 2003.* Profile.

Saver, J. L., & Rabin, J. (1997). The neural substrates of religious experience. *Neuropsychiatry of Limbic and Subcortical Disorders, 9*(3), 498–510.

Schjoedt, U. (2009). The Religious Brain: A General Introduction to the Experimental Neuroscience of Religion. *Method & Theory in the Study of Religion, 21*, 310–339.

Seeram, E. (2006). Nobel Prize for CT and MRI pioneers: Historical article. *Radiographer, 53*(1), 4.

Wolfe, T. (Feb, 1997). Sorry, but your soul just died. *Forbes ASAP*, 210–219.

6

Origins

Triggers of Spiritual Experience

Spiritual experiences often come unbidden, leaving those who have them surprised and wondering where they came from. Yet in other cases, at least the proximal trigger of the experience is known, such as meditation or prayer. Contemporary neuroscientist Jill Bolte Taylor described her powerful spiritual experience in her book, *My Stroke of Insight* (2009). The trigger of the experience, however, was not one of the more typical examples from meditation or mindfulness retreats—–it was a hemorrhagic stroke in the left side of her brain. In her book, Taylor re-creates her experience of the stroke in minute-by-minute detail:

> By this point I had lost touch with much of the physical three-dimensional reality that surrounded me. My body was propped up against the shower wall and I found it odd that I was aware that I could no longer clearly discern the physical boundaries of where I began and where I ended. Instead, I now blended in with the space and flow around me. (Taylor, 2009, p. 42)

As a neuroscientist in her 30s, Taylor was simultaneously amazed and overwhelmed by the experience on a personal level while trying to diagnose what was happening in her brain on an intellectual level. "What is happening in my brain?" she kept asking herself. Despite having an idea of the neurological origin of what was happening to her, she reported that the experience transformed her life. While the experience was physically traumatic and emotionally difficult, she ultimately referred to her experience as a "gift." For Taylor, knowing the origin of her spiritual experience did nothing to diminish her appreciation for it.

Most spiritual experiences do not have a trigger as obvious as Taylor's stroke, so where *do* spiritual experiences come from? How are they triggered? There is, of course, a theological/philosophical level and a more practical level to this question. If spiritual experiences are assumed supernatural

The Varieties of Spiritual Experience. David B. Yaden and Andrew B. Newberg, Oxford University Press. © David Yaden and Andrew Newberg 2022. DOI: 10.1093/oso/9780190665678.003.0006

and *only* supernatural, then they would presumably only come under the purview of religion/spirituality and would be entirely beyond scientific inquiry. But even if they have a supernatural origin, one might argue that there are still likely to be physiological effects in the brain and body of the person having the experience. After all, if the person hears the voice of God, and even if it truly is the voice of God, it is likely that the auditory cortex becomes activated along with the language centers of the brain that help to interpret what that voice is saying. On the other hand, if such experiences are assumed to be purely the product of brain function or malfunction, then they should be studied only in clinical contexts and classified as a symptom or sequelae of mental illness. But as we have seen many times now, we can take the Jamesian approach of setting aside questions regarding supernatural origin and scientifically study the conditions that seem to make these experiences more likely and evaluate the meaning that they hold for those who have them.

A number of different dispositions, circumstances, and activities have been identified as common triggers for spiritual experiences. In our Varieties Survey, we asked participants to indicate what they believed triggered their experience (Figure 6.1).

We address each trigger in turn, drawing on existing studies conducted by psychologists as well as our own research.

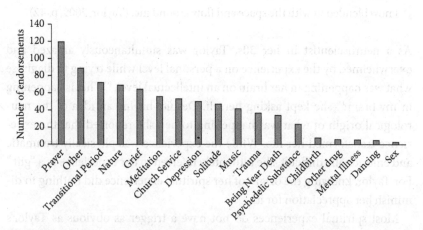

Figure 6.1 Triggers for spiritual experiences. The *y*-axis shows the number of times participants chose each category. Note that participants could choose more than one trigger. Drawn by David B. Yaden.

Spontaneous

Most spiritual experiences don't seem to have a trigger at all--that is, they feel spontaneous. In our Varieties Survey, we found that about the majority, 68% of participants, indicated that their experience felt like it came on spontaneously (Figure 6.2).

James included several personal accounts of spontaneous spiritual experiences in *The Varieties* (1902/2009). This description is from the autobiography of John Trevor, a Unitarian Universalist minister:

> For nearly an hour I walked along the road. . . . Suddenly, without warning, I felt that I was in Heaven—an inward state of peace and joy and assurance indescribably intense, accompanied with a sense of being bathed in a warm glow of light. . . (James, 1902/2009, p. 301)

Many people report experiences like Trevor's, which can seem to come out of nowhere and occur in the most unlikely of places. While many people report that their experiences came on spontaneously, sometimes a closer look at each particular case will show that there were some contextual or circumstantial factors in the life or mind of the individual perhaps influencing the onset of the experience. In one U.K. sample, 50% of the participants who reported that their experience was "spontaneous"

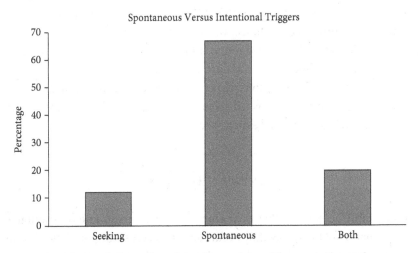

Figure 6.2 Types of trigger for spiritual experience. The *y*-axis shows the percentage endorsement of each type of trigger. Drawn by David B. Yaden.

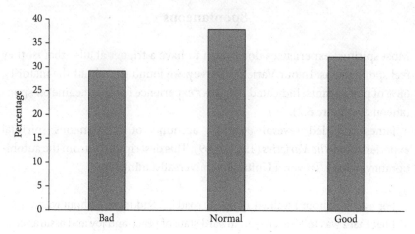

Figure 6.3 Life circumstances when the experience occurred. The *y*-axis shows the percentage endorsement of each type of trigger. Drawn by David B. Yaden.

also reported that they had been markedly "distressed and ill at ease" during the days and weeks before their experience (Hay, 1982). Another U.K. study found that about one third of the sample reported depression, despair, illness, or interpersonal differences around the time of their experience (Hardy, 1979). While truly spontaneous experiences do seem to occur, many may have been influenced by various hidden psychosocial circumstances (Beit-Hallahmi & Argyle, 1997, p. 85; Hay, 1982). Even so, about 34% of some samples insist that there was "nothing special" going on before their spiritual experiences occurred.

In our Varieties Survey, we found a balance between life circumstances being particularly good, bad, and normal (Figure 6.3).

The substantial diversity in terms of the specific triggers, spontaneity, and balance of circumstances has led scientists to look for other clues to understand what triggers spiritual experiences.

Personality Types

While most people feel that their spiritual experiences came on spontaneously, that is not to say that they occur randomly across the population. Some people seem to be predisposed to having spiritual experiences due to certain their personal characteristics, or their *psychological traits*. James speculated that those who tend to have spiritual experiences may have an unusual degree of access to the realm of one's imagination, or the subliminal regions of the mind, his term for the mental region from which dreams and epiphanies seem to come from.

This early psychological perspective has been somewhat supported by modern scientific research. There are now a number of different psychological constructs that describe an active inner life of the mind. A major area of study in psychology is *personality psychology*, which attempts to discover the basic and measurable personal characteristics and psychological traits that can explain differences in behavior. Psychologists arrive at personality traits by administering hundreds of questions about feelings, thoughts, and behaviors. Then, using a procedure called *factor analysis*, they are able to identify major clusters of questions (or "items") that group together. We use the method of factor analysis to establish the evidence-based classification of spiritual experience described throughout Part II.

Factor analysis of self-report survey questions has resulted in several well-known personality inventories, the best known of which is the five factor model (FFM), or its nickname, the "Big 5." The Big 5 consist of five major traits, which together form the acronym OCEAN: openness to experience, conscientiousness, extraversion, agreeableness, and neuroticism. Here are example items for each of the Big 5 traits:

- Openness to experience: "I am full of ideas."
- Conscientiousness: "I get chores done right away."
- Extraversion: "I feel comfortable around people."
- Agreeableness: "I sympathize with others' feelings."
- Neuroticism: "I have frequent mood swings."

The only Big 5 personality trait consistently related to the general tendency to have spiritual experiences is, as the name might suggest, *openness to experience*. Openness to experience is marked by tendencies for curiosity, creativity, appreciation of art, interest in ideas, and a preference for variety in experience.

Psychologist Scott Barry Kaufman (2018) has found that openness to experience has some facets that relate more strongly to *intellectual interests* and other facets more related to the *tendency to engage in interesting experiences*, and it is the latter facet is more strongly related to spiritual experience. Perhaps it is not surprising that the tendency to have spiritual experiences is associated with the tendency to seek novel and interesting experiences in general.

There are some traits that studies have shown are *not* related to spiritual experience. In a research article "Religiosity and Personality: Are Mystics Introverted, Neurotic, or Psychotic?" the results showed that spiritual experiences were *not* related to any of these three particular traits (Caird, 1987). The author of this study described how these findings contradict some prevalent stereotypes of people who report spiritual experiences. Here is more evidence that having spiritual experiences is not generally associated with mental illness. (Note: Introversion is, of course, not a mental illness.)

One of the most traits most predictive of having a spiritual experience is called absorption. *Absorption*, first described by psychologists Tellegen and Atkinson (1974), is an openness to inner experiences as well as the capacity to have one's attention entirely engaged to the point that everything else fades away from one's awareness. Here are some items from the Tellegen Absorption Scale. Most readers would probably agree that these items apply at least *somewhat* to themselves:

- When I listen to music, I can get so caught up in it that I don't notice anything else.
- I can be greatly moved by eloquent or poetic language.
- I can be deeply moved by a sunset.

Other items on this scale, though, involve more unusual inner experiences. These items apply to a smaller subset of people and will likely leave some readers nodding in agreement while others might raise their eyebrows incredulously:

- Different colors have distinctive and special meanings for me.
- If I wish, I can imagine (or daydream) some things so vividly that they hold my attention as a good movie or story does.
- I sometimes "step outside" my usual self and experience an entirely different state of being.

Anthropologist Tanya Luhrmann was interested in the question of whether people who score higher on the Absorption Scale have more spiritual experiences during prayer. She conducted a study of this in which she had people take a survey that included both the Absorption Scale as well as items having to do with spiritual experiences during prayer. She found that, indeed, evangelical Christians who scored higher in absorption were more likely to have spiritual experiences. In her book *When God Talks Back* (2012), Luhrmann wrote:

> There was another interesting thing the absorption scale predicted. If people answered "true" to at least half the items on the absorption scale, their chances of reporting that they had heard God's voice or felt God's touch or seen the wing of an angel or had a sensory perception of something supernatural (like hearing God say "I will always be with you" from the backseat of a car) was six times as high as for those who had said "true" to less than half the statements. (p. 197)

Openness to experience and absorption are thus the two psychological traits most associated with spiritual experience. Of these, absorption is the most predictive (Lifshitz et al., 2019). By way of inference, we have reason to suppose that other traits highly associated with openness to experience and absorption might also be related to spiritual experience.

Genetics

If certain people are psychologically predisposed to spiritual experiences, we should also consider how this predisposition is manifested biologically, in terms both of brain structure and function and of genetics. One method of addressing this question is to study identical twins raised together versus twins who are raised apart. This method allows researchers to study the extent to which environment impacts one's psychology as opposed to genetic influences. Identical twins have the same genes, so similarities between twins raised apart can be inferred to result from genetics. Twin research of this kind showed that spiritual beliefs and spiritual experience were roughly (41% in women and 37% in men; Kirk, Eaves & Martin, 1999, p. 86). This suggests that some individuals can be genetically predisposed to have spiritual experiences.

Further research conducted by geneticist Dean Hamer described, in a book called *The God Gene* (2005), suggested a particular gene is associated with spiritual beliefs and experiences, here measured by Cloninger's Self-Transcendence Scale (Cloninger et al., 1993). This scale was created by

Robert Cloninger in order to capture insights from the field of transpersonal psychology (Cloninger, 2004). This Self-Transcendence Scale measures the tendency for a person to experience going beyond the self and becoming more intimately connected, or absorbed, with another object, such as God. The gene associated with this scale codes for the VMAT2 receptor in the brain, which regulates serotonin and dopamine neurotransmitters. While providing a potentially important piece of information regarding the predisposition for spiritual experiences, this research has been criticized because of the very small magnitude of the relationship between differences in VMAT2 and scores on the self-transcendence measure, as it explains only about 1% of the differences in scores on the spiritual experience measure. However, this research provides support for at least some degree of a genetic predisposition for spiritual experience.

This kind of research rests on gene-wide association studies (GWASs), which correlate a number of genes with various traits in individuals for which researchers have genetic and self-report data. These studies need very large samples in order to identify genes associated with psychological traits. Recently, these research samples have grown much larger as a result of international collaborations between researchers. We can thus expect more specificity on the particular genes that explain the heritability of spiritual experience in years to come.

Brain Processes

While all of the various experiences described in this chapter involve brain processes (as all experiences do), there are particular aspects of brain activity that are worth describing in more detail. Brain imaging research has found differences in the brains of believers and nonbelievers (Harris et al., 2009), as well as differences in those who have performed spiritual practices for many years compared to those who have not (Newberg & d'Aquili, 2008). The research on believers and nonbelievers suggests that a number of structures might be involved in the predisposition for religious and spiritual beliefs.

For example, the frontal lobes are an important region in this regard. Popular author Sam Harris, who was trained in neuroscience, showed that belief in general—religious or nonreligious—was associated with greater activation in the ventromedial prefrontal cortex (Harris et al., 2009). Research by Kapogiannis et al. (2009) indicated several other structures might be involved with religious beliefs in particular. They argued that religious beliefs (in the Western traditions) are organized cognitively along three dimensions: (1) God's involvement; (2) God's emotion; and (3) the source of religious knowledge, ranging from doctrinal to experiential. The neural correlates of these dimensions include those involving understanding the actions and intent of others (referred to as theory of mind and including the inferior frontal gyrus and temporal lobes); emotion-related processes and emotional regulation (including the middle temporal and middle frontal gyrus); and abstract thought processing and imagery (including the inferior and superior temporal regions).

Other kinds of changes in frontal lobe activity may lead to spiritual experiences. Specifically, a temporary reduction in the activity in frontal regions of the brain may lead to experiences that feel overwhelming and "out of one's control" (sometimes referred to as the "transient hypofrontality theory"). Alternately, it may not be merely a reduction in frontal lobe activity but rather the *magnitude of the decrease* that is associated with intense spiritual experiences (Newberg & Waldman, 2016). The structure and function of the frontal lobe is a promising area for future research that may lead to information about individuals who are more likely to have spiritual experiences (Brewer et al., 2011).

Several studies have shown that dopamine is involved with spiritual practices and experiences. For example, a study of patients with Parkinson disease, a neurodegenerative disorder that causes a depletion of dopamine, showed that dopamine reductions were associated with decreased religiosity (Giaquinto et al., 2011). Additionally, a functional magnetic resonance imaging (fMRI) study of Mormons attending to specific beliefs and religious feelings found that activity in a main dopamine area (the nucleus accumbens) preceded peak spiritual feelings.

Religiosity, Spirituality, and Mindset

Is one more likely to have a spiritual experience simply by desiring one more? While this is not yet known, those who identify as religious or spiritual, who one might think are more likely to desire a spiritual experience, do indeed report more instances of spiritual experiences than those who identify as atheist, agnostic, or "none." It would seem intuitive that religious and spiritual experiences would occur more often to religious and spiritual individuals, and this is indeed broadly the case. Several studies showed that being spiritual—but not necessarily being religious—increased the odds that one has positive emotional and spiritual experiences (Yaden, Kaufman, et al., 2019; Yaden, Giorgi, et al., 2021). The reasons for why spiritual experiences are more likely to occur in those individuals who consider themselves spiritual remains unclear. It could be that individuals who are more likely to have these kinds of experiences are more drawn to spirituality and religion in the first place, or it could be that religious and spiritual practices and rituals make one more likely to have a spiritual experience (which we have also seen is indeed the case).

Luhrmann argued that religious and spiritual individuals unknowingly train their own minds to have spiritual experiences (2012):

> In effect, people train the mind in such a way that they experience part of their mind as the presence of God. They learn to reinterpret the familiar experiences of their own minds and bodies as not being their own at all— but God's. They learn to identify some thoughts as God's voice, some images as God's suggestions, some sensations as God's touch or the response to his nearness. They construct God's interactions out of these personal mental events. (p. xxi)

This may help to explain why religious or spiritual individuals tend to have more spiritual experiences, because they build up their expectancies for such experiences and then interpret ambiguous stimuli along these lines. However, a religious or spiritual believer might retort that they have merely opened themselves to these experiences of other parts of reality through their belief. Also, this theory does not explain why atheists and agnostics with little to no religious or spiritual training sometimes report spiritual experiences.

Circumstances

Some circumstances seem to make spiritual experience more likely to occur due to the religious or spiritual significance they hold for some people. Some religious and spiritual traditions, such as the Celtic tradition, talk about "thin places," or sacred spots where spiritual experiences are more likely to happen (McCall, 2015). But this has not been investigated empirically. Researchers might study pilgrims to holy places, like Muslims on their hajj to Mecca, visitors to Lourdes in France, Jews touching the Western Wall, Buddhists visiting Sarnath, and Hindus wading in the Ganges. The intense meaning that such places hold to some people could be a factor that makes these individuals more likely to have spiritual experiences.

One setting that has been investigated empirically and shown to help elicit spiritual experiences is nature. James noticed this association between natural settings and spiritual experience, writing "Certain aspects of nature seem to have a peculiar power of awakening such mystical moods. Most of the striking cases which I have collected have occurred out of doors" (James, 1902/2009, p. 298). James included a spiritual experience triggered by nature that was recounted by his family's old friend, the famous naturalist and author of *Walden*, Henry David Thoreau:

> Once, a few weeks after I came to the woods, for an hour I doubted whether the near neighborhood of man was not essential to a serene and healthy life. To be alone was somewhat unpleasant. But, in the midst of a gentle rain, while these thoughts prevailed, I was suddenly sensible of such sweet and beneficent society in Nature, in the very pattering of the drops, and in every sight and sound around my house, an infinite and unaccountable friendliness all at once, like an atmosphere, sustaining me. (James, 1902/2009, p. 209)

Contemporary psychologist Ralph Hood conducted a study of whether solitude in nature reliably triggers spiritual experiences. He studied participants in a wilderness retreat program that included spending a day and night alone in the forest (Hood, 1977). This "solitude in nature" condition was compared to another group who went on a whitewater canoe trip. Hood found that the participants who were alone in the forest reported more mystical experiences. Furthermore, he found that expectations were related to the incidence of spiritual experience. Specifically, it was not stress or the lack of stress that predicted whether one would have a mystical experience while alone in the forest—but rather if there was a mismatch between expected stress and experienced stress. In other words, if a participant expected that she would not be stressed during her time in the forest but when she was out there she felt a lot of stress, then she was more likely to have a mystical experience than other participants who got what they expected—and vice versa. This points to a potential interaction between "set and setting," or one's mindset and one's surroundings.

Near-Death Experiences and Trauma

Being near death and experiencing other forms of trauma can also prompt spiritual experiences in some cases. Neurologist Kevin Nelson, in his book *The Spiritual Doorway in the Brain* (2010), took trauma as a key starting point for his theory of spiritual experience. Nelson related the story of a missionary who had a spiritual experience that was prompted, literally, by being in the jaws of a lion:

> When David Livingstone, the famous Scottish missionary and explorer, found himself in a lion's jaw, the shock, he wrote, "caused a sense of dreaminess in which there was no sense of pain or feeling of terror, though [I was] quite conscious of all that was happening . . . merciful provision by our benevolent Creator for lessening the pain of death. (Nelson, 2010, p. 1999)

Being on the brink of death is a well-known trigger of spiritual experience—often called a "near-death experience" (NDE). James cited one such experience in *The Varieties* from someone who felt the presence of God and who desired to remain rather than return back to their life:

> I felt him streaming in like light upon me. . . . I cannot describe the ecstasy I felt. Then, as I gradually awoke from the influence of the anaesthetics, the old sense of my relation to the world began to return, the new sense of my relation to God began to fade. . . . "Why did you not kill me? Why would you not let me die?" (James, 1902/2009, p. 296)

To cite a more contemporary example, the actor Sharon Stone reported a spiritual experience while her brain was hemorrhaging. She described her experience in terms of its positive effects on her life:

> It's a very . . . loving, and gentle, and OK [feeling], and there's nothing to be afraid of. . . . I had a real journey with this, that took me to places both here and beyond that affected me so profoundly, that my life will never be the same. . . . This kind of giant vortex of white light was upon me and I kind of—poof! Sort of took off into this glorious, bright, bright, bright white light and I started to see and be met by some of my friends. But it was very fast—whoosh! Suddenly, I was back. I was in my body and I was in the room. (cited in Spencer, 2011, p. 199)

Near-death experiences have been studied in both the psychological and medical literature. One of the unique characteristics of NDEs is the claims from patients that they were able to see aspects of their surgical procedure from the ceiling or some other vantage point beyond their physical body. These are known as *out-of-body experiences*.

Psychologist Susan Blackmore had an out-of-body experience herself and then devoted many years to studying them. In her work, she analyzes studies that involve putting signs with letters and numbers on top of cabinets in operating rooms, above where patients can see from their beds. If a patient reports an out-of-body experience wherein they claim to have looked down at their own body during the surgery, they are then asked by the researchers if they saw the top of the cabinet and what the sign said. No one has been able to accurately describe what was on the sign in these studies (Blackmore, 1996). So, at the moment, the evidence that people are able to actually gain a perspective outside of their body is still being studied since many people report that they feel this to be the case. Of course, even if some claims about out-of-body experiences have not been borne out by research that is not to say that such experiences are not meaningful for those who have them.

Near-death states are likely associated with intense autonomic nervous system activity. It may be, as in other spiritual experiences, that there is unusual activity in the temporal and parietal lobes that are involved in helping establish the spatial representation of the self (Newberg & d'Aquili, 2008). Thus, as these areas lose function during the dying process, we might expect that there is a loss of the sense of self and the potential for an out-of-body experience.

In one of the few neuroimaging studies related to NDEs, when subjects meditated on their experience, they activated brain regions such as the orbitofrontal cortex, right medial prefrontal cortex, right superior parietal lobule, visual areas, and temporal lobe (Beauregard et al., 2009). However, this study should be qualified by the fact that it focused on memories of NDEs and not actual occurrences of spiritual experiences triggered by being near death.

Rites of Passage and Transformative Festivals

Rites of passage are rituals that typically mark a transition from one life role to another, such as from adolescence to an adulthood. Although they are largely absent from contemporary society, these rituals appear to frequently induce spiritual experiences in participants in places where they did occur. Anthropologist Victor Turner (1969), in the context of discussing rites of passage, used the term "liminality" to describe periods of time that diverged from the daily, routine, more socially structured parts of life. The ritual process is described as first involving a period of separation, then a period of liminality, and finally a return to one's social circumstances and daily routine. The period of liminality could be considered a kind of transitional period, albeit within the ritual context itself. Note that "transitional periods of life" was a primary trigger of spiritual experience in our Varieties Survey.

Comparative religion scholar Mircea Eliade described an adolescent rite of passage in the Aboriginal Kurnai tribe of Australia. Participants in this rite of passage are brought to a room that is considered sacred, whereupon they are forced to the ground and covered by rugs and left there for several days (Eliade, 1958, p. 7). Lying for many hours in silence is difficult, getting covered by lots of heavy rugs is certainly different, and symbolically this ritual is meant to convey a rebirth—the adolescent self "dies," and the participant emerges as an adult. These three "d's" of liminality (difference, difficulty, and death) often seem to occur in rites of passage.

Traditional rites of passages often seem intended to trigger spiritual experiences. However, more modern rites of passage are often missing elements of traditional ones—most graduations, communions, and bat/bar mitzvahs basically amount to a few speeches and a family party (hardly much different from any holiday celebration).

Military boot camp could be seen as a contemporary rite of passage. Boot camp, as anyone who has been through it will tell you, is difficult, and it is different from daily life. There could be an aspect of symbolic death as well since participants are referred to as "recruits" and are not allowed to use their name or the first person (they refer to themselves as "this recruit" or "this candidate"). Graduates of basic training are then referred to as "soldiers" and are treated as symbolically differentiated from their previous "civilian" selves. Obviously, spiritual experience is not a goal of military training, but some recruits report a kind of spiritual experience from the synchrony of movement that occurs during marches. In his book *The Happiness Hypothesis* (2006), psychologist Jonathan Haidt underscored this aspect of military behavior by quoting the words of a soldier describing marching while in basic training:

Words are inadequate to describe the emotion aroused by the prolonged movement in unison that drilling involved. A sense of pervasive well-being is what I recall; more specifically, a strange sense of personal enlargement; a sort of swelling out, becoming bigger than life, thanks to participation in collective ritual. (Haidt, 2006, p. 237)

James seems to have noticed this propensity for an upwelling of fellow feeling and selflessness that can arise from military drilling and even combat. As Steven Pinker noted in *The Better Angels of Our Nature: Why Violence Has Declined*, James was *not* one of those 19th-century thinkers to get caught up in romanticized visions of war and violence (Pinker, 2012). But James did think about trying to replicate the states of selflessness and esprit de corps that can be aroused during war, though James was interested in how this could be done through nonviolent means:

What we now need to discover in the social realm is the moral equivalent of war: something heroic that will speak to men as universally as war does, and yet will be as compatible with their spiritual selves as war proved itself to be incompatible. (James, 1902/2009, p. 278)

Additionally, festivals, or "transformational festivals" as they are sometimes called, can elicit spiritual feelings. Durkheim referred to the state that can be brought about from social gatherings as "collective effervescence" and viewed it as an essential component of social bonding (Durkheim, 1912). More recently, journalist Barbara Ehrenreich has described the history of such social settings and the feelings that they tend to elicit in her book *Dancing in the Streets* (2007). Empirical research from psychologist Molly Crockett and her research team, who collected data at festivals such as Burning Man and others, has provided support for the notion that such experiences are more frequent at these events (Forstmann et al., 2020). Of course, mass gatherings can also be turned toward immoral ends as well; one need only think of the Nazi rallies at Nuremberg for a stark reminder of collective fellow feeling channeled toward the destruction of other people.

Religious Rituals

Many rites of passage are part of the larger category of rituals. Rituals can take both secular and spiritual forms, though they are largely associated with religions. Rituals play an important part of the yearly, weekly, or even daily life of many religious individuals (Yaden, Zhao, Peng, & Newberg, 2019). Rituals are generally done in a group setting, most commonly in a building devoted to that purpose—a church, temple, or mosque. Looking at the United States, the Pew religious landscape survey (2014) found that about 36% of Americans go to church at least once a week, 33% go a few times a year (on major holidays), and 30% of Americans never go. This puts America's church attendance around the average for countries with substantial Christian populations. In terms of church attendance, Russia, France, and Belgium have the lowest attendance, while Nigeria, Zambia, and Chad have the highest rates. Religious attendance has been dropping in the United States for a number of years, but attendance is still higher in the United States than it is in other more economically developed nations.

A large number of research studies have revealed that attending religious services is associated with modest mental and physical health benefits. In one study it was found that church attendance slightly increased longevity (Li et al., 2016), and others have found decreased rates of suicide, depression, and addiction (Koenig & Cohen, 2002). There are even some indications that nonreligious individuals can benefit from these effects by attending religious services with their families. This raises the question of the mechanisms through which religious services convey their health benefits.

Religious services are a somewhat frequent setting for spiritual experiences, though this depends on the sect and denomination. For example, in Christianity, Pentecostal Christians habitually speak in tongues and collapse during services, while Presbyterians—another branch of Protestant Christianity—might go to church every Sunday and never see this kind of behavior in their lives.

Tanya Luhrmann's work on an evangelical Christian church provides a visceral description of a time when speaking in tongues broke out among the congregation:

> The young man shared his testimony, which was beautiful and stirring. . . . One fellow, Tim, started bouncing. His arms flung out and he fell over, but one of his hands accidentally hit a mike [sic] stand and he took it down with him. He was tangled up in the cord with the mike next to his mouth. Then he began speaking in tongues, so the sound went throughout the gymnasium. . . . The majority of young people were shaking and falling over. At one point it looked like a battlefield scene—bodies everywhere, people weeping, wailing and speaking in tongues, much shouting and loud

behavior. And there was Tim in the middle of it all, babbling into the micro-phone. (Luhrmann, 2012, p. 31)

The collective coordination involved in religious rituals seems particularly important for their capacity to induce spiritual experiences. This quality, sometimes referred to as "synchrony," is common in rituals—from Muslims circling the Kaaba stone in Mecca, to Sufis twirling together, to a monastery full of Buddhist monks meditating in neat rows and columns, to Christians singing hymns together in pews. Group synchrony has been shown to strengthen social bonds and even reduce pain (Hove & Risen, 2009; Tarr et al., 2014). It appears likely that group synchrony can also make spiritual experiences more likely to occur.

Practices

Practices can be defined, for our purposes, as a kind of ritual that people can—and usually do—engage in alone. Meditation and prayer are the most common forms of religious or spiritual practices. Both of these practices have been shown to increase the likelihood of having spiritual experiences.

Prayer. Prayer is remarkably common. Almost 90% of Americans report engaging in prayer practices, and 76% report that they pray daily (Poloma & Gallup, 1991). While the type and the intensity of prayer are quite variable, these statistics suggest that prayer is a widespread practice. In fact, it appears that Americans engage in prayer more often than sexual intercourse. While substantial psychological theory and research has been devoted to sex, it is perhaps notable note that comparatively little research has been devoted to studying prayer.

Prayer practices can be differentiated on the basis of the form that they take as well as their goal. In terms of form, researchers have differentiated prayer practices into different types. Here are some kinds of prayer and items for measuring them (Hood et al., 1993):

- *Contemplative prayer.* "When you pray or meditate, how often do you seek to be one with God or ultimate reality?"
- *Liturgical prayer.* "When you pray or meditate, how often do you read from sacred texts?"

- *Petitionary prayer.* "When you pray or meditate, how often do you seek blessings for others?
- *Material prayer.* "When you pray or meditate, how often do you seek material things for yourself?"
- *Conversational prayer.* "When you pray or meditate, how often do you simply talk with God?"

There are clearly a number of different reasons for prayer and kinds of prayer. In terms of spiritual experience, it has been found that of these forms of prayer, contemplative prayer is particularly suited to trigger spiritual experiences (Poloma & Gallup, 1991).

In *When God Talks Back,* Luhrmann (2012) described her experience of living with and worshipping alongside evangelical Christians in the United States who converse with God as part of their prayer practice. Congregants are told to "listen for the leading of the Holy Spirit. Look for indications of the presence of the Holy Spirit (crying, peace, warmth, tingling, muscle spasms)" (Luhrmann, 2012, p. 50). Here is one congregant named Aisha describing an experience that she had that was triggered by prayer:

> As I was praying, I looked up, and it was cloudy and the sun shone through the clouds. . . . Everything was very intimate. I remember walking into the water, and I saw myself doing it. It's the most mystical thing that's ever happened to me. By far it's the most spiritual experience I've ever had. . . . I was really scared, really scared, but afterward I was so happy. (Luhrmann, 2012, p. 151)

Thus, prayer is usually directed at a divine entity (e.g., God), and conversational prayer actually takes the form of something like a dialogue. Perhaps unsurprisingly, brain regions related to social interaction are active during this type of prayer (Mohandas, 2008). More contemplative prayer practices are associated with a complex interaction between a variety of brain structures (e.g., see Ferguson et al., 2019). During the attention-focusing part of prayer (i.e., when you focus on repeating the prayer or on the image of God), frontal lobe activity is typically increased. If a prayer practice is associated with a sense of communion, connection, or oneness with God, the parietal lobe regions typically have reduced activity (Newberg et al., 2003). In this situation, there is a concomitant reduction in the sense of self, a blurring of the spatial boundary between self and other, and the experience of oneness.

Meditation. There is no clear dividing line between prayer and meditation. But in general, modern connotations are that prayer involves a *sequential* process through words and/or images, whereas meditation is more often associated with a more *repetitious* practice, in which one continuously returns to an object of focus in order to clear one's mind.

One of the most well-known forms of meditation is "mindfulness meditation." The roots of this practice have been traced back 2,500 years to Hindu philosophical traditions but have been most discussed in and associated with Buddhist contexts. Mindfulness is usually described as a form of non-judgmental, open awareness of the present moment (Kabat-Zinn & Hanh, 2009). This practice has been formalized as mindfulness-based stress reduction (MBSR), which takes 8 weeks of practicing for 20 minutes twice a day. This form of mindfulness has reached a surprising degree of popularity in the United States.

There are a few simple instructions for how to practice mindfulness, adapted from Kabat-Zinn and Hanh's (2009) book *Full Catastrophe Living* in the work of Pickert (2014):

1. Sit cross-legged on a cushion on the floor or in a chair. Keep your back straight and let your shoulders drop. Take a deep breath and close your eyes if you wish.
2. Notice your breath. Don't change your breathing, but focus on the air moving in and out of your lungs.
3. As thoughts come into your mind and distract you from your breathing, acknowledge those thoughts and then return to focusing on your breathing each time.
4. Don't judge yourself or try to ignore distractions. Your job is simply to notice that your mind has wandered and to bring your attention back to your breathing.
5. Start by doing this 10 minutes a day for a week. The more you meditate regularly, the easier it will be to keep your attention where you want it.

Unlike most prayer practices, this kind of meditation practice does not require any kind of theological or metaphysical commitments. In this form it is secularized, in the sense that it is apart from religion and can be practiced by anyone regardless of their beliefs. For this reason, mindfulness has been utilized in psychotherapeutic and healthcare contexts. It has been shown to effectively (though with effects of a fairly small magnitude) reduce depression

(Hofmann et al., 2010), help with anxiety disorders (Hoge et al., 2018), and reduce chronic pain (Grossman et al., 2007). Mindfulness has also been shown to boost well-being (Carmody & Baer, 2008).

Other secularized forms of meditation have also emerged, mostly from Buddhism. For example, *Mettā* is a Pali word that has been translated as "loving kindness." Psychologist Barbara Fredrickson and her team (2008) have conducted a series of experiments using loving kindness meditation in order to effectively induce positive emotions like love in study participants. Another form of secularized meditation that is more emotion focused is compassion meditation, which involves a repetitive wishing of happiness on other people.

Meditation is a reliable trigger of spiritual experiences. Neuroimaging studies of Tibetan meditators have shown that they can reliably put themselves into a state of oneness with the universe (Newberg, Alavi, et al., 2001). In general, rituals and practices like prayer and meditation are among the most common triggers of spiritual experience, as we saw in our Varieties Survey.

Psychopharmacology

The practice of using psychedelic substances to help induce spiritual experiences goes back thousands of years, and yet this practice is currently controversial since such substances are illegal in many countries. In a number of contexts through history, however, the religious establishment endorsed them. In ancient Athens, there is evidence that the Eleusinian Mysteries, a religious rite held once a year, may have involved a psychedelic substance (Muraresku, 2020). The psychedelic substance may have been derived from a fungal parasite on rye grain, which contains alkaloids that are precursors to LSD (lysergic acid diethylamide). An ancient Indian text, the Veda, mentions a substance called "soma," which, though quite speculative, some scholars think may have been a psychedelic substance. Indigenous people in South America have been continuously using ayahuasca since at least the 16th century, when Spanish missionaries described the practice in written reports (and attempted to outlaw the practice by force).

As described previously, a small group of researchers passed through a period of enthusiasm about the potential of these substances, but, as we discussed previously, breaches of professional ethics and an unwarranted government response led to the field being forced into dormancy for several decades (Baumeister & Placidi, 1983; Lattin, 2010). Now, modern research is demonstrating that psychedelic substances are indeed fairly reliable triggers of spiritual experiences through rigorous and ethical research designs (Yaden, Yaden, & Griffiths, 2021).

Substances considered to be "psychoactive" are able to act on the central nervous system and impact perception, mood, and/or behavior. These psychoactive substances, or drugs, include everything from caffeine to cocaine. But only a subset of psychoactive drugs is considered "psychedelic." Psychedelic substances can be broken down further into groups. The group that we focus on, called "classic psychedelics," is also referred to as "entheogens" by some people who emphasize their capacity to trigger spiritual experiences. These classic psychedelics include psilocybin, LSD, psilocybin (the psychoactive substance in "magic mushrooms"), and N,N-dimethyltryptamine (DMT). These substances result in psychoactive effects primarily through their interaction with particular serotonin receptors (5-HT$_{2A}$).

Psychopharmacologist Roland Griffiths, Matthew Johnson, and researchers at Johns Hopkins Center for Psychedelic and Consciousness Research (also including Frederick Barrett, Albert Garcia-Romeu, Bill Richards, Mary Cosimano, and others) have made breakthrough progress on the study of psilocybin's ability to induce spiritual experiences. For the most part, these spiritual or mystical-type experiences are rated as among the most meaningful and spiritually significant experiences in a person's life (Griffiths et al., 2006). These experiences have also been associated with subsequent improvements in symptoms of anxiety and depression in some individuals (Carhart-Harris et al., 2016; 2021; Davis et al., 2021; Griffiths et al., 2016).

DMT has a markedly different time course than the other two psychedelics. While LSD and psilocybin last for around 6–12 hours, DMT lasts for under 30 minutes. While not long lasting, the subjective effects of DMT are more intense. DMT researcher Rick Strassman described the experience in the following way:

> Extraordinarily powerful feelings surge through our consciousness. We are ecstatic, and the intensity of this joy is such that our body cannot contain it—it seems to need a temporarily disembodied state. While the bliss is pervasive, there's also an underlying peace and equanimity that's not affected

by even this incredibly profound happiness. . . . There is a searing sense of the sacred and the holy. (Strassman, 2000, p. 235)

There are a number of indicators that psychedelics may be on the cusp of becoming a major form of treatment for substance use and mood disorders. Michael Pollan's bestselling book *How to Change Your Mind* (2019) recently provided an accessible introduction to the topic of psychedelic research. A side effect of psychedelic treatment—or perhaps part of the therapeutic mechanism—is the capacity of psychedelics to trigger spiritual experience (Yaden & Griffiths, 2020). We cover psychedelics in much more detail in Chapter 18.

Neurostimulation

Spiritual experiences may someday be triggered through directly modulating the brain's activity. The notion that direct manipulations to the brain can create predictable changes to subjectivity is not new. In the 1940s and 1950s, neurosurgeon Wilder Penfield was able to map the primary motor cortex and the primary somatosensory cortex using electrical probes on the brains of patients about to undergo neurosurgery (Penfield & Jasper, 1954). Through this process, he was able to determine the specific brain locations responsible for motion and sensation in particular areas of the body. Penfield also found that when certain areas in the temporal lobe were stimulated, patients experienced hallucinations, dream-like states, and out-of-body experiences.

Pioneering research by Persinger and Healey (2002) purported to create the feeling of a "sensed presence" in the room with study participants. This was done by using what's known as the "God helmet," a device placed on a person's head that emits weak electrical fields. Basing his theory on temporal lobe epilepsy, Persinger recorded what he called "temporal lobe transients," or temporal lobe microseizures, and attempted to reproduce these patterns using stimulation with what he called "complex magnetic fields" over the temporal lobes of subjects.

Persinger's studies have not been successfully replicated, however. Critics have commented that this stimulation method is probably not sufficiently powered to pass through the skull (by some estimates, Persinger's technique was approximately 5,000 times weaker than contemporary transcranial magnetic stimulation technology), and a more recent replication of the study failed to yield significant results (Granqvist et al., 2005). The authors of the replication ultimately attributed Persinger's initial findings to suggestion resulting from the lack of a double-blind condition. It therefore appears that this particular method was not effective, but more research is needed on this and related technologies.

Brain stimulation (and related technologies like neurofeedback) is a quickly developing area, so we are keeping our eye on technologies such as transcranial magnetic stimulation (TMS) as a potential future trigger of spiritual experiences (Yaden Eichstaedt, & Medaglia, 2018). TMS works by passing a magnetic pulse through the skull, which can briefly increase or decrease the activation levels of targeted brain regions. Emerging neurostimulation technologies, similar to TMS, may eventually become capable of inducing spiritual experiences with even more specificity than pharmacological agents. But as of now, psychedelic substances are the most reliable means to elicit spiritual experiences in controlled laboratory settings.

Conclusion

There are a number of circumstances, dispositions, mindsets, rituals, practices, psychoactive substances, and, perhaps in the near future, neurotechnologies that make spiritual experiences more likely to occur. This list is not comprehensive. As psychologist Ralph Hood put it: "Survey research has long established that a variety of triggers can elicit mystical experiences. Although some triggers are consistently reported—prayer; church attendance; significant life events, such as births and deaths; and experiences associated with music, sex, and entheogens—one seeks in vain for a common characteristic shared by such diverse triggers" (Hood et al., 2018, p. 389). In Part II, we discuss additional triggers that are associated with specific spiritual experiences, but for now we move from the triggers of spiritual experience to the impact that they have on the lives of those who have them.

References

Baumeister, R. F., & Placidi, K. S. (1983). A social history and analysis of the LSD controversy. *Journal of Humanistic Psychology*, 23(4), 25–58.

Beauregard, M., Courtemanche, J., & Paquette, V. (2009). Brain activity in near-death experiencers during a meditative state. *Resuscitation, 80*(9), 1006–1010.

Beit-Hallahmi, B., & Argyle, M. (1997). *The psychology of religious behaviour, belief and experience.* Taylor & Francis.

Blackmore, S. J. (1996). Near-death experiences. *Journal of the Royal Society of Medicine, 89*(2), 73–76.

Brewer, J. A., Worhunsky, P. D., Gray, J. R., Tang, Y. Y., Weber, J., & Kober, H. (2011). Meditation experience is associated with differences in default mode network activity and connectivity. *Proceedings of the National Academy of Sciences of the United States of America, 108*(50), 20254–20259.

Caird, D. (1987). Religiosity and personality: Are mystics introverted, neurotic, or psychotic? *British Journal of Social Psychology, 26*(4), 345–346.

Carhart-Harris, R. L., Bolstridge, M., Rucker, J., Day, C. M., Erritzoe, D., Kaelen, M., . . . Nutt, D. J. (2016). Psilocybin with psychological support for treatment-resistant depression: An open-label feasibility study. *Lancet Psychiatry, 3*(7), 619–627.

Carhart-Harris, R., Giribaldi, B., Watts, R., Baker-Jones, M., Murphy-Beiner, A., Murphy, R., . . . Nutt, D. J. (2021). Trial of psilocybin versus escitalopram for depression. *New England Journal of Medicine, 384*(15), 1402–1411.

Carmody, J., & Baer, R. A. (2008). Relationships between mindfulness practice and levels of mindfulness, medical and psychological symptoms and well-being in a mindfulness-based stress reduction program. *Journal of Behavioral Medicine, 31*(1), 23–33.

Cloninger, C. R. (2004). *Feeling good: The science of well-being.* Oxford University Press.

Cloninger, C. R., Svrakic, D. M., & Przybeck, T. R. (1993). A psychobiological model of temperament and character. *Archives of General Psychiatry, 50*(12), 975–990.

d'Aquili, E. G., & Newberg, A. B. (1999, August). *The mystical mind: Probing the biology of religious experience.* Fortress Press.

Davis, A. K., Barrett, F. S., May, D. G., Cosimano, M. P., Sepeda, N. D., Johnson, M. W., . . . Griffiths, R. R. (2021). Effects of psilocybin-assisted therapy on major depressive disorder: A randomized clinical trial. *JAMA Psychiatry, 78*(5), 481–489.

Durkheim, E. (1912). *The elementary forms of the religious life.* The Free Press.

Ehrenreich, B. (2007). *Dancing in the streets: A history of collective joy.* Macmillan.

Eliade, M. (1958). *Rites and symbols of initiation* (W. R. Trask, Trans.). Harper & Row.

Ferguson, M. A., Nielsen, J. A., King, J. B., Dai, L., Giangrasso, D. M., Holman, R., Korenberg, J. R., Anderson, J. S. (2018). Reward, salience, and attentional networks are activated by religious experience in devout Mormons. *Social Neuroscience, 13*(1), 104–116. doi:10.1080/17470919.2016.1257437.

Forstmann, M., Yudkin, D. A., Prosser, A. M., Heller, S. M., & Crockett, M. J. (2020). Transformative experience and social connectedness mediate the mood-enhancing effects of psychedelic use in naturalistic settings. *Proceedings of the National Academy of Sciences of the United States of America, 117*(5), 2338–2346.

Fredrickson, B. L., Cohn, M. A., Coffey, K. A., Pek, J., & Finkel, S. M. (2008). Open hearts build lives: Positive emotions, induced through loving-kindness meditation, build consequential personal resources. *Journal of Personality and Social Psychology, 95*(5), 1045.

Giaquinto, S., Bruti, L., Dall'Armi, V., Palma, E., & Spiridigliozzi, C. (2011). Religious and spiritual beliefs in outpatients suffering from Parkinson disease. *International Journal of Geriatric Psychiatry, 26*(9), 916–922.

Granqvist, P., Fredrikson, M., Unge, P., Hagenfeldt, A., Valind, S., Larhammar, D., & Larsson, M. (2005). Sensed presence and mystical experiences are predicted by suggestibility, not by the application of transcranial weak complex magnetic fields. *Neuroscience Letters, 379*(1), 1–6.

Griffiths, R. R., Johnson, M. W., Carducci, M. A., Umbricht, A., Richards, W. A., Richards, B. D., . . . Klinedinst, M. A. (2016). Psilocybin produces substantial and sustained decreases in depression and anxiety in patients with life-threatening cancer: A randomized double-blind trial. *Journal of psychopharmacology, 30*(12), 1181–1197.

Griffiths, R. R., Richards, W. A., McCann, U., & Jesse, R. (2006). Psilocybin can occasion mystical-type experiences having substantial and sustained personal meaning and spiritual significance. *Psychopharmacology, 187*(3), 268–283.

Grossman, P., Tiefenthaler-Gilmer, U., Raysz, A., & Kesper, U. (2007). Mindfulness training as an intervention for fibromyalgia: Evidence of postintervention and 3-year follow-up benefits in well-being. *Psychotherapy and Psychosomatics, 76*(4), 226–233.

Haidt, J. (2006). *The happiness hypothesis: Finding modern truth in ancient wisdom.* Basic Books.

Hamer, D. H. (2005). *The God gene: How faith is hardwired into our genes.* Anchor.

Hardy, S. A. (1979). *The spiritual nature of man: A study of contemporary religious experience.* Clarendon Press.

Harris, S., Kaplan, J. T., Curiel, A., Bookheimer, S. Y., Iacoboni, M., & Cohen, M. S. (2009). The neural correlates of religious and nonreligious belief. *PLoS One, 4*(10), e0007272. doi:10.1371/journal.pone.0007272

Hay, D. (1982). *Exploring inner space: Scientists and religious experience.* Penguin Books.

Hofmann, S. G., Sawyer, A. T., Witt, A. A., & Oh, D. (2010). The effect of mindfulness-based therapy on anxiety and depression: A meta-analytic review. *Journal of Consulting and Clinical Psychology, 78*(2), 169.

Hoge, E. A., Bui, E., Palitz, S. A., Schwarz, N. R., Owens, M. E., Johnston, J. M., . . . Simon, N. M. (2018). The effect of mindfulness meditation training on biological acute stress responses in generalized anxiety disorder. *Psychiatry Research, 262,* 328–332.

Hood, R. W., Jr. (1977). Eliciting mystical states of consciousness with semistructured nature experiences. *Journal for the Scientific Study of Religion, 16,* 155–163.

Hood, R. W., Jr., Hill, P. C., & Spilka, B. (2018). *The psychology of religion: An empirical approach.* Guilford Publications.

Hood, R. W., Jr., Morris, R. J., & Harvey, D. K. (1993). *Religiosity, prayer, and their relationship to mystical experience.* In: Annual meeting of the Religious Research Association, Raleigh, NC.

Hove, M. J., & Risen, J. L. (2009). It's all in the timing: Interpersonal synchrony increases affiliation. *Social Cognition, 27*(6), 949–960.

James, W. (1902/2009). *The varieties of religious experience: A study in human nature. eBooks@Adelaide.* https://csrs.nd.edu/assets/59930/williams_1902.pdf

Kabat-Zinn, J., & Hanh, T. N. (2009). *Full catastrophe living: Using the wisdom of your body and mind to face stress, pain, and illness.* Delta.

Kapogiannis, D., Barbey, A. K., Su, M., Zamboni, G., Krueger, F., & Grafman, J. (2009). Cognitive and neural foundations of religious belief. *Proceedings of the National Academy of Sciences of the United States of America, 106,* 4876–4881.

Kaufman, S. B. (2018). Self-actualizing people in the 21st century: Integration with contemporary theory and research on personality and well-being. *Journal of Humanistic Psychology.* https://doi.org/10.1177/0022167818809187

Kirk, K. M., Eaves, L. J., & Martin, N. G. (1999). Self-transcendence as a measure of spirituality in a sample of older Australian twins. *Twin Research and Human Genetics, 2*(2), 81–87.

Koenig, H. G., & Cohen, H. J. (Eds.). (2002). *The link between religion and health: Psychoneuroimmunology and the faith factor.* Oxford University Press.

Lattin, D. (2010). *The Harvard Psychedelic Club: How Timothy Leary, Ram Dass, Huston Smith, and Andrew Weil killed the Fifties and ushered in a new age for America.* HarperOne/HarperCollins.

Li, S., Stampfer, M. J., Williams, D. R., & VanderWeele, T. J. (2016). Association of religious service attendance with mortality among women. *JAMA Internal Medicine, 176*(6), 777–785.

Lifshitz, M., van Elk, M., & Luhrmann, T. M. (2019). Absorption and spiritual experience: A review of evidence and potential mechanisms. *Consciousness and Cognition, 73*, 102760.

Luhrmann, T. M. (2012). *When God talks back: Understanding the American evangelical relationship with God.* Vintage.

McCall, T. D. (2015). Hope and eternity: God as transcendent presence in the ordinary. In D. B. Yaden, T. D. McCall, & J. H. Ellens (Eds.), *Being called: Scientific, secular, and sacred perspectives* (pp. 193–202). Praeger.

Mohandas, E. (2008). Neurobiology of spirituality. *Mens Sana Monographs, 6*(1), 63.

Muraresku, B. C. (2020). *The immortality key: The secret history of the religion with no name.* St. Martin's Press.

Nelson, K. (2010). *The spiritual doorway in the brain: A neurologist's search for the God experience.* Penguin.

Newberg, A., & d'Aquili, E. G. (2008). *Why God won't go away: Brain science and the biology of belief.* Ballantine Books.

Newberg, A., B., Pourdehnad, M., Alavi, A., & d'Aquili, E. (2003). Cerebral blood flow during meditative prayer: Preliminary findings and methodological issues. *Perceptual and Motor Skills, 97*, 625–630.

Newberg, A. B., Alavi, A., Baime, M., Pourdehnad, M., Santanna, J., & d'Aquili, E. (2001). The measurement of regional cerebral blood flow during the complex cognitive task of meditation: A preliminary SPECT study. *Psychiatry Research: Neuroimaging, 106*(2), 113–122.

Newberg, A. B., d'Aquili, E. G., Rause, V. P. (2001). *Why God won't go away: Brain science and the biology of belief.* Ballantine Books.

Newberg, A. B., & Waldman, M. R. (2016). *How enlightenment changes your brain: The new science of transformation.* Penguin Random House.

Pew Research Center. (2014). *Religious Landscape Study.* Washington, D.C. https://www.pewforum.org/religious-landscape-study/attendance-at-religious-services/

Penfield, W., & Jasper, H. (1954). *Epilepsy and the functional anatomy of the human brain.* Little Brown.

Persinger, M. A., & Healey, F. (2002). Experimental facilitation of the sensed presence: Possible intercalation between the hemispheres induced by complex magnetic fields. *Journal of Nervous and Mental Disease, 190*(8), 533–541.

Pickert, K. (2014). The mindful revolution. *Time, 3*, 34–48.

Pinker, S. (2012). *The better angels of our nature: Why violence has declined.* Penguin Group USA.

Pollan, M. (2019). *How to change your mind: What the new science of psychedelics teaches us about consciousness, dying, addiction, depression, and transcendence.* Penguin Books.

Poloma, M. M., & Gallup, G. H. (1991). *Varieties of prayer.* Trinity.

Spencer, L. R. (2011). *1001 things to do while you're dead.* Lulu.

Strassman, R. (2000). *DMT: The spirit molecule: A doctor's revolutionary research into the biology of near-death and mystical experiences.* Simon & Schuster.

Tarr, B., Launay, J., & Dunbar, R. I. (2014). Music and social bonding: "self-other" merging and neurohormonal mechanisms. *Frontiers in Psychology, 5,* 1096.

Taylor, J. B. (2009). *My stroke of insight.* Hachette UK.

Tellegen, A., & Atkinson, G. (1974). Openness to absorbing and self-altering experiences ("absorption"), a trait related to hypnotic susceptibility. *Journal of Abnormal Psychology, 83*(3), 268.

Turner, V. (1969). Liminality and communitas. *The Ritual Process: Structure and Anti-structure, 94*(113), 125–130.

Yaden, D. B., Eichstaedt, J. C., & Medaglia, J. D. (2018). The future of technology in positive psychology: Methodological advances in the science of well-being. *Frontiers in Psychology, 9,* 962.

Yaden, D. B., Giorgi, S., Kern, M. L., Adler, A., Ungar, L. H., Seligman, M. E., & Eichstaedt, J. C. (2021). Beyond beliefs: Multidimensional aspects of religion and spirituality in language. *Psychology of Religion and Spirituality.* https://doi.org/10.1037/rel0000408

Yaden, D. B., & Griffiths, R. R. (2020). The subjective effects of psychedelics are necessary for their enduring therapeutic effects. *ACS Pharmacology & Translational Science, 4*(24), 568–572.

Yaden, D. B., Kaufman, S. B., Hyde, E., Chirico, A., Gaggioli, A., Zhang, J. W., & Keltner, D. (2019). The development of the Awe Experience Scale (AWE-S): A multifactorial measure for a complex emotion. *Journal of Positive Psychology, 14*(4), 474–488.

Yaden, D. B., Yaden, M. E., & Griffiths, R. R. (2021). Psychedelics in psychiatry—Keeping the renaissance from going off the rails. *JAMA Psychiatry, 78*(5), 469–470.

Yaden, D. B., Zhao, Y., Peng, K., & Newberg, A. B. (2019). *Rituals and practices in world religions.* Springer.

7

The Pragmatic Principle

Positive and Pathological Experiences

Fyodor Dostoevsky, the Russian novelist who wrote *Crime and Punishment*, *The Brothers Karamazov*, and *Notes from the Underground*, had spiritual experiences of his own in addition to writing about them in his novels. His spiritual experiences were almost always triggered by, or accompanied by, seizures. A certain emotional state usually preceded the seizures, as he explained to his friend: "I am penetrated by an immense happiness, which cannot be experienced in normal circumstances" (cited in Baumann et al., 2005). One particular night, Dostoevsky was walking with two friends and he began to have a spiritual experience during a seizure as the local bell tower began ringing for midnight:

> The air was filled with a big noise and I tried to move. I felt the heaven was going down upon the earth and that it had engulfed me. I have really touched God. He came into me myself, yes God exists, I cried, and I don't remember anything else. (cited in Alajouanine, 1963, p. 212)

Dostoevsky was well aware that his spiritual experiences were caused by, or at least related to, his epileptic seizures. Like Jill Bolte Taylor's experience described in the previous chapter, this did nothing to lessen his appreciation of his experience. He acknowledged this point in his writings, praising his experiences in the highest possible terms:

> You all, healthy people . . . can't imagine the happiness which we epileptics feel during the second or so before our fit. . . . I don't know if this felicity lasts for seconds, hours or months, but believe me, for all the joys that life may bring, I would not exchange this one. (cited in Alajouanine, 1963, p. 212)

Dostoevsky, like James, made the point that knowing the origin of a spiritual experience does not invalidate its value. But if not their origin, on what basis *should* one judge the merits of a spiritual experience?

The Varieties of Spiritual Experience. David B. Yaden and Andrew B. Newberg, Oxford University Press. © David Yaden and Andrew Newberg 2022. DOI: 10.1093/oso/9780190665678.003.0007

As we have seen, James's position was that outcomes should be the basis for judging spiritual experience, not their origins. He wrote, borrowing part of a biblical phrase: "In the end it had to come to our empiricist criterion: By their fruits ye shall know them, not by their roots" (James, 1902/2009, p. 19). Again, according to James, it is not the *origin* (roots) of the experience that ought to determine the value of each experience for each individual, but rather the *outcomes* (fruits) of an experience.

In order to illustrate this point further, James drew on the example of genius. At the time, some physicians viewed creative genius as a symptom of mental illness. According to this perspective, which was held by at least some of James's contemporaries, genius was thought to be "allied to moral insanity," and that "as a rule, the greater the genius, the greater the unsoundness" of mind (James, 1902/2009, p. 17). James thought that this view was absolutely absurd. In the same way that no diagnosis of physical or mental illness could, or should, keep us from enjoying Beethoven's symphonies, the origin of a spiritual experience should do nothing to limit our appreciation of their effects.

However, we must acknowledge that while focusing on the pragmatic results of spiritual experiences is useful from a psychological perspective, religious and spiritual individuals might argue that the roots are, in fact, fundamentally important. Within the Christian tradition, for example, it has very often been debated whether spiritual experiences are derived from God or from the Devil. Since we cannot use science to clarify such controversies, it is important for us to at least acknowledge them, though we leave them to further in this book to consider more fully.

The Pragmatic Principle

James had deep philosophical reasons for emphasizing outcomes, largely stemming from a philosophical view that he helped to create and popularize called "pragmatism." After writing *The Varieties* (1902/2009), James turned his attention to defending this philosophical position, writing a book called *Pragmatism: A New Name for Some Old Ways of Thinking* (1907/1975), which was published just a few years before his death.

Pragmatism grew out of an extraordinary philosophical discussion group. This group, called the "Metaphysical Club," for a time rivaled the influence of the later "Vienna Circle" in its impact on philosophy. Aside from James, the cocreator of pragmatism, Charles Sanders Peirce (scientist, mathematician, and logician), and Oliver Wendell Holmes Jr. were active members (Holmes would become among the most cited Supreme Court justices in the country's history). Another member, Chauncy Wright, who the others in the group affectionately referred to as "the Cambridge Socrates," was a mathematician who added flair to the already lively conversations with his eccentricity and encyclopedic mind. The discussions of this group of decidedly empirically minded thinkers in Cambridge, Massachusetts, can be counted as the birthplace of pragmatism (Menand, 2001; note that these and other philosophical issues are covered in more detail in Chapter 16).

This view, defined in slightly different ways by Peirce (who James credited as the founder of pragmatism), James, philosopher John Dewey, and others, has become an entrenched view in philosophy and persists to the present. The thrust of this view is the emphasis on the practical consequences when determining the value of a particular belief, action, or state of affairs. One of the practical results of taking a pragmatic approach in *The Varieties* was an emphasis on the outcomes of spiritual experiences.

James considered a number of positive and pathological spiritual experiences in *The Varieties*. However, evaluating spiritual experiences is complex, and they rarely fit neatly into one of these two simple categories. To begin with, positive and pathological effects from spiritual experiences can overlap and interrelate in complex ways. While modern psychology and medicine have tended to take an overly pathological approach to spiritual experiences, we think that some of this bias can be corrected by considering James's views as well as examining the empirical evidence, which on balance tends to point in the positive direction. But the question is sometimes complex and is best evaluated on a case-by-case basis.

All this emphasis on consequences raises the question: If we should, as James claims, judge spiritual experiences by their outcomes, then what qualifies as a good outcome? James offered some ideas. He wrote: "*Immediate luminousness*, in short, *philosophical reasonableness*, and *moral helpfulness* are the only available criteria" (James, 1902/2009, p. 17). James attempted more specific explanations for these three criteria, but they seem to boil down to beneficial consequences as judged by one's self and others. According to James, if a spiritual experience increases one's own happiness and that of others', then the experience has value. So, do spiritual experiences influence happiness? For James, the answer was an emphatic "yes!" followed quickly by "usually." That is, spiritual experiences often, but not always, lead to beneficial outcomes.

However, in a move typical of James, he made sure to emphasize a contrasting perspective: "We cannot possibly ignore these pathological aspects of the subject" (James, 1902/2009, p. 11). That is, spiritual experiences can also be triggered by, associated with, or result in, mental illness. It was well known among clinicians at the time (as it is today) that those who are suffering from psychosis or other forms of mental illness often refer to religious/spiritual topics. Accordingly, after his thorough-going discussion of those spiritual experiences that resulted in an abundance of happiness, James turned to experiences that exert a more negative influence:

> But more remains to be told, for religious mysticism is only one half of mysticism. The other half has no accumulated traditions except those which the text-books on insanity supply. Open any one of these, and you will find abundant cases in which "mystical ideas" are cited as characteristic symptoms of enfeebled or deluded states of mind. In delusional insanity, paranoia, as they sometimes call it, we may have a diabolical mysticism, a sort of religious mysticism turned upside down. (James, 1902/2009, p. 323)

James acknowledged and emphasized in several places how some spiritual experiences are related to psychopathology. In contemporary scientific investigations, it has been shown that religious/spiritual content plays a small part in psychopathological conditions, but there is evidence to support some role in some disorders (Peteet et al., 2011). For example, less than 5% of patients with seizures express unusual religious beliefs (Devinsky & Lai, 2008). And between 25% and 50% of patients with psychotic disorders have religious delusions or hallucinations, but it is important to note that patients with psychotic disorders make up a very small percentage of the overall population (Peteet et al., 2011). Thus, there is a relationship, but the specifics of how and when unusual religious and spiritual experiences arise in patients with psychopathology remains unanswered.

Psychiatrists frequently characterize the thought content of patients experiencing psychosis or mania as "religious preoccupation." This term refers to the spiritual content that some patients experience in the midst of intense internal experiences. Although at times frightening, like in the case of a patient fearing demonic possession, spiritual content can also be seen as comforting—even when experienced in the setting of a manic or psychotic episode.

For instance, a qualitative study of patients with bipolar disorder showed the positive impact that spiritual experiences can have during manic episodes. Patients often acknowledge both the spiritual importance of these experiences and understand that they occur in instances of disease or psychological decompensation (Ouwehand et al., 2018). Many patients who experience religious content during episodes of illness argue for its existential importance and meaning, even in cases when it is also associated with psychopathology. For James, a spiritual experience that brings comfort—even in the midst of an otherwise harmful and pathological state—would still be considered valuable.

Furthermore, James reiterated the fact that *some* spiritual experiences result in psychopathology does not diminish the effects of *all* spiritual experiences—particularly not those that cause happiness. He wrote:

> To the medical mind these ecstasies signify nothing but suggested and imitated hypnoid states, on an intellectual basis of superstition, and a corporeal one of degeneration and hysteria. Undoubtedly these pathological conditions have existed in many and possibly in all the cases, but that fact tells us nothing about the value for knowledge of the consciousness which they induce. To pass a spiritual judgment upon these states, we must not content ourselves with superficial medical talk, but inquire into their fruits for life. (James, 1902/2009, p. 313)

James also acknowledged there are some mixed cases. That is, for example, experiences that are positive at the time of the experience, but end up being ultimately detrimental, as well as those experiences that are difficult at the time but become ultimately valuable. In particular, spiritual experiences can sometimes come as a resolution to difficult periods of life. In order to cite evidence contrary to the prevailing medical perspective of his day, which held that such experiences were generally explained by pathology, James cited personal accounts and famous historical examples that began in difficulty and ended in well-being:

> Saint Augustine . . . emerged into the smooth waters of inner unity and peace, and I shall next ask you to consider more closely some of the peculiarities of the process of unification, when it occurs. It may come gradually,

or it may occur abruptly; it may come through altered feelings, or through altered powers of action; or it may come through new intellectual insights, or through experiences which we shall later have to designate as 'mystical.' However it come, it brings a characteristic sort of relief. . . . Easily, permanently, and successfully, it often transforms the most intolerable misery into the profoundest and most enduring happiness. (James, 1902/2009, p. 133)

In sum, James acknowledged that some spiritual experiences are related to psychopathology, and some may cause suffering. In general, though, James speculated that spiritual experiences more often cause happiness for individuals and for others around such people and that this should be of great scientific and practical interest. He agreed with Starbuck's assessment of the value of spiritual experience: that they can result in "a changed attitude towards life, which is fairly constant and permanent, although the feelings fluctuate . . . " (Starbuck cited in James, 1902/2009, p. 228).

Moral Transformation

James also noticed reports of altruistic impulses after spiritual experiences. James used happiness and altruism together as primary outcomes by which to weigh the value of spiritual experience. These outcomes are put forward as key ways to differentiate pathological from positive spiritual experiences. He wrote, addressing pathological and positive spiritual experiences, respectively, "while selfishness characterizes the one, the other is marked by altruistic impulses" (James, 1902/2009, p. 212).

To characterize these different impulses, the selfish and the altruistic, James referred to "higher" (altruistic) and "lower" (selfish) aspects of the self. The term "homoduplex" refers to a duality of human motives. (Note: This term was later used by Durkheim to refer to the profane and sacred levels of human life.)

James illustrated these conflicting higher and lower moral impulses with the Christian Saint Paul's line: "What I would, that do I not; but what I hate, that do I" (James, 1902/2009, p. 130). This quotation illustrates how different motivations can conflict within a person. James's exemplar for the concept of homoduplex and the conflicted self is the Christian Saint Augustine, who famously described his alternating drunken debaucheries followed by self-condemnations, and his eventual salvation in his autobiography, *Confessions*

(Augustine, 1876). Augustine eventually found a resolution and unification to these two aspects of himself.

In many places in *The Varieties*, James referred to the lower and higher centers of moral motivation. This insight is central to James's treatment of spiritual experience, as he believed that these mental states are capable of raising one's moral habits from the lower to one's higher moral self. To James, these upward shifts are a core aim of religion and spirituality in general.

> The fundamental pillar on which it [religion] rests is nothing more than the general basis of all religious experience, the fact that man has a dual nature, and is connected with two spheres of thought, a shallower and a profounder sphere, in either of which he may learn to live more habitually. (James, 1902/2009, p. 76)

James suggested that spiritual experiences are capable of lifting one's motivations from the lower self to the higher moral self. It is worth noting that his examination on this division of moral motivations is not driven by an interest in understanding the essence of religion, but is rather motivated by a scientific interest in human psychology more broadly.

> Were we writing the story of the mind from the purely natural-history point of view, with no religious interest whatever, we should still have to write down man's liability to sudden and complete conversion as one of his most curious peculiarities. (James, 1902/2009, p. 176)

Shifts in moral motivations usually occur in more gradual ways, James acknowledged. The fact that these changes can occur so dramatically may be a unique feature of spiritual experience, consisting of one the most interesting characteristics of these mental states.

> The older medicine used to speak of two ways, lysis and crisis, one gradual, the other abrupt, in which one might recover from a bodily disease. In the spiritual realm there are also two ways, one gradual, the other sudden. (James, 1902/2009, p. 141)

James did not dismiss more gradual forms of moral changes as unimportant, but he did take a deeper scientific interest in the sudden shifts caused by spiritual experience. He acknowledged that both types, while differing in their timescale, have a similar general effect.

The shift from the lower to the higher moral self is characterized as toward "the elimination of selfishness" (James, 1902/2009, p. 98). But do these moral transformations, deeply felt or not, really matter? That is, do they really impact behavior in noticeable and lasting ways? And, if so, how long do these changes last?

James equivocated in his answers to these questions. One might guess, with all of the buildup to the fruits of spiritual experiences, that he would make a bold statement about the value of the changes spiritual experiences tend to produce. But, at first, his assessment was somewhat lukewarm. He wrote: "Converted men as a class are indistinguishable from natural men; some natural men even excel some converted men in their fruits" (James, 1902/2009, p. 181). In other words, there seems to be little to no noticeable moral difference between those who have had and those who have not had a spiritual experience.

Having first offered this fairly bland assessment of the value of spiritual experiences, James then offered a bolder thesis. While, for James, there was no great dividing line between the experiential "haves" versus the "have-nots" in terms of well-being or moral motivation—that does not necessarily mean that spiritual experiences are irrelevant. He wrote:

> Dismiss it with a pitying smile at so much "hysterics." Psychologically, as well as religiously, however, this is shallow. It misses the point of serious interest, which is not so much the duration as the nature and quality of these shiftings of character to higher levels. (James, 1902/2009, p. 196)

James readily acknowledged that moral changes resulting from spiritual experiences do not always last, commenting: "Men lapse from every level— we need no statistics to tell us that" (James, 1902/2009, p. 196). But James asked his readers to consider the possibility that some people may still be at relatively lower levels of happiness and moral behavior *had they not had their experiences*. That is, spiritual experiences may have kept some people from sinking into despair who otherwise would have. James wrote: "When we live in our own highest centre of energy, we may call ourselves saved, no matter how much higher someone else's centre may be" (James, 1902/2009, p. 193).

In general, James advocated for evaluating spiritual experiences in terms of their effects on well-being and moral outcomes. His method of evaluation, though, relies on examining written accounts. Modern methods provide more quantitative means of evaluating the outcomes of spiritual experiences.

Contemporary Approaches to Evaluating Pathological Outcomes

Mental illness is among the leading causes of disability and poor health around the world. It is also shockingly prevalent, as almost one in four individuals worldwide will experience a mental health problem at some point in their lives (World Health Organization, 2001). Mental illnesses range from manageable chronic conditions to completely debilitating, and they collectively account for a large proportion of the suffering in the world. Thus, mental illness is an important challenge for both psychology and psychiatry to help the billions of people who are seeking assistance with their suffering.

In terms of brain-based illnesses relevant to spiritual experience, there are several prominent examples worth mentioning. We have already considered temporal lobe epilepsy in the case of Dostoevsky and a number of other individuals. Seizures in the temporal lobes appear to be associated with either unusual religious experiences or hyperreligious activity by the individual. This is sometimes referred to as Geschwind syndrome after the influential neurologist and consists not only of hyperreligious behavior, but also increased verbal output, increased sexuality, and irritability (Gainotti, 2017). More recent studies have observed that patients with injury (i.e., trauma or tumors) in the parietal lobes are more likely to express feelings of self-transcendence compared to patients with injury to other brain areas (Urgesi et al., 2010).

The *Diagnostic and Statistical Manuel of Mental Disorders* (*DSM-5*; American Psychiatric Association, 2013) is an important tool for the understanding, study, and treatment of mental illness. This book is the result of large teams of psychologists and psychiatrists collaborating to try to capture the field's consensus regarding the definition and classification of mental illness. The *DSM* (as well as its more international counterpart, the *International Classification of Diseases*) has been met with well-founded criticism with each of its revisions. Now on its fifth edition, the *DSM*'s earlier issues had significant problems, such as including psychoanalytic theories, pathologizing normal human differences, and failing to appreciate cross-cultural differences. The newest version is the culmination of many

hundreds of empirical studies and represents substantial progress over previous editions, but the *DSM* remains very much a work in progress.

Defining mental illness is more difficult that one might imagine. The definition of a mental disorder is lengthy and attempts to both be sensitive to
cross-cultural differences and to avoid imposing a socially normative framework on an individual.

> A mental disorder is a syndrome characterized by clinically significant
> disturbance in an individual's cognition, emotion regulation, or beha-
> vior that reflects a dysfunction in the psychological, biological, or devel-
> opmental processes underlying mental functioning. Mental disorders are
> usually associated with significant distress or disability in social, occupa-
> tional, or other important activities. An expectable or culturally approved
> response to a common stressor or loss, such as the death of a loved one, is
> not a mental disorder. Socially deviant behavior (e.g., political, religious,
> or sexual) and conflicts that are primarily between the individual and so-
> ciety are not mental disorders unless the deviance or conflict results from
> a dysfunction in the individual, as described above. (American Psychiatric
> Association, 2013, p. 20)

The *DSM* definition of mental illness includes a Jamesian emphasis on
outcomes. This is no accident, one of the founders of modern psychiatry,
Adolf Meyer of Johns Hopkins, explicitly supported James's philosophy of
pragmatism. Therefore, James's thought has been quietly absorbed into some
core components of contemporary psychiatry (Lamb, 2014). Illustrating the
emphasis on outcomes, a mental illness diagnosis requires that "the disturbance causes clinically significant distress or impairment in social, occu-
pational, or other important areas of functioning" (American Psychiatric
Association, 2013, p. 21). This suffering and dysfunction can be measured
using standardized instruments, such as self-report surveys and/or structured interviews with trained clinicians. The systematic and standardized
measurement of the effects of various mental illnesses, and the effectiveness
of various therapies at treating them, represent important steps toward progress in reducing the suffering of those people with mental illnesses.

Of the many possible diagnoses within the *DSM*, the mental illnesses
that are the most relevant to spiritual experience include schizophrenia and
other psychotic disorders, manic episodes, dissociative disorders, and an
additional category called "religious or spiritual problem." Each of these is

detailed in Part II of this book, as specific disorders generally pertain more to some kinds of spiritual experience than others.

One illuminating example of negative experiences comes in the form of near-death experiences (NDEs). We have previously mentioned that NDEs often have a variety of positive elements, such as seeing deceased relatives; entering into the realm of light, blissful feelings; and a lack of fear about dying (Ring, 1980, 1984). However, there is an entirely different group of NDEs associated with horribly negative elements, including perceptions of pain, bodies being ripped apart, and extreme fear (Zaleski, 1987). These "hellacious" experiences have been noted in both medieval and modern descriptions. It is unclear why some people have negative NDEs and others have positive ones.

Reading through this section, one can easily get the impression that spiritual experience is likely a symptom of a mental illness, it's just not clear which one. This concern is especially apparent when one gets used to viewing human nature through the lens of psychopathology. Approaching human experience in this way runs the risk of erring on the side of thinking that anything unusual is likely the result of mental illness.

However, mentions of spiritual experiences in the *DSM* come in the context of cross-cultural differences. The *DSM* contains lines like the following:

- "Hallucinations may be a normal part of religious experience in certain cultural contexts" (American Psychiatric Association, 2013, p. 87).
- "Cultural and religious background must be taken into account when considering whether beliefs are delusional" (American Psychiatric Association, 2013, p. 95).
- "In some cultures, visual or auditory hallucinations with religious content (e.g., hearing God's voice) are a normal part of a religious experience" (American Psychiatric Association, 2013, p. 103).

However, at least two facts complicate this perspective that spiritual experiences can be excluded from being seen as pathological based entirely on one's cultural and religious background. The first is that spiritual experiences are surprisingly prevalent in mainstream U.S. culture as well as most—perhaps all—cultures. How does this fact square with the caveat about "cross-cultural backgrounds"? In what cultures are these experiences *not* normative? There has not been a culture identified that does not have some substantial prevalence of spiritual experience, thus suggesting that spiritual experiences may, in fact, be cross-culturally normative.

Second, aspects of spiritual experience may not merely be normative but may actually usually be positively beneficial to mental health. Benefits from spiritual experience can even be seen in cases that are initially difficult to mentally process and which may require some therapeutic support. One could imagine the *DSM* noting that spiritual experiences with difficult or even delusional content, when properly integrated through therapeutic support, can be growth inducing and beneficial for individuals.

To return to James for a moment, it is important to reiterate that he fully acknowledged the relationship with psychopathology. While some scholars suggest that James did not sufficiently address this issue, he definitely discussed it (recall the quotation from James in this chapter about how such experiences fill the pages of "text-books on insanity"). James described many of the spiritual experiences that we review throughout Part II, but here he also described how spiritual experiences can sometimes have the appearance of nightmares:

> The same sense of ineffable importance in the smallest events, the same texts and words coming with new meanings, the same voices and visions and leadings and missions, the same controlling by extraneous powers; only this time the emotion is pessimistic: instead of consolations we have desolations; the meanings are dreadful; and the powers are enemies to life. It is evident that from the point of view of their psychological mechanism, the classic mysticism and these lower mysticisms spring from the same mental level, from that great subliminal or transmarginal region of which science is beginning to admit the existence, but of which so little is really known. (James, 1902/2009, p. 323)

When it comes to outcomes from spiritual experience, the positive and pathological are clearly both possibilities. Contemporary anthropologist Tanya Luhrmann summarized the research showing that some spiritual experiences seem to be the result of psychopathology, whereas others do not seem to originate or result in psychopathology (though, again, some people may need temporary support with integrating their experience). She put it like this:

> It seems, then, that there is good empirical evidence for two different patterns of hallucination-like phenomena in the population. One is the result of a psychotic process associated with schizophrenia and other psychiatric disorders. In this pattern, hallucinations are frequent, extended, and distressing. . . . Then there is the ordinary, nonpathological pattern in which sensory overrides are rare, brief, and not distressing. (Luhrmann, 2012, p. 242)

This raises the question of proportion. How many experiences require therapeutic support? In our survey, we found that the vast majority of our participants (90%) did not require any assistance from healthcare professionals (although some did; see Figure 7.1).

We examine more evidence in Part II regarding the relationship between distinct kinds of spiritual experience and some kinds of mental illness. Despite the known association between some spiritual experience and some psychopathology, it is important to note that *most spiritual experiences are not associated with mental illness.* On the contrary, it appears that most spiritual experiences are profoundly positive.

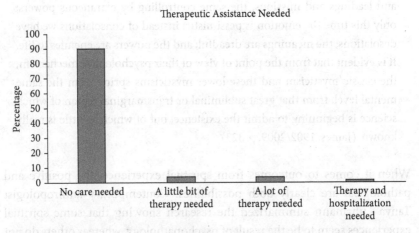

Figure 7.1 Assistance from healthcare professional required. Drawn by David B. Yaden.

Contemporary Approaches to Evaluating
Positive Outcomes

As the newly elected American Psychological Association (APA) president, psychologist Martin Seligman made a speech that has become historic in the field of psychology. He called on psychologists to study not only the negative aspects of human experience, like psychopathology, but also the positive side of human nature (Seligman, 2004). He drew on previous theoretical work in humanistic psychology and related fields but advocated a more rigorously experimental and generally cognitive approach (see Kaufman, 2021). He articulated a research agenda that would elucidate the behaviors, traits, and mental states that protect people from mental illness and provide them with better relationships, more meaning in life, and more happiness. He called it "positive psychology."

Positive psychology was formed as a reaction to a too one-sided view of human nature that is overly focused on mental illness to the exclusion of protective, enjoyable, or otherwise beneficial aspects of human experience. To be clear, positive psychology is *not* intended as a replacement or even a critique of the *DSM* or mental health services. On the contrary, positive psychology seeks to supplement this essential research and clinical work by helping to find ways in which patients exceed getting back to "neutral" and to take positive steps toward increasing their well-being. There are three main pillars of positive psychology (Seligman, 2004): the studies of positive traits, positive institutions, and positive mental states—the last of these is clearly relevant to the study of spiritual experiences.

Positive psychology encourages researchers to consider the beneficial aspects that spiritual experiences may cause in the lives of those who have them. This research perspective might measure one's level of happiness, whether one's relationships get worse or better, one's degree of engagement with their social community, how much stress one experiences on a daily basis, how helpful one seems to their coworkers, how meaningful one feels their life to be, and so on. By measuring positive as well as pathological aspects of spiritual experience, a more holistic picture of spiritual experience can emerge.

Some research is already beginning to show the positive aspects of spiritual experience. In one study that we conducted, for example, those reporting a religious, spiritual, or mystical experience (RSME), reported less fear of death, improvements to their relationship with their family, and better health (Yaden et al., 2017).

In our Varieties Survey, we asked our participants to describe their experiences in several ways relevant to positive and pathological considerations. We include figures of the data as they become relevant throughout this section. To begin with, we simply asked participants whether they would characterize their experiences as "positive." We see in Figure 7.2 that they did, and overwhelmingly so.

The field of positive psychology offers a few key measures of well-being, which, when complemented by measures of mental illness mentioned in the previous section, are useful for studying the effects of spiritual experience. One of the major operationalizations of well-being is called subjective well-being (SWB), which is thought to comprise three main features: more positive emotion, less negative emotion, and an overall satisfaction with one's life (Diener, 1984).

Negative emotions, such as anger, fear, and sadness, tend to result in a narrowing of attention on the cause of the negative emotion as well as a focus on one's self. Such emotions are often followed by social withdrawal. Of course, negative emotions are adaptive in many situations: It is appropriate (and clearly important) to feel fear from a wild fire, anger at a corrupt politician, and sadness during mourning. However, it is equally obvious that there are situations where negative emotions are inappropriate, and the suffering that they cause unnecessary. Both too many and too few negative

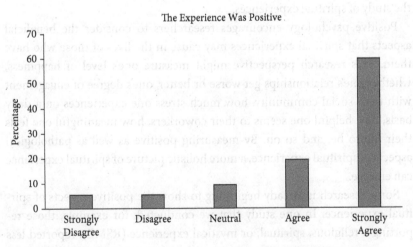

Figure 7.2 Overall valence of the experience. Drawn by David B. Yaden.

emotions are maladaptive in the long term, but in general fewer negative emotions than positive emotions (within reasonable bounds) over time is associated with higher SWB and a number of beneficial life outcomes. If considered "positive," then we would expect most spiritual experiences to result in fewer average unnecessary negative emotions afterward. Common self-report measures of negative emotion ask participants how "sad," "distressed," or "angry" they have been recently (Watson & Clark, 1999).

Positive emotions, such as happiness, excitement, and love, are associated with quite different effects than negative emotions. Psychologist Barbara Fredrickson introduced the "broaden and build" theory of positive emotions (Fredrickson, 2001). While experiencing positive emotion, one's attention can be "broadened" to notice more in one's environment. The "build" part of the theory refers to social resources, as positive emotions tend to enhance relationships with other people. While experiencing far too many positive emotions can be associated with manic states (Gruber, 2011), experiencing more positive emotions is generally associated with increased SWB. Common self-report measures of positive emotion ask participants how "happy," "content," or "excited" they have been recently (Watson & Clark, 1999). Participants in our Varieties Survey indicated that they had more positive emotions (Figure 7.3) and fewer negative emotions after their spiritual experience.

Satisfaction with life is a measure that has been used across dozens of countries and millions of people (Diener et al., 1985). This measure taps

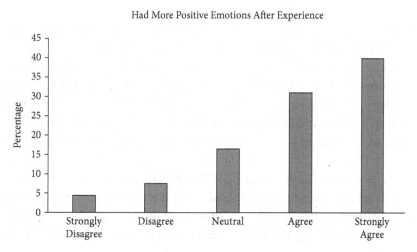

Figure 7.3 Positive emotions after experience. Drawn by David B. Yaden.

one's overall cognitive evaluation of their life as a whole. Satisfaction with life predicts a number of important life outcomes, such as health, relationships, income, and many others. Here is the Satisfaction With Life Scale (Diener et al., 1985):

In most ways my life is close to my ideal.
(Strongly Disagree, Somewhat Disagree, Neutral, Somewhat Agree, Strongly Agree)

The conditions of my life are excellent.
(Strongly Disagree, Somewhat Disagree, Neutral, Somewhat Agree, Strongly Agree)

I am satisfied with my life.
(Strongly Disagree, Somewhat Disagree, Neutral, Somewhat Agree, Strongly Agree)

So far I have gotten the important things I want in life.
(Strongly Disagree, Somewhat Disagree, Neutral, Somewhat Agree, Strongly Agree)

If I could live my life over, I would change almost nothing.
(Strongly Disagree, Somewhat Disagree, Neutral, Somewhat Agree, Strongly Agree)

While there are a number of measures of well-being, the three components of SWB are widely used and considered the gold standard. The sense of meaning or purpose in life is another measure that is highly related to well-being, but has more to do with feeling part of something beyond one's self. Contemporary psychologist Crystal Park has organized research on this topic in an article, "Making Sense of the Meaning Literature" (2010). The sense of meaning in life describes the feeling of connection to our loved ones and the higher ideals and values that we aspire to fulfill in life. Spiritual experiences seem highly related to SWB as well as the sense of meaning in life. Using a measure adapted from Roland Griffith's research on psychedelics, we asked participants in our survey whether their spiritual experience could be ranked among the top five most meaningful experiences of their entire lives (Figure 7.4).

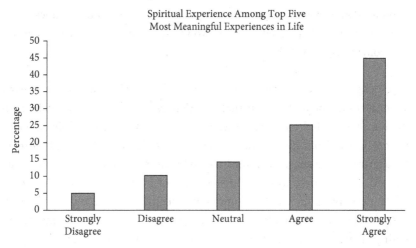

Figure 7.4 Most meaningful experiences. Drawn by David B. Yaden.

We introduce other measures as they become relevant to discussing outcomes of specific spiritual experiences in Part II.

Twelve-Step Programs

There is one area of clinical and medical research where the term "spiritual experience" is more commonly used: addiction (now generally referred to as a "substance use disorder"). If you open to the first chapter of what members of Alcoholics Anonymous (AA) call the "Big Book," which is essentially a guide to treating a substance use disorder, you will see "Bill's Story." Bill Wilson, the founder of AA, described his slow but steady descent into alcohol addiction, eventually resulting in days-long binges, losing jobs, disrupting his family life, and frequent unsuccessful attempts at quitting. The only solution to hitting rock bottom was, according to Wilson, a spiritual experience. Recent scholarship has revealed that Wilson had this experience while undergoing medical treatment using the psychedelic substance belladonna (also called "deadly nightshade," this psychedelic is rarely used to its higher levels of toxicity; Miller, 2019). Wilson summed up his situation and his deliverance:

How dark it is before the dawn! In reality that was the beginning of my last debauch. I was soon to be catapulted into what I like to call the fourth dimension of existence. I was to know happiness, peace, and usefulness, in a way of life that is incredibly more wonderful as time passes. (Alcoholics Anonymous, 2001, p. 25)

Psychologist Carl Gustav Jung, who we have previously described as an early advocate of the benefits of spiritual experiences, ratified this approach to addiction. An alcoholic named Rowland Hazard visited Jung while suffering tremendously from his substance use disorder. After attempting treatment for a year with no success, Hazard was to be discharged. In a state of despair, Hazard asked if there was any further hope for his recovery. Jung's response (note: perhaps apocryphal in some of its specifics; see Bluhm, 2006) forms the basis of the AA program: "No, there is none—except that some people with your problem have recovered if they had a transforming experience of the spirit" ("Letter to the Editor," 1993). In a letter to Bill Wilson, Jung wrote: "You see, Alcohol in Latin is 'spiritus' and you use the same word for the highest religious experience as well as for the most depraving poison. The helpful formula therefore is: spiritus contra spiritum" (Schoen, 2009, p. 20). This view was anticipated by James. In *The Varieties*, James included a quotation that he described as having overheard a contemporary clinician say regarding "dipsomania," which was the term used then for alcoholism: "The only radical remedy I know for dipsomania is religiomania" (James, 1902/ 2009, p. 203).

It is difficult to overstate the centrality that the concept of spiritual experience holds in 12-step programs. The final step of 12-step programs reads: "Having had a *spiritual experience* as the result of these steps, we tried to carry this message to alcoholics, and to practice these principles in all our affairs" (emphasis added; Alcoholics Anonymous, 2001, p. 82). Positioning spiritual experience as the solution to addiction underscores the question: What is the mechanism by which spiritual experiences relate to addiction?

The answer provided by 12-step programs is a reduction in selfishness, or self-centeredness, which can be achieved through a transformative spiritual experience (Alcoholics Anonymous, 2001, p. 84). Spiritual experiences may absorb the attention of the individual on the road to sobriety, but they are ultimately supposed to be integrated into one's daily life: "We have found nothing incompatible between a powerful spiritual experience, and a life of sane and happy usefulness" (Alcoholics Anonymous, 2001, p. 161).

Contemporary addiction research could benefit from some of the insights provided by James, Jung, and 12-step programs. Psychedelic research, in particular, has been promising. Work conducted by Matthew Johnson at the Johns Hopkins Center for Psychedelic and Consciousness Research showed that psilocybin can reduce tobacco addiction better than any known treatment (Johnson et al., 2017), and other promising studies involving alcohol, opiate, and cocaine use are ongoing (e.g., Bogenschutz et al., 2015). While most addiction research is advancing by finding specific pharmacological treatments for particular addictions, psychedelic treatments appear to work across multiple substance use disorders (e.g., alcohol and tobacco), suggesting that it is tapping into a common pathway. This common pathway may well involve in some way the spiritual experience they reliably elicit. The findings from this research suggest that psychedelics and 12-step programs may share a common underlying mechanism capable of releasing people from the grip of addictions.

While 12-step programs have some empirical support for their efficacy (Kelly et al., 2020), they also pose some challenges for successful treatment. Medication-assisted treatments (MATs) are demonstrating substantial effectiveness in the treatment of addiction (Kampman, 2019); on the other hand, 12-step recovery programs often do not condone using any medications that mimic the effect of the substances of abuse (so-called agonist or partial agonist treatments) to treat addictions. This is compelling as Bill Wilson not only experienced healing through the use of belladonna but also experimented with LSD later in his life (Yaden et al., 2021). This conflict, between the methods of 12-step community programs and proponents of MAT, provides an example of a larger problem with some groups that promote spiritual-type experiences at the expense of seeking evidence-based treatments. We return to these issues, and to Bill's story, in Chapter 18.

Conclusion

The approach advocated by James in *The Varieties*, to look to the outcomes of spiritual experience in order to judge their value, is a useful perspective with which to proceed with their scientific study. The *DSM* and the field of positive psychology both provide measures with which to examine the outcomes of spiritual experience quantitatively. AA, the largest addiction support program in the world, places spiritual experience at its center, and psychedelic treatments may work, at least in part, due to the spiritual experiences that they trigger. Part II examines the various types of spiritual experience, some of which have quite different relationships with pathological and positive outcomes. However, it is worth emphasizing that the vast majority of spiritual experiences are associated with positive outcomes.

References

Alajouanine, T. (1963). Dostoiewski's epilepsy. *Brain, 86*(2), 209–218.

American Psychiatric Association. (2013). *Diagnostic and statistical manual of mental disorders* (5th ed.; *DSM-5*).

Anonymous. (2001). *Alcoholics anonymous*. Hazelden Publishing.

Augustine, S. (1876). *The confessions*. Clark.

Baumann, C. R., Novikov, V. P., Regard, M., & Siegel, A. M. (2005). Did Fyodor Mikhailovich Dostoevsky suffer from mesial temporal lobe epilepsy? *Seizure, 14*(5), 324–330.

Bluhm, A. C. (2006). Verification of C. G. Jung's analysis of Rowland Hazard and the history of Alcoholics Anonymous. *History of Psychology, 9*(4), 313–324.

Bogenschutz, M. P., Forcehimes, A. A., Pommy, J. A., Wilcox, C. E., Barbosa, P. C. R., & Strassman, R. J. (2015). Psilocybin-assisted treatment for alcohol dependence: A proof-of-concept study. *Journal of Psychopharmacology, 29*(3), 289–299.

Devinsky, O., & Lai, G. (2008). Spirituality and religion in epilepsy. *Epilepsy and Behavior, 12*(4), 636–643.

Diener, E. (1984). Subjective well-being. *Psychological Bulletin, 95*(3), 542.

Diener, E., Emmons, R. A., Larsen, R. J., & Griffin, S. (1985). The Satisfaction With Life Scale. *Journal of Personality Assessment, 49*(1), 71–75.

Fredrickson, B. L. (2001). The role of positive emotions in positive psychology: The broaden-and-build theory of positive emotions. *American Psychologist, 56*(3), 218.

Gainotti, G. (2017). Can different mechanisms underpin the "Geschwind syndrome" in temporal lobe epilepsy and in temporal lobe variant of frontotemporal degeneration? *Cortex, 96*, 134–136. https://doi.org/10.1016/j.cortex.2017.06.025

Gruber, J. (2011). Can feeling too good be bad? Positive emotion persistence (PEP) in bipolar disorder. *Current Directions in Psychological Science, 20*(4), 217–221.

James, W. (1902/2009). The varieties of religious experience: A study in human nature. *eBooks@Adelaide*. https://csrs.nd.edu/assets/59930/williams_1902.pdf

James, W. (1975). *Pragmatism: A new name for some old ways of thinking*. Harvard University Press. (Original work published 1907)

Johnson, M. W., Garcia-Romeu, A., & Griffiths, R. R. (2017). Long-term follow-up of psilocybin-facilitated smoking cessation. *American Journal of Drug and Alcohol Abuse, 43*(1), 55–60.

Kampman, K. K. (2019). General introduction: Issues and perspective on medication assisted treatment. In S. M. Evans (Ed.), *APA handbook of psychopharmacology* (pp. 471–479). American Psychological Association.

Kaufman, S. B. (2021). *Transcend: The new science of self-actualization*. Penguin.

Kelly, J. F., Humphreys, K., & Ferri, M. (2020). Alcoholics Anonymous and other 12-step programs for alcohol use disorder. *Cochrane Database of Systematic Reviews, 3*(3), CD012880.

Lamb, S. D. (2014). *Pathologist of the mind: Adolf Meyer and the origins of American psychiatry.* JHU Press.

Luhrmann, T. M. (2012). *When God talks back: Understanding the American evangelical relationship with God.* Knopf.

Letter to the editor. (1993). *New York Times.* https://www.nytimes.com/1993/12/03/opinion/l-jung-s-insights-formed-basis-of-a-a-101693.html

Menand, L. (2001). *The metaphysical club.* Macmillan.

Miller, J. (2019). *US of AA: How the twelve steps hijacked the science of alcoholism.* Chicago Review Press.

Ouwehand, E., Muthert, H., Zock, H., Boeije, H., & Braam, A. (2018). Sweet delight and endless night: A qualitative exploration of ordinary and extraordinary religious and spiritual experiences in bipolar disorder. *International Journal for the Psychology of Religion, 28*(1), 31–54.

Park, C. L. (2010). Making sense of the meaning literature: An integrative review of meaning making and its effects on adjustment to stressful life events. *Psychological Bulletin, 136*(2), 257.

Peteet, J. R., Lu, F. G., & Narrow, W. E. (2011). *Religious and spiritual issues in psychiatric diagnosis: A research agenda for* DSM-V. American Psychiatric Association.

Ring, K. (1980). *Life at death: A scientific investigation of the near-death experience.* Quill.

Ring, K. (1984). *Heading toward omega: In search of the meaning of the near-death experience.* Morrow.

Seligman, M. E. (2004). *Authentic happiness: Using the new positive psychology to realize your potential for lasting fulfillment.* Simon & Schuster.

Schoen, D. E. (2009). *The war of the gods in addiction: C. G. Jung, Alcoholics Anonymous, and archetypal evil.*: Spring Journal Books.

Watson, D., & Clark, L. A. (1999). *The PANAS-X: Manual for the positive and negative affect schedule—Expanded form.* University of Iowa.

World Health Organization. (2001). *Mental disorders affect one in four people.* World Health Report.

Urgesi, C., Aglioti, S. M., Skrap, M., & Fabbro, F. (2010). The spiritual brain: Selective cortical lesions modulate human self-transcendence. *Neuron, 65*(3), 309–319.

Yaden, D. B., Berghella, A. P., Regier, P. S., Garcia-Romeu, A., Johnson, M. W., & Hendricks, P. S. (2021). Classic psychedelics in the treatment of substance use disorder: Potential synergies with twelve-step programs. *International Journal of Drug Policy, 98,* 103380.

Yaden, D. B., Le Nguyen, K. D., Kern, M. L., Wintering, N. A., Eichstaedt, J. C., Schwartz, H. A., Buffone, A. E., Smith, L. K., Warlman, M. R., Hood, R. W., & Newberg, A. B. (2017). The noetic quality: A multimethod exploratory study. *Psychology of Consciousness: Theory, Research, and Practice, 4*(1), 54.

Zaleski, C. (1987). *Otherworld journeys: Accounts of near-death experience in medieval and modern times.* Oxford University Press.

PART II
THE VARIETIES

So far in this book, we have explored the influences that William James brought to *The Varieties* and how he recommended that a scientific study of spiritual experience should proceed. As we saw, the research methods used to explore this topic required a number of advances—conceptually, statistically, and technologically. Then, looking at research findings using contemporary methods, we examined some of the primary triggers of spiritual experience as well as some of their major outcomes. However, the outcomes from spiritual experience depend, to a significant extant, *on the kind of spiritual experience that one has.* This chapter explores various typologies that researchers have attempted to use to distinguish various kinds of spiritual experience from one another. We then offer our own evidence-based typology of spiritual experience based on a statistical procedure called factor analysis.

In the following chapters of Part II, we describe James's perspective on each particular experience as well as a few major pieces of relevant scholarship. This is followed by descriptions of the psychological research that has been done on each type of experience, including findings related to pathological and positive aspects of each kind of experience. We then describe the relevant physiological and neuroimaging research. The goal of this part of the book is to provide a kind of scientific guide to the varieties of spiritual experience using a 21st-century scientific approach.

8

Types of Spiritual Experience

So far, we have used spiritual experience as an umbrella term to refer to a general class of experience. In Part I, we made a number of generalizations about spiritual experiences, and indeed spiritual experiences are often measured as though they are all the same, as we saw, for example, in the items used by Gallup. However, it would be more accurate not to ask what spiritual experience *is*, but rather what spiritual experiences *are*, as implied by the word "varieties" in the title of this book. Part II of this book focuses on distinguishing the various different kinds of spiritual experiences.

The idea that there are varieties of spiritual experience is important for several reasons. The first is that it is misleading, and maybe even cross-culturally insensitive, to think that everyone who has had a spiritual experience is describing the *same* experience. On the one hand, many spiritual experiences have unique characteristics that vary between individuals and cultures. On the other hand, there may be certain elements that are common among some or all types of spiritual experiences. Written descriptions that we gathered from participants of our Varieties Survey (as well as thousands of such written descriptions from our other studies) clearly demonstrate that no two descriptions of spiritual experiences are exactly identical. However, some descriptions of spiritual experiences are clearly similar to others. Between the extremes of complete similarity and complete difference is the perspective that spiritual experience can be classed into a number of broad categories, and that each experience varies across people and cultures to some degree.

Recognizing a broader plurality of spiritual experiences has significant implications for research. If spiritual experiences were all lumped together into one category, then any differences between them—in terms of triggers, subjective qualities, neural correlates, or outcomes—would be impossible to discover. As an analogy, consider "mental illness" as an umbrella term capturing all kinds of disorders in a single category. The term "mental illness" is undoubtedly useful, but it is also generally acknowledged that making subdivisions between depression, addiction, schizophrenia, and others is

The Varieties of Spiritual Experience. David B. Yaden and Andrew B. Newberg, Oxford University Press. © David Yaden and Andrew Newberg 2022. DOI: 10.1093/oso/9780190665678.003.0008

crucial to effective treatment. According to fifth edition of the *Diagnostic and Statistical Manual of Mental Disorders* (*DSM*): "Reliable diagnoses are essential for guiding treatment recommendations, identifying prevalence rates for mental health service planning, and documenting important public health information such as morbidity and mortality rates" (American Psychiatric Association, 2013, p. 5). A similar rationale applies to the usefulness of differentiating and categorizing spiritual experience.

We won't reiterate all of our definitions here, but some more specific restatements are needed in order to show that each specific spiritual experience that we describe still belongs to a broader category. First, spiritual experiences are *mental states*. Whether spiritual experiences are purely mental states or whether they also involve a supernatural component is a larger philosophical and theological discussion that we are setting aside for the purpose of empirical research (but which we address further in the book). Spiritual experiences typically involve a fairly dramatic shift in one's perceptions, emotions, and cognitions--what is sometimes called an "altered state of consciousness." We get more specific about the qualities of altered states of consciousness considered spiritual experiences throughout this part of the book. Importantly, these criteria exclude beliefs from consideration— merely thinking about some doctrine is not a spiritual experience under this definition.

Second, and really a clarification of the first point, *spiritual experiences are not merely emotions*. They may involve emotions, and emotions often follow, but the experience itself cannot be described only in emotional terms. Similarly, spiritual experiences are not only thoughts, but also involve cognitive processes and can frequently alter thoughts or beliefs after the fact. This criterion is a long-standing guideline in the study of such states. According to psychologist Ralph Hood in his *Handbook of Religious Experience* (1995), "That religious experience is not merely belief, not merely emotion; not merely the interaction of belief and emotion is the organizing theme that will clarify the empirical literature on the facilitation of religious experience" (p. 574). This requirement excludes a number of more routine kinds of mental states from consideration and helps us to focus on intensely altered states of consciousness.

Third, spiritual experiences include *some content having to do with some aspect of reality beyond appearances*. That is, one feels as if he or she has contacted something deeper than everyday life. One of James's definitions of religion involved connection to an "unseen reality," and this may come as close as possible to describing this criterion. This criterion is a bit broader than his stipulation about being in relation to something deemed "divine." The *unseen* aspect is what allows people to have a spiritual experience around other people, and yet other people do not perceive the same thing that the experiencer is perceiving. The *reality* aspect requires that some underlying, often essence-like component of existence is perceived. Most often, this involves some kind of mind—a god, gods, or other supernatural entities— but it can also involve a perception of an underlying oneness or even beauty in existence. Note that we are not claiming that the unseen reality that is perceived in fact exists, but only that it *seems* to exist to the one having the experience. Spiritual experiences typically involve deep feelings of connectedness to the unseen order that is perceived.

Here again, the line between whether these experiences are best considered perceptions of something real or hallucinations of the mind blurs and trails off into mystery. Beliefs are relevant to this definition, but it is often not clear exactly how. For example, an atheist can have an experience in which they feel as if they have perceived God, yet they choose to interpret the experience as a hallucination. Similarly, a religious person can have an experience of oneness, in which unity was the dominant feature of the experience, yet afterward can interpret the experience in a way that emphasizes their beliefs about God. One's beliefs influence the triggers, subjective qualities, and outcomes of spiritual experiences, but we believe that discovering the various different types of spiritual experience and their subjective qualities is an important step before reevaluating the role of belief (as we do in Part III).

James on Typologies of Experiences

James offered contrasting perspectives on the question of whether experiences could be categorized. On the one hand, he provided some important conceptual distinctions in *The Varieties* (James, 1902/2009). In terms of experiences, James distinguished between conversion experiences and mystical experiences. Conversion experiences are typically defined by a moral transformation, often from an unwanted state of being—such as depression or addiction—to a state of salvation and happiness. Mystical experiences are characterized by more specific criteria (note: these, for James, were ineffability, a noetic quality, passivity, and transiency, as we discuss at length) and also seem to be marked by a sense of unity. But James did not seem to mark out a strict distinction between different types of experiences. At some points, however, James seems to suggest that spiritual experiences could be categorized into types:

> One must read Saint Teresa's descriptions and the very exact distinctions that she makes, to persuade one's self that one is dealing, not with imaginary experiences, but with phenomena which, however rare, follow perfectly definite psychological types. (James, 1902/2009, p. 313)

James was, of course, adamant that spiritual experiences are a *subjectively* real phenomenon, and, in the above quotation at least, seemed to claim that the experiences can be divided into different types. On the other hand, in other places, James seemed skeptical at the possibility of finding a comprehensive typology. He wrote: "I imagine that these experiences can be as infinitely varied as are the idiosyncrasies of individuals" (James, 1902/2009, p. 309). James was being (characteristically) contradictory here, but the statements are also potentially reconcilable. He may have meant that some broad types are possible to establish, as long as these categories are not interpreted in a way that requires experiences in different individuals to feel exactly the same.

A Scholarly Debate: Perennialism and Constructivism

An important scholarly debate has emerged since *The Varieties* was published, especially in the field of religious studies (a field that recognizes James as a foundational influence). As mentioned, much of the weight of James's argument in *The Varieties* rests on the many personal accounts of spiritual experiences that he included. For most readers, these descriptions do seem to convey a definite, yet fuzzy, "family resemblance." That is, James's subject becomes quite clear through these examples. However, some scholars have challenged this view and argued that when read closely, these personal accounts of experiences diverge in many ways. This debate is between the "perennialists," who hold that experiences are largely similar across cultures, and the "constructivists," who hold that experiences are different across cultures.

Perennialism holds that spiritual experiences are a human universal— essentially the same across time and place, a view that James tended toward and in some places seemed to endorse. For example, he wrote (regarding mystical experiences marked by a sense of unity):

> In mystic states we have both become one with the Absolute and we become aware of our oneness. This is the everlasting and triumphant mystical tradition, hardly altered by differences of clime or creed. (James, 1902, p. 318)

According to perennialism, people everywhere have the same basic experiences, but they are described using different language, a view that *The Varieties* helped to inspire. After James, a number of scholars—Evelyn Underhill in *Mysticism* (1911), Rudolf Otto in *The Idea of the Holy* (1958), Aldous Huxley in *The Perennial Philosophy* (1945/2014), and Walter Stace in *Mysticism and Philosophy* (1960) to name just a few—all undertook efforts to gather together accounts of spiritual experiences from more diverse cultural contexts. Each of these books is considered an example of perennialism. While they vary in their degree of nuance, they all make more sweeping claims than James did regarding the universality of mystical or spiritual experiences.

However, when taken to its extreme, perennialism ignores real differences in cultural concepts that are invoked in descriptions of spiritual experiences. For example, most spiritual experiences in the United States involve Jesus, whereas most spiritual experiences in Nepal involve Buddha, and cultural differences can explain why the situation is not reversed. James seemed only mildly aware of this critique. Scholar Wayne Proudfoot wrote regarding this point: "James . . . does not draw the implication that a person's explanation of her experience might itself be an ingredient in the experience" (Proudfoot in preface to *The Varieties*; James, 1902/2004, p. xxix). Thus, it is obvious that at least some features of spiritual experience are conditioned, or constructed, by one's culture.

Scholars who emphasize differences between accounts, the constructivists, argue that all experiences are completely conditioned by cultural influences. According to this line of thinking, peoples' psychological experiences are made distinct according to their cultural contexts. To illustrate this view, it is not that there are merely different words for "drinking a glass of water," "feeling pain from a stubbed toe," or "having an orgasm" in, say, China and India—but these different cultures make peoples' actual subjective experience of these things different. According to this view, the experience of drinking water would be fundamentally different for a person who grew up in China and a person who grew up in India due to the differences in culture.

This view becomes a little absurd, though, when pushed to its extremes. For example, if one considers the difference in experiences between a person in London and a person in Paris drinking a glass of water, we start to see that these experiences can't be entirely different, even given the cultural differences. What about differences in drinking a glass of water between even closer cities with only minor cultural differences, such as Philadelphia and Baltimore? As these examples suggest, there appear to be undeniable similarities in the subjective experiences of people drinking a glass of water regardless of cultural differences. While there are differences in language and culture, the effects these cultural differences have on subjective experience are likely fairly minor in many cases. However dubious on the grounds of science and common sense the constructivist view becomes when taken to its extreme, it also contains an important objection to James's approach to spiritual experience in this view to consider. There are indeed differences between spiritual experiences—differences that spring from differences in culture, language, and beliefs—that are important to acknowledge.

Constructivism offers an especially valid critique of *naïve* forms of perennialism. In his book *Mysticism and Philosophical Analysis* (1978), Steven Katz, a leading constructivist scholar, articulated increasingly sophisticated perennialist views, beginning with one that is obviously wrong, to more nuanced views (each of which he finds incorrect). Here is the first, most naïve form of perennialism according to Katz:

> I. All mystical experiences are the same; even their descriptions reflect an underlying similarity which transcends cultural or religious diversity. (Katz, 1978, p. 23)

This view is obviously too simplistic. Different cultures and religions often have quite different concepts due to differences in history and language. Almost no serious scholars hold this view (though it can be found in popular spirituality books). The second view is slightly more tenable:

> II. All mystical experiences are the same but mystics' reports about their experiences are culturally bound. Thus they use the available symbols

of their cultural-religious milieu to describe their experience. (Katz, 1978, p. 24)

This view describes how two people from different cultures might experience something the same way but describe it differently, using words and concepts from their own cultures. But it still claims that the experiences themselves are the same. The following view is, according to Katz, the most sophisticated form of perennialism:

III. All mystical experience can be divided into a small class of "types" which cut across cultural boundaries. Though the language used by mystics to describe their experience is culturally bound, their experience is not. (Katz, 1978, p. 24)

This view acknowledges the possibility of different types of experiences. In more recent years, an even more minimal version of perennialism has been advanced, called the "modified common core theory." This quasi-perennialist view takes the constructivist critiques into account. This view, defended by Ralph Hood, holds that people from all cultures report spiritual experiences that appear to have some real similarities, but it must also be acknowledged that culture plays an important role in influencing and creating these experiences (e.g., Chen et al., 2011).

Our own view would admit even more influence of cultural constructivism, which we might call the common clusters model (note the plural "clusters"). To us, there appears to be common clusters of similar features, even in cross-cultural reports of spiritual experiences, despite the fact that a great number of differences also exist. In our view, these common clusters consist of reliable statistical groupings of subjective qualities—but, crucially, no one subjective quality is necessary or sufficient, and these clusters can change across cultures.

Our common clusters model attempts to balance the insights of perennialism and constructivism while making room for empirical investigation to furnish more specific details. Thus, the linguistic and cross-cultural components have become an important part of the study of spiritual experiences and it is clear that no simple claims to universality that do not take these cultural issues into account can be correct. On the other hand, the sweeping skeptical conclusion that experiences cannot be compared at all due to cultural differences is equally untenable. In further chapters we show how contemporary scientists address cross-cultural and linguistic variation in research.

Contemporary Typologies of Experiences

Scientists since James have been split on providing typologies of spiritual experience, particularly on the question of whether there is one, a few, several, or many kinds of experiences. The most simplistic version of the perennialist view, that there is just one experience that occurs across time and culture, has been largely dismissed. This claim simply does not hold up to scrutiny: People definitely describe their experiences differently across cultures and religious belief systems. On the opposite end of the spectrum, some scholars remain skeptical that a typology could be developed at all. However, many researchers defend the idea that, despite the uniqueness of each individual experience as well as cross-cultural differences, *there are several broad types that cover the major subjective qualities of a majority of experiences—* and this is the view that we advance here.

A few typologies of spiritual experience of this kind have been attempted. These classification systems are generally based on researchers analyzing written descriptions of spiritual experiences and creating categories. That is, for example, participants in a typical study of this kind would be presented with a loose definition of a religious, spiritual, or mystical experience (or these terms would simply be listed) and are then asked to indicate whether they have had such an experience. If so, participants are asked to write about their experience.

A distinction used by anthropologists that is useful here—that between "emic" and "etic" approaches. Emic approaches rely on the terms and categories of a particular social group, whereas etic approaches use technical terms brought in by the observer. When it comes to spiritual experience, the emic approach would use labels for experiences most familiar to the participants. For example, a researcher using the emic method might ask a Christian if they have felt the "presence of Christ," whereas a researcher using the etic method might ask if they have "felt a nonphysical mind surround them." One can see the trade-offs here in terms of intelligibility but imprecision in the emic approach, whereas the etic approach might be more precise but the abstractions and jargon might make it harder to understand.

Regardless of whether taking an emic or etic approach, researchers then analyze the writings from study participants and try to sort them into various categories based on themes found in the descriptions. This is a form of qualitative research that relies more on meaning and themes than numeric information. The primary textbook in the field of the psychology of religion and spirituality speaks to this process of reading written reports of spiritual experiences (we have read many thousands of these reports collected through the course of our research): "Access to these materials by scholars has led to numerous classification systems, few of which have been rigorously established by methodological or statistical means" (Hood et al., 2009, p. 306).

Alister Hardy, the English researcher who gathered thousands of accounts of spiritual experiences, provided a classification system based on the major five senses (Hardy, 1979). This early attempt has the merit of providing a typology with a firm conceptual foundation, but it ultimately failed to provide much insight or differentiation. Most of the experiences in his collection were associated with vision and hearing, while a few also mentioned touch. But many of the senses were involved in many of the experiences, which limited its value.

David Hay, a psychologist who carried on work at the Alister Hardy foundation, created a classification that diverged from the sensory-based perspective. In this line of research, Hay circulated a survey (much like Starbuck's) with the following question: "Have you ever been aware of or influenced by a presence or power, whether you call it God or not, which is different from your everyday self?" (A version of this question was also used by Gallup, as seen in a previous chapter). The results of one such study provide some insight into different types of experiences. Participants responded to this question and described their experience in writing. Then the researchers sorted the answers into several categories: "presence of or help from God (28%), assistance via prayer (9%), intervention by presence not identified as God (13.5%), presence or help from deceased (9%), premonitions (10%), meaningful patterning of events (10%), and miscellaneous (8%) (Hay & Morisy, 1985, p. 217)" (Hood et al., 2009, p. 343).

Roland Fischer (1971), an experimental psychologist, described what he referred to as a "cartography" of mental states, based on the degree of physiological arousal. His article, which was published in the prestigious academic journal *Science*, begins with the following bold statement: "In this age so concerned with travel in outer space as well as inner space, it is strange that, while

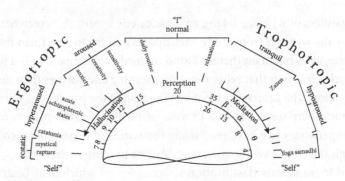

Figure 8.1 From Roland Fischer (1971). From Fischer, R. (1971).
A Cartography of the Ecstatic and Meditative States: The experimental and
experiential features of a perception-hallucination continuum are considered.
Science, *174*(4012), 897–904. Reprinted with permission from AAAS.

we have detailed charts of the moon, we have no cartography of the varieties of human experience" (p. 897). According to Fischer's model (Figure
8.1), either extreme arousal or relaxation results in a continuum of altered
states of consciousness. When arousal or relaxation are driven to extremes,
then various spiritual experiences tend to occur. Though grounded in physiology, this is nonetheless a speculative and theoretical perspective. However,
it cannot explain why all highly arousing or highly relaxing experiences do
not reliably trigger spiritual experience. Also, it does not carefully define or
seek to measure the various spiritual experiences supposedly underpinned
by changes in arousal.

The work of Eugene d'Aquili, along with one of us (Andrew Newberg;
d'Aquili & Newberg, 1999), proposed that there is mutual activation of both
arms of the autonomic nervous system. They argued that during intense
states of arousal or quiescence, there is a breakthrough of the other side
leading to brief experiences of combined arousal or energy and blissfulness.
There has been some interesting evidence pointing to this process playing an
important role in intense spiritual, or even mystical, experiences (Hugdahl,
1996; Newberg & Iversen, 2003).

Based on her anthropological fieldwork, Tanya Luhrmann proposed three
types of experiences "that appear around the world in different faiths" (2012,
p. 377), which is a quasi-perennialist claim. These three types are (1) spiritual seizures, (2) sensory overrides, and (3) trance phenomena. *Spiritual
seizures* involve "dramatic, transformative events like mystical experiences,

near-death experiences, and out-of-body phenomena" (Luhrmann, 2012, p. 377). *Sensory overrides*, on the other hand, involve hallucinations or perceptions of nonphysical entities. *Trance phenomena*, according to Luhrmann, include intense prayer practices like speaking channeling spirits and speaking in tongues (glossolalia).

Last, there is an emerging classification system with substantial promise for future work advanced by religious studies professor Ann Taves. Her work on the Inventory of Non-Ordinary Experiences (INOE) is still in development, so we cannot provide much information here. This framework takes the concerns of the cultural constructivists very seriously, who emphasize differences across cultures, and yet the INOE attempts to find the elements of experiences that may be shared (Taves, 2020). It utilizes a "building block" approach wherein various subjectivity qualities may be identified and tagged to a particular experience, but it does not attempt to create a typology. Taves and her team are attempting to develop items referring to highly abstract qualities that will appear across cultural differences. We return to a discussion of this kind of approach in Chapter 19.

In general, each of these classifications systems or typologies has been derived through top-down, researcher-derived categories. This is largely unavoidable when access to statistical methods or instruments is limited. However, modern quantitative methods provide some ways to improve on this process and to make categorization somewhat less subject to researcher opinion or bias.

Modern Classification Methods

When contemporary researchers want to examine how many components there are in a given psychological construct, they often use a method called "factor analysis." Factor analysis is a statistical method that can be applied to self-report surveys; the analysis identifies clusters of items that constitute subdimensions of a broader construct. This technique can be applied to self-report questions ("items") to reduce them to just a few major clusters for easier interpretation. One textbook on factor analysis states: "Reducing the number of variables to a more reasonable subset is often a prime goal of a factor analysis" (Gorsuch, 1983, p. 90). In other words, this technique allows one to reduce many variables into just a few clusters, which are easier to work with.

Research on intelligence using the intelligence quotient (IQ) represents one well-known application of factor analysis and provides an illustrative example. Some intelligence researchers claim that all of the various aspects of intelligence can be combined into a single general intelligence factor, referred to as "*g*." Other researchers, however, claim that breaking out individual factors, or subdimensions, of intelligence yields important insights. For example, verbal intelligence and mathematical intelligence are highly correlated, but they are also distinct. William Gibson, author of science fiction classic *Neuromancer*, reportedly had an almost perfect score on the verbal portion of the SAT (Scholastic Aptitude Test) but scored among the lowest percentiles in the mathematical portion (Sale, 2003). Reducing intelligence to a single factor may be more parsimonious, but cases in which these two aspects come apart—such as Gibson's case—would be missed.

A great number of psychological constructs have been factor analyzed in order to reveal important subdimensions (the Big 5 personality model—described in Chapter 6—is another example). Factor analysis has also been used in the physical and biological sciences to reduce many variables into a smaller number of clusters, which can then be treated as variables. This technique does not provide a final answer about how many parts of a construct are "really" there—the answer depends on the level of simplicity or complexity that is desired. When using factor analysis with self-report survey data, the results are dependent on the items that go into the analysis as well as the sample of individuals who answer the items.

Factor analysis has the virtue of quantitatively identifying the responses that tend to be associated with one another. The categories derived from intelligence and personality research are relatively reliable. This method also has the scientific benefit of being falsifiable; a theorist could claim, for example, that extraversion is identical to openness to experience, but that theorist could be proven wrong by conducting a factor analysis.

Factor Analyzing Spiritual Experience

In the context of studying spiritual experience, it appears that factor analysis can be utilized to better characterize various types. In order to conduct factor analysis on spiritual experiences, one would first ask many people if they have had a spiritual experience, and if so to describe it in writing, and finally to answer many questions related to their spiritual experiences. These questions, or items, can then be reduced into smaller clusters of answers using factor analysis. We did just this with our data from the Varieties Survey.

As previously described, in our Varieties Survey, we asked 461 people to write about their intense experience (which could be called religious, spiritual, mystical, peak, transcendent, peak, etc.). Here are some examples of the kinds of descriptions that we received:

> I was traveling. I had woken up very early in the morning to watch the sunrise over one of the most beautiful cities in the world. I climbed to the top of a hill, and watched as the sun came up. I then went inside a religious building that was also at the top of the hill. As I sat there, out of nowhere I felt this overwhelming sense that there was something MORE. I have no idea how to explain it, but it was powerful enough that it made me start to cry.

> I had a vision of a deity during meditation and my body began to shake as though I were terrified, yet at the same time there was an overwhelming sense of peace. Afterwards, I felt mentally clear and at peace.

> The moment my daughter died. We felt her leaving. It felt like the opposite of creation, of birth. It felt like a thinning of the veil. I felt very connected to God and everyone in the room. It was like nothing else.

We then asked participants to respond to a long battery of questions about their experience. We created these items after reading thousands of written descriptions of spiritual experiences that we gathered in other studies. The items we created addressed different distillations of the "unseen realities" in our definition of spiritual experience. We administered a great number of items, related to perceptions of god/gods, feelings of oneness, voices, visions, perceptions of great beauty, epiphanies, and encounters with other supernatural entities. We derived these items from topics that were frequently mentioned in written descriptions of spiritual experiences after reading several thousand accounts of spiritual experience as well as items from previous measures.

We considered how to begin each item. We thought that "I perceived . . ." as in "I perceived God" might be interpreted as requiring participants to endorse a particular belief. How would someone answer who felt the presence of something that felt like God, but who interpreted their experience as entirely deriving from their brain? Instead, then, we decided to keep the items feeling focused. Thus, the stem of each item begins with "I felt . . .," a decision that was made after discussion with a number of scholars and scientists. The chair of religious studies at Penn, Justin McDaniel, described the importance of conveying how these are subjective sensations—not beliefs or interpretations. "Felt" is a fairly neutral word in respect to claiming that something is either true, on the one hand, or an illusion, on the other hand. We think that the word "felt" is brief, understandable, and neutral.

After generating these items, we then conducted what is called exploratory factor analysis, which is described in the next section. We also later conducted what is called confirmatory factor analysis on a sample of 8,126 people who reported having had a spiritual experience (in collaboration with Ryan Niemic at the VIA Institute of Character). This additional study allowed us to test our models to ensure that the models presented below represent an adequte fit of the data, which they do.

Results of the Factor Analysis

The factor analysis process produced findings that could perhaps help to ground some theoretical and speculative debates in more concrete data. There are a number of metrics that researchers pay attention to when doing factor analysis. (Note: We thank University of Pennsylvania psychologist Jer Clifton for assisting with the initial factor analysis.)

The most well-known criterion for identifying the number of factors is called a scree plot. A *scree plot* is named after the rock and loose gravel that collects at the bottom of cliffs or steep mountainsides, called "scree." In terms of factor analysis, the first few factors explain most of the variance in the data and are represented as the higher points in the graph. Each subsequent factor is able to explain less of the total variance, so each new factor descends on the graph, creating the impression of a steep cliff. At some point, the amount of variance explained reaches a point of diminishing returns. This point, which is often referred to as the "elbow" of the graph, and right before the elbow is usually where researchers will mark the number of factors.

In our data, the scree plot seems to suggest that there are three factors. As you can see in the graph of Figure 8.2, the elbow (the point before the line becomes essentially flat) is on Component 4, so it is standard practice to retain the factors to the left of that point. In this case, the scree plot suggests a three-factor solution.

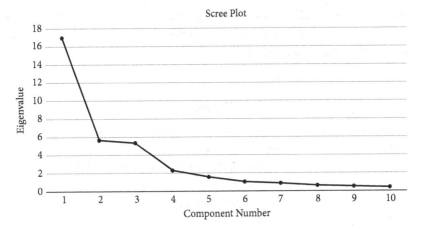

Figure 8.2 A scree plot can show which factors account for the most variance in the data. In this case, the first three factors account for the most variance. Drawn by David B. Yaden.

While the three-factor solution may be the most parsimonious (at least according the scree plot) other quantitative criteria can provide other estimates for the number of factors. For example, an algorithm called parallel analysis indicated 11 factors here. Parallel analysis works by comparing the real data to a randomly generated data set. The algorithm then extracts factors in the original data set until additional factors are indistinguishable from noise, such as the data in the randomly generated data set. Of course, this is just a summary of how the algorithm works, but the end result is an indicator that often provides a higher estimate of the number of factors to extract. These factors were then examined more closely to ensure that the items cluster together sufficiently well and that there are at least three items to constitute a factor. Factors that fail to meet these criteria are removed. In this case, this process resulted in *a nine-factor solution.*

For the three-factor solution, we label the resulting types: Numinous Experiences (involving the presence of God), Mystical Experiences (involving feelings of unity), and Paranormal Experiences (involving the presence of deceased relatives or other nonphysical beings). We have already seen a number of examples of experiences involving God and unity, as these are commonly associated with the term "spiritual experience." The third factor, Paranormal Experience, includes items related to seeing deceased friends or relatives. While this topic is not usually part of the academic discourse on spiritual experience, it appears that many people in the normal population report these experiences, and that they are in some way distinct from God and Unity experiences.

Factor 1

0.83	I felt God's presence.
0.82	I felt the presence of an all-powerful being.
0.81	I felt that I communed with God.
0.79	I felt that I encountered God.
0.79	I felt that I encountered the divine.

Factor 2

0.81	I felt a sense of oneness with all things.
0.8	I felt wonder for the natural world.
0.79	I felt awe for the natural world.
0.78	I felt at one with all things.
0.77	I felt a sense of unity with my surroundings.

Factor 3

0.82	I felt that I encountered a ghost of someone I knew.
0.79	I felt that I encountered a ghost.
0.78	I felt that I was visited by a dead friend or relative.
0.77	I felt that I saw a recently deceased friend or relative.
0.71	I felt a ghostly presence.

For the nine-factor solution, recommended by parallel analysis after removing error factors, there were more fine-grained experience types. More specifically, the Numinous, Mystical, and Paranormal experience factors split into several other categories (Figure 8.3). The first factor,

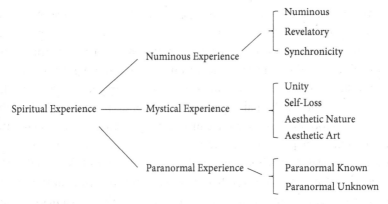

Figure 8.3 Description of factor analyses. The three factors (God, Unity, Ghost) represent the factors suggested by the scree plot. The nine factors indicate those produced by iteratively producing factors to the number suggested by parallel analysis until an error factor was reached. Drawn by David B. Yaden.

Numinous Experience, specifically refers to the feeling of the presence of God. The second factor, *Unity Experience*, refers to feelings of connectedness. The third factor, *Revelatory Experience*, refers to hearing voices or seeing inner visions that seem to come from beyond the self. The fourth factor, *Synchronicity Experience*, has to do with detecting a personal meaning in events that coincide, which outside observers may consider coincidences. The fifth factor, *Aesthetic Nature Experience*, involves witnessing beauty or feeling awe at the natural world. The sixth factor, *Paranormal Known Experience*, involves experiencing a deceased friend or relative. The seventh factor, *Aesthetic Art Experience*, involves feeling moved by beautiful or excellent art or a performance of some kind. The eighth factor, *Self-Loss Experience*, includes feeling as though one's sense of self temporarily fades in some way. Finally, the ninth factor, *Paranormal Unknown Experience*, involves witnessing a ghost or otherwise nonphysical being of some kind.

Interpreting the Factor Analysis

What do the results of this factor analysis mean? One way to interpret these findings is that when people mention having a spiritual experience, they are probably referring to sensing the presence of God, feeling at one with all things, or perceiving an apparition of someone who has died. These three kinds of experiences explain the most variance (the three-factor solution). The nine-factor solution provided more granular details about different kinds of experiences. From this perspective, people who say they have had a spiritual experience may be referring to 1) feeling the presence of God, 2) hearing a voice or receiving a vision, 3) a coincidental event that holds a special significance, 4) feeling a sense of unity, 5) feeling the self fade away, 6 & 7) being moved by art or nature, or 8 & 9) feeling the presence of someone who has died, who is either known or unknown to the experiencer . There are likely many other kinds of experiences that do not fit neatly within these categories; of course, but that does not diminish the value of these categories which appear to cover a large number of cases. However, it is important to remember that this is merely a rough—yet still a convenient and quantitative—way to classify different types of spiritual experience.

Another distinction is important to mention, as described in detail in our further chapter on mystical experiences, is that self-loss and unity split apart from one another. This was surprising because they seem like two comple-mentary aspects of the same experience. But the finding that self-loss and unity were not as associated as we thought they were has spurred us to ex-amine this distinction in further work (Yaden et al., 2017). Distinguishing be-tween these two subcomponents resulted in some counterintuitive findings related to how unity and self-loss can result in very different outcomes when it comes to well-being.

In the coming chapters, we have collapsed a few types of experiences that are easier to discuss in tandem. For example, we discuss unity and self-loss together (which we call "Mystical Experience"), in addition to aesthetic experiences of art and nature ("Aesthetic Experience"), as well as known and unknown paranormal experiences ("Paranormal Experience"). The factor analysis shows that while such experiences can be distinguished, we have grouped them in a way that balances thorough-ness with brevity. While we treat them together, we distinguish them when appropriate. Figure 8.4 shows the prevalence of the types of spiritual ex-perience from our survey, shown here grouped as we discuss them in the coming chapters of Part II.

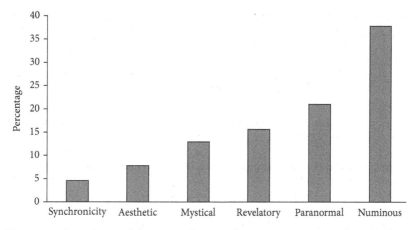

Figure 8.4 Prevalence of the types of spiritual experiences. Drawn by David B. Yaden.

Conclusion

The typology described here provides a data-driven way to distinguish between various types of experiences generally considered "spiritual." We feel that this is an important contribution from modern psychometric methods that were simply not available to James when he was writing *The Varieties*. This updated approach allows for better understanding the varieties of spiritual experiences. In each particular type of experience, as well as with spiritual experience in general, there is no set of necessary and sufficient conditions to determine with certainty whether a particular experience fits a particular type, but there do seem to be certain clusters of subjective qualities across the varieties of spiritual experiences that are worth examining.

However, we must emphasize that these clusters represent very rough categories for these experiences. Some experiences might fall completely into one category, but many experiences might overlap across two or more categories. James himself may have balked at too strict of a classification system, but we believe he would have agreed that classification of some kind, even a rough one, is required in order to make scientific progress. We believe that this data-driven factor analysis will help to drive some progress in the scientific study of spiritual experience. However, as time goes on, we fully expect improvements to the ways in which we can categorize the varieties of spiritual experiences.

References

American Psychiatric Association. (2013). *Diagnostic and statistical manual of mental disorders* (5th ed.; DSM-5).

Chen, Z., Hood, R. W., Jr., Yang, L., & Watson, P. J. (2011). Mystical experience among Tibetan Buddhists: The common core thesis revisited. *Journal for the Scientific Study of Religion, 50*(2), 328–338.

d'Aquili, E. G., & Newberg, A. B. (1999). *The mystical mind: Probing the biology of religious experience.* Fortress Press.

Fischer, R. (1971). A cartography of the ecstatic and meditative states. *Science, 174*(4012), 897–904.

Gorsuch, R. L. (1983). *Factor analysis* (2nd ed.). Erlbaum.

Hardy, A. (1979). *The spiritual nature of man. A study of contemporary religious experience.* Oxford University Press.

Hay, D., & Morisy, A. (1985). Secular society, religious meanings: A contemporary paradox. *Review of Religious Research*, 213–227.

Hood, R. W., Jr. (1995). *Handbook of religious experience.* Religious Education Press.

Hood, R. W., Jr., Hill, P. C., & Spilka, B. (2009). *The psychology of religion: An empirical approach.* Guilford.

Hugdahl, K. (1996). Cognitive influences on human autonomic nervous system function. *Current Opinion in Neurobiology, 6*, 252–258.

Huxley, A. (1945/2014). *The perennial philosophy.* McClelland & Stewart.

James, W. (1902/2009). The varieties of religious experience: A study in human nature. *eBooks@Adelaide.* https://csrs.nd.edu/assets/59930/williams_1902.pdf

Katz, S. T. (1978). *Mysticism and philosophical analysis.* Oxford University Press.

Luhrmann, T. M. (2012). *When God talks back: Understanding the American evangelical relationship with God.* Knopf.

Newberg, A. B., & Iversen, J. (2003). The neural basis of the complex mental task of meditation: Neurotransmitter and neurochemical considerations. *Medical Hypothesis, 61*(2), 282–291.

Otto, R. (1958). *The idea of the holy.* Oxford University Press.

Sale, J. (2003, June 19). Passed/failed: William Gibson, novelist and scriptwriter. *Independent.* https://www.independent.co.uk/news/people/profiles/passedfailed-william-gibson-novelist-and-scriptwriter-109559.html

Stace, W. T. (1960). *Mysticism and philosophy.* Tarcher.

Taves, A. (2020). Mystical and other alterations in sense of self: An expanded framework for studying nonordinary experiences. *Perspectives on Psychological Science, 15*(3), 669–690.

Underhill, E. (1911). *Mysticism.* Methuen.

Yaden, D. B., Haidt, J., Hood, R. W., Jr., Vago, D. R., & Newberg, A. B. (2017). The varieties of self-transcendent experience. *Review of General Psychology, 21*(2), 143–160.

9

Numinous Experiences

Encountering Divinity

During a nearly yearlong illness, a Catholic nun in 16th-century Spain began to have a series of spiritual experiences during which she felt the presence of God surrounding her. This nun, known today as Saint Teresa of Avila, described several stages that were involved in her spiritual experiences in her autobiography, *The Interior Castle*. According to Teresa, these stages involve a withdrawal from one's outward senses, surrendering one's will to a higher power, intense feelings of love for God, and, finally, what she referred to as "ecstasy." In this final ecstatic phase, she described feeling entirely absorbed in God.

Saint Teresa's descriptions of her experiences prominently featured a feeling of the presence of God and unity with God. Scholars often draw a distinction between experiences predominantly involving the presence of divinity, termed "numinous," and experiences predominantly involving union, termed "mystical." Religious scholar Rudolph Otto made such a contrast and described numinous experience as "an awareness of a 'holy other' beyond nature" (Otto, 1917). Saint Teresa's experiences blur this line, as they often involved feelings of union, albeit with the presence of God. But overall, because of the prominence of God in her experiences, we think they would fall into the category of numinous experience.

Numinous experience, the feeling of being in touch with divinity or God, may constitute the prototypical religious or spiritual experience. Our own research data show that numinous experiences are the most prevalent kind of experience that people report when asked to describe their most intense spiritual experience.

The feeling of divine "presence" is difficult to define, as it suggests something sensory-like, but most people often report that it doesn't quite involve a specific sensory system. This feeling of sensing a nonphysical presence is therefore sometimes described as "extrasensory" for this reason. This may provide some clues about the psychological processes involved with these

The Varieties of Spiritual Experience. David B. Yaden and Andrew B. Newberg, Oxford University Press. © David Yaden and Andrew Newberg 2022. DOI: 10.1093/oso/9780190665678.003.0009

experiences. Here are the items used to measure divinity experiences on our survey:

- I felt God's presence.
- I felt that I encountered God.
- I felt that I communed with God.

In the following chapter, as well as each of the chapters in this part, we describe William James's perspective on the particular type of experience as well as a few major pieces of scholarship related to James's perspective. This is followed by sections on contemporary psychological research, including findings related to pathological and positive aspects of each experience. Finally, we turn to neuroscience research on each type of experience.

James on Numinous Experience

In *The Varieties*, James (1902/2009) specifically discussed the case of Saint Teresa. James was well aware of the criticisms made by the Church toward many saints who described their spiritual experiences. As prophets, seers, and sages through the ages have found, spiritual experiences can be dangerous when they are seen to undermine the traditional authority of the church. This is perhaps especially the case for women, whose immediate experience of God or spiritual scholarship was more often viewed as heretical. (Note: Relatedly, in his lecture series "Exceptional Mental States" a few years before his Gifford Lectures, James argued that historically it was not generally the "witches" who were mentally ill, but rather their accusers who showed signs of paranoia in addition to their misogyny.)

James (1902/2009) also argued against a general tendency to see individuals who report spiritual experience as lacking in will or intellect. This is yet another form of reflexive pathologizing spiritual experience, which James challenged. James provided counterexamples against this view by describing saints who demonstrated a kind of spiritual genius that was matched by other intellectual strengths and virtues. James described Teresa as having "a powerful intellect of the practical order" (James, 1902/2009, p. 263), James was adamant that numinous experiences occur to individuals of all kinds and resisted the implication that these experiences are associated with psychopathology or unsoundness of mind.

James (1902/2009) included a number of other accounts involving the presence of God. Here are just a few more:

God surrounds me like the physical atmosphere. He is closer to me than my own breath. (p. 57)

In that time the consciousness of God's nearness came to me sometimes. I say God to describe what is indescribable. A presence, I might say, yet that is to suggestive of personality, and the moments which I speak did not hold the consciousness of a personality, but something made me feel myself a part of something bigger than I, that was controlling. (p. 298)

These highest experiences that I have had of God's presence have been rare and brief—flashes of consciousness which have compelled me to exclaim with surprise—God is here!—or conditions of exaltation and insight, less intense, and only gradually passing away. (p. 301)

While mystical experiences of unity have received more scholarly attention over the past hundred years, James devoted a larger portion of *The Varieties* to experiences involving divinity. Yet again, we refrain from describing James's views on the metaphysical reality or unreality of these experiences until further in this book.

Contemporary Numinous Experience Measures

Numinous experiences involving God or some sense of divinity occur in contemporary settings as well. In *Fingerprints of God*, journalist Barbara Hagerty (2009) described a numinous experience that she had while interviewing a cancer patient. She wrote:

Gradually, and ever so gently, I was engulfed by a presence I could feel but not touch. I was paralyzed. I could manage only shallow breaths. After a minute, although it seemed longer, the presence melted away. We sat quietly, while I waited for the earth to steady itself. I was too spooked to speak, and yet I was exhilarated, as the first time I skied down an expert slope, terrified and oddly happy that I could not turn back. Those few moments, the time it takes to boil water for tea, reoriented my life. The episode left a mark on my psyche that I bear to this day. (Hagerty, 2009, p. 3)

Experiences like these are surprisingly common. Most of the large-scale survey questions asked by companies like Gallup and the General Social Survey focus on the feeling of the presence of God (this is for historical reasons having to do with the early influence of Hardy and the Oxford Researcher Center). Recall that about 35% of participants in these large-scale polls will agree that they have felt the presence of God. A recent study from Columbia psychologist Lisa Miller and her team involved collecting narratives of spiritual experiences from 6,112 participants, which we cite throughout this part of the book. In this study, 54% of U.S. narratives, 79% Indian narratives, and 41% of Chinese narratives contained a reference to a religious figure or religious force suggestive of a numinous experience (Lau et al., 2020).

Beyond the single-item measures used in large-scale surveys, researchers use several scales to measure numinous experience. The most well-known scale is the *Index of Core Spiritual Experience* (INSPIRIT; Kass et al., 1991). This measure was inspired by the researchers' observations that many individuals report spiritual experiences while engaging in relaxation practices like meditation (Benson & Klipper, 1975), writing that during these relaxation practices: "Many patients reported what we came to call 'core spiritual experiences'" (Kass et al., 1991, p. 204).

The creators of the INSPIRIT explicitly aimed to measure experiences rather than beliefs; however, this is belied by the authors' description of the scale as measuring experiences that "convince a person that God exists and evoke feelings of closeness with God" (Kass et al., 1991, p. 205), suggesting a strong belief-based component. This emphasis on belief is also obvious from the instructions for the measure: "The following list describes spiritual experiences that some people have had. Indicate if you have had any of these experiences and the extent to which each of them has affected your belief in God." The following is a sample item from the measure:

Have you ever had an experience that has convinced you that God exists?

The INSPIRIT scale thus covers a wide range of experiences (including items related to experiencing God, angels, communication with a deceased relative, feelings of unity) as well as the degree to which each experience led to a stronger belief in God. The broad range of experiences is not a strength of the scale, we argue, but rather a significant weakness. All of the conceptual differentiation that James engaged in to distinguish beliefs and experiences is lost, as these are conflated in this scale. Also, all of the statistical differentiation made possible through our factor analysis is lost in this scale as it includes all of these kinds of experiences on a single dimension.

Another common scale is the *Daily Spiritual Experiences Scale* (DSES; Underwood & Teresi, 2002). This measure was created from a process of interviews and focus groups of people of various belief systems (Christian, Jewish, Muslims, Buddhists, Hindus, agnostics, and atheists). The instructions for this measure are fairly typical of all scales that measure spiritual experiences, attempting to refer to spiritual experience while trying to be vague enough to capture various kinds: "The list that follows includes items which you may or may not experience, please consider how often you directly have this experience, and try to disregard whether you feel you should or should not have these experiences. A number of items use the word God. If this word is not a comfortable one for you, please substitute another idea which calls to mind the divine or holy for you" (Underwood & Teresi, 2002, p. 25). Despite the purported influence of individuals across various belief systems during the creation of the scale, it appears to use specifically monotheistic concepts. For example, here are two items from this measure: "I feel God's presence" and "I feel God's love for me directly."

The DSES is treated as a single factor, though it includes a diverse array of experiences in addition to experiences featuring God or divinity, such as unity experiences (e.g., "I experience a connection to all life"). The scale also includes items related to beliefs (about drawing strength from one's faith) and practices (e.g., prayer). This raises all of the same problems mentioned regarding the INSPIRIT. The conceptual distinction between experiences and belief is lost, and the distinctions between different types of spiritual experience are also obscured.

Additionally, the DSES includes several mentions of positive emotions in the scale (e.g., "I feel thankful for my blessings"). At first glance this might seem like a step away from the inappropriate pathologization of spiritual experience, but it actually makes it impossible for researchers to establish whether or not spiritual experiences are associated with mental illness or well-being. In this case, if a scale score includes measures of well-being, then it's little wonder if it positively correlates with well-being—the two variables are tautologically related!

Both the INSPIRIT and the DSES also suffer from another problem: They may measure experiences so subtle that they would not be the topic of James's investigation (or ours). This issue is particularly relevant with numinous experiences, as it is particularly difficult to differentiate experiences from beliefs with this category of experience. For example, many people who be- lieve in God interpret many aspects of their daily lives in religious terms. Luhrmann (2012) even found among her evangelical Christian subjects that some would attribute finding a good parking spot to divine intervention— and thus label this an experience of God. As we have made clear, these kinds of subtle and daily kinds of experiences are not our focus here. Instead, our focus is on intensely altered states of consciousness.

"Sacred Moments" in Clinical Contexts

Clinical contexts are one particularly controversial context where numinous experiences reportedly occur, in the form of both intensely altered states of consciousness and subtle, more belief-based forms. Most contemporary healthcare and therapeutic environments are secular, indicating that there is an attempt to remain neutral with respect to one's religious/spiritual beliefs. Clinicians are taught to respect their patients' or clients' belief systems. Thus, clinicians generally do not delve into their patients' belief systems—or experiences that seem related to religion/spirituality—out of an abundance of caution, unless, or course, they directly relate to a diagnostic category.

Contemporary clinical psychologist Ken Pargament of Bowling Green State University, coined the term "sacred moments" for numinous experiences that occur in clinical contexts. Pargament argued that these experiences are already occurring in therapy rooms, and that they can ac- tually enhance the therapeutic process when explicitly acknowledged. In an article, "Sacred Moments in Psychotherapy From the Perspectives of Mental Health Providers and Patients" (2014), he and his coauthors described sev- eral of these sacred moments. Here is one from a patient:

> I also felt safe because I knew my therapist was/is there for me and that she has my best interests at heart. She was very supportive and loving. She extended my session by another hour and made sure I was safe to go home. This moment brought us closer and deepened my trust in her. [This moment] was sacred to me because I knew, all the way to my spirit that I was not alone in this anymore and that I had not only my therapist on my side but it brought home that God was pained by what I went through. (Pargament et al., 2014)

Pargament et al. (2014) also made the point that it's not only the patients, but also the clinicians who can experience such sacred moments. Here is one therapist describing an experience that occurred while the patient was expressing gratitude about the therapeutic process:

> He said I was different than all other providers in the sense that I was genuinely caring about him and paying attention to what he was saying and also to what he was not saying. It was like time had stopped and we were two vulnerable human beings connected at a very deep level. A "sacred" moment. (Pargament et al., 2014)

Pargament and his colleagues also addressed the mental health benefits of spiritual experiences outside of the clinical office. They found that experiences of spiritual experiences (what he called sacred moments) are associated with less caregiving burden and greater relationship satisfaction among family caregivers of adults with dementia (Wong, Pargament & Faigin, 2018) and greater growth in the aftermath of spiritual struggles in an adult sample (Wilt et al., 2019).

While Pargament convincingly argued that such experiences occur and can be beneficial for the therapeutic process, these topics speak to deep and difficult issues for clinicians. The secular nature of most healthcare and therapeutic settings has been hard won. It is not so long ago that such contexts were explicitly and necessarily dominated by particular religions; what some religious individuals do not adequately acknowledge is that *secularism actually protects religious freedoms* for all individuals, especially those who don't happen to be in the dominant religious group.

Bringing religious and spiritual beliefs into a therapeutic context raises a number of important considerations when patients describe their spiritual experiences. But some clinicians argue that in some cases religious/spiritual beliefs and experiences should be explicitly brought into the clinical context when appropriate (Koenig, Peteet, & VanderWeele, 2020). For example, some have suggested that mental health providers working with some contemporary Native American individuals might regard spirituality as inseparable from their client's daily life, presentation of pathology, and treatment options (see King & Trimble, 2013). Clearly, these issues often require a finely tuned sense of cultural sensitivity from clinicians (Koenig, Peteet, & VanderWeele, 2020). We touch on these issues again in Chapter 15, which covers the interpretation and integration of spiritual experiences.

Positive and Pathological

The *Diagnostic and Statistical Manual of Mental Disorders* (*DSM*) launched a task force to grapple with these difficult religious and spiritual issues. One compendium of research recommendations for the *DSM* called *Religious and Spiritual Issues in Psychiatric Diagnoses* (2011) includes contributions from influential psychiatrists and psychologists, such as George Vaillant, Harold Koenig, David Lukoff, and others.

The book pays special attention to the topic of religious and spiritual content in psychosis and delusions, yet the generally positive outcomes of spiritual experiences is repeatedly acknowledged. Furthermore, the book emphasizes how spiritual experiences that require clinical care are generally easy to identify. Koenig wrote: "Members of religious communities today seldom have difficulty distinguishing normative, culturally sanctioned religious belief, experience, and practice from psychotic symptoms with religious content" (Koenig, 2011, p. 32). Generally, the distinguishing characteristic is the lack of insight about the incredible claims being made by the person who has had the spiritual experience. In a more typical instance of a healthy spiritual experience, the individual will indicate an awareness that the experience may seem unusual or difficult to believe, whereas a pathological instance will more often involve a grandiose aspect about one's "specialness."

As we have mentioned many times, spiritual experiences requiring clinical care do occur, and religious and spiritual content can arise in the context of mental illness. Most clinicians who work with individuals suffering from mental illness will have seen patients who report religious and spiritual content as part of their delusions. This can sometimes create the impression that there is something inherently pathological about spiritual experience, which we have seen is certainly not the case. However, religious and spiritual content does show up in delusions and psychosis. Across several studies in the United States, about 25%–39% of patients with schizophrenia exhibited some kind of religious/spiritual content in their delusions (Koenig, 2011, p. 34). The percentage of religious/spiritual content was slightly lower in bipolar disorder (the manic phase can include delusions), at about 15% to 22% (Koenig, 2011, p. 34).

The degree to which religious or spiritual content occurs in schizophrenia or bipolar disorder varies across cultures. While the averages just given are for the United States, Europe has somewhat lower levels of religious or spiritual content in delusions, likely due to the lower levels of religious belief compared to the United States. These differences can be quite large. For example, the prevalence of religious/spiritual delusions in the Afro-Cuban populations is around 80%, while it is only about 7% in Japan (Koenig, 2011). One study has shown that religious or spiritual content in delusions is predicted by the amount of religious activity that individual had been engaged in (Siddle et al., 2002), suggesting that, like dreaming, the content of one's delusions is furnished in part by the details of one's daily life.

The kind of religious or spiritual content that occurs in delusions is shaped by culture as well. Religious and spiritual content in the United States and Europe is generally related to the Judeo-Christian God—an omniscient, omnipresent, and benevolent being. In Chinese contexts, individuals tend to report delusions containing culturally situated content, such as "Buddhist gods, Taoist gods, historical heroic gods" (Yip, 2004, cited in Koenig, 2011, p. 34). These gods would fit into the category of numinous experience.

A number of other studies have found similar associations between experiences of God and positive outcomes for religious individuals (Miner et al., 2014), in samples of heterogeneous religious identification (Byrd et al., 2000; Ellison & Fan, 2008) and for youth (Cotton et al., 2006). In the study by Ellison and Fan (2008), the authors used the DSES, which contains questions that tap into the degree to which people feel God's presence or God's love directly or through others (p. 253). The authors found that scores on the DSES were strongly related to positive psychological outcomes such as happiness, satisfaction with self, optimism, and excitement with life.

In our Varieties Survey data, we found that numinous experiences were associated with well-being more than any other kind of spiritual experience (see Table 9.1). We report these same outcomes for each of the types of experience throughout this part of the book. The numbers are Pearson's r, which is a measure of effect size or - how related two variables are from 0 to 1. Generally, a .1 to .2 is considered a small effect size, a .2 to .4 is considered medium, and .4 to .6 is considered large (Meyer et al., 2001). (Note: Correlations above a .6 are rarely seen in social science research and usually indicate a tautology is present.) The asterisks in the table indicate statistical significance, which means that: assuming that there is no relationship between the variables, there is a low probability that an equivalent or more extreme value would be observed, given the data in this sample (Lakens, 2021).

Table 9.1 Numinous Experience With Well-Being, Mental Health, and Faculties of Consciousness

	Numinous Experience
Well-Being Outcomes	
More positive emotions	.48**
Better personal relationships	.43**
Greater sense of meaning in life	.51**
Mental Health Outcomes	
Depression	−.17**
Anxiety	−.27**
Faculties of Consciousness	
Sense of space changed	.20**
Noetic quality	.33**
Sense of time changed	.23**

*p < .05. **p < .01.

Mind Perception

In the various numinous experiences described in this chapter, the core of the experience involves direct contact with an ultimate kind of "mind." This may seem like an abstract way of putting it, but *mind perception* is a psychological process that can help us understand the mental processes involved with this aspect of numinous experiences.

Mind perception is a relatively automatic mental process that assesses whether other things are conscious or not (Wegner & Gray, 2017). For example, when you look out across a crowded room, how do you differentiate between the furniture in the room and the people in it? This immediate, basically automatic process is called mind perception. Mind perception is related to the somewhat better known mental process called theory of mind, which refers to the capacity to understand the mental states and intentions of others. Mind perception is more fundamental insofar as it refers to the perception of whether or not another object/entity is conscious at all—before even considering what particular mental states or intentions that a given mind might contain.

The question of what we deem conscious or not is an ancient issue that is becoming increasingly complex. In their book *The Mind Club*, psychologists Dan Wegner and Kurt Gray (2017), described how people deem different entities as more or less conscious. Gray and Wegner described mind perception across two different dimensions: experience (or the capacity to feel pleasure or pain) and agency (the capacity to make decisions and take actions). When Gray and Wegner asked people to rate the minded-ness of various things on these two dimensions, certain assessments diverged. For example, dogs were judged to have a capacity for experience but not so much for agency. Interestingly, God was judged to have high agency but low experience (see Figure 9.1).

When Kurt Gray and colleagues (2011) administered this assessment to individuals diagnosed with various mental illnesses, they found that mind perception changed as a function of these disorders (Figure 9.2). They found that people with autism were less likely to perceive agency in others but just as likely to perceive the capacity for experiencing pleasure and pain. (Note: People with autism are often referred to as neurodiverse, and many do not consider autism to be a mental illness. We certainly would not equate

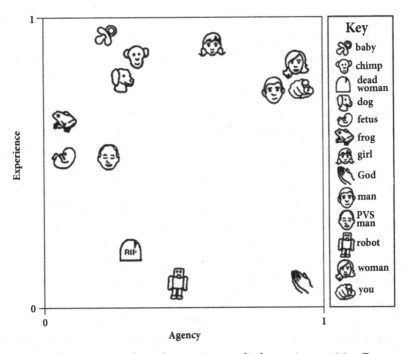

Figure 9.1 Dimensions of mind perception applied to various entities. From Heather M. Gray, Kurt Gray, Daniel M. Wegner. (2007). Dimensions of Mind Perception. *Science*, 315(5812). Reprinted with permission from AAAS.

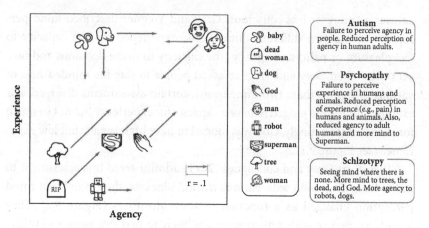

Figure 9.2 Dimensions of mind perception applied to various entities in people with autism, psychopathy, and schizotypy. From Gray, K., Jenkins, A. C., Heberlein, A. S., & Wegner, D. M. (2011). Distortions of mind perception in psychopathology. *Proceedings of the National Academy of Sciences, 108*(2), 477–479. Reprinted with permission from PNAS.

the various kinds of mental illness measured in this study, as each has its own very different dynamics and meaning.) Individuals with psychopathy, on the other hand, were less likely to perceive the capacity for experience in others, which may relate to why such individuals commit violent crimes at higher rates. Individuals with schizotypy (a milder form of schizophrenia) perceived more mind across both dimensions in most objects and entities.

Animals offer a complicated case when it comes to mind perception. Historically, animals have sometimes been considered gods or in some way god-like. In India, cows continue to be treated as sacred. Many Native American hunters prayed or pray to the representative god of each creature that was killed. There is also a belief system often known as animism—as in there is an animating spirit in all things. In contemporary Western culture, pets like dogs and cats are not theologically sacred but are treated as sacred-like in practice. Most contemporary Americans would respond with shock to eating a cat or a dog but eat other mammals almost daily with no issues. In particular, Americans eat cow (sacred, in India) and pig (more intelligent than dogs) at astounding rates. These patterns derive from historical practices that persist today as social norms and are related to the way that we attribute mind.

Artificial intelligence (AI) offers another interesting case of mind percep-tion. As algorithms become more and more capable of learning, and even show the early beginnings of true problem-solving, AI may eventually reach a point at which it becomes worthy of its name. At this point, we may be able to carry out mostly fluent conversations with AI. Indeed, British scien-tist Alan Turing, who was famous for breaking Nazi codes in World War II and played a primary role in making modern computing possible, conceived of a test to determine whether AI is truly intelligent, now called the Turing test. In this test, still carried out at a yearly programming conference, one must converse virtually with a chat bot and not be able to tell if their conver-sation partner (conveyed through text) is human or computer. Imagine, for a moment, that a program passes this test—is it conscious? Would it have the capacity for agency and experience?

Mind perception also offers one way to think about the question of whether or not God exists. One of our current conceptualizations of how consciousness comes into being involves the mind arising as an emergent property from a sufficiently complex set of neurobiological processes. Could, in a similar way as how mind arises from the brain, an ultimate kind of mind (i.e., God) emerge from the complex physical system that is the universe? We find such questions fascinating, but ultimately, they are well beyond our capacity to test or even address scientifically. When applied to the mind that is perceived during spiritual experiences, mind perception is merely another way to wonder whether the experience is an accurate perception or a mental projection—reality or illusion.

Mind perception does, though, provide a useful scientific concept to help parse out how much and what kind of mind we attribute to various entities, such as animals, objects, and artificial intelligence. Even our gold standard of an entity in which mind is percieved—other human beings—is questioned in some cases. Dehumanization, often used in genocidal campaigns, pushes people to act in unthinkable ways by portraying other human beings as less than human (less minded).

This discussion of mind perception is relevant because God is com-monly understood as a mind, albeit an ultimate kind of mind. Therefore, when people are having numinous experiences, they are perceiving a vast and special kind of mind, but a mind nonetheless. As Figure 9.2 shows, dif-ferent mental illnesses result in changes to mind perception (Gray et al., 2011). While this has not been tested, we believe that people who have had a spiritual experience may perceive more mind across each of these objects and entities.

The Hypersensitive Agency Detection Device

Mind perception appears to be the process through which any mind is perceived, but how could this occur in the specific case of numinous experience? One theory from psychologist Justin Barrett, which is often invoked by influential atheist thinkers like Richard Dawkins, involves what has been called the hypersensitive agency detection device (HADD; Barrett, 2007). According to this theory, it has been evolutionarily advantageous for humans to perceive agency in ambiguous situations (contexts in which it is unclear whether or not another agent, or being, is present). To illustrate, if a hunter–gatherer hears a rustle in the bushes, they would be better off believing it is a being of some kind (rather than, say, just the wind) to be better prepared for a potential predator. The thinking here goes that because we have a cognitive module called the HADD, we are predisposed for evolutionary reasons to believe in and experience God due to our more general tendency to attribute mind to ambiguous stimuli. Accordingly, spiritual experiences may consist of ambiguous stimuli, either in one's sensory experience or driven by dramatic autonomic changes, to which mind is then attributed and interpreted in terms of culturally available religious beliefs about nonphysical mind. This is the most prevalent evolutionary account of numinous experiences. Note that while the originator of theory, Justin Barrett, has argued that the HADD theory is likely more relevant to experiences of ghosts or spirits than all-pervading numinous experiences, it has been used by others (e.g., Richard Dawkins, Daniel Dennett) to apply to numinous type experiences.

However, there are some problems with this theory. The most serious problem is why, if HADD evolved as a threat detection mechanism, are most spiritual experiences involving the presence of God felt as positive? One would, according to this theory, expect feelings of fear to predominate. Additionally, numinous experiences typically involve a feeling of presence that is all pervading. The term used by Durkheim to describe feelings of bonding during sacred rituals, "collective effervescence," illustrates the idea. Philosopher Martin Buber's (1937) conception of moving from an "I-it" kind of stance to an "I-thou" stance toward the world helps to provide a picture of the abstract and often all-encompassing nature of mind in numinous experiences. This contrasts starkly with a biological predator detection mechanism.

The problems with HADD, then, as it applies to numinous experiences, are that numinous experiences do not involve a distinct entity (like a predatory animal), and they do not typically involve feelings of fear and threat coupled with the desire to fight or flee. Another evolutionary view involving mind perception is also possible. While the need to detect predators was no doubt essential for early human survival, so was the ability bond with other friendly minds. Most importantly, spiritual experiences often involve overwhelming feelings of peace, love, and compassion—the very opposite of the feelings that one would predict would flow from a cognitive module designed to alert one to predators. It seems more likely that an attachment-related module is involved here than a threat detection module. Overall, while the ability to detect other mind is essential for numinous experience, it is unclear how HADD illuminates numinous experience or how it would "debunk" such experiences (show them to be delusory).

Psychologist Bering (2002) called this perception of all-pervading mind the "existential theory of mind." Existential theory of mind is a way of relating to the world as if reality itself had agency and experience (i.e., a mind). It should be noted that this need not be a belief; it can also be understood as a feeling state. Spiritual experiences may represent transient, yet intense, experiences of existential theory of mind—or what we could call massive mentalization events. That is, during spiritual experiences, normally dead-seeming matter may seem take on a mind of its own, and we may feel an attachment to this seemingly minded world. This theory involves describing cognitive modules that allow us to perceive mind in general, yet it is silent regarding whether or not the mind that is perceived really exists (we return to these issues in Chapter 19).

Neuroscience

There have been a number of neuroscience studies on numinous experiences, generally using neuroimaging. Some individuals, often monastics or other people who have devoted many hours to practices like meditation or prayer and who generally believe in God, are reportedly able to put themselves into a state of mind where they feel in touch with divinity. These individuals have then been asked to put themselves into this state while in a neuroimaging scanner (certainly an added challenge).

In a study by Beauregard and Paquette (2006), the researchers examined the brains of Carmelite nuns who were asked to relive a time when they were "subjectively in a state of union with God" (p. 186). The functional magnetic resonance imaging (fMRI) results from Beauregard and Paquette's (2006) study showed the average patterns of activation across 15 nuns. They showed that a wide array of brain areas were activated during recall of these mystical states, but there was a pattern of activation that was similar across participants. The researchers found that areas of the brain implicated during these mystical states were those that are also involved with changes in perception of visual imagery, cognition regarding the self, and the processing of emotion.

Because numinous experiences involve seeming contact with a mind, many results show that brain regions associated with social cognition are activated during such experiences. That is, at a neuronal level, feeling the presence of another human being and feeling the presence of God have a great deal of similarity (Azari et al., 2001; Miller et al., 2019). Brain regions implicated in social interaction include the medial frontal as well as parietal (inferior) areas (Mohandas, 2008). One study found that when people were asked to think about emotions that God might feel (e.g., love), brain regions related to social cognition were activated (Kapogiannis et al., 2009). This suggests that on the neurological level, people respond to God as they would another person, suggesting the underlying process of mind perception may be occurring in both cases.

There thus appears to be a strong social aspect in numinous experience that is observable in neuroimaging studies. For example, in the image of a brain scan from Kapogiannis and colleagues (2009), the area of the brain that was active when a participant was imagining the love that God might feel is *also* the brain region that is active when we experience positive emotional states in general.

Finally, one of us (A. B. N.) performed a small neuroimaging study of Franciscan nuns performing a type of prayer called centering prayer (Newberg et al., 2003). In centering prayer, by bringing the mind's focus to a specific prayer or phrase from the Bible, over time, the individual experiences a powerful connection with God. The name centering prayer was taken from Thomas Merton's description of intense contemplative prayer that is "centered entirely on the presence of God." Hence, this type of prayer might be regarded as facilitating a numinous experience. In our study, we found two

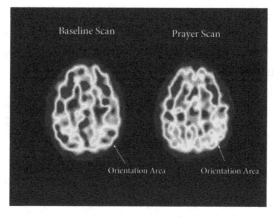

Figure 9.3 Brain scans of Christian centering prayer showing prefrontal regions. From Andrew Newberg.

particularly relevant findings. The nuns were found to have increased activity in the prefrontal cortex associated with the increased focus of attention during the centering prayer (Figure 9.3).

The nuns also had decreased activity in the parietal lobe, consistent with the blurring of the boundary between the self and God and associated with the feeling of deeply connecting with God. In addition, since centering prayer is a verbally based practice, the nuns had increased activity in the language areas, which is distinguished from other, nonverbal, practices that involve elements such as visualization of sacred objects or attention to the breath (Figure 9.4).

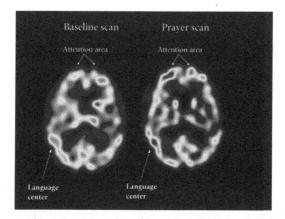

Figure 9.4 Brain scans of Christian centering prayer showing language regions. From Andrew Newberg.

Such findings, along with the other neuroimaging findings described previously, support the notion that there is a complex neurobiological pattern associated with numinous experiences. As we shall see in the chapters to come, this pattern of neuroimaging findings shares certain similarities with other spiritual experiences and has certain unique features.

Conclusion

Numinous experiences, involving the presence of God or divinity, are among the most prevalent and impactful spiritual experiences. While it is somewhat difficult to differentiate between beliefs about and experiences of God, intensely altered states of consciousness involving the presence of God do occur. Some psychiatric disorders, such as schizophrenia and mania, can include religious or spiritual content related to numinous experiences—but most numinous experiences are positive. Neuroscience studies show us that there are neural correlates to feeling the presence of God, and that many of these correlates seem to align with the experience of feeling the presence of another human being and establishing an intimate type of relationship. Brain scans have demonstrated that when participants are asked to consider God, areas of the brain important for social processing, or the perception of mind, become active.

References

Azari, N. P., Nickel, J., Wunderlich, G., Niedeggen, M., Hefter, H., Tellmann, L., Herzog, H., Stoerig, P., Birnbacher, D., & Seitz, R. J. (2001). Neural correlates of religious experience: Brain activity and religious experience. *European Journal of Neuroscience, 13*(8), 1649–1652. https://doi.org/10.1046/j.0953-816x.2001.01527.x

Barrett, J. L. (2007). Cognitive science of religion: What is it and why is it? *Religion Compass, 1*(6), 768–786.

Beauregard, M., & Paquette, V. (2006). Neural correlates of a mystical experience in Carmelite nuns. *Neuroscience Letters, 405,* 186–190.

Benson, H., & Klipper, M. Z. (1975). *The relaxation response* (p. 240). New York: Morrow.

Bering, J. M. (2002). The existential theory of mind. *Review of General Psychology, 6*(1), 3–24.

Buber, M. (1937). *I and thou* (W. Kaufman, Trans.) New York: Scribner.

Byrd, K. R., Lear, D., & Schwenka, S. (2000). Mysticism as a predictor of subjective well-being. *International Journal for the Psychology of Religion, 10*(4), 259–269.

Cotton, S., Zebracki, K., Rosenthal, S. L., Tsevat, J., & Drotar, D. (2006). Religion/spirituality and adolescent health outcomes: A review. *Journal of Adolescent Health, 38,* 472–480.

Ellison, C. G., & Fan, D. (2008). Daily spiritual experiences and psychological well-being among U.S. adults. *Social Indicators Research, 88*, 247–271.

Gray, K., Jenkins, A. C., Heberlein, A. S., & Wegner, D. M. (2011). Distortions of mind perception in psychopathology. *Proceedings of the National Academy of Sciences of the United States of America, 108*(2), 477–479.

Hagerty, B. B. (2009). *Fingerprints of God: The search for the science of spirituality.* Penguin.

James, W. (1896/1984). *On exceptional mental states: The 1896 Lowell lectures.* University of Massachusetts Press.

James, W. (1902/2009). The varieties of religious experience: A study in human nature. *eBooks@Adelaide.* https://csrs.nd.edu/assets/59930/williams_1902.pdf

Kapogiannis, D., Barbey, A. K., Su, M., Zamboni, G., Krueger, F., & Grafman, J. (2009). Cognitive and neural foundations of religious belief. *Proceedings of the National Academy of Sciences, 106*(12), 4876–4881.

Kass, J. D., Friedman, R., Leserman, J., Zuttermeister, P.C., & Benson, H. (1991). Health outcomes and a new index of spiritual experience. *Journal for the Scientific Study of Religion, 30*(2), 203–211.

King, J., & Trimble, J. E. (2013). The spiritual and sacred among North American Indians and Alaska Natives: Mystery, wholeness, and connectedness in a relational world. In K. I. Pargament, J. J. Exline, & J. W. Jones (Eds.), *APA handbook of psychology, religion and spirituality (Vol. 1): Context, theory and research* (pp. 565–580). American Psychological Association.

Koenig, H. G. (2011). Schizophrenia and other psychotic disorders. In J. R. Peteet, F. G. Lu, & W. E. Narrow (Eds.), *Religious and spiritual issues in psychiatric diagnosis: A research agenda for DSM-V.* American Psychiatric Pub.

Koenig, H. G., Peteet, J. R., & VanderWeele, T. J. (2020). Religion and psychiatry: Clinical applications. *BJPsych Advances, 26*(5), 273–281.

Lakens, D. (2021). The practical alternative to the p value is the correctly used p value. *Perspectives on Psychological Science, 16*(3), 639–648.

Lau, E., McClintock, C. H., Graziosi, M., Nakkana, A., Garcia, A., & Miller, L. (2020). Content analysis of spiritual life in contemporary USA, India and China. *Religions, 11*, 286. https://doi.org/10.3390/rel11060286

Luhrmann, T. M. (2012). *When God talks back: Understanding the American evangelical relationship with God.* Knopf.

Meyer, G. J., Finn, S. E., Eyde, L. D., Kay, G. G., Moreland, K. L., Dies, R. R., . . . Reed, G. M. (2001). Psychological testing and psychological assessment: A review of evidence and issues. *American Psychologist, 56*(2), 128.

Miller, L., Balodis, I. M., McClintock, C. H., Xu, J., Lacadie, C. M., Sinha, R., & Potenza, M. N. (2019). Neural correlates of personalized spiritual experiences. *Cerebral Cortex, 29*(6), 2331–2338. https://doi.org/10.1093/cercor/bhy102

Miner, M., Dowson, M., & Malone, K. (2014). Attachment to God, psychological need satisfaction, and psychological well-being among Christians. *Journal of Psychology and Theology, 42*(4), 326–342.

Mohandas, E. (2008). Neurobiology of spirituality. *Mens Sana Monographs, 6*(1), 63.

Newberg, A., Pourdehnad, M., Alavi, A., & d'Aquili, E. (2003). Cerebral blood flow during meditative prayer: Preliminary findings and methodological issues. *Perceptual and Motor Skills, 97*, 625–630.

Otto, R. (1917). *The Idea of the Holy*, trans. by John W. Harvey. New York: Galaxy Book.

Pargament, K., Lomax, J., Mcgee, J., & Fang, Q. (2014). Sacred moments in psychotherapy from the perspectives of mental health providers and patients. *Spirituality in Clinical Practice, 1*(4), 248–262.

Peteet, J. R., Lu, F. G., & Narrow, W. E. (2011). *Religious and spiritual issues in psychiatric diagnosis: A research agenda for DSM-V*. American Psychiatric Pub.

Siddle, R., Haddock, G., Tarrier, N., & Faragher, E. B. (2002). Religious delusions in patients admitted to hospital with schizophrenia. *Social Psychiatry and Psychiatric Epidemiology, 37*(3), 130–138.

Teresa, S. (1588/1979). *The interior castle*. Paulist Press.

Underwood, L. G., & Teresi, J. A. (2002). The daily spiritual experience scale: Development, theoretical description, reliability, exploratory factor analysis, and preliminary construct validity using health-related data. *Annals of Behavioral Medicine, 24*, 22–33.

Wegner, D. M., & Gray, K. (2017). *The mind club: Who thinks, what feels, and why it matters*. Penguin.

Wilt, J. A., Pargament, K. I., & Exline, J. J. (2019). The transformative power of the sacred: Social, personal, and religious/spiritual antecedents and consequents of sacred moments during a religious/spiritual struggle. *Psychology of Religion and Spirituality, 11*(3), 233–246.

Wong, S., Pargament, K. I., & Faigin, C. A. (2018). Sustained by the sacred: Religious and spiritual factors for resilience in adulthood and aging. In *Resilience in aging* (pp. 191–214). Springer, Cham.

10

Revelatory Experiences

Voices, Visions, and Epiphanies

In 1971, David Lukoff was just 23 years old when he dropped out of his graduate program in anthropology at Harvard. He gave away all of his possessions and began traveling around the country, staying with friends. One day, looking in the mirror, he saw that parts of his body seemed to be glowing and the thought came to him that he was somehow related through reincarnation to both Buddha and Jesus Christ. Over the next week, he heard the voices of various religious leaders (Buddha and Christ), philosophers (Locke and Hobbes), artists (Bob Dylan and Cat Stevens), and other scholars (Freud and Margaret Mead). He wrote the results of these conversations down into what was to become a new "holy book," which he sent out to family and friends. Based on their concern, Lukoff was committed to a psychiatric hospital (Lukoff, 2015).

At this point of his story, one might be tempted to feel a sense of sympathy and sadness at the delusions of a confused young man. But Lukoff's story does not end there. Lukoff began participating in a number of different therapeutic processes to better understand his experience, and as he did this he believed that many parts of his experience were delusory. Eventually, he came to see his experience as complicated, yet still among the most important and meaningful of his life—despite, and even perhaps because of, the fact that he spent time in a psychiatric hospital. He came to see that this part of his experience helps him to better empathize with people going through similar experiences. Lukoff became a clinical psychologist and contributed to the scientific understanding of the hazy boundary between pathological and positive spiritual experiences. Decades later, he contributed the previously mentioned *Diagnostic and Statistical Manual of Mental Disorders* (*DSM*; American Psychiatric Association, 2013) category "religious or spiritual problem," which refers to psychological troubles stemming from joining or leaving a religion (Lukoff et al., 1992).

The Varieties of Spiritual Experience. David B. Yaden and Andrew B. Newberg, Oxford University Press. © David Yaden and Andrew Newberg 2022. DOI: 10.1093/oso/9780190665678.003.0010

Like Lukoff, the founders of most of the world's major religions heard voices and saw visions. Moses received the Ten Commandments from God on Mt. Sinai. Jesus heard the voice of God during his baptism, which he took as his calling to begin his ministry. Mohammad received the Koran from a voice he referred to as the archangel, Gabriel. Arjuna, a main figure in the mythological Hindu text the Mahabharata, described extended conversations with the god Krishna, about whether or not he should fight in a war. During his enlightenment, Buddha heard the voice of a demon called Mara who tempted him from his goal with worldly pleasures. Other important historical figures had similar experiences—recall that the philosopher Socrates described a *daimon*, or voice of wisdom, that spoke to him and kept him from acting unethically. Innumerable other prophets and holy people have also described hearing voices—Joan of Arc, to name just one well-known example among many, both heard and saw angels.

Yet now most people would be alarmed if a loved one told them that they were "hearing voices" or "seeing things" that other people cannot hear or see. In popular parlance, these phrases are almost synonymous with serious mental illness. But this is precisely what occurs during *revelatory experiences*, defined here as *voices, visions, or epiphanies that seem to come from a source beyond the self.* How can the fact that so many venerated historical figures heard voices be squared with the modern assumption of psychopathology?

Here are some items related to revelatory experiences as described in our survey:

- I felt that I received information from beyond my usual sense of self about what I should do with my life.
- I felt that I received my calling in life from a source beyond my usual sense of self.
- I felt called to a particular life path by a force beyond my usual sense of self.

James on Revelatory Experiences

James cited several examples of hearing voices, from both biblical examples and his contemporaries. He returned to the New Testament story of Saint Paul on the road to Damascus. Here is the key passage from Saint Paul, whose name was Saul before his conversion to Christianity:

Now as he journeyed he approached Damascus, and suddenly a light from heaven flashed about him. And he fell to the ground and heard a voice saying to him, "Saul, Saul, why do you persecute me?" And he said, "Who are you, Lord?" And he said, "I am Jesus, whom you are persecuting; but rise and enter the city, and you will be told what you are to do." (Acts 9:3–6, cited in Proudfoot, 1985, p. 115)

James also mentioned the story of Saint Augustine, a Christian thinker and writer of central importance to the history of Christianity in general, but especially Catholicism. In the midst of what seems like a nervous breakdown or crisis of faith, Augustine's revelatory experience converted him to Christianity:

He heard a voice in the garden say, "Sume, lege" (take and read), and opening the Bible at random, saw the text, "not in chambering and wantonness," etc., which seemed directly sent to his address, and laid the inner storm to rest forever. (James, 1902/2009, p. 131)

James also included several accounts from his contemporaries of individuals who heard voices with religious content. For example, he included one experience in which someone heard specific words spoken:

The very instant I heard my father's cry calling unto me, my heart bounded in recognition. I ran, I stretched forth my arms, I cried aloud, "Here, here I am, my Father." Oh, happy child, what should I do? "Love me," answered my God. (James, 1902/2009, p. 55)

James's view of the experience of hearing voices drew from the psychoanalytic tradition, of which he was usually more dismissive. He referred to the "wonderful explorations" of Freud and his mentors (e.g., Binet, Breur, and Charcot) "of the subliminal of patients with hysteria" which had "revealed to us whole systems of underground life" (James, 1902/2009, p. 179). For James, the voices heard in these experiences derived from these "systems of underground life" in the mind—or one's unconscious. James wrote: " . . . one's ordinary fields of consciousness are liable to incursions from it of which the subject does not guess the source, and which, therefore, take for him the form of . . . hallucinations of sight or hearing" (James, 1902/2009, p. 178).

Other psychologists since James wrote extensively about hearing voices, though generally from a perspective of identifying the psychopathological process that underlies it. One exception to this trend is Jung, who himself experienced revelatory experiences and wrote about his own experience of hearing a divine voice:

> The voice . . . always pronounces an authoritative declaration or command, either of astonishing common sense and truth, or of profound philosophic allusion. It is nearly always a definite statement, usually coming toward the end of a dream, and it is, as a rule, so clear and convincing that the dreamer finds no argument against it. It has, indeed, so much the character of indisputable truth that it often appears as the final and absolutely valid summing up of a long unconscious deliberation and weighing of arguments. (Jung, 1938, p. 45)

Jung saw a positive potential in such mental states. He wrote: "I have to admit the fact that the unconscious mind is capable at times of assuming an intelligence and purposiveness which are superior to actual conscious insight" (Jung, 1938, p. 45). Here again we see an experience that is generally pathologized by psychologists, but for which Jung saw the positive potential and about which James tended to describe from a more neutral perspective based on the outcomes in a given case.

A Source Beyond Self

As with other varieties of spiritual experience, it may be easy to suspect that such mental states remain historical curiosities. But this is not the case. Luhrmann's work with American evangelical Christians showed that revelatory experiences are still common. She related the story of Stanley, a 10-year-old child whose parents had just gotten divorced:

> I woke up in the middle of the night at some point, and there was this overwhelming [sense] of peace and calm. There were these words that just kept coming to my mind, over and over again: "I will never leave you, I will always be with you." Just sort of over and over again. I have never felt that way before and then rarely felt that way afterward. (Luhrmann, 2012, p. 287)

Most people understand that revelatory experiences go well beyond the kind of internal monologue and daydreams that, for most of us, constantly chatter in the background of our awareness. Revelatory experiences are not merely the kind of internal monologue that delineates our "to-do" lists or the songs that we silently sing to ourselves. In other words, one's usual stream of consciousness (a phrase, remember, coined by William James) is not in itself a revelatory experience because these thoughts feel as if they come from one's self. Revelatory experiences seem to come from somewhere—or someone— else (e.g., God.). Some people who hear voices even reflexively turn their heads to see who is speaking because the voice seems to come from someone standing nearby. Others hear voices in their own minds, but they report that the tone of the voice and the content of what it says seems so alien that it may just as well be spoken by someone else.

Similarly, visions (imagery or symbols) can span from full hallucinations perceived to exist outside of one's body to thoughts that seem to come from elsewhere. Epiphanies involve more abstract or complex content, such as a solution to a problem. These, too, when they seem to come from some source beyond one's self, could be considered a revelatory experience. Here, as with other varieties of spiritual experiences, the previously mentioned "orgasm test" is instructive—if you're not sure whether or not you had one, then you probably did not.

A voice speaking while no one else is present or a voice inside one's own mind can be uncanny. While spiritual experiences often seem to suppress one's capacity to question the experience, many people still report actively questioning the meaning or source of a voice. As anthropologist Luhrmann related, the biblical character of Samuel was confused about the voice he heard until he decided that it was God who was speaking to him (Luhrmann, 2012, p. 334). In some cases, the voice may even directly address its hearer by name. For example, in the Old Testament story, Moses saw a bush on fire that called out to him, saying: "Moses, Moses." The bush (i.e., God) then proceeded to tell him how he would lead his people out of Egypt. There is an interesting theological problem that has to do with the presumed origin of voices that people receive in such cases. In the previous example, the individual perceived the voice to be from God; however, some religious individuals might argue that such voices are actually produced by the Devil.

A once well-known theory of consciousness prominently involved hearing voices. Psychologist Julian Jaynes's book, *The Origin of Consciousness in the Breakdown of the Bicameral Mind* (1976/2000) articulated the theory that humans used to constantly experience what we now feel to be our thoughts as inner voices issuing commands. These voices were, according to Jaynes, interpreted as coming from a leader in the society or from a god. Modern society consists of a different environment for brain development, leading people now to instead interpret most of their thoughts as belonging to their own selves. For Jaynes, the exceptions to experiencing our thoughts as our own in modern society are those with schizophrenia, mystics, and some artists who are still able to hear inner voices as coming from beyond ourselves in the way that our ancestors did.

Jaynes's interesting, though highly speculative, theory is largely unfalsifiable, as the truth of the matter lies in the long-dead heads of our ancestors. This theory does, however, underscore the important role of culture in the inner voices that one hears and how they are interpreted.

Sensory Overrides

Anthropologist Tanya Luhrmann offered a more modern explanation of voices with the concept of "sensory overrides," or instances in which one's perception of their experience differs from their physical circumstances. She takes a learning-centered approach that emphasizes the roles of both culture and expectation; that culture should play an important role in such experiences makes intuitive sense. People raised in an Islamic context tend not to have experiences of Buddha, for example. One learns from one's culture, and particularly one's religion, about how to interpret experiences like a voice speaking in one's mind.

The important influence of expectation on experience requires some brief explanation of how perception works. The naïve view of perception suggests that it works like a video camera. That is, if you were to look up from these words, it could seem as if your visual and auditory system is providing an entirely accurate, faithful "recording" of the world. But this impression, tempting as it is, is not the case. Only a relatively small region of the visual field is highly attuned to one's surroundings at any one time. The rest of the scene is held in memory and generated through what the mind *expects* will be there. Thus, many of the things you think you see clearly are actually reconstructions built by your mind. Thus, expectation plays an important role in perception.

This view is supported by observations of the brain's structure. In *Surfing Uncertainty* (2015), philosopher of cognitive science Andy Clark described a view of the brain that is constantly filling in the details of perception and trying to anticipate what will happen next. He illustrated this point by describing part of the anatomy and physiology of the eye. The eyes and the brain have a number of circuits connecting them—information from the eye leads to the brain (to convey visual impressions) and then commands from the brain lead back to the eye (i.e., about where to look). However, and here is the interesting twist, there are many more pathways leading down to the eye than up to the brain. The implication is that much of our visual field may be created by expectation. This is often put in terms of "bottom-up" as opposed to "top-down" processing. Bottom-up processing emphasizes the data coming to the brain through sensory systems, whereas top-down processing emphasizes the role of beliefs and expectation on the perception of sensory data. Both processes are intimately involved in perception.

Luhrmann's sensory override theory takes these observations about perception and applies them to subjective experiences like hearing inner voices. According to her theory, one learns from one's culture about the kinds of things one might hear from a disembodied voice, then, at least on some level, expects to hear them. Finally, under certain conditions where uncertainty is high—due to the strangeness of either one's external or internal circumstances—this expectation becomes a perception. Here, Luhrmann described just how common these experiences are:

> The first finding about sensory overrides is how remarkably common they are. Our initial questionnaires asked our subjects a simple question: "Have you ever heard an audible voice when you were alone, or a voice that no one else present could hear, like someone calling your name?" Nearly half of them said yes. Half. (Luhrmann, 2012, p. 209)

Such experiences are not only rather common, but also some religious communities actively seek them out. Luhrmann described particular practices designed to help trigger a revelatory experience. According to her, these practices essentially supercharge cultural learning and expectation. She provided one account of an individual who bought a kind of how-to book for hearing voices:

The book I picked up in a weekend course on how to speak with God, *Dialogue with God*, was the clearest in laying out this progression. The first step is learning what God's voice sounds like when spoken within (reading your Bible so that you recognize the kinds of things God says and when he says them). The second is knowing how to go to a quiet place and still one's own thoughts and emotions. The third is attending carefully in the mind, and to images and thoughts and dreams. The fourth is writing out the dialogue, so that it is clear, external, and remembered: real. (Luhrmann, 2012, p. 159)

There are some cases in which one becomes less an interlocuter with a voice—but rather a conduit. That is, in some cases, one seems to speak the words of the voice without stopping to consider their meaning. The words that a person speaks during such an experience are often disowned afterward. One might say that the words that they spoke were not their own. Some practices seek to induce the experience of a divine voice seeming to speak through someone. These are not as esoteric as they may seem, either. A number of Christian churches in the United States regularly practice speaking in tongues, called *glossolalia*. The practice is fairly widespread; there are videos of several contemporary U.S. senators participating in this practice. In this ritual, God is invited to speak through the worshipper. In such experiences, individuals do not so much hear a voice as speak in a "language" that does not correspond to any known language, and some researchers have speculated is meant to approximate the sounds of both laughing and crying. We describe some of the underlying brain changes involved in these experiences further in this chapter.

Visions

Audible words are not the only form of communication that can occur in revelatory experiences. For some people, the experience is primarily visual. In the Lau et al. (2020) study of cross-cultural spiritual experience narratives, 27% of U.S. narratives, 16% of Indian narratives, and 20% of Chinese narratives contained a reference to some kind of "apparitional" or visual experience. Again, there was no clear distinction here between a vision or hallucination that appears to be in one's environment or an inner image that is part of one's own mental life. The essence of the revelatory experience involves perceiving an image that seems to come from beyond one's self, from an unseen reality of some kind, that other people cannot see. Thus, visions are those symbols, signs, or images that come as a kind of communication from a source beyond the self.

The Roman emperor Constantine provided a well-known historical example of a vision. During a battle to determine who would rule the whole of Rome, Constantine reportedly saw a vision of an enormous cross made out of light above the sun with Greek words proclaiming "Through this sign, you shall conquer." Constantine did, in fact, go on to conquer Rome and declared Christianity its official religion, providing a foundation for Christianity's eventual spread through Europe.

James provided an account from one of his contemporaries of a vision that prominently featured a kind of divine light. In this case, the light did not appear to derive from the sun or any obvious usual source of light:

> All at once the Glory of God shone upon and round about me in a manner almost marvelous. . . . A light perfectly ineffable shone in my soul, that almost prostrated me on the ground. . . . This light seemed like the brightness of the sun in every direction. It was too intense for the eyes. (James, 1902/ 2009, p. 191)

Visions are also reported in contemporary contexts. Luhrmann provided a case of an Evangelical woman called Aisha who saw a hand in the sky:

> As I was praying, I looked up, and it was cloudy and the sun shone through the clouds, and it looked like a hand. . . . Everything was very intimate. I remember walking into the water, and I saw myself doing it. It's the most mystical thing that's ever happened to me. By far it's the most spiritual experience I've ever had. . . I was really scared, really really scared, but afterward I was so happy. (Luhrmann, 2012, p. 121)

James's take on visions was similar to his view of voices. He believed that they emerge from the "margins of consciousness." Visions, then, are part of one's own mental processes—just parts that are usually hidden from conscious awareness. In fact, these parts are so hidden from our usual awareness that they seem altogether different.

James also focused in particular on the experience of seeing an otherworldly light, as the report of light makes a frequent appearance in visions. For this, he specifically invoked the concept of seeing lights, called "photisms":

There is one form of sensory automatism which possibly deserves special notice on account of its frequency. I refer to hallucinatory or pseudo-hallucinatory luminous phenomena, photisms, to use the term of the psychologists. Saint Paul's blinding heavenly vision seems to have been a phenomenon of this sort; so does Constantine's cross in the sky. (James, 1902/2009, p. 191)

For Luhrmann, visions are another form of "hallucination" that, just like voices, are relatively common and can be explained through her concept of sensory overrides. She reported that when she surveyed a population about how many hallucinations they have had—about 14% of the sample reported a "visual, auditory, or tactile" hallucination. Of those, the vast majority (84%) contained some visual element (Luhrmann, 2012, p. 238). Also, similar to voices, she described guidebooks that aim to instruct individuals on how to see a vision. She wrote: "These writings do imply an important psychological hypothesis: that mental imagery practice will lead to visionary experience" (Luhrmann, 2012, p. 171).

There are also simple techniques that allow individuals to experience visual imagery. Perhaps the most ancient form of inducing revelatory experience is through the traditional practice of yoga, which in Patañjali's system involves eight hierarchical practices (or *eight limbs*) of progressive withdrawal from external stimulation, increasing focus on and control of the body and breath, and eventually achieving a single-pointed consciousness or awareness where the distinction between subject and object disappear, often called absorption or *samadhi* (Braud, 2008). As a yogi proceeds through the eight limbs, the yogi is purported to gain powers, or *siddhis,* which include but are not limited to: "a vision of perfected ones . . . spontaneous intuitive flashes based in hearing, touching, seeing, tasting, and smelling" (Braud, 2008, p. 229). It is important to note that Patañjali warns that these siddhis are ultimately a distraction from achieving a state of absorption (samadhi, which is likely closer to the mystical experiences described in Chapter 12) and that they should be largely ignored.

Another reliable trigger of revelatory experience, particularly visions, is the use of a sensory isolation tank (Hood et al., 2009). Isolation tanks are environments that deprive individuals of nearly all sensory input. Typically, they involve room temperature, heavily salinized (salted) water tanks that allow people to float without effort (as is the case in any body of water with a high salt content, like the Dead Sea). The sensory deprivation tank is kept dark and is almost entirely soundproof. This allows people to have an uninterrupted experience of their own mind and body. The imagery people see in isolation tanks can include light, geometric forms, cartoon figures, and, notably, religious figures (Hood et al., 2009, p. 278).

Other methods can also trigger visual imagery. Psychedelics are a prominent example. Research has compared the imagery seen in isolation tanks with that seen while using psychedelics, and the result is that the various categories of imagery are experienced at roughly similar rates. For example, religious imagery is quite common in the midst of psychedelic experiences, even when individuals do not classify their own experience as "religious" (Masters & Houston, 1966, cited in Hood et al., 2009, p. 285).

Epiphanies and Callings

Voices and visions are quite concrete and specific; with epiphanies, the content becomes more abstract. Epiphanies can contain complicated content, especially in cases in which the epiphany provides solutions for difficult personal or professional problems. Here, as previously discussed, it is essential that such experiences seem to derive from a source beyond the self during a substantially altered state of consciousness in order for them to count as revelatory experiences. The subcategory of epiphanies is useful for those instances in which the content seems more complex or abstract than hearing a voice or seeing a vision.

Sometimes individuals use words like I "saw" or "received" the answer in a more metaphorical manner (as in when one "sees the solution"). James provided some accounts of individuals who described "conversations" with God. The answers or replies described, however, do not seem to be quite auditory or visual—yet information appears to be received nonetheless. To illustrate this, one individual included in *The Varieties* wrote:

> God is quite real to me. I talk to him and often get answers. Thoughts sudden and distinct from any I have been entertaining come to my mind after asking God for his direction. (James, 1902/2009, p. 56)

Here, the individual is receiving information from beyond the self (i.e., from God), but it seems to come in the form of a thought. It is not specified whether the thought was in auditory or visual form, so we can imagine that the information may be more abstract than these concrete categories of perception.

Other examples provide realizations or understandings that seem even less obviously derived from any one particular statement of a voice. For example, psychiatrist R. M. Bucke, author of *Cosmic Consciousness* (which James cited several times in *The Varieties*), describes an experience that exemplifies the abstract complexity of the information that can be contained in an epiphany. Even though the author explicitly called the experience a vision, and it involved a feeling of presence, the complex nature of the information conveyed in the experience made it appear more like what we refer to as an epiphany:

> Like a flash there is presented to his consciousness a conception (a vision) of the meaning and drift of the universe. He does not come to believe merely; but he sees and knows that the cosmos, which to the self-conscious mind seems made up of dead matter, is in fact far otherwise—is in truth a living presence. He sees that life which is in man is eternal . . . that the foundation principle of the world is what we call love. . . . Especially does he obtain such a conception of the whole—as makes the old attempts mentally to grasp the universe and its meaning petty and ridiculous. (Bucke, 1923, p. 73)

This experience appears to convey a particular view about the meaning and nature of the universe. It is not personalized information. For Bucke, it was a revelation about the truth of the universe, but it does not appear to be tied to a particular sensory system.

Some epiphanies (like Bucke's) are abstract, but others can be quite personal. Some experiences can even change one's life in a particular way. One special form of revelatory experience, which occurs when the content of the revelation refers to the direction of one's life, is known as a *calling experience*. The items that represented revelatory experience in our factor analysis ended up mostly representing what we might refer to as calling experiences. These experiences are worth special mention due to the influence they can have on the course of one's entire life.

It's a rare person who, when choosing their vocation, creates a large spreadsheet complete with skills, strengths, interests, possible occupations, and realistic opportunities. (Note: While some readers will have indeed done this, they will most likely be economists or future economists . . .) More often, the route to one's life work is more winding and filled with chance occurrences. Additionally, a not insignificant portion of people point to single moments as "turning points" on the way to their vocation. When these vocational turning points come in the form of substantially altered states of consciousness that involve information that seems to come from beyond the self, we can all this subtype of revelatory experience a calling experience.

Calling experiences can come in the form of an epiphany that conveys information about their lives' work should be. In the book *Being Called: Scientific, Secular, and Sacred Perspectives* (Yaden et al., 2015), a number of scientists and scholars representing a wide spectrum of belief systems (religious, spiritual but not religious, agnostic, and atheist), described distinct experiences that led them to their current vocations. In many cases, these were revelatory experiences containing some information about what one should do.

For example, psychologist Martin Seligman, one of the founders of positive psychology, reported an experience of this type. After a conversation over lunch with psychiatrist Aaron Beck about his future in research, whether to pursue a career conducting animal or human studies, Seligman described a "numinous dream" in which he received information about what he would do with his life:

> I find myself in the Guggenheim Museum slowly walking up the curving ramp. There are rooms off to the right every few paces and in the rooms people are playing with cards. I ask, "why is everyone playing with cards?" Whereupon the roof of the museum opens and the godhead appears.... He says—unforgettably, "Seligman, at least you are starting to ask the right questions." (Seligman cited in Yaden et al., 2015, p. 4)

There is some evidence that calling experiences really do tend to lead to more personally meaningful work. Psychologists Brian Dik, Ryan Duffy, and Michael Steger measured what we call the "transcendent sense" of callings. According to this view, a calling consists of "a transcendent summons, experienced as originating beyond the self" (Duffy et al., 2011). This form of calling is also associated with higher work motivation and more meaning in life.

Lukoff, whose story we discussed at the beginning of this chapter, described his revelatory experience as the event that led him to his life's work. Lukoff wrote: "Many individuals feel an inner longing, perhaps a Calling, to find a sense of direction, for renewal after crisis, or discover their true life path" (Lukoff, 2015, p. 176). More research is required to learn how frequently these experiences result in one finding personally meaningful work and how to integrate such experiences in a sensible and beneficial way.

Positive and Pathological Revelatory Experiences

There has long been a concern that individuals who are hearing voices or "seeing things" are experiencing symptoms of a mental illness. This may be the case for revelatory experience more than maybe any other form of spiritual experience. One classic psychological study took advantage of the common association between hearing voices and psychopathology to dramatic effect. In what is called the "pseudopatient experiment," psychologist David Rosenhan (1973) enlisted several colleagues to check themselves into psychiatric institutions with one complaint: that they were hearing voices (though they were in fact not). If asked to describe the content of the voices, they were told to reply that the voices said words like "empty" and "hollow," without further elaboration. They were told to answer all of the other questions as they would from the perspective of a "normal" person (someone not currently suffering from mental illness) and to act otherwise entirely as they normally would. (Note: Of historical interest, psychologist Martin Seligman was a participant in Rosenhan's study.)

Despite being entirely healthy and answering all other questions normally, the single report of hearing a voice was enough for all of these individuals to be admitted for at least a couple of weeks, with most of them being diagnosed with schizophrenia. Rosenhan argued that the study demonstrated the problems with psychiatric diagnostic criteria. However, most psychologists now agree that the study merely showed that it is difficult to tell patients suffering from actual mental illness from those who are *faking* a mental illness. For our purposes, it shows that merely mentioning that one is hearing voices—with no other apparent symptoms of mental illness—is enough to be admitted to psychiatric care. It demonstrates the close association our society has between hearing voices and mental illness.

It is worth emphasizing that there is good reason for this association on the part of healthcare professionals. Hearing voices, particularly those that seem to keep running commentary on one's thoughts and actions or hearing several voices speaking at once—is indeed a reliable sign of the onset of schizophrenia. Schizophrenia is an often debilitating and degenerative form of mental illness that usually manifests in late adolescence or early adulthood.

Hearing voices can also occur episodically in other mood disorders, such as major depression or bipolar disorder that can be disturbing or debilitating. For this reason, many have argued that the healthcare professionals in the pseudopatient study were actually correct to admit these pseudopatients for observation.

If an individual hearing voices is suffering from the onset of schizophrenia or another mental disorder, then it is important for them to receive care from a healthcare professional. In a recent longitudinal study of 1,800 adolescents from the general population, it was found that the longer that psychotic features such as auditory hallucinations persist over time, the more likely an individual is to experience negative outcomes, including delusions, emotional disturbance, and increased risk for clinical psychosis (De Loore et al., 2011). Individuals who hear voices or see visions have also been shown to be at greater risk for suicide (Bromet et al., 2017). Even in a condition such as Alzheimer disease, researchers have found that hallucinations and delusions are related to worse outcomes, such as cognitive and functional decline, higher rates of institutionalization, and higher mortality (Scarmeas et al., 2005).

In the vast majority of cases individuals hearing voices or seeing visions are not dangerous to other people; however, in some cases when severe thought disorganization or impairment occurs, individuals can endanger themselves or others, necessitating emergency psychiatric care. The *DSM* includes hearing voices and seeing visions in several categories. For example, the *DSM-5* category for schizophrenia requires two of the following symptoms:

(1) delusions
(2) hallucinations
(3) disorganized speech (e.g., frequent derailment or incoherence)
(4) grossly disorganized or catatonic behavior
(5) negative symptoms (i.e., affective flattening, alogia, or avolition)

Voices and visions can also be associated with dissociative disorders. For example, the *DSM* states regarding individuals suffering from dissociative disorder: "Such individuals may also report perceptions of voices (e.g., a child's voice; crying; the voice of a spiritual being" (American Psychiatric Association, 2013, p. 293).

Common psychotic delusions that are not experienced as frank hallucinations are called "thought insertion" and share some phenomenological overlap with revelatory experiences. Thought insertion refers to a delusion that a particular thought, idea, or revelation was inserted into your mind by someone or something outside of one's self. In the case of paranoia, this may take the form of the delusion that the government or a nefarious agency is "inserting ideas" into one's mind.

The *DSM* does, however, make exceptions related to cultural context. It notes that if an experience is "normal," given the cultural context, then the voice need not be treated as pathological. However, this is complicated by Luhrmann's findings that hearing voices is normative among a large percentage of American evangelical Christians. Revelatory experiences are in the interesting cultural position of being often assumed pathological, while also being statistically normative.

Additionally, it is important to consider and understand what it means for one to have revelatory experiences *within* their culture, rather than just tolerate the fact that in some cultures these experiences happen. In Bali, "initiatory madness" (p. 14), which resembles psychosis, is often an indication that one is destined to become a traditional healer (or *Balian*) and can be distinguished from mental illness by the "positive nature of the imagery and voices" (p. 23) (Stephen & Suryani, 2000). In Chinese culture, some aspects of religious expression have been regulated by the government (Edgell, 2012); yet, in the study by Lau and colleagues (2020), many people in China endorsed that it was culturally appropriate to experience a relationship involving some communication with deceased ancestors.

Taken together, we've seen that in Western countries, the assumption of psychopathology is often the predominant reaction to individuals claiming to hear voices or see visions. Yet there have also been many individuals, from religious or spiritual leaders to contemporary psychiatrists and psychologists, who pointed to the benefits such experiences can have for some people. Jung wrote, summarizing this view: "If somebody has a vision it doesn't mean that he is necessarily insane. Perfectly normal people can have visions in certain moments" (Jung, 2021, p. 380).

Again, we must refer to James's pragmatic principle. *What are the fruits (outcomes) of the experience?* If the experience causes suffering and dysfunction in one's life, then it may be branded pathological; if it contributes to one's sense of well-being and their functioning in work and family life, then it is viewed as positive. There are also instances in which the experience is culturally normative, with neutral effects on one's mental health.

It is also quite possible to adapt to hearing voices in such a way as to make what was a negative experience become neutral or even positive by normalizing the experience through talking to others about it. One organization doing this work is the Hearing Voices Network. The organization's mission statement reads: "People of all ages and backgrounds can hear voices at some point in their life, for many different reasons. Whilst some are distressed by their experiences, people can—and do—find ways of living with them" (http://www.hearing-voices.org/).

In addition to outcomes, there are often experiential differences between the kinds of voices heard in the context of mental illness such as dissociative disorders and psychosis and those that are supportive of well-being. Luhrmann differentiated the two types as follows:

> It seems, then, that there is good empirical evidence for two different patterns of hallucination-like phenomena in the population. One is the result of a psychotic process associated with schizophrenia and other psychiatric disorders. In this pattern, hallucinations are frequent, extended, and distressing. They are primarily auditory, and they are often accompanied by strange, fixed beliefs (delusions) not shared by other people. . . . Then there is the ordinary, nonpathological pattern in which sensory overrides are rare, brief, and not distressing. (Luhrmann, 2012, p. 242)

In our survey data, we found that revelatory experiences were associated with various mental health outcomes at similar levels to numinous experiences (see Table 10.1).

Further complicating any easy distinctions between pathological and positive, there can be cases in which an individual is suffering from a mental illness but they have an experience that is healing and restorative. Also, voices, visions, and epiphanies convey informational content in a way that separates them from other varieties of spiritual experience. Can the content of these experiences be useful?

The Muses Speak

Revelatory experiences intersect with creativity. How can one disambiguate spiritual experience, psychopathology, and the creative process? We inevitably revert back to James's criteria of looking to outcomes, but outcomes

Table 10.1 Revelatory Experience With Well-Being, Mental
Health, and Faculties of Consciousness

	Revelatory Experience
Well-Being Outcomes	
More positive emotions	.43**
Better personal relationships	.49**
Greater sense of meaning in life	.49**
Mental Health Outcomes	
Depression	−.05
Anxiety	−.13**
Faculties of Consciousness	
Sense of space changed	.32**
Noetic quality	.38**
Sense of time changed	.34**

$*p < .05.$ $**p < .01.$

need not necessarily be limited to mental health or well-being; creativity is one benefit that people frequently report.

Poet Naomi Shihab Nye was traveling with her husband when her poem "Kindness" came to her in the form of what amounts to a revelatory experience. One day during their honeymoon, Nye and her husband returned to their room to find that their luggage had been stolen. While her husband traveled to the next town for replacement travel documents, Nye sat in the town's square, watching people as they passed by. She described the words of her poem coming to her, as if they were "floating across the square" for her to dictate.

Other revelatory experiences that result in creative output are more ambiguous. A number of individuals in the arts report revelatory experiences that fuel their creativity. Some even developed means to make these experiences more frequent. Jung advocated a technique to see visions that he called "active imagination." One way to access a mental state in which voices, visions, and epiphanies would come to him was to sit in a darkened room, close his eyes, and imagine digging a hole in the ground. Then, he would try to imagine the digging process in greater and greater detail while trying, as much as possible, to imagine that he was really digging a hole. After spending some time engaging in this practice, voices and visions would, according to Jung, appear on their own (Jung et al., 2009).

The book *The Creative Process* (Ghiselin, 1985) argued that there is a three-step progression that is common to creative epiphanies. First, there is an immersion period, in which one actively learns as much as possible about a given topic. Second, there is an incubation period, in which one thinks about other topics for some period of time (though contemporary research has complicated this step, showing that it is not necessary or even brief distractions can suffice). Last, there is the revelatory step—in which an idea can present itself fully formed to the conscious mind. There are a number of instances throughout the history of philosophy and science, in addition to the arts, in which an individual received an image or heard a voice that seemed to come from beyond themselves that guided an actual scientific discovery. The third step of this creative process could be what is occurring in some revelatory experiences.

Importantly, just because information is conveyed through a revelatory experience does not mean that it is necessarily true or useful. All information, regardless of where it comes from, should be subjected to critical and ethical analysis. Revelatory experiences are no exception.

Neuroscience

Neurologically, there are several lines of evidence that might help elucidate part of the process involved in revelatory experiences. Our group has performed neuroimaging studies of people speaking in tongues in which individuals felt that how they acted and what they perceived was being guided from outside of their own body and mind—particularly, by the spirit of God (Newberg et al., 2006).

One of the common findings in brain scans is a decrease in frontal lobe function (see Figure 10.1). We would expect that a decrease in frontal lobe function would be associated with a sense of losing purposeful control of a person's actions and a sense of surrendering one's conscious control. In the case of Christians speaking in tongues, they enter a trance state in which they no longer feel in control of what is happening. The vocalizations and the information flowing through them is not perceived as created by their own volition. This lack of purposeful action, and specifically agency, likely contributes to the "spiritual" and revelatory nature of the experience. It feels not only like it comes from outside the person, but also like it comes from something or someone unseen.

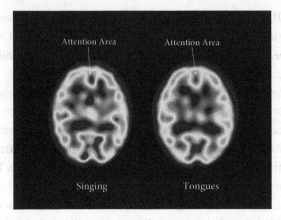

Figure 10.1 On the left is the subject performing gospel singing in English, and on the right, the subject is speaking in tongues. The red areas in the frontal lobe (top of the screen) are markedly reduced while speaking in tongues. You will also notice that the initial asymmetry in the thalamus (the red spot in the middle) is altered during speaking in tongues. From Andrew Newberg.

In addition, people who are speaking in tongues gain new insights into both personal problems and religious or spiritual beliefs. If such information is received, it would seem likely that areas of the brain associated with memory and reality processing are involved. In one of our prior works (Newberg & Waldman, 2017), we made the argument that alterations in the thalamus, a central structure that coordinates brain processes between cortical areas and also between the sensory organs and the brain, might be essential for changing a person's belief system and overall approach to life. There is some evidence that supports altered thalamic function associated with intense spiritual experiences (Newberg & d'Aquili, 2000).

Additionally, we conducted a neuroimaging study that compared a group of successful, or "eminent," creatives across a number of different fields, such as math, music, and comedy. (Note: This was done in collaboration with the Imagination Institute at the University of Pennsylvania, led by Martin Seligman and Scott Barry Kaufman.) We compared these highly creative people to a group of people matched for age and gender balance. We found a similar pattern of brain activity as the study on speaking in tongues. We found that the prefrontal lobe region was less active than other areas of the brain when eminent creators were engaged in creative thinking compared to controls (Chrysikou, Jacial, et al., 2020; Chrysikou, Wertz, et al., 2020).

Overall then, it appears that revelatory experiences are more likely to occur when the frontal lobe is less active and may occur through similar brain processes as creativity.

Conclusion

"Hearing voices" and "seeing things" may be common symptoms of mental illness, but as we have seen in this chapter, the value of these experiences is sometimes more complex. Hearing voices or experiencing hallucinations is a symptom of emerging schizophrenia or other psychotic disorders, so someone reporting these symptoms would probably be advised to see a healthcare provider. However, the majority of instances in which one has visions or hears voices are not related to mental illness. Indeed, many cases result in elevated well-being, more meaning, and, sometimes, even creative breakthroughs. Sometimes such experiences help people find their calling in life. Each of these revelatory experiences is united by the common thread that they involve some kind of communication from a source beyond one's self.

References

American Psychiatric Association. (2013). *Diagnostic and statistical manual of mental disorders (DSM-5).*

Braud, W. G. (2008). Patañjali Yoga and siddhis: Their relevance to parapsychological theory and research. In K. R. Rao, A. C. Paranjpe, & A. K. Dalal (Eds.), Handbook of Indian *psychology* (pp. 217–243). Cambridge University Press India/Foundation Books.

Bromet, E. J., Nock, M. K., Saha, S., Lim, C. C., Aguilar-Gaxiola, S., Al-Hamzawi, A., . . . de Girolamo, G. (2017). Association between psychotic experiences and subsequent suicidal thoughts and behaviors: A cross-national analysis from the World Health Organization World Mental Health Surveys. *JAMA Psychiatry, 74*(11), 1136–1144.

Bucke, R. M. (1923). *Cosmic consciousness: A study in the evolution of the human mind.* EP Dutton.

Chrysikou, E. G., Jacial, C., Yaden, D. B., van Dam, W., Kaufman, S. B., Conklin, C. J., . . . Newberg, A. B. (2020). Differences in brain activity patterns during creative idea generation between eminent and non-eminent thinkers. *NeuroImage, 220*(15), 117011.

Chrysikou, E. G., Wertz, C., Yaden, D. B., Kaufman, S. B., Bacon, D., Wintering, N. A., . . . Newberg, A. B. (2020). Differences in brain morphometry associated with creative performance in high-and average-creative achievers. *NeuroImage, 218*, 116921.

Clark, A. (2015). *Surfing uncertainty: Prediction, action, and the embodied mind.* Oxford University Press.

De Loore, E., Gunther, N., Drukker, M., Feron, Sabbe, B., Deboutte, D., van Os, J., & Myin-Germeys, I. (2011). Persistence and outcome of auditory hallucinations in adolescence: A longitudinal general population study of 1800 individuals. *Schizophrenia Research, 127,* 252–256.

Duffy, R. D., Dik, B. J., & Steger, M. F. (2011). Calling and work-related outcomes: Career commitment as a mediator. *Journal of Vocational Behavior, 78*(2), 210–218.

Edgell, P. 2012. A cultural sociology of religion: New directions. *Annual Review of Sociology, 38,* 247–265.

Ghiselin, B. (Ed.). (1985). *The creative process: Reflections on the invention in the arts and sciences.* University of California Press.

Hood, R. W., Hill, P. C., & Spilka, B. (2009). *The psychology of religion: An empirical approach.* Guilford Press.

James, W. (1902/2009). *The varieties of religious experience: A study in human nature.* eBooks@Adelaide. https://csrs.nd.edu/assets/59930/williams_1902.pdf

Jaynes, J. (2000). *The origin of consciousness in the breakdown of the bicameral mind.* Houghton Mifflin Harcourt. (Original work published 1976)

Jung, C. G. (1938). *Psychology and religion.* Yale University Press.

Jung, C. G. (2021). CG Jung Letters, Volume 2: 1951–1961. Princeton University Press.

Jung, C. G., Shamdasani, S. E., Kyburz, M. T., & Peck, J. T. (2009). *The red book: Liber novus.* Norton.

Lau, E., McClintock, C., Graziosi, M., Nakkana, A., & Garcia, A. (2020). Content analysis of spiritual life in contemporary USA, India, and China. *Religions, 11,* 286.

Luhrmann, T. M. (2012). *When God talks back: Understanding the American evangelical relationship with God.* Knopf.

Lukoff, D. (2015). Calling of a wounded healer: Psychosis, spirituality, and shamanism. In D. B. Yaden, T. McCall, J. H. Ellens (Eds.). *Being called: Secular, scientific, and sacred perspectives.* Praeger.

Lukoff, F. Lu, & R. Turner. (1992). Toward a more culturally sensitive *DSM-IV*: Psychoreligious and psychospiritual problems. *Journal of Nervous and Mental Disease, 180*(11), 673–682.

Newberg, A. B., & d'Aquili, E. G. (2000). The neuropsychology of religious and spiritual experience. *Journal of Consciousness Studies, 7*(11–12), 251–266.

Newberg, A., & Waldman, M. R. (2017). *How enlightenment changes your brain: The new science of transformation.* Penguin.

Newberg, A. B., Wintering, N. A., Morgan, D., & Waldman, M. R. (2006). The measurement of regional cerebral blood flow during glossolalia: A preliminary SPECT study. *Psychiatry Research: Neuroimaging, 148*(1), 67–71.

Proudfoot, W. (1985). *Religious experience.* University of California Press.

Rosenhan, D. L. (1973). On being sane in insane places. *Science, 179*(4070), 250–258.

Scarmeas, N., Brandt, J., & Albert, M. (2005). Delusions and hallucinations are associated with worse outcome in Alzheimer disease. *Archives of Neurology, 62*(10), 1601–1608.

Stephen, M., & Suryani, L. K. (2000). Shamanism, psychosis and autonomous imagination. *Culture, Medicine, & Psychiatry, 24,* 5–40.

Yaden, D. B., McCall, T. D., & Ellens, J. H. (Eds.). (2015). *Being called: Scientific, secular, and sacred perspectives.* ABC-CLIO.

11

Synchronicity Experiences

"Everything happens for a reason"

The term "synchronicity," referring to a meaningful pattern of events, is generally associated with the work of Carl Gustav Jung. Jung (1952) used a story to illustrate a synchronicity experience that was drawn from his clinical practice. He described a highly educated client who was unable to engage in treatment due to what Jung described as an overly rationalistic approach to life. At one point in treatment, this client was describing a dream in which she was given a piece of jewelry in the shape of a golden scarab beetle. While his client described her dream, Jung was distracted by a tapping sound on the window of his office. When Jung got up and opened the window to investigate its source, a beetle with a gold-green sheen flew into the room. Jung caught the beetle in his hand and turned to his patient saying: "Here is your scarab." This seemingly meaningful coincidence is taken to be a quintessential synchronicity experience.

There is another, earlier story about Jung that also demonstrates his tendency to experience a deeper meaning in what to some people may seem like mundane events. When he was meeting Freud for the first time, the two are said to have talked for 13 hours straight. During the course of these conversations (the content of which, unfortunately, is largely lost to history), the two heard a knocking sound in the wall next to them. Jung then predicted that they would hear the sound again and believed that the sound was somehow related to the content of the conversation. They indeed heard the knocking sound again—but Freud dismissed any meaning in the event, thinking that the sound resulted from the wood walls moving slightly as a result of a change in temperature. Jung would continue to put stock in such meaningful coincidences, or synchronicity experiences, for the rest of his life.

In *Synchronicity: An Acausal Connecting Principle* (1952/2010), Jung wrote extensively about these synchronicities. For Jung, the story of the scarab beetle represented more than a coincidence; it is rather evidence that there are some parts of our minds that are woven into reality in a way beyond

The Varieties of Spiritual Experience. David B. Yaden and Andrew B. Newberg, Oxford University Press. © David Yaden and Andrew Newberg 2022. DOI: 10.1093/oso/9780190665678.003.0011

our physical actions. Of course, these speculations are based in beliefs that are essentially spiritual in nature and thus become a topic for theology or philosophy, but some parts of reports of these experiences can be studied scientifically.

Most contemporary people will have heard or spoken the phrase "everything happens for a reason." By this statement, people usually seem to mean that there is an underlying purpose, or even some kind of divine authorship to all events. It is usually used to provide consolation, such as to express the idea that suffering serves a greater purpose and that things will, ultimately, end well. In some cases, this phrase is not merely a belief, but rather consists of an intensely altered state of consciousness in which there seems to be an imminent sense of meaningfulness in the events currently unfolding around the experiencer. We refer to this as a synchronicity experience. The following items were derived from the factor analysis having to do with such moments:

I felt that I knew the meaning behind a seemingly random event.
I felt that I knew the hidden meaning of a certain coincidence.
I felt that a seeming coincidence had a special meaning.

James on Synchronicity Experiences

James, as a general rule, was far more careful than Jung in the conclusions that he drew about spiritual experiences, synchronicity experiences being no exception. He was also fascinated by related mental states, like feelings of déjà vu, which he described as "that sudden feeling, namely, which sometimes sweeps over us, of having 'been here before,' as if at some indefinite past time, in just this place, with just these people, we were already saying just these things" (James, 1902/2009, p. 289). James made this comment in *The Varieties* in the context of describing a continuum of increasing feelings about the meaningfulness of surrounding events.

James offered a psychological explanation that can help us understand at least some experiences that seem to have a deeper meaning. He pointed out that we tend to impose our own expectations and interpretations on our sensory impressions and went on to describe how we can perceive entirely random patterns, *and even know that they are random*, but nonetheless derive meaning from them. He wrote:

If I should throw down a thousand beans at random upon a table, I could
doubtless, by eliminating a sufficient number of them, leave the rest in almost any geometrical pattern you might propose to me, and you might
then say that the pattern was the thing prefigured beforehand, and that the
other beans were mere irrelevance and packing material. Our dealings with
nature are just like this. (James, 1902/2009, p. 332)

That is, we have a general tendency to see meaning in almost anything—even
in randomness that we know is random. But for most people, synchronicity
experiences do not consist of only a mundane meaning, but also usually a
transcendental or divine one. God or some other underlying religious or
spiritual reality seems to be behind these events. In some cases, one can be
struck or even overwhelmed by the seeming significance of a specific event,
creating an intensely altered state of consciousness.

James provided some examples of people who viscerally feel the sense of
meaning behind "the veil" of physical reality, such as the following:

When I walk the fields, I am oppressed now and then with an innate feeling
that everything I see has a meaning, if I could but understand it. And this
feeling of being surrounded with truths which I cannot grasp amounts to
indescribable awe sometimes. (James, 1902/2009, p. 290)

Such experiences are felt on an intuitive level and occur without deliberation
or intent—that is, they seem to happen *to* one—and go beyond mere rationalistic interpretations of events. These synchronicity experiences no doubt
exist on a spectrum of intensity, spanning from a vague and subtle feeling of
déjà vu to overwhelming altered states in which feelings of the meaningfulness of events are highly salient.

Contemporary Synchronicity Experiences

British psychologist David Hay defined synchronicity experiences as "an
extraordinary coincidence or . . . a vague sense that somehow one's life has
an unfolding pattern to it. It is often very vague, sensed intuitively, and discovered rather than planned" (Hay, 1990, p. 41). While narrower and more
specific definitions of synchronicity exist, we take a wide view of the phenomena in this chapter. There is an abundance of contemporary examples

of this general kind of experience. One individual described a synchronicity experience with an explicit attribution of God as behind the events:

> The experiences of the last six months have ... confirmed my deep conviction that God is directly and indirectly guiding my life. ... The pattern of my life seems to be a mosaic, in which everything, including seeming disasters, eventually turn to good (e.g., a mental breakdown, frequent eye trouble, the giving up of my career after thirty years to come home to look after my parents ...). (Hay, 1990, p. 43)

In a study by Lau and colleagues (2020), the authors used the phrase *intuitive impressions* to capture the idea of synchronicity and déjà vu in spiritual narratives collected from participants. In their sample, these intuitive impressions were reported in 27% of U.S. narratives, 21% of Indian narratives, and 32% of Chinese narratives. While many acknowledge that God or some kind of divine force is responsible for the events, in other descriptions it is the uncanniness of the coincidence(s) that elevate the meaning of an experience. The following is an excerpt from one U.S. participant:

> My car had broken down, overheated. For some unknown reason, I had a jug of water in the back, which I never normally kept. I poured the water into the radiator, and it got me just far enough as it began to overheat again, to coast with the engine off into a parking lot. That lot happened to be an auto parts store. In addition, by the door of the store stood a man with a tool bag on the ground by his side. As it turned out, he was a mechanic, who had just gotten off duty. Also, as it turned out, he specialized in my make of car. Also, as it turned out, he troubleshot the problem and the store happened to have the hose he needed to repair my car. Also, as it turned out, the kind parts store owner did not charge me for the part. Also, as it turned out, I had 40 dollars cash on me, which I rarely carry, but was more than happy to pay that off-duty mechanic after he repaired my car and I was on my way. (p. 21)

The question of whether or not there is, in fact, a deeper meaning to a given event—or events in general—is a question for philosophy or theology. From a religious or spiritual perspective, perhaps the simplest answer for the believer is that God or some other supernatural agent is, in fact, controlling the universe. And, we can see that control if we only look. Perhaps we can see an unseen meaning guiding events more clearly in particular moments. Of course, a skeptic could respond that this is a form of the "God of the gaps" argument, in which people infer a divine cause to anything beyond their understanding. As scientific knowledge advances, presumably the possible places in which God can intervene would become fewer and fewer, or so the skeptic would argue.

Some people interested in having synchronicity experiences have developed techniques to make these experiences seem more likely to occur. These techniques are framed with a belief that denies the randomness of any part of the universe and instead encourages people to look for a meaning behind every event, no matter how mundane. One online guide that promises to make synchronicity experiences more likely to occur in one's life suggests that one should pick some feature of normal life in which one can look for meaningful coincidences, suggesting that readers "choose a medium with a high refresh rate," giving the example of car license plates (Alves, 2014). The idea here is that one will begin to notice certain numbers more frequently than others, and then one is encouraged to mentally expand on the meanings that the numbers might hold. The guide then suggests that individuals can then check numerology guides on the various meanings that spiritual authors have ascribed to different numbers, or one can think about what meaning that number might hold for one's self. The key, according to this guide, is to interpret the number as a message from God. This technique could either be seen as a way to understand divine messages in everyday life, or it could be seen as a way to leverage the many biases in our mind to see more meaning in randomness.

While meaning from numbers in license plates may strike most people as a clear case of delusion, the experience of noticing a seemingly meaningful coincidence can be quite compelling to those perceiving it. The story of Nobel Prize–winning economist John Nash demonstrates the complicated relationship between noticing meaning that does not exist (a delusion) and perceiving meaning that could come to exist. As portrayed in the movie and book *A Beautiful Mind*, Nash suffered from a psychotic disorder that led him to believe that a far-reaching government conspiracy was going on around him. When Nash was asked why he found this conspiracy theory so convincing, he responded that the delusions came from the same mental place as did his mathematical solutions (which were often true).

Culture is an important consideration in the discussion of perceiving meaning in what appears to some to be randomness. For instance, in some Native American cultures, all events are imbued with meaning (King &

Trimble, 2013). Depending on the culture, nurturing the ability to perceive patterns may help to foster a deeper understanding and connection with the natural world.

However, the world is also filled with clear examples in which people perceive seemingly meaningful correlations between events that do not, in fact, have any relationship in reality. In many cases, any meaning perceived is simply not accurate. In fact, much of the scientific process is intended to undercut the propensity in human psychology to see illusory meaning. The scientific method provides a way to test a relationship in the world that avoids the trap of confirmation bias, which is the tendency to find evidence to support one's preexisting beliefs and to deny or ignore evidence that contradicts with one's beliefs.

People develop all manner of superstitious beliefs about meaningful patterns emerging from random processes. In fact, this drive seems to cut across species. B. F. Skinner demonstrated that "superstitious behavior" would arise in pigeons if they were given noncontingent reinforcement at random intervals. That is, birds in some studies would engage in random sequences of behavior in order to receive a reward, when really the reward was given at random regardless of their behavior (Skinner, 1947).

There are cases in which it is less clear whether an event is truly random or not. For example, people often have the experience of thinking of a friend or family member and then receiving a call from that person. One could explain this in terms of random chance. Thoughts about family and friends are very common, so it is very likely that eventually we will receive a phone call from someone that we had just been thinking about. This "hit," however, is then celebrated as a moment of synchronicity, while all of the "misses" (times when thinking about that person but not receiving a call from them) are forgotten. One could also explain these coincidences in nonrandom terms that nonetheless involve more mundane forces. It could be, for example, that the reason that both friends thought of one another was that they typically talk at certain intervals (say, once every 2 weeks) and so enough time had lapsed that one could reasonably expect the call.

One way to think about synchronicity is through the lens of signal detection theory. This idea was developed by British radar operators in World War II to identify whether the blips on their screen were incoming German bombers or random "noise." In such conditions of making decisions under uncertainty, a threshold needs to be set in order to establish how many "false positives" will be accepted in order to identify "true positives"—as well as how many "false negatives" will be accepted in order to find "true negatives." In different cases, the threshold for what makes for a true positive can be adjusted to be stricter or looser, depending on the costs of missing a possible true positive. This is related to two kinds of errors when using scientific methods: Type 1 errors are false positive (thinking something is true when it is false), whereas Type 2 errors are false negatives (thinking something is false when it is in fact true). One can adjust the threshold to reduce the risk of false positives (while accepting a risk of increased false negatives) or vice versa. Regarding the incoming bomber example, one can have more false alarms (but be more likely to be prepared when they are really coming) or can have fewer false alarms (but sometimes be caught by surprise when the bombers are really incoming).

In synchronicity experiences, there is usually no way to prove the truth of the matter one way or another. A seeming coincidence could be either a random occurrence or a meaningful sign. Interpreting the reality of such occurrences then becomes quite complex and ultimately relegated to the domain of theology or philosophy rather than science.

Apophenia—Meaning in Randomness

Psychologically, there seems to be a continuum along which people find patterns in the world. One study observed that when different people viewed pictures that were intentionally made extremely blurry, some participants were able to perceive the original objects and shapes while others could only see random elements (Krummenacher et al., 2010). The point is that some people can find patterns more easily than others, and sometimes these patterns represent something real. In other words, the tendency to see more patterns can sometimes help people accurately perceive real patterns in the world, and sometimes it makes people see patterns that are not really there. The data from this study further suggest that dopamine, an important neurotransmitter in the brain for emotions and motor activity, might also be involved in whether people see more or fewer patterns.

Despite the difficulty in establishing the truth of many events deemed meaningful in synchronicity experiences, there are some pretty straightforward cases in which the perceived meaning is in fact randomness. For example, if a random number generator is used to produce a long string of digits, then the fact that the day and month of your birthday is contained in that set of numbers should not indicate any special meaning.

The psychological trait that describes the tendency to ascribe meaning to randomness is *apophenia*, coined by German neurologist Klaus Conrad (1958). Apophenia "refers to the perception of connections or meaning in unrelated events" (Fyfe et al., 2008, p. 1317). Note that this concept takes a position on the reality of such perceptions in any given case and classifies them as delusions.

Apophenia has been linked to changes in theory of mind and mentalization. For example, in one study, Blakemore et al. (2003) presented a video of shapes moving in synch with one another and another video of shapes moving out of synch in a random manner. Individuals scoring high on apophenia rated the movements of the shapes in both videos as equally in synch. The individuals scoring high on apophenia were also more likely to suffer from "persecutory delusions," which are personalized conspiracy theories directed against oneself. Individuals who see more meaning in randomness are also more likely to perceive intentions from other minds in general where there is none.

This relates to the work on mind perception described in Chapter 9. Apophenia—and synchronicity experiences—could be characterized as overmentalizing or perceiving mind in ongoing events. Whereas in numinous experiences mind perception seems to occur as a sense of presence surrounding one's self, synchronicity experiences seem to involve a perception that the causal flow of events is being impacted by an external mind of some kind. Of course, depending on one's metaphysical beliefs, these experiences could also be accurate perceptions of an unseen order of meaningfully connected events.

There appears to be a relationship between synchronicity and creativity. In an article "Must One Risk Madness to Achieve Genius?" (2012), psychologist Scott Barry Kaufman (note: We met Kaufman in Chapter 4 in the context of his work on updating humanistic psychology) reviewed the literature on personality, creativity, and mental illness, with a particular emphasis on apophenia. Kaufman reviewed evidence that in cases where one's intellect is high (a personality trait related to intellectual interests and critical thinking) and apophenia is also high, creativity can result. However, if apophenia is high without an accompanying high degree of intellect, then psychopathology is more likely to result. It thus appears that some degree of apophenia can promote creativity, although too much can result in psychopathology.

As with synchronicity experiences, creativity depends on the perception of possible connections; this brings the creative process perilously close to an aspect of mental illness. However, creativity is also thrilling and supportive of well-being. Philosopher Bertrand Russell wrote: "Reason is a harmonizing, controlling force rather than a creative one. Even in the most purely logical realm, it is insight that first arrives at what is new" (1914/1985, p. 165). Additionally, underscoring this creative process, German scientist Max Planck wrote: "When the pioneer in science sends forth the groping fingers of his thoughts, he must have a vivid, intuitive imagination, for new ideas are not generated by deduction, but by an artistically creative imagination" (Happold, 1970, p. 28). Thus creativity, spiritual experience, and delusions share a complicated set of relationships.

Positive and Pathological

Apophenia appears in both schizophrenia, in the related but generally milder and nonpathological psychological trait called schizotypy, and in other various psychotic disorders (Fyfe et al., 2008). In clinical contexts, when the meaning found in patterns from apophenia refer to one's self, they are called ideas of reference. Colloquially, we call this "paranoia," which refers to finding nefarious or threatening intent in individuals, behaviors, or neutral stimuli in one's surroundings.

Morrison and Cohen (2014) found that when *perceived intentionality* is high (e.g., "a social-cognitive bias for interpreting people's actions . . . as being directed at oneself"; p. 529), a person was more likely to exhibit higher levels of paranoia and more ideas of reference. Just as synchronicity may involve the perception of the influence of an unseen beneficent mind, the same perceived intentionality may occur in the appraisals of other individuals in reference to the self in psychosis.

The casino is a good place to witness the perception of meaning in randomness in action. Many people have a "knowing feeling" that the big win is in the next hand of cards, spin of the roulette wheel, or pull on the lever of the slot machine. This has sometimes been called the "gambler's fallacy," when people get the feeling that the chance for a win increases after a string of losses (even though each event is independent from one another from the standpoint of probability). A recent study found that apophenia can even impact multiple-choice examination performance among college students, with students being unable to tolerate a string of more than three identical answers in a row (Paul et al., 2014).

Conspiracy theories are another common place to see apophenia at work. When one adheres to a conspiracy theory, especially an encompassing one, then all information can be interpreted through this lens. However, there are also a number of cases in history in which investigators have uncovered real conspiracies after many people thought they were delusional, so the issue of adjudicating truth in these cases often becomes quite complex.

Paranoia can be debilitating. In a study of 147 individuals with schizophrenia, those with paranoia tended to have more hostile and accusatory behavior and had greater difficulties with real-life social interaction and interpersonal relationships than nonparanoid participants (Pinkham et al., 2016). Paranoid delusions and conspiracy theories about malevolent forces (which can involve governments, secret societies, or supernatural forces like demons) coordinating against one can be absolutely terrifying. Every new event, no matter how random—the time on a clock, a van passing by on the road, several swans flying over a river—can be taken as "evidence" to support the conspiracy theory or to hold a special, private meaning to the individual. To return to John Nash, the Princeton mathematician who won the Nobel Prize for his work on game theory and who suffered from schizophrenia, apophenia played a large role in his illness. While Nash heard voices, he also interpreted special meanings in numbers and random phrases that he came across in his life. He believed, for example, that parts of articles in the New York Times were coded messages to him sent from aliens.

In general, if an individual begins to report seeing complicated meanings or special messages in events that seem coincidental to other people, then it is a good idea to have them speak with a mental health professional. While some individuals may engage with apophenia regularly (as in the case of schizotypal personality traits), when these behaviors or thought patterns emerge suddenly or out of the blue, it may be a sign of an emerging mental health crisis (Blain et al., 2020). However, one might wonder whether some of the great religious figures of history like Moses could have been considered to have apophenia as they interpreted so many of their experiences as coming from angels or God.

Ideas of reference can also occur in mania and other forms of psychosis. Mania is marked by hyperactive speech and other "approach" behaviors. People suffering from mania can feel an overabundance of positive emotions, yet the behaviors triggered by this state—often involving risky gambling, sex, or drug use—can cause substantial suffering to individuals. On the other hand, for some, mania can be a positive experience. In a study of 196 outpatients at a bipolar disorder clinic in the Netherlands, 66% characterized their manic experience as religious (Ouwehand et al., 2019). Furthermore, of the 66% participants who viewed their experience as religious, only 15% viewed their mania as solely pathological. Psychosis can also be a symptom of severe depression. Individuals suffering from depression often have very negative beliefs about themselves, their future, and the world as a whole, in addition to extreme fatigue and sadness. When psychosis enters the picture, then these beliefs take on a delusional character, creating a subjective world with the character of a nightmare. In such cases, the meaning of various objects and events leads to a highly negative interpretation, perhaps reflecting the work of the Devil.

The opposite of paranoia is called "pronoia." In paranoia, it seems as if people are conspiring to hurt you—but in pronoia, it seems as if other people are secretly conspiring for your well-being. In synchronicity experiences, this perspective may sometimes be raised to the level of reality itself, as it can seem as if all things are working toward one's personal benefit. Synchronicity experiences are generally closer to pronoia than paranoia, which fits the general rule that spiritual experiences are more often positive than negative.

Pronoia can result in extreme gullibility in people and a dangerous overabundance of trust, yet in many contexts giving other people the benefit of the doubt can also be helpful. And, notably, those who claim that events are essentially conspiring for their benefit, there is no way to demonstrate that they are not. That is, maybe the meaning is real and in synchronicity experiences one peers into a deeper, underlying meaning in reality. As the old saying about paranoia goes "You're not paranoid if they really are all out to get you," one could say of pronoia, "It's not pronoia if the world really is working toward the good of all things."

Synchronicity experiences can provide a beautiful and wondrous perspective of the world. These experiences can suddenly make the world seem like it makes good sense. Psychological research on the sense of meaning in life seems related to the kind of meaning perceived during synchronicity experiences. Some meaning researchers emphasize the idea of "coherence" and argue that being able to create a sensible narrative of one's life is an important part of well-being (Adler et al., 2007; Waters & Fivush, 2015). We do this all the time in the form of telling stories about our lives to loved ones or when we explain life occurrences to ourselves. We find a way to believe that it was really for the best that we lost our last job (and maybe it was!). Experiencing a larger meaning in an event is not really so different from finding "the silver lining" in otherwise unexpected or challenging events.

Each of these traits discussed in this chapter so far—apophenia, ideas of reference, paranoia, pronoia, and the sense of meaning in life—involve perceiving significance in what other people may consider randomness. However, synchronicity experiences are *brief* moments involving an intensely altered state, which may or may not fit with a general tendency to perceive meaning in this manner.

A number of religious teachings advocate for finding a divine meaning in events. The Babylonian Talmud, a central text in rabbinic Judaism compiled of the legal rulings of Jewish scholars in what is now the state of Iraq, discusses how dreams should be interpreted. One such scholar, Rav Hisda, posited that: "A dream not interpreted is like a letter not read" (Berakhot, 55a). This kind of thinking may assume that the universe is filled with meaning that we can discover—or it could mean that the universe is filled with possible meanings that we can create.

In our survey data, we found that synchronicity experiences were associated with outcomes of a lower magnitude than numinous or revelatory experiences, perhaps suggesting that these experiences are less intense overall and hence less impactful (see Table 11.1).

Table 11.1. Synchronicity Experience With Well-Being, Mental Health, and Faculties of Consciousness

	Revelatory Experience
Well-Being Outcomes	
More positive emotions	.33**
Better personal relationships	.31**
Greater sense of meaning in life	.33**
Mental Health Outcomes	
Depression	−.05
Anxiety	−.10*
Faculties of Consciousness	
Sense of space changed	.24**
Noetic quality	.27**
Sense of time changed	.20**

$*p < .05. **p < .01.$

Neuroscience

If the search for meaning is a fundamentally human expression, there should be some evidence from neuroscience that indicates what is going on in the brain during these experiences. Like revelatory experiences, the nature of synchronicity experiences is difficult to capture in a laboratory. A person's experience may last only minutes and then fade away. Recall the excerpt previously in this chapter about a participant's car breaking down. One would be hard pressed to replicate these experiences with fidelity in a controlled neuroimaging environment. Instead, the research on more general tendencies to see patterns and imbue meaning, such as apophenia, ideas of reference, and paranoia, do lend themselves to neuroscientific investigation.

In Scott Barry Kaufman's (2012) review of apophenia as it pertains to creativity, he highlighted the dopaminergic system as it relates to the "openness to experience" trait. There is some evidence to support the role of dopamine in this trait, recall, in the study by Krummenacher and colleagues (2010) where dopamine was implicated as having a role in the ability of some participants to perceive shapes in otherwise random stimuli. How might dopamine be involved? Psychologist Colin DeYoung (2013) describes how motivation to act in order to gather reward or information is impacted by dopamine. That is to say, while dopamine may be implicated in one's *motivation* to seek patterns and meaning in apophenia, the degree to which these explanations elicit positive or negative or mixed emotional states cannot be explained by dopaminergic activity alone.

Another possibility may lie in a theory that ties beliefs in synchronicity or paranormal phenomena to one's inherent ability to experience surprise regarding remarkable coincidences (Hadlaczky & Westerlund, 2011). That is, some people may tend to see coincidences as more important than others due to their disposition to experience surprise at different levels of intensity. If such an emotional response is, in part, responsible for attribution of synchronicity, perhaps it is mediated by dopamine function (Valenti et al., 2018).

In their article mapping brain systems to psychotic symptoms, Strik and colleagues (2017) pointed out that in psychosis, there is a "psychotic communication breakdown" that they described in the following way:

"Psychotic communication breakdown" . . . can be broken down and operationally distinguished by its elements: the loss of a common frame of reference, the incapacity to realize this loss, ignorance or neglect of its negative consequences, and the drive to fight for solitary ideas, attitudes, or intentions, or, alternatively, to retreat from interpersonal contacts to avoid conflicts. Such a communication breakdown is not limited to verbal arguments but can affect any major human communication domain including emotions and motor behavior. (p. 104)

The authors also pointed out that this communication breakdown has its source in disruptions in areas of the brain related to language, such as Broca's area and Wernicke's area, which are brain regions heavily implicated in the production of language and comprehension of language respectively.

Strik and colleagues (2017) also cited evidence that connects the "experiences of existential threat or of supernatural power" (p. 109) in psychosis to regions in the limbic system (e.g., amygdala-ventral striatum). Other authors have likewise found links to the limbic system in paranoid schizophrenia. For instance, a study by Williams and colleagues (2004) found diminished amygdala and medial prefrontal activity in participants with paranoid schizophrenia; this activity exceeded that of both healthy controls and participants with nonparanoid schizophrenia.

Synchronicity experiences may somtimes involve the misattribution of mental causation to physical causation and such misattributions may sometimes stem from problems with causal reasoning in general (Wiseman & Watt, 2006). Research shows that believers in synchronicity do not perform as well on logical tests compared to nonbelievers (Wiseman & Watt, 2002). However, part of the problem with this conclusion is that the content of the logic questions in this study can take various forms, some of which mix supernatural beliefs into the "logic" questions themselves. To this point, one study showed that if the logical problems are consistent with a person's beliefs, then both believers and nonbelievers actually perform just as well (Feather, 1967).

It is not known with specificity how any of these cognitive processes are situated within the brain. It may be that a combination of prefrontal lobe and cerebellar function helps people to create various probabilistic models of reality (Blackwood et al., 2004; Demanuele et al., 2015). Whether altered functioning in these areas determines the likelihood that someone will have a synchronicity experience remains to be determined.

Overall, while synchronicity experiences are virtually impossible to study in a controlled lab setting (though psychedelic research may make this possible in the near future), for now it is helpful to look at similar but more general tendencies such as apophenia, ideas of reference, paranoia, and pronoia. The neuroscience seems to point to three main findings regarding synchronicity experiences: first an increased level of dopaminergic activity that motivates one to search for and see more patterns; second, disruptions in areas of the brain responsible for language and abstract thought that might be making frames of reference more malleable to change; and, third, changes in activity in the limbic system and in particular the amygdala. More research is needed to determine if during synchronicity experiences brain activity changes in a similar, but perhaps more fleeting, way.

Conclusion

Synchronicity experiences involve the feeling that one is peering into the deeper meaning of events. The reality of this meaning is up for philosophical and theological debate, but it is clear that people report feeling that there is a deeper significance to certain events that others might see as mere coincidences. While the tendency to have these experiences has been linked to some mental illnesses, the majority of these experiences are not only nonpathological, but can provide a deep sense of wonder and reverence for the workings of the world and our interconnected lives.

References

Adler, J. M., Wagner, J. W., & McAdams, D. P. (2007). Personality and the coherence of psychotherapy narratives. *Journal of Research in Personality, 41*(6), 1179–1198.

Alves, N. (2014, April 26). Synchronicity: What it is, and how to experience it. *Medium.* https://medium.com/energy-and-consciousness/ synchronicity-what-it-is-and-how-to-experience-it-a5dab660d68c

Berakhot 55a–55b. *The William Davidson Talmud.* https://www.sefaria.org/ Berakhot?lang=bi

Blackwood, N., Ffytche, D., Simmons, A., Bentall, R., Murray, R., & Howard, R. (2004). The cerebellum and decision making under uncertainty. *Brain Research Cognitive Brain Research, 20*(1), 46–53. https://doi.org/10.1016/j.cogbrainres.2003.12.009

Blain, S. D., Longenecker, J. M., Grazioplene, R. G., Klimes-Dougan, B., & DeYoung, C. G. (2020). Apophenia as the disposition to false positives: A unifying framework for openness and psychoticism. *Journal of Abnormal Psychology, 129*(3), 279–292.

Blakemore, S.-J., Sarfati, Y., Bazin, N., & Decety, J. (2003). The detection of intentional contingencies in simple animations in patients with delusions of persecution. *Psychological Medicine, 33,* 1433–1441.

Conrad, K. (1958). *Die Beginnende Schizophrenie.*

Demanuele, C., Kirsch, P., Esslinger, C., Zink, M., Meyer-Lindenberg, A., & Durstewitz, D. (2015). Area-specific information processing in prefrontal cortex during a probabilistic inference task: A multivariate fMRI BOLD time series analysis. *PLoS One, 10*(8), e0135424. https://doi.org/10.1371/journal.pone.0135424

DeYoung, C. G. (2013). The neuromodulator of exploration: A unifying theory of the role of dopamine in personality. *Frontiers in Human Neuroscience, 7*, 762.

Feather, N. T. (1967). Evaluation of religious and neutral arguments in religious and atheist student groups. *Australian Journal of Psychology, 19*, 3–11.

Fyfe, S., Williams, C., Mason, O. J., & Pickup, G. J. (2008). Apophenia, theory of mind and schizotypy: Perceiving meaning and intentionality in randomness. *Cortex, 44*(10), 1316–1325.

Hadlaczky, G., & Westerlund, J. (2011). Sensitivity to coincidences and paranormal belief. *Perceptual and Motor Skills, 113*(3), 894–908. https://doi.org/10.2466/09.22. PMS.113.6.894-908

Happold, F. C. (1970). *Mysticism: A Study and an Anthology.* Harmondsworth: Penguin.

Hay, D. (1990). *Religious experience today: Studying the facts.* Mowbray.

James, W. (1902/2009). The varieties of religious experience: A study in human nature. *eBooks@Adelaide.* https://csrs.nd.edu/assets/59930/williams_1902.pdf

Jung, C. G. (2010). *Synchronicity: An acausal connecting principle* (Vol. 598). (From Vol. 8. of the collected works of C. G. Jung) (New in Paper). Princeton University Press. (Original work published 1952)

Kaufman, S. B. (2012). Must one risk madness to achieve genius. *Psychology Today.* https://www.psychologytoday.com/us/blog/beautiful-minds/201201/must-one-risk-madness-achieve-genius-0

King, J., & Trimble, J. E. (2013). The spiritual and sacred among North American Indians and Alaska Natives: Mystery, wholeness, and connectedness in a relational world. In K. I. Pargament, J. J. Exline, & J. W. Jones (Eds.), *APA handbook of psychology, religion and spirituality (Vol. 1): Context, theory and research* (pp. 565–580). American Psychological Association.

Krummenacher, P., Mohr, C., Haker, H., & Brugger, P. (2010). Dopamine, paranormal belief, and the detection of meaningful stimuli. *Journal of Cognitive Neuroscience, 22*(8), 1670–1681.

Lau, E., McClintock, C., Graziosi, M., Nakkana, A., Garcia, A., & Miller, L. (2020). Content analysis of spiritual life in contemporary USA, India, and China. *Religions, 11*(6), 286.

Morrison, S. C., & Cohen, A. S. (2014). The moderating effects of perceived intentionality: Exploring the relationships between ideas of reference, paranoia and social anxiety in schizotypy. *Cognitive Neuropsychiatry, 19*(6), 527–539.

Nasar, S. (2011). *A beautiful mind.* Simon and Schuster.

Ouwehand, E., Braam, A. W., Renes, J. W., Muthert, J. K., & Zock, H. T. (2019). Holy apparition or hyperreligiosity: Prevalence of explanatory models or religious and spiritual experiences in patients with bipolar disorder and their associations with religiousness. *Pastoral Psychology, 69*, 29–45.

Paul, S. T., Monda, S., Olausson, M., & Reed-Daley, B. (2014). Effects of apophenia on multiple-choice exam performance. *SAGE Open, October–December,* 1–7.

Pinkham, A. E., Harvey, P. D., & Penn, D. L. (2016). Paranoid individuals with schizophrenia show greater social cognitive bias and worse social functioning than non-paranoid individuals with schizophrenia. *Schizophrenia Research: Cognition, 3*, 33–38.

Russell, B. (19141985). The collected papers of Bertrand Russell (Vol. *12*). R. A. Rempel, A. Brink, & M. Moran (Eds.). Routledge.

Skinner, B. F. (1947). "Superstition" in the Pigeon. *Journal of Experimental Psychology, 38*, 168–172.

Strik, W., Stegmayer, K., Walther, S., & Dierks, T. (2017). Systems neuroscience of psychosis: Mapping schizophrenia symptoms onto brain system. *Neuropsychobiology, 75*, 100–116.

Valenti, O., Mikus, N., & Klausberger, T. (2018). The cognitive nuances of surprising events: Exposure to unexpected stimuli elicits firing variations in neurons of the dorsal CA1 hippocampus. *Brain Structure and Function, 223*(7), 3183–3211. https://doi.org/10.1007/s00429-018-1681-6

Waters, T. E. A., & Fivush, R. (2015). Relations between narrative coherence, identity, and psychological well-being in emerging adulthood. *Journal of Personality, 83*(4), 441–451.

Williams, L. M., Das, P., Harris, A. W. F., Liddell, B. B., Brammer, M. J., . . . Gordon, E. (2004). Dysregulation of arousal and amygdala-prefrontal systems in paranoid schizophrenia. *American Journal of Psychiatry, 161*(3), 480–489.

Wiseman, R., & Watt, C. (2006). Belief in psychic ability and the misattribution hypothesis: A qualitative review. *British Journal of Psychology, 97*(Pt. 3), 323–338.

Wiseman, R., & Watt, C. (2002). Experimenter differences in cognitive correlates of paranormal belief and in psi. *Journal of Parapsychology, 66*, 371–385.

12

Mystical Experiences

Unity and Ego-Dissolution

Mystical experiences are among the most well-studied kind of spiritual experience. They are defined by a fading of the sense of self and/or deep feelings of connectedness. These kinds of feelings go well beyond what we feel in our normal, daily awareness. In our ordinary consciousness, there is the impression that there is a *me* on the one hand, and *everything* (and *everyone*) *else*, on the other. This sense of singleness, of "me-ness," is the essence of being a self, an individual, a person. Under some circumstances, however, this sense can be inverted: One's sense of self can fade into the background and become *a part of*, rather than *apart from*, everything else.

The experience of unity has been a core part of the academic study of religious experience ever since *The Varieties* was published (James, 1902/2009). This kind of experience has been the subject of scholarship and research in recent decades more than other varieties of spiritual experience. This may be due, at least in part, to the fact that these experiences do not necessarily require supernatural beliefs. Mystical experiences of unity may or may not involve religious beliefs, which makes them somewhat easier to study by scientific researchers who are not interested in dealing with the complexities of metaphysical beliefs.

The following items were derived from our factor analysis as describing mystical experiences. Recall that two different factors emerged—one related to unity and the other related to self-loss:

Unity
- I felt a sense of oneness with all things.
- I felt at one with all things.
- I felt completely connected to everything.

Self-loss
- I felt my sense of self temporarily fade.
- I felt my self-boundaries temporarily fade away.

The Varieties of Spiritual Experience. David B. Yaden and Andrew B. Newberg, Oxford University Press. © David Yaden and Andrew Newberg 2022. DOI: 10.1093/oso/9780190665678.003.0012

- I did *not* feel my usual sense of self temporarily fade away. (this item is reverse scored)

Einstein expressed well the vantage point gained during this kind of experience:

> A human being is a part of the whole called by us "Universe," a part limited in time and space. He experiences himself, his thoughts and feeling as something separated from the rest—a kind of optical delusion of his consciousness. (Sullivan, 1972)

During mystical experiences, this sense of separation (what Einstein referred to as an "optical delusion") is temporarily removed and one feels themselves as part of a larger whole.

Mysticism in *The Varieties*

The chapter "Mysticism" is probably the most read chapter of The Varieties. James spent a considerable amount of time describing experiences of unity and what he called "self-surrender," which he often referred to under the term "mystical experience." His work on mysticism created its own lineage of research and scholarship. Part of the reason for its popularity may derive from the importance that James himself placed on this kind of experience. For James, these experiences were at the core of religious/spiritual experience and were described as the most subjectively intense. He wrote:

> One may say truly, I think, that personal religious experience has its root and centre in mystical states of consciousness; so for us, who in these lectures are treating personal experience as the exclusive subject of our study, such states of consciousness ought to form the vital chapter from which the other chapters get their light. (James, 1902/2009, p. 286)

James then reiterated his earlier claim that he himself had never had such an experience. However, he then insisted that he would try to be "objective and receptive" (James, 1902/2009, p. 286) when considering these experiences and would try to relate his thoughts on what he took to be their "paramount importance" as a psychological function. Here again James, unlike many scientists, took seriously the testimony of people describing their subjective experiences.

The word "mysticism," much like the word "spiritual," has been used in many different ways over time, making it such a broad and vague word that it runs the risk of being unhelpful. James commented on how the term had been used to refer to spiritualist and occultist beliefs, which is *not* how he used the term. James then turned to what he did mean here:

> The words "mysticism" and "mystical" are often used as terms of mere reproach, to throw at any opinion which we regard as vague and vast and sentimental, and without a base in either facts or logic. . . . So, to keep it useful by restricting it, I will do what I did in the case of the word "religion," and simply propose to you four marks which, when an experience has them, may justify us in calling it mystical for the purpose of the present lectures. (James, 1902/2009, p. 286)

Again, James was referring to *experiences* here, not beliefs. Similarly, he was *not* advocating antirationalism, as the word mysticism is sometimes used in other contexts. James proposed four criteria to help define what he meant by mystical experience (although these apply to many of the other varieties of spiritual experiences that we discuss in addition to mystical experience):

- Ineffability
- Noetic quality
- Transiency
- Passivity

Ineffability means that the experience goes beyond one's capacity to express it in language (Yaden et al., 2016). James wrote: "The subject of it immediately says that it defies expression, that no adequate report of its contents can be given in words" (James, 1902/2009, p. 287). He then described mystical experiences as closer to "states of feeling than states of intellect" (James, 1902/2009, p. 287)—that is, they are experiences, not merely thoughts or beliefs. James then compared mystical experiences to listening to music or being in love: How could one adequately describe moments such as these to someone who has not experienced them?

The *noetic quality* emphasizes a kind of insight, even though the specific knowledge remains "inarticulate" (see the previous quality of ineffability).

The experiences seem to carry a kind of authority even after the experience has ended. That is, those who have these experiences feel as if, though they often cannot say quite what, they nonetheless have learned *something* from the experience. Furthermore, this criterion means that these experiences feel real (even somehow "realer than real", see Yaden et al., 2017) and seem to go well beyond mere dreams or flights of the imagination.

Transiency is the third criterion. Transiency means that mystical experiences tend to be brief and passing. James observed: "Mystical states cannot be sustained for long. Except in rare instances, half an hour, or at most an hour or two, seems to be the limit beyond which they fade into the light of common day" (James, 1902/2009, p. 287). Our data, as well as other large-scale survey research, have made James's initial estimate more precise (our data suggest the average spiritual experience lasts about 18 minutes).

Passivity describes how mystical experiences seem to happen *to* the experiencer—the individual feels as if it is happening to them in a way that is usually felt to be overwhelming and out of their direct control. These states can generally not be voluntarily forced, only invited, though it may be possible that very advanced contemplatives (e.g., long-term meditators and monastics) can encourage the onset of these experiences. But even in such a circumstance, once it begins to happen, the person feels as if he or she is going along for the ride and surrendering to it.

These are somewhat vague and broad criteria for mystical experiences, and James admitted as much. He wrote: "The range of mystical experience is very wide, much too wide for us to cover in the time at our disposal" (James, 1902/2009, p. 288). However, these criteria are similar to the ones given by scholars who came after James in an attempt to define mystical experience, and most scholars build explicitly on the criteria provided by James. These criteria also apply to each of our varieties of spiritual experience, so they are not specific to mystical experiences according to our classification.

Ninian Smart, in *Dimensions of the Sacred: An Anatomy of the World's Beliefs* (1999), tried to differentiate mystical experiences across traditions. According to Smart, individuals coming from traditions associated with experiences of unity, such as Buddhism and Hinduism, typically have "mystical" experiences, whereas individuals from monotheistic traditions who connect with God or some supernatural being are considered to have "numinous" experiences. This insight points to the role that expectations, which are often derived from cultural influences, can impact spiritual experience. While we support this distinction in terms of types of experiences, as we see it in our data, we note that individuals from any religious (or nonreligious) tradition can have any kind of spiritual experience. It is also worth reiterating that the boundaries between our categories are fuzzy; one could certainly have an experience with features from multiple categories.

All spiritual experiences, for James, fell along a spectrum of intensity. As mentioned, James consciously attempted to discuss mostly extreme examples. The following provides a taste of how more intense mystical experiences in particular are described. James prefaced the account by saying: "A much more extreme state of mystical consciousness is described by J.A. Symonds; and probably more persons than we suspect could give parallels to it from their own experience." James (1902/2009, p. 290) then quoted Symonds's report:

> I cannot even now find words to render it intelligible. It consisted in a gradual but swiftly progressive obliteration of space, time, sensation, and the multitudinous factors of experience which seem to qualify what we are pleased to call our Self. In proportion as these conditions of ordinary consciousness were subtracted, the sense of an underlying or essential consciousness acquired intensity. (James, 1902/2009, p. 291)

There is no question that James emphasized mystical experiences in *The Varieties*, which often appear to be marked by the loss of self-boundaries and a feeling of unity. While his account is no doubt overly simplistic, his attention to this topic has helped to spur scholarship and scientific research on these experiences.

Contemporary Study of Mystical Experience

Other scholars have added more elements to James's initial group of four criteria. Philosopher W. T. Stace, in a book called *Mysticism and Philosophy* (1960), took James's initial idea and both expanded on and more succinctly defined mystical experience, emphasizing feelings of unity and describing its concomitants—a sense of timelessness, spacelessness, and selflessness. (Note: Stace also described a uniformity to the state, reasoning that if one feels no time, no space, and no self, then there is no room for content that could differentiate such states from one another. This would seem to make all true mystical experiences the same across history and culture. Stace was therefore an extreme perennialist, and his work provoked a reaction from other scholars critical of this view, cultural constructivists, who argue that culture inevitably impacts the content of spiritual experience.)

The psychologist Ralph Hood, who described a more intermediate position between the perennialist and constructivist positions with his "modified common core" (Chen et al., 2011) theory (though which still leans perennialist, and is described in Chapter 8), developed the Mysticism Scale, or M-Scale (Hood, 1975).

The M-Scale has been tested across several cultures, such as Iranian Muslims and Tibetan Buddhists, in addition to Christians in the United States. The M-Scale has several factors, or subcomponents, that capture some of the phenomenological qualities that tend to occur. The first factor is called introvertive mysticism, which describes a sense of unity with ultimate reality wherein everything becomes one abstract whole. The second factor, extrovertive mysticism, refers to feelings of connection with the various people and objects in one's environment, which retain some degree of differentiation from one another. Both of these factors come from Stace's theoretical work (which itself is largely based on *The Varieties*). The third and final factor of this scale is "interpretive," which has to do with whether or not one attributes religious or spiritual significance to the experience.

Hood's M-Scale asks whether one has *ever* experienced any of the aspects of mystical experiences listed. This scale is thus best used to determine whether or not one has or has not had a mystical experience at some point over the course of one's life. There are also some problems with the scale, such as the inclusion of reverse-scored items, which many people find difficult to understand, as it results in highly abstract double negatives (e.g., "I have never had an experience that was both timeless and spaceless").

It is also possible that the scores on this scale and other similar measures have led to misleading estimates on the overall prevalence of full mystical experiences. For example, Thomas and Cooper (1978) found that when they applied the full criteria for mystical experiences from James during follow-up interviews, only 2% of their sample were classed as full mystical experiences. This is much lower than the about 35% figure that has been suggested by most self-report research.

A related but slightly different scale of mystical experience, the Mystical Experience Questionnaire (MEQ; Barrett et al., 2015), has recently been created by Fred Barrett, Matt Johnson, and Roland Griffiths—researchers at Johns Hopkins in the Center of Psychedelic and Consciousness Research.

The MEQ is intended to measure recent mystical experiences, such as those induced in the laboratory from psychedelic substances. The MEQ is slightly different from the M-Scale, as it has removed the problematic reverse-scored questions, and the items are designed to measure an experience that one has just had. The MEQ has four factors: Mystical, Positive Mood, Space/Time, and Ineffability. Items from each factor of the MEQ include the following:

- Mystical: "Experience of unity with ultimate reality" (MEQ; Barrett et al., 2015. P. 1186)
- Positive Mood: "Experience of ecstasy" (MEQ; Barrett et al., 2015. P. 1186)
- Space/Time: "Loss of your usual sense of time" (MEQ; Barrett et al., 2015. P. 1186)
- Ineffability: "Sense that the experience cannot be described adequately in words" (MEQ; Barrett et al., 2015, p. 1186)

The MEQ has been used to predict beneficial long-term outcomes from psychedelic sessions. That is, the higher participants score on the MEQ on the day that they received a psychedelic, the more likely they will be to benefit from the psychedelic session long term. The fact that this self-report scale predicts outcomes related to well-being and addiction months after the psychedelic experience proves that it is picking up on something important (Yaden & Griffiths, 2020). But what features of mystical experiences matter most? Some psychedelic studies have found that it is the first "mystical" factor, which includes items related specifically to feelings of unity, that is most predictive of later positive outcomes like well-being (Barrett et al., 2015).

It is worth noting that participants can have a difficult time answering items from these scales. Remember, one criterion that James provided for mystical experience is ineffability—or being beyond language. In the religious realm, ineffability is often illustrated with a line from the Tao Te Ching, "The Tao that can be named is not the eternal name" (Nuyen, 1995, p. 487): How does one name the unnamable? Yet others have observed that many people will claim an experience is ineffable and then go right ahead describing it at length using language (Yaden et al., 2016). This has led some scholars to suggest that claiming that an experience is beyond language is really a way to underscore how important the experience was for them, some even making the claim that it is impossible for any experience to be entirely ineffable (Blum, 2012). While it seems that there is something about mystical

experiences that is indescribable, there are many experiences that are difficult to describe (and impossible to fully capture), such as feelings of deep
grief or love.

Philosopher William Alston, who is discussed more in Chapter 16 on
beliefs, had this to say about ineffability:

> These repeated assertions have led James to include ineffability among his
> four distinguishing marks of mysticism. Nevertheless, I feel that this is
> blown out of all proportion. Despite statements like those just quoted, our
> subjects manage to say quite a lot about their experiences and about what
> they take themselves to be experiencing. (Alston, 1993, p. 32)

That is, despite participants claiming that their experience is beyond language, they usually then go right ahead and describe their experience using
language (Yaden et al., 2016).

But even if such experiences are not, strictly speaking, entirely beyond language, they are still difficult to describe. Self-report survey scales can accordingly be difficult for participants to respond to. Here is how author Michael
Pollan described, in his book *How to Change Your Mind*, taking the MEQ
after a psychedelic experience (2019).

> Some items were easy to rate: "Loss of your usual sense of time." Check;
> five. "Experience of amazement." Uh-huh. Another five. "Sense that the ex-
> perience cannot be described adequately in words." Yup. Five again. "Gain
> of insightful knowledge experienced at an intuitive level." Hmmm. I guess
> that platitude about being would qualify. Maybe a three? But I was unsure
> what to do with this one: "Feeling that you experienced eternity or infinity."
> The language implies something more positive than what I felt when time
> vanished and terror took hold; NA, I decided. (Pollan, 2019, p. 283)

Pollan seems to feel that some of items on the MEQ captured his experience
quite well, while others seemed to not apply or required further clarification.
This is typical of most self-report survey scales and is especially the case when
the scales are intended to measure highly subjective states like spiritual experience. There are real trade-offs when using these measurement instruments.
On the one hand, it is the standardization across participants and the numeric data that these methods provide that allows them to predict certain
outcomes. On the other hand, these questions do not allow participants to

go into great depth about their experiences. Throughout this book we have attempted to balance quantitative data from scales like these with qualitative data from written accounts of experiences.

Another ongoing issue is how these measures intersect with beliefs. The term "mystical experience" tends to have an explicitly religious connotation to many (despite its definition in the scholarly literature as referring to feelings of unity rather than beliefs), which can cause problems when people have them who do not have religious or spiritual beliefs. A number of attempts have been made to provide more neutral terms capable of covering religious, spiritual, *and* secular interpretations. James mentioned one such attempt by Richard Maurice Burke to provide a label with no religious or spiritual connotations, "cosmic consciousness." Psychologist Abraham Maslow, founder of humanistic psychology and transpersonal psychology, called them "peak" experiences. We have used the term "self-transcendent experiences" as an umbrella term to capture a spectrum of mental states.

Self-Transcendent Experiences

We teamed up with psychologists Ralph Hood, David Vago, and Jonathan Haidt to write a comprehensive review of self-transcendent experiences (Yaden et al., 2017). We defined self-transcendent experiences as mental states involving a temporary fading of the self and/or enhanced connectedness, which is how we have described mystical experiences in this chapter. Jonathan Haidt is an expert on the social psychology of these experiences; Ralph Hood is an expert on the psychometric measure of mystical experience; and David Vago is an expert on the neuroscience of mindfulness meditation.

Together, we noticed that a number of common psychological states include an aspect of self-transcendence. We aimed to situate mystical experiences on a spectrum with these more widely studied psychological constructs. We examined the scientific literature to find constructs that involve a degree of self-loss/unity in items used to measure them and have over several thousand citations. We identified several that fit these criteria:

- Mindfulness
- Flow
- Awe

- Peak experience
- Mystical experience

Mindfulness is defined as an open and nonjudgmental state of attention to the present moment (Dahl & Davidson, 2019). The mental state of mindfulness involves a "decentering" of the sense of self and a focus on one's surroundings. People experience the mental state of mindfulness during and after meditation, but can also experience it in quiet moments with a cup of tea or, perhaps, while reading a book and becoming aware of one's immediate surroundings for a moment or two.

Flow is a mental state characterized by a lack of self-consciousness and focused attention on a particular task (Csikszentmihalyi, 1997). Flow is usually triggered by a task that is both interesting and challenging. During flow, people often lost track of time. Most people have had the experience of being so absorbed in a particular task that they look up at the clock in surprise to realize that hours have passed. Flow has been connected to a number of important outcomes related to work. For example, one is more likely to report high job satisfaction if they have frequent experiences of flow throughout the day (Maeran & Cangiano, 2013).

Positive emotions, and awe in particular, covered in a further chapter (on aesthetic experience), have an important aspect of self-loss and unity. But each of these experiences is relatively common and of lower intensity than the mystical experiences of unity that we focus on in this chapter. That goes for mindfulness and flow as well. These experiences are relatively common for many people, whereas the experiences that we focus on here are rarer.

This discussion again raises the idea that many of the experiences discussed throughout this part of the book can be placed along a spectrum of intensity. In the specific case of experiences of unity, one of us (A. B. N.) has described "the unitary continuum," which describes increasing feelings of self-loss and connectedness (Newberg & d'Aquili, 2000). On this continuum, flow, mindfulness, and positive emotions would be relatively low. Some emotions of awe might be placed closer to the middle of the continuum. The experiences that we focus on for the rest of the chapter would go much higher (Figure 12.1).

Through the course of this project, and as reflected in the factor analysis for this book, we noticed two components of self-transcendent experiences that *seem* like logical corollaries, but which can be conceptually differentiated: self-loss and connectedness. Intuitively, it makes sense that if an individual felt connected to everything, then their sense of self would also fade

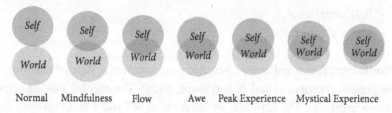

Figure 12.1 The unitary continuum. Drawn by David B. Yaden.

away, almost as if these two feelings are two sides of the same coin. But it turns out that differentiating these two aspects is important, as they are likely underpinned by different neurobiological systems that could be dissociated, and they predict different psychological outcomes. The wife of one of us (D. B. Y), psychiatrist Mary "Bit" Yaden, MD, coined two poetic terms to describe these two components: the "annihilational" (self-loss) and the "relational" (connectedness) forms of self-transcendent experience.

Aspects of Self-Transcendence: The Annihilational

The *annihilational component* refers to how people report feelings of the self temporarily fading away. In *The Varieties*, James referred to this aspect of self-loss as "self-contradiction" or "self-surrender," writing about "that vertigo of self-contradiction which is so dear to mysticism" (James, 1902/ 2009, p. 233).

Contemporary psychologists have hundreds of words for different aspects of the self, and it is unclear which aspects of the self fade during these experiences. For example, is it one's sense of self-control? One's memories about their life and identity? The boundaries that separate one from everything else? The answers to these questions are largely unknown, but it is certain that many people describe the self temporarily disappearing during some spiritual experiences. Psychologist Mark Leary described "hypo-egoic states" in which the sense of self fades away (Leary & Guadagno, 2011) and provided some discussion about which parts of the self may be most impacted by such states.

In *Waking Up: A Guide to Spirituality Without Religion* (2014), atheist Sam Harris described a spiritual experience prominently involving self-loss.

As I gazed at the surrounding hills, a feeling of peace came over me. It soon grew to a blissful stillness that silenced my thoughts. In an instant, the sense of being a separate self—an "I" or a "me"—vanished. Everything was as it had been—the cloudless sky, the brown hills sloping to an inland sea, the pilgrims clutching their bottles of water—but I no longer felt separate from the scene, peering out at the world from behind my eyes. Only the world remained. (Harris, 2014, p. 81)

Interestingly, Harris described his experience entirely in terms of self-loss, yet also then indicated that he would have interpreted the experience in religious terms were he religious: "If I was Christian I would have no doubt interpreted the experience in Christian terms" (Harris, 2014, p. 81). This points to the ever-present role of beliefs and interpretations in spiritual experiences (the point of emphasis for the constructivists), in addition to their basic phenomenological qualities (the point of emphasis for the perennialists).

Of course, belief systems and culture also shape the way that such experiences are felt and described. For instance, in some indigenous knowledge systems, the very idea of self-loss loses its footing because the "self" is inherently connected to all things, so essentially there would be nothing to lose according to this worldview. For example, King and Trimble (2013) described a term used by the Muscogee Creek Nation to mean " 'all my relations'—male, female, human and nonhuman, known and unknown, all part of a continuum of energy that is at the heart of the universe" (King & Trimble, 2013, p. 569; see also Graziosi, Armstrong, Cole, & Reilly, 2021). There are therefore ways of understanding self and connection that link them in complex and potentially inseparable ways in some understandings. In Buddhism, a core tenet is the concept of anatman, or "no-self". According to Buddhism, therefore, feeling the self disappear is tantamount to an illusion ceasing to exist (Yaden et al., 2018).

The experience of self-loss involving the transient loss of self-boundaries that Harris described is different from other forms of self-loss. For example, *out-of-body experiences* involve seeming to see one's own body from a position from outside of the body (Blackmore, 2017). As with other experiences in this book, the trait of absorption has been linked to a higher probability of having an out-of-body experience (Gabbard & Twemlow, 1984). To illustrate out-of-body experiences, a participant from India in the Lau et al. (2020)

study described the experience in the following way, which highlights the mystical and spiritual content that these experiences may sometimes have:

> One day I woke up, and I realized everything has changed. As I looked around, I felt like I was looking through someone else's eyes. Everything looked as if I've never seen it before. Later that day, I began walking. As I passed people, I suddenly felt an emotional and spiritual connection, unlike anything I've ever felt before. I felt as if I wasn't controlling my body. As if I was just simply a spectator to my own life, or watching my life through another person's eyes. It was like a natural high or a euphoria. As I passed people, I could feel their emotions, and understand them as a person. I have become more aware of my feelings, thoughts, actions, speech, and impact. I don't know how else to explain it. It's almost frightening to an extent. I feel more connected to myself and to others. (p. 21)

Most experiences of self-loss don't involve an out of body experience, but rather consist of reduced attention to the more abstract features of the self, such as one's inner narrative or sense of separateness from the world. As mentioned, it is difficult to pin down just what part of the self people mean when they refer to experiences of self-loss; nonetheless, these reports are quite common in the context of mystical experience. Some aspect of self-loss, or ego dissolution, is almost always associated with mystical experience. As psychologist Jonathan Haidt (2006) put it in a summary remark: "Mystical experience is an 'off' button for the self" (p. 236). And that is often just how people who have had this experience describe it.

Aspects of Self-Transcendence: The Relational

The *relational component* refers to experiences of connectedness, up to and including feelings of complete unity. James pondered the possibility of these ultimately unifying experiences in *The Varieties*, writing "Yet it makes one ask the question: Can there in general be a level of emotion so unifying, so obliterative of differences between man and man, that even enmity may come to be an irrelevant circumstance and fail to inhibit the friendlier interests aroused?" (James, 1902/2009, p. 216). For James, this question is largely rhetorical, as he left no room for doubt in other statements:

You will then be convinced, I trust, that these states of consciousness of "union" form a perfectly definite class of experiences, of which the soul may occasionally partake, and which certain persons may live by in a deeper sense than they live by anything else with which they have acquaintance. (James, 1902/2009, p. 92)

James also included several experiences of this type. The following is an excerpt from an account from a clergyman in Starbuck's study:

I remember the night, and almost the very spot on the hill-top, where my soul opened out, as it were, into the Infinite, and there was a rushing together of the two worlds, the inner and the outer. (James, 1902/2009, p. 52)

A wife–husband team of contemporary psychologists, Elaine and Arthur Aron, developed the concept of self–other overlap (Aron et al., 1992). This idea was formed from the study of romantic partners who come to identify with one another. Under such conditions, two "I's" can become one "we" in a sense that sits somewhere between literal and figurative language. Their Inclusion of Other in the Self Scale is meant to relate to romantic relationships, but it can also help to illustrate the pervading kind of connectedness that can occur during spiritual experiences.

The question of what one feels connected to can change the quality of the experience considerably. There appears to be a continuum of experiences associated with increasing feelings of connectedness. On one end of the continuum is perhaps a sense of "self-fullness," which might be akin to the notion of narcissism or solipsism. During such an experience, the self is the focus of the person's view of the universe, and everything else is viewed in relation to the self. Moving along the continuum, we experience an increasing sense of connection to other people and things. The degree of connection eventually goes beyond simple acquaintance to feelings of love—even to complete strangers. Sometimes, in such states, people feel that they are connected with the entire universe or all of existence. For example, neurologist Kevin Nelson described how common feelings of connectedness are during near-death experiences (NDEs): "A sizable 42 percent of our research subjects felt 'united, one with the world' during their near-death experience" (Nelson, 2010, p. 221).

Unity can also extend to the perception of (believers would say the presence of) divinity—God or gods. For some, unity with God might seem to be at the exclusion of all else—all worldliness drops away. Others experience unity with all that is, which might include all that is *and* God, underscoring how these categories of experience can and frequently do overlap with one another. Remember the inherent fuzziness of our phenomenological categories as they apply to particular cases.

Positive and Pathological

As we have seen, feelings of connectedness and self-loss occur across a range of mental states. Some of these mental states typically result in positive outcomes, but some are more often associated with psychopathology and result in negative outcomes. This section describes how these experiences can relate to positive, pathological, or mixed outcomes.

Lower intensity self-transcendent experiences already described, such as mindfulness, flow, and awe, are generally associated with positive outcomes, especially increased well-being and prosocial behaviors (for a review, see Yaden et al., 2017). While each of these mental states is otherwise quite different from the others, they all involve some degree of self-loss and/or connectedness, and each generally results in positive outcomes.

However, there are complications to this picture even in these lower intensity cases. After all, it is rare indeed for any psychological construct to be *only* associated with positive outcomes. Mindfulness meditation practice, which has myriad benefits and is generally innocuous even when it is not effective, can still be aversive for some people. One study interviewed 30 male participants in the United Kingdom and found that for several of the participants meditation was associated with negative experiences, as well as worsening mental health (Lomas et al., 2015). One participant described the experience with an advanced meditation technique meant to "deconstruct the self" (p. 855) in the following way:

> I crashed, lying on the floor sobbing. I had a really strong sense of impermanence without the context, with-out the positivity. The crushing experience of despair was very strong. . . . You just feel like you don't exist, you're nothing, there's nothing really there. It's nihilistic, pretty terrifying. (Lomas et al., 2015, p. 855)

These adverse reactions are especially likely when meditation is practiced intensely for long periods of time. Willoughby Britton, a professor of psychiatry, started what she called "The Dark Night Project," which catalogues aversive and sometimes even traumatic experiences from practicing forms of meditation like mindfulness. Here is how one meditation retreat participant described their difficult experience with meditation:

> It basically felt like whatever personality I thought I had before just disintegrated. And it wasn't an expansive disintegration into unity or bliss or anything like that. It was a disintegration into dust. And I really had the feeling of being in a very, very, very narrow, small, limited psychological space. (Lindahl & Britton, 2019, p. 164)

It is easy to be overly simplistic when thinking in terms of positive or negative outcomes. When we argue that the preponderance of data suggests that spiritual experiences are positive, we don't mean to erase negative experiences from discussion. As we have seen time after time after time, James was careful to balance his positive assessment by acknowledging the complicated picture of positive and negative outcomes. When one considers mindfulness as purely positive, one may miss some negative and aversive reactions that can also occur. On the other hand, however, when one considers mindfulness negative on the basis of some negative cases, then they can miss how the vast majority of mindfulness experiences are positive and beneficial to some degree (or at least not harmful). The goal is to create an accurate picture based on the evidence, without falling into one extreme or the other in one's overall assessment. Transcending this kind of black-and-white thinking and replacing it with a more nuanced and data-informed way of thinking is a major goal of this book.

Negative experiences of self-loss or feelings of merging into one's environment are generally described as depersonalization, which falls under dissociative disorder. Depersonalization is related to another condition in dissociative disorder called derealization, in which the external world feels unreal. Dissociative disorders are a serious form of mental illness; here is one definition in the fifth edition of the *Diagnostic and Statistical Manual of Mental Disorders* (*DSM-5*; American Psychiatric Association [APA], 2013) that is particularly relevant to self-loss:

Depersonalization: Persistent or recurrent experiences of feeling detached from, and as if one were an outside observer of, one's mental processes or body (e.g., feeling as though one were in a dream; feeling a sense of unreality of self or body or of time moving slowly). (p. 272)

It appears that many of the accounts in The Dark Night Project relate to dissociative disorders. In many of these cases, it is unclear whether meditation triggered the depersonalization directly, or whether the individual would have suffered from depersonalization regardless (i.e., they had a predisposition) or some combination.

A 2007 study looked at the relationship between childhood trauma, depersonalization, and mindfulness, where mindfulness was defined as "being in touch with the present moment" (Michal et al., 2007, p. 693). In both clinical and nonclinical samples in this study, childhood trauma was associated with a higher severity of depersonalization and lower degree of mindfulness. In the nonclinical sample, even childhood emotional maltreatment produced this same pattern. The authors suggested that developmental factors and early childhood experiences may impact a person's predisposition for depersonalization, as well as their ability to be mindful.

Some participants in Britton's project described their experiences explicitly in these terms:

In some ways I felt like I was—what's that . . . is it called depersonalization? Yeah, the state in which one's thoughts and feelings seem unreal or not to belong to oneself. So I felt like I wasn't connected to what I was feeling. (Lindahl & Britton, 2019, p. 164)

In high-intensity self-transcendent experiences such as peak and mystical experiences, the kinds of subjective effects described in the quotation—both positive and negative—can be amplified. However, as with the lower intensity experiences, it seems that the vast majority of intense peak and mystical experiences are positive and a much smaller number are negative. For example, in psychedelic research most experiences are rated as highly meaningful, and positive outcomes are seen in the vast majority of cases (Yaden & Griffiths, 2020). While some negative experiences do occur, these do not seem to have any lasting negative effects (Griffiths et al., 2006, 2008). We revisit these issues, with a focus on psychedelics, in Chapter 18 on applications of spiritual experience in the clinical domain.

Last, emerging research is beginning to find a difference between the annhilational and relational aspects of self-transcendent experience. As mentioned, these two elements seem as if they are two ways of saying the same thing, but in fact they can be differentiated from one another quite reliably using factor analysis. Furthermore, when they are broken apart and correlated with outcomes they show different patterns of relationships. It appears that the annhilational aspect (self-loss or ego dissolution) is *less* associated with well-being, whereas the relational aspect (connectedness or unity) is *more strongly* associated with well-being. Therefore, it may be that theories that rely on ego dissolution will not help to explain the positive outcomes of mystical experiences, whereas feelings of connectedness may represent an important clue about why these experiences benefit those who have them.

In our survey data, we found that unity experiences were associated with more positive outcomes than self-loss experiences. Both unity and self-loss experiences result in more altered faculties of consciousness than any of the previous experiences (see Table 12.1).

Table 12.1 Mystical Experience With Well-being, Mental Health, and Faculties of Consciousness

	Unity Experience	Self-Loss Experience
Well-Being Outcomes		
More positive emotions	.45**	.31**
Better personal relationships	.38**	.26**
Greater sense of meaning in life	.45**	.34**
Mental Health Outcomes		
Depression	−.11*	−.06
Anxiety	−.22**	−.10*
Faculties of Consciousness		
Sense of space changed	.46**	.44**
Noetic quality	.39**	.34**
Sense of time changed	.44**	.46**

$^*p < .05$. $^{**}p < .01$.

Neuroscience

We have already introduced one early study on mystical experiences of unity, which is the study on the Tibetan meditators and Franciscan nuns described in Chapter 5 (Newberg et al., 2001). This neuroimaging study found that feelings of unity were associated with decreased activity in the superior parietal lobe (Figure 12.2). This brain region is typically associated with mapping self–other boundaries, so it makes straightforward neurological sense that a deactivation of this region would be associated with feelings of connection with things beyond the self when the line delineating differences is dissolved. However, the single-photon emission computed tomographic (SPECT) imaging technology used in this study is known for its somewhat poor spatial resolution, meaning that the areas of activation in the brain that were measured are rather large and non-specific .

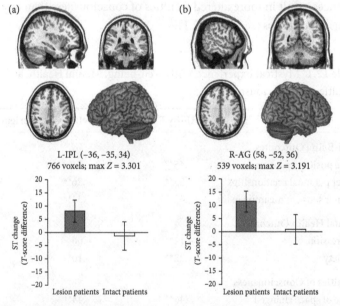

Figure 12.2 Lesions in the inferior parietal lobe result in increased self-transcendent experience. Reprinted from Neuron 65(3), Urgesi, C., Aglioti, S. M., Skrap, M., & Fabbro, F. The spiritual brain: selective cortical lesions modulate human self-transcendence, 309–319. Copyright (2011), with permission from Elsevier.

More recent research by Urgesi and colleagues (2010), using techniques with better spatial resolution, found that it might be the inferior parietal region (slightly lower and closer to the temporal lobes) that is associated with mystical experience. This study used Cloninger's Self-Transcendence Scale to measure the tendency of participants to have experiences of unity before and after they underwent surgery to have cancerous tumors removed from their brain. A side effect of this operation is that the brain regions where the tumor was removed were cut (or "lesioned") and the resulting tissue damage would make these regions less active. When lesions occurred in areas in the inferior parietal lobe (and even more specifically a region called the angular gyrus), then participants reported more experiences of unity in the weeks and months after the surgery.

Neuroscientist Olaf Blanke has targeted the right angular gyrus (one of the regions identified in the Urgesi study) using brain stimulation and was able to produce reports of out-of-body experiences (Blanke et al., 2004).

Furthermore, in a review of the literature on depersonalization disorder, Simeon (2004) commented on the confluence of neuroimaging findings: "These all coalesce in suggesting a unique role for the inferior parietal lobule and other transmodal sensory cortical areas in mediating depersonalisation-like experiences" (p. 348). Therefore, it seems that in unity experiences, and their pathological counterparts, the inferior parietal lobe has a significant part to play.

In addition to the inferior parietal lobe findings, it might be that there are even more specific changes in the brain related to mystical experience. With respect to the parietal lobe, there may be differences between the functions of the left and right hemispheres. There is some possibility that the left hemisphere is more involved with the sense of self while the right hemisphere is more involved with the general sense of space (d'Aquili & Newberg, 1999). If this is the case, it may help explain the difference between the annihilational (loss of self related to the left parietal lobe) and relational aspects (connectedness or unity related to the right parietal lobe). Such hemispheric differences, though highly speculative at this point, might help to explain why one might experience either of these feelings, or both, depending on which parietal lobe is involved.

With respect to the other aspects of mystical experiences, several elements might also be readily tied to underlying neurophysiology. Given the elements we considered previously (ineffability, noetic quality, and passivity), there is evidence to support changes in other brain structures as well.

Frontal lobe function is also associated with a sense of purposeful behaviors and thoughts. We have described previous neuroimaging studies from our team that have shown decreased frontal lobe activity during experiences that are more passive and feel as if they are happening to the person (Newberg et al., 2006). Finally, the noetic quality might be associated with both limbic system areas, such as the hippocampus, that are involved in memory and the thalamus, which is involved with general higher order processing of cognitive data among cortical regions (Newberg & Iversen, 2003; Newberg & Waldman, 2016).

Conclusion

Mystical experiences feature feelings of unity and self-loss, which are themselves differentiable from one another, as shown in our factor analysis. It appears that feelings of unity may be more related to well-being and positive outcomes than self-loss, though more research is needed to carefully differentiate these aspects and to examine their underlying mechanisms. Mystical experiences are among the most studied varieties of spiritual experience, probably because the unseen reality involved with them is not necessarily supernatural and is therefore easier to fit within a naturalistic worldview; however, mystical experiences may also involve unity with a sense of divinity. Brain regions most associated with this experience involve inferior parietal or temporoparietal regions related to mapping physical self-other boundaries.

References

Alston, W. P. (1993). *Perceiving God: The epistemology of religious experience.* Cornell University Press.

American Psychiatric Association. (2013). *Diagnostic and statistical manual of mental disorders* (5th ed.).

Aron, A., Aron, E. N., & Smollan, D. (1992). Inclusion of other in the self scale and the structure of interpersonal closeness. *Journal of Personality and Social Psychology,* 63(4), 596.

Barrett, F. S., Johnson, M. W., & Griffiths, R. R. (2015). Validation of the revised Mystical Experience Questionnaire in experimental sessions with psilocybin. *Journal of Psychopharmacology, 29*(11), 1182–1190.

Blackmore, S. (2017). *Seeing myself: The new science of out-of-body experiences.* Robinson.

Blanke, O., Landis, T., Spinelli, L., & Seeck, M. (2004). Out-of-body experience and autoscopy of neurological origin. *Brain, 127*(2), 243–258.

Blum, J. (2012). Radical empiricism and the unremarkable nature of mystic ineffability. *Method & Theory in the Study of Religion, 24*(3), 201–219.

Chen, Z., Hood, Jr, R. W., Yang, L., & Watson, P. J. (2011). Mystical experience among Tibetan Buddhists: The common core thesis revisited. *Journal for the Scientific Study of Religion, 50*(2), 328–338.

Csikszentmihalyi, M. (1997). *Finding flow: The psychology of engagement with everyday life*. Basic Books.

Dahl, C. J., & Davidson, R. J. (2019). Mindfulness and the contemplative life: Pathways to connection, insight, and purpose. *Current Opinion in Psychology, 28*, 60–64.

d'Aquili, E. G., & Newberg, A. B. (1999, August). *The mystical mind: Probing the biology of religious experience*. Fortress Press.

Gabbard, G. O., & Twemlow, S. W. (1984). *With the eyes of the mind: An empirical analysis of out-of-body states*. Praeger.

Graziosi, M., Armstrong, C., Cole, A.B., & Reilly, E. (2021). The Spiritual Dimension of American Indian Life: Considerations for Clinical Practice. *Behavior Therapist, 44*(2), 134–143.

Griffiths, R. R., Richards, W. A., McCann, U., & Jesse, R. (2006). Psilocybin can occasion mystical-type experiences having substantial and sustained personal meaning and spiritual significance. *Psychopharmacology, 187*(3), 268–283.

Griffiths, R. R., Richards, W. A., Johnson, M. W., McCann, U. D., & Jesse, R. (2008). Mystical-type experiences occasioned by psilocybin mediate the attribution of personal meaning and spiritual significance 14 months later. *Journal of Psychopharmacology, 22*(6), 621–632.

Haidt, J. (2006). *The happiness hypothesis: Finding modern truth in ancient wisdom*. Basic Books.

Harris, S. (2014). *Waking up: A guide to spirituality without religion*. Simon & Schuster.

Hood, R. W., Jr. (1975). The construction and preliminary validation of a measure of reported mystical experience. *Journal for the Scientific Study of Religion, 14*, 29–41.

James, W. (1902/2009). The varieties of religious experience: A study in human nature. *eBooks@Adelaide*. https://csrs.nd.edu/assets/59930/williams_1902.pdf

King, J., & Trimble, J. E. (2013). The spiritual and sacred among North American Indians and Alaska Natives: Mystery, wholeness, and connectedness in a relational world. In K. I. Pargament, J. J. Exline, & J. W. Jones (Eds.), *APA handbook of psychology, religion and spirituality (Vol. 1): Context, theory and research* (pp. 565–580). Washington, DC: American Psychological Association.

Lau, E., McClintock, C., Graziosi, M., Nakkana, A., Garcia, A., & Miller, L. (2020). Content analysis of spiritual life in contemporary USA, India, and China. *Religions, 11*(6), 286.

Leary, M. R., & Guadagno, J. (2011). The role of hypo-egoic self-processes in optimal functioning and subjective well-being. In K. M. Sheldon, T. B. Kashdan, & M. F. Steger (Eds.), Designing positive psychology: Taking stock and moving forward (pp. 135–146). Oxford University Press.

Lindahl, J. R., & Britton, W. B. (2019). 'I Have This Feeling of Not Really Being Here': Buddhist Meditation and Changes in Sense of Self. *Journal of Consciousness Studies, 26*(7-8), 157–183.

Lomas, T., Cartwright, T., Edginton, T., & Ridge, D. (2015). A qualitative analysis of experiential challenges associated with meditation practice. *Mindfulness, 6*, 848–860.

Maeran, R., & Cangiano, F. (2013). Flow experience and job characteristics: Analyzing the role of flow in job satisfaction. *TPM–Testing, Psychometrics, Methodology in Applied Psychology, 20*(1), 13–26.

Michal, M., Beutel, M. E., Jordan, J., Zimmermann, M., Wolters, S., & Heidenreich, T. (2007). Depersonalization, mindfulness, and childhood trauma. *Journal of Nervous and Mental Disease, 195*(8), 693–696.

Nelson, K. (2010). *The spiritual doorway in the brain: A neurologist's search for the God experience.* Penguin.

Newberg, A., Alavi, A., Baime, M., Pourdehnad, M., Santanna, J., & d'Aquili, E. (2001). The measurement of regional cerebral blood flow during the complex cognitive task of meditation: A preliminary SPECT study. *Psychiatry Research: Neuroimaging, 106*(2), 113–122.

Newberg, A. B., & d'Aquili, E. G. (2000). The neuropsychology of religious and spiritual experience. *Journal of Consciousness Studies, 7*(11–12), 251–266.

Newberg, A. B., & Iversen, J. (2003). The neural basis of the complex mental task of meditation: Neurotransmitter and neurochemical considerations. *Medical Hypothesis, 61*(2), 282–291.

Newberg, A. B., & Waldman, M. R. (2016). *How enlightenment changes your brain: The new science of transformation.* Penguin Random House.

Newberg, A. B., Wintering, N. A., Morgan, D., & Waldman, M. R. (2006). The measurement of regional cerebral blood flow during glossolalia: A preliminary SPECT study. *Psychiatry Research: Neuroimaging, 148*(1):67–71.

Nuyen, A. T. (1995). Naming the unnameable: The being of the Tao. *Journal of Chinese Philosophy, 22*(4), 487–497.

Pollan, M. (2019). *How to change your mind: What the new science of psychedelics teaches us about consciousness, dying, addiction, depression, and transcendence.* Penguin.

Simeon, D. (2004). Depersonalisation disorder: A contemporary overview. *CNS Drugs, 18*(6), 343–354.

Smart, N. (1999). *Dimensions of the sacred: An anatomy of the world's beliefs.* University of California Press.

Stace, W. T. (1960). *Mysticism and philosophy.* Tarcher.

Sullivan, W. (1972). The Einstein papers: A man of many parts. *New York Times,* 19. https://www.nytimes.com/1972/03/29/archives/the-einstein-papers-a-man-of-many-parts-the-einstein-papers-man-of.html

Thomas, L. E., & Cooper, P. E. (1978). Measurement and incidence of mystical experiences: An exploratory study. *Journal for the Scientific Study of Religion,* 433–437.

Urgesi, C., Aglioti, S. M., Skrap, M., & Fabbro, F. (2010). The spiritual brain: Selective cortical lesions modulate human self-transcendence. *Neuron, 65*(3), 309–319.

Yaden, D. B., Eichstaedt, J. C., Schwartz, H. A., Kern, M. L., Le Nguyen, K. D., Wintering, N. A., . . . Newberg, A. B. (2016). The language of ineffability: Linguistic analysis of mystical experiences. *Psychology of Religion and Spirituality, 8*(3), 244.

Yaden, D. B., & Griffiths, R. R. (2020). *The subjective effects of psychedelics are necessary for their enduring therapeutic effects.* ACS Pharmacology & Translational Science.

Yaden, D. B., Haidt, J., Hood, R. W., Jr., Vago, D. R., & Newberg, A. B. (2017). The varieties of self-transcendent experience. *Review of General Psychology, 21*(2), 143–160.

Yaden, D. B., Le Nguyen, K. D., Kern, M. L., Wintering, N. A., Eichstaedt, J. C., Schwartz, H. A., . . . Newberg, A. B. (2017). The noetic quality: A multimethod exploratory study. *Psychology of Consciousness: Theory, Research, and Practice*, 4(1), 54.

Yaden, D. B., Meleis, M., Newberg, A. B., Vago, D. R., & McDaniel, J. (2018). Cross-cultural contributions to psychology and neuroscience: Self, mind, and mindfulness in Buddhism. *Pacific World*, 3(19), 53–68.

13

Aesthetic Experiences

Awe and the Sublime

Think back to the most awe-inspiring experience of your life involving nature, a moving piece of art, or elevating music. What features were most striking to you? How did you feel? What were you thinking, if anything, during the experience? What changes do you currently feel in your mind and body as you consider the experience? While only some of our readers will have had any of the spiritual experiences described in previous chapters, we believe that almost everyone has had an aesthetic experience.

Based on our factor analysis, people who had aesthetic experiences described them in the ways listed next. Think about your own experience as you consider these items and try to determine how much you agree with them:

Nature
- I felt speechless by the beauty of the natural world.
- I felt speechless by natural beauty.
- I did *not* feel overwhelming awe for the natural world. (this item is reverse scored)

Art
- I felt awe from a work of art.
- I felt moved by the beauty of a work of art.
- I felt an excellent performance move me at a deep level.

Taken from a study on the experience of awe, here are a few examples of contemporary individuals describing experiences that would fit within this category:

> The moment I set my eyes on the view of the lake during the winter holidays I was immediately in awe. My jaw literally dropped and I was just blown away. The view was jaw-droppingly beautiful. My eyes lit up and my face

The Varieties of Spiritual Experience. David B. Yaden and Andrew B. Newberg, Oxford University Press. © David Yaden and Andrew Newberg 2022. DOI: 10.1093/oso/9780190665678.003.0013

was all grinning from intense amounts of joy, relief, and awe at the spectacle in front of my eyes.

I was watching Elon Musk give his speech on his intention to send humans to Mars. As he went through the different stages required to build the requisite infrastructure, including a mission to land supplies on Mars, I felt completely floored. I was both amazed and stunned at the size and scope of what he was proposing.

The time that I felt intense awe was when my wife and I went into the Rocky Mountains for our honeymoon. I had never been outside the state of Missouri and couldn't contemplate something being as large as the mountains are.

Aesthetic experiences seem to be triggered most often by natural scenery or works of art. Something like *beauty* or the *sublime* would be the "unseen order" at the heart of this experience. This unseen aspect of the experience brings aesthetic experiences under the umbrella of spiritual experience, even though these kinds of experiences may be a borderline case, as it is not always clear that an unseen aspect is perceived. However, people write about aesthetic experiences when we ask them to report spiritual experiences, demonstrating that many people do indeed consider these experiences from art and nature "spiritual."

According to Irish novelist James Joyce, there are two kinds of art. There is "true" art, defined by its capacity to produce a state of stillness in the mind, much like the sense of harmony just described—and then there is everything else. According to Joyce, the kind of art that does not still the mind could be considered a kind of "pornography" because it produces desire, in either attracting or repelling the mind (Joyce, 1916). In other words, for Joyce, true art triggers a kind of spiritual experience—a state of "aesthetic arrest." Joyce had this to say about aesthetic experiences:

> The instant wherein that supreme quality of beauty, the clear radiance of the esthetic image, is apprehended luminously by the mind which has been arrested by its wholeness and fascinated by its harmony is the luminous silent stasis of esthetic pleasure, a spiritual state. (Joyce, 1916, p. 213)

Aesthetic experiences occur from nature as well as art. John Muir, the naturalist, founder of the Sierra Club, and writer who has been called the poet laureate of America's national parks, would often carry a copy of one of

Emerson's books with him on his long hikes through Yosemite and other forests. Eventually, Emerson visited Muir. After looking out at the vast tract of forests and mountains, Emerson said: "The greatest wonder is that we can see these trees and not wonder more" (cited in Thayer, 1884/1971, p. 108).

Aesthetic experiences form a bridge between more common kinds of moments that most people will be familiar with and the more otherworldly seeming spiritual experiences described in previous chapters.

James's Perspectives on Aesthetic Experiences

James includes several accounts of aesthetic experiences in The Varieties, 1902/2009) arising from the perception of beauty in natural settings, as well as those arising from the arts, music, or poetry. Here is an account of someone walking in nature amidst the blooming of spring:

> . . . it was the first perfume of the year. I felt all the happiness destined for man. . . . I know not what shape, what analogy, what secret of relation it was that made me see in this flower a limitless beauty. (James, 1902/2009, p. 360)

James also asked his readers to recall a case of aesthetic experience they may have had from poetry:

> Most of us can remember the strangely moving passages in certain poems read when we were young, irrational doorways as they were through which the mystery of fact, the wildness and pang of life, stole into our hearts and thrilled them. (James, 1902/2009, p. 288)

Aesthetic experiences, as will be the case with many other experiences described in this section, can only be roughly distinguished. In many cases, here and elsewhere, the trigger and the experience itself seem bound up with one another.

In a footnote in The Varieties, James cited an article published in the Atlantic in 1900, which was written by Ethel D. Puffer. This passage describes how it is possible, psychologically and physiologically, for one's awareness to seem momentarily divorced from one's body during intense aesthetic experiences. Here is James describing Puffer's breathtakingly perceptive work:

Miss Ethel D. Puffer explains that the vanishing of the sense of self, and the feeling of immediate unity with the object, is due to the disappearance, in these rapturous experiences, of the motor adjustments which habitually intermediate between the constant background of consciousness (which is the self) and the constant foreground, whatever it may be. (paraphrasing an article in the *Atlantic Monthly* by Ethel D. Puffer, James, 1902/2009, p. 299)

Puffer was a graduate student at Harvard in psychology and James's contemporary who has not received nearly enough credit for her work. She briefly studied at the University of Freiburg under psychologist Hugo Munsterberg, who she followed to Harvard to assist with running the first psychology laboratory in the United States, the one founded by William James (note that the first official psychology lab was at Johns Hopkins, but James started a small lab for his own research at Harvard first). Despite the excellent work that Puffer did there, attested to by many professors, she was not granted a degree by Harvard—one of the many shameful challenges put in her way (and in the way of countless other female scientists) by institutionalized and systemic sexism (note: as well as racism, homophobia, and other obstacles that countless aspiring scientists suffered and unfortunately continue to suffer) throughout the history of science.

Puffer later wrote a book called *The Psychology of Beauty* (1906) that anticipated some of the work described in this chapter. But her thinking also anticipated one of the broadest conclusions that we will make—namely, that spiritual experiences frequently involve a temporary mismatch between one's mental representation of their body in space (described in the findings related to the inferior parietal lobe in the previous chapter). We believe that Puffer's point here is fundamental to the neuroscientific study of spiritual experience and is only beginning to be fully unpacked. We return to this observation in a further discussion of altered states of consciousness in Chapter 19.

The Emotion of Awe

Aesthetic experience is related to contemporary psychological and neuroscientific research on awe. Darwin wrote one of the first books on the scientific study of human emotions, *The Expression of the Emotions in Man and Animals* (1872), and he had much to say about emotions related to awe: "In my journal I wrote that whilst standing in the midst of the grandeur of a Brazilian forest, 'it is not possible to give an adequate idea of the higher feelings of wonder, admiration, and devotion which fill and elevate the mind'" (1892, p. 60).

Psychologist Paul Ekman launched an influential research paradigm based on Darwin's work on emotions. According to Ekman, emotions are a coordinated set of subjective, cognitive, physiological, and behavioral reactions to the world and other people (Ekman, 1992). Ekman and his colleagues discovered that certain facial muscles were associated with specific subjective feelings, allowing researchers to chart out a number of specific emotions (joy, sadness, fear, anger, disgust, and surprise), each with distinct subjective features, behavioral outcomes, and facial expressions (Ekman, 1993). More recently, psychologist Carroll Izard mapped out several more discrete emotions: interest, joy, surprise, sadness, anger, disgust, contempt, self-hostility, fear, shame, shyness, and guilt (2013). Determining the degree to which each of these emotions are truly cross-culturally universal is still very much a scientific work in progress, and some researchers (see Barrett, 2017) are skeptical of these distinctions among emotions. In any case, Ekman's and colleagues' emotion research laid the foundation for work on the emotion most relevant to aesthetic experience—awe.

Psychologists Dacher Keltner and Jonathan Haidt identified awe as a specific positive emotion that they believe is important in its own right. In their seminal paper, "Approaching Awe: A Moral, Spiritual, and Aesthetic Emotion" (2003), they defined awe as consisting of (1) an appraisal of vastness and (2) a need to accommodate that perception of vastness into existing mental structures. Notably, this vastness can be either perceptual or conceptual. Perceptual vastness refers to seeing something enormous—like a sweeping mountain range—while conceptual vastness can refer, for example, to encountering grand ideas, like proposals to travel to Mars or witnessing great skill, like at a classical music concert, or great virtue, like an activist standing up against injustice at great personal cost.

There are several additional aspects of awe that have been empirically derived. The Awe Experience Scale (AWE-S) is a psychometric measure created by one of us (D. B. Y.) in collaboration with psychologists Scott Barry Kaufman, Dacher Keltner, and others (Yaden et al., 2019). This scale measures six different aspects of awe: perception of vastness, need for accommodation, altered sense of time, self-diminishment, connectedness, and physiological changes. Each of these elements can similarly be applied to aesthetic experiences.

Call to mind the experience that you thought about at the beginning of this chapter and try to indicate the extent to which you would agree with the following items from the AWE-S:

- Vastness: I felt that I was in the presence of something grand.
- Accommodation: I struggled to take in all that I was experiencing at once.
- Time: I noticed time slowing.
- Self-Loss: I felt that my sense of self was diminished.
- Connectedness: I had the sense of being connected to everything.
- Physiological: I had goosebumps.

Vastness refers to perceiving literal or figurative greatness, as described previously. The need for accommodation involves paying attention to the experience and mentally processing it. For example, the first few times on an airplane are awe inspiring for many people, but over time people tend to lose the need to mentally process the experience and begin to take it for granted—it is no longer surprising or salient. Alterations to the subjective sense of time are an indicator that awe alters one's state of consciousness in a way that is more profound than many other emotions (Wittmann, 2016). In the case of awe, people tend to report that time seemed like it temporarily slowed down. This is called "time dilation."

Due to the fact that awe decreases self-focus and increases feelings of connectedness, awe is classified as a "self-transcendent experience," which we described in the previous chapter on mystical experience. Awe is at the border between what we might consider an emotion and a more intensely altered state of consciousness. As Haidt wrote: "Awe is *the* emotion of self-transcendence" (Haidt, 2006, p. 202). Writing elsewhere he stated: "Something about the vastness and beauty of nature makes the self feel small and insignificant, and anything that shrinks the self creates an opportunity for spiritual experience" (Haidt, 2006, p. 200). The most common triggers for such feelings of awe are nature and art (Yaden et al., 2019).

But the emotion of awe is closely related to a few other emotions. Haidt has also described the emotion of "elevation," which is specifically triggered by witnessing moral excellence (Algoe & Haidt, 2009). Another emotion, which is often associated with awe and elevation, but that could arguably consist of a separate emotion unto itself, has been called "kama muta" by anthropologist

Alan Fiske and his colleagues (Zickfield et al., 2019). This is a "welling up" or the kind of tearing up that occurs from feeling deeply moved. Haidt conveyed this feeling well with the words of a Unitarian Universalist minister named David Whitford:

> There's another kind of tear. This one's less about giving love and more about the joy of receiving love, or maybe just detecting love (whether it's directed at me or at someone else). It's the kind of tear that flows in response to expressions of courage, or compassion, or kindness by others. (Haidt, 2006, p. 198)

The relationships and distinctions between these various mental states have not been established with any exactitude in either psychology or cognitive neuroscience. But it seems as if these various emotions bear an important connection with the other spiritual experiences. They form a kind of bridge between our "normal" emotional reactions to daily life and the extraordinary experiences that are our subject. In fact, a study by Graziosi and Yaden (2021) found that even close loved ones can invoke feelings of awe in everyday contexts, albeit to a lesser intensity than awe experienced in nature. The authors concluded: "Perhaps awe, while an ordinary response to the extraordinary, is also an extraordinary response to the ordinary" (p. 7).

The Overview Effect

There are some examples of stimuli that create both perceptual *and* conceptual vastness. One such instance is an experience that only 600 or so human beings have experienced—viewing Earth from outer space. The psychological experience of viewing Earth from orbit (or beyond) has been called "the overview effect" by author Frank White (1998), and we have attempted to ground this experience in the psychological mechanisms that are likely involved (Yaden et al., 2016).

Astronauts are perhaps not the type of people one usually thinks of as overly susceptible to aesthetic experiences, as they are highly technically inclined and not often the artistic type that one might tend to associate with this kind of experience. But when we examined hundreds of descriptions from astronauts describing their experience of viewing Earth from space and the kinds of emotions that it brought up within them, we found most experiences involved (a) the appreciation and perception of profound beauty, (b) unexpected and powerful emotions, and (c) feelings of connection to other people and Earth as a whole (Yaden et al., 2016). Here are some examples of astronauts from countries all over the world describing their experiences of viewing Earth from space:

> It's hard to explain how amazing and magical this experience is. First of all, there's the astounding beauty and diversity of the planet itself, scrolling across your view at what appears to be a smooth, stately pace. . . . I'm happy to report that no amount of prior study or training can fully prepare anybody for the awe and wonder this inspires. (NASA Astronaut Kathryn D. Sullivan; Sullivan, 1991, p. 12)

> You identify with Houston and then you identify with Los Angeles and Phoenix and New Orleans . . . and that whole process of what it is you identify with begins to shift when you go around the Earth. . . . You look down and see the surface of that globe you've lived on all this time, and you know all those people down there and they are like you, they are you—and somehow you represent them. You are up there as the sensing element, that point out on the end. . . . You recognize that you're a piece of this total life. (NASA Astronaut Rusty Schweikart, as cited in White, 1998, p. 12)

> The feeling of unity is not simply an observation. With it comes a strong sense of compassion and concern for the state of our planet and the effect humans are having on it. It isn't important in which sea or lake you observe a slick of pollution or in the forests of which country a fire breaks out, or on which continent a hurricane arises. You are standing guard over the whole of our Earth. (Russian Cosmonaut Yuri Artyuskin, as cited in Jaffe, 2011, p. 9)

> From space I saw Earth—indescribably beautiful with the scars of national boundaries gone. (Syrian Astronaut Muhammad Ahmad Faris, as cited in Hassard & Weisberg, 1999, p. 1)

> I had another feeling, that the earth is like a vibrant living thing. The vessels we've clearly seen on it looked like the blood and veins of human beings. I said to myself: this is the place we live, it's really magical. (Chinese Space Program Astronaut Yang Liu, as cited in Chen, 2012, p. 288)

> You've seen pictures and you've heard people talk about it. But nothing can prepare you for what it actually looks like. The Earth is dramatically beautiful when you see it from orbit, more beautiful than any picture you've ever seen.

> It's an emotional experience because you're removed from the Earth but at the
> same time you feel this incredible connection to the Earth like nothing I'd ever
> felt before. (NASA Astronaut Sam Durrance, as cited in Redfern, 1996, p. 1)

As is apparent from these quotations from a diverse array of astronauts, there were many mentions of the immense beauty and the connectedness of Earth and the shifts in feelings and thoughts that this experience produced within people. Many astronauts report that "Earthgazing" is one of the most enjoyable and meaningful activities that they engage in while aboard the International Space Station. One crew (Skylab 4) even staged a kind of brief protest because the work schedule was so rigorous, and, at least in part, there was not enough time available for simply viewing Earth and processing the experience. These experiences seem to really have an impact on astronauts' lives, as they often report engaging in environmental and humanitarian causes after their experiences.

The overview effect may even be a helpful concept in thinking about how spiritual experiences result in positive outcomes. While the overview effect is usually taken to describe the experience of astronauts viewing Earth, in a more metaphorical sense it could be taken to describe the experience of viewing one's own self and life from a different vantage point.

In *How to Change Your Mind* (2019), journalist Michael Pollan invoked the overview effect in a metaphorical way to describe the therapeutic effects of psychedelic substances.

> I thought about this so-called overview effect during my conversations
> with volunteers in the psilocybin trials, and especially with those who
> had overcome their addictions after a psychedelic journey—to inner
> space, if you will. . . . It sounded as though the psychedelic experience
> had given many of them an overview effect on the scenes of their own
> lives, making possible a shift in worldview and priorities that allowed
> them to let go of old habits, sometimes with remarkable ease. (Pollan,
> 2019, p. 359)

These shifts in perspective are reported in many spiritual experiences, and the overview effect provides a compelling metaphor for this heightened (or at least altered) vantage on one's life and self.

The Sublime

Most of our research showed that awe experiences, and aesthetic experiences more generally, are usually positive. However, in terms of awe, a "dark" side of the emotion has been identified. In our research examining emotions related to awe, we found that in addition to many positive emotions, the emotional cluster of being "stressed-overwhelmed" was also correlated with awe experiences (Yaden et al., 2019).

Additionally, a psychological study by Gordon and colleagues (2017) found that some awe experiences that are associated with threatening stimuli, such as thunderstorms, can be felt as negative emotions. Qualitative research by Kirk Schneider also underscored this negative emotional aspect of awe (Schneider, 2017).

This finding coheres with philosophical work on the "sublime," which has been described as having a positive, ecstatic element as well as a frightening tone. There is a rich philosophical history of the sublime. The philosopher Edmund Burke differentiated beauty and the sublime from one another, with the latter capable of moving the mind to both awe and terror (1757/2019). Immanuel Kant also noted the differences between beauty and the sublime, believing that the sublime was associated with a sense of "boundlessness" (1789/2019). Schopenhauer provided concrete examples of beauty and different levels of the sublime (1818/2019). For beauty, he provided the example of a flower. For the sublime, he gave the example of viewing a storm from safety. The highest level of the sublime, according to Schopenhauer, involves contemplating the size or timescale of the universe itself.

In research conducted with a philosopher of the sublime, Robert Clewis, and Italian psychologist Alice Chirico, we found some overlap and some differences between the way that psychologists operationalize awe and philosophers conceptualize the sublime (Clewis et al., 2021; Table 13.1). The study also provided some new possibilities for psychologists to consider. For example, one of the major areas that philosophers of the sublime consider is "the expansion of the imagination." This is an example of how philosophy can contribute substantially to psychological studies.

In general, the way psychologists describe awe appears highly related to the way philosophers conceptualize the sublime. James would have known about this philosophical tradition of analyzing the sublime but he did not mention it in *The Varieties*. It is worth noting that in some cases aesthetic

Table 13.1 Philosophers of the Sublime and Their Views on Its Subjective Qualities

Author	Does the Person Feel Significant and Have Sense of Smaller Self?	Does One Experience a Feeling of Connectedness and Belonging?	Is the Experience Primarily Sensory–Perceptual or Cognitive?	Is the Elicitor Typically Art (artifact) or Natural?	Does One Reflect on Oneself (Consciously, Reflexively) During the Experience?	Is the Imagination Activated and Expanded?	Does One Have a Sense of Freedom and Rising Above Ordinary Affairs?
Burke (1757/2019)	Unclear	No, separation from the object of delightful terror	Primarily sensory–perceptual	Either	No	Unclear	Unclear
Kant (1789/2019)	No, one feels significant on account of reason	Yes, belonging to the moral world	Can be either	Typically natural	Yes (according to standard interpretation)	Yes	Yes
Schopenhauer (1818/2019)	Yes, one feels insignificant/smaller self (yet oneness with the world)	Yes, belonging to a universe or world (metaphysically)	Can be either	Either (e.g., dramatic tragedy)	Yes, sometimes, but it is not necessary	Unclear	Yes
Hegel (1835/2019)	Yes, one feels insignificant/smaller self	No, separation from the infinite (or supernatural higher power)	Primarily cognitive	Typically art (especially religious poetry)	Unclear	Unclear	Unclear

experiences can serve as triggers to other kinds of experiences. For example, here is how one man described an experience while listening to a symphony:

> Rapt in Beethoven's music, I closed my eyes and watched a silver glow which shaped itself into a circle with a central focus brighter than the rest. . . . The peace that passes all understanding and the pulsating energy of creation are one in the centre in the midst of conditions where all opposites are reconciled. (Happold, 1970, p. 133)

Here we see an aesthetic experience blending into a profound experience that has some resemblance to numinous and mystical experiences. Again, it is important to note that these types represent merely rough distinctions, and the experiences often overlap with one another.

Religious Aestheticism

Religion and aestheticism share a long history. A massive amount of the artwork that has been collectively created by humanity explicitly references or at the very least has been inspired by religion. Even the earliest cave paintings may have served a largely religious or spiritual function portraying spiritual experiences and aspects of religious mythologies (Whitley, 2009). Many Greek and Roman statues are of various gods and goddesses. By the Middle Ages, the religious influence of Christianity on European art was ubiquitous. In some cases, such as for Michelangelo, religious faith motivated the creation of the art. In other cases, such as Leonardo da Vinci, the religious aspect may have served as a fundable and socially sanctioned subject for art through which to experiment with mechanics of the art form that were of interest to the artist, such as form and color.

Religious architecture provides numerous examples of attempts to invoke awe and the sublime in the viewer. From the ornate and massive ceilings at the Vatican, to huge statues of the Buddha in Japan, to the Golden Temple of the Sikh religion, and to the square black Kaaba in the Great Mosque of Mecca—there are numerous examples of sublime and/or beautiful places for religious worship. Sacred architecture takes aesthetics one step further by directly connecting the sense of vastness to a religious or spiritual context. Thus, the Vatican is not only beautiful and vast in its architecture, but it is also filled with religious symbols, such as the sculpture of *The Pieta*. By combining these elements, individuals may have aesthetic experiences that are directly linked to a particular religious belief system.

Sometimes, places of worship are not particularly massive but are nonetheless deeply moving for their other aesthetic qualities. For example, a small white chapel on a mountain in Santorini Greece relies on its position among awe-inspiring natural surroundings rather than its own architecture. In some other cases, the aesthetic qualities can be quite subtle. For example, a small Quaker meeting room in Chestnut Hill, Pennsylvania, is built around a sky window that was positioned by artist James Turrell to provide a view of the changing colors of light at sunset for quiet contemplation in the chapel.

Aesthetic experiences also occur outside of religious contexts, of course. Many people seek natural settings and scenery for their intrinsically rewarding aesthetic value. Contemporary philosopher Alain de Botton (2012) recommended that atheists seek out aesthetic experiences of art as a kind of replacement for the awe and wonder to which religious people may have more ready access due to their places of worship. Research has found that even tall buildings that are *not* affiliated with religious contexts, such as skyscrapers, can elicit feelings of awe and lead to a perceptual and behavior freezing akin to "aesthetic arrest" described by Joyce in the beginning of this chapter (Joye & Dewitte, 2016). Certainly, many of us are familiar with the sight of tourists gazing up at skyscrapers in awe, while city dwellers pass by without a second glance.

There may be another less conscious reason for the relationship between religious and spiritual traditions and aesthetic experience, which is that people tend to report more agreement with religious and spiritual beliefs after aesthetic experiences—*even in cases where there is no explicitly religious or spiritual content surrounding the trigger for the experience.* Positive emotion researcher Barbara Fredrickson found that positive emotions in general result in more beliefs about the "benevolence" of the universe (Van Cappellen et al., 2013). Research on awe similarly showed that individuals see more meaning in random stimuli after awe-inspiring experiences (Valdesolo & Graham, 2014). While we continue to hold off on an in-depth discussion of the role of beliefs, it is worth mentioning that even the type of experience that seems least related to religious/spiritual beliefs cannot entirely escape the influence of such beliefs and one's culture.

Positive and Pathological

While some negative aspects have also been identified in the case of awe, our research suggests that the vast majority of awe experiences are rated as feeling positive. Fredrickson included awe in the class of 10 representative positive emotions, along with joy, gratitude, serenity, interest, hope, pride, amusement, inspiration, and love (Fredrickson, 2013). As described in a previous chapter, positive emotions are generally conducive to desirable life outcomes. The tendency to experience awe more often, for example, has been linked to higher life satisfaction (Rudd et al., 2012).

The experience of awe also causes more prosocial behavior. In one study, one group of participants was taken to gaze at an awe-inspiring view on campus while another group was taken to view a normal part of campus. The participants who were exposed to the awe-inspiring view were more likely to help a stranger passing by (actually a member of the study team) pick up something that she dropped (Piff et al., 2015).

Mental health risks have been identified for positive emotions in general. As mentioned previously, researchers have found that there is an upper range for positive emotions, above which they can provide a risk to mental health. If one experiences much too many positive emotions, with few or no negative emotions, then this could trigger a manic episode (Gruber et al., 2008). Mania, recall, can cause risk-taking behavior such as excessive gambling, drug/alcohol use, or sexual risk-taking (American Psychological Association, 2013). It is also often associated with a rush of unwanted thoughts and even delusions.

Mania (or the less intense but nonetheless sometimes risky hypomania) may sometimes take on the quality of a religious or spiritual experience; this has led researchers to begin to call for a better integration of spiritual themes in the treatment of manic and psychotic states (Ouwehand et al., 2013). In a qualitative study by Lobban and colleagues (2010), a participant described their manic state, which verged on an aesthetic experience:

> It's almost as if it opens up something in the brain that isn't otherwise there, and er [sic] I see colour much more vividly than I used to. . . . So I think that my access to music and art are something for which I'm grateful to bipolar for enhancing. It's almost as it's a magnifying glass that sits between that and myself. (p. 207)

The finding that too many positive emotions can trigger mania has not been elaborated in the domain of awe, but it is worth bearing in mind that positive emotions are not always "positive" in all ways. As with most things in psychology and neuroscience, this is not a case of more is always better. In fact, the participant from Lobban and colleagues (2010) mentioned earlier, did acknowledge that these positive manic states do come with a "price," so to speak:

> It's a two-edged sword, because the very gift is also a curse but the gift in itself was simply wonderful at times. (p. 208)

Mania and hypomania, to be clear, are mental disorders that result in a great deal of suffering for individuals who have these conditions. It is important not to romanticize such states. While there does seem to be a connection between these states and some kinds of more positive spiritual experiences, the nature of this connection is complex and at present unclear.

In our survey data, we found that aesthetic experiences involving art and nature were only moderately related to our outcomes. These experiences, like synchronicity experiences, may be generally less intense and thus less positively impactful. It also appears that aesthetic experiences involving nature have slightly more positive outcomes, perhaps also because they tend to be more intensely felt (see Table 13.2).

Table 13.2 Aesthetic Experience With Well-Being, Mental Health, and Faculties of Consciousness

	Art	Nature
Well-Being Outcomes		
More positive emotions	.24**	.34**
Better personal relationships	.19**	.28**
Greater sense of meaning in life	.20**	.35**
Mental Health Outcomes		
Depression	.05	−.14**
Anxiety	−.01	−.20**
Faculties of Consciousness		
Sense of space changed	.38**	.36**
Noetic quality	.22**	.30**
Sense of time changed	.30**	.36**

$*p < .05. **p < .01.$

Neuroscience

Although intense aesthetic experiences are hard (like all spiritual experiences) to elicit in a laboratory, there has been some work done on milder states of aesthetic appreciation. One of the founding works in this field was done by Kawabata and Zeki, "Neural Correlates of Beauty" (2004). By imaging participants' brains while viewing artwork, they were able to find differences in brain patterns elicited by "beautiful" versus "ugly" pieces. Interestingly, they found the medial orbitofrontal cortex, known to be involved in the perception of rewarding stimuli, to be more activated when seeing "beautiful" (according to the observer's taste) artwork. This suggests that viewing art, and potentially aesthetic experiences in general, may have a rewarding quality.

Neurologist Anjan Chatterjee at the University of Pennsylvania studies the "neuroscience of aesthetics" at the Penn Center for Neuroaesthetics (Chatterjee, 2014). While he focuses more on how the brain processes beauty and the perceptual aspects of art, there is some overlap with aesthetic experience as we mean it here. In his book, *The Aesthetic Brain* (2014), Chatterjee described how the brain evolved to appreciate certain kinds of forms and patterns. He began with attractiveness, the perception of beauty in other people. He presented evidence from many studies conducted by others that what we find attractive in other peoples' faces has much to do with their symmetry. Specifically, symmetrical faces are judged to be more attractive than asymmetrical faces.

The brain's sensitivity to symmetry has interesting implications in the religious sphere. Many religious symbols, iconography, and architecture are symmetrical. One need only look at the front façades of places of worship to see this tendency toward symmetry. And symbols such as the cross, stars, or circles feature prominently in various spiritual traditions. One of us (A. B. N.) conducted a study exploring the impact of religious symbols on the brain. Participants were shown five different sets of pictures of various symbols:

1. Religious symbols with positive emotional content, such as a cross or dove.
2. Religious symbols with negative emotional content, such as a snake or devil.
3. Nonreligious symbols with positive emotional content, such as a smiling face.

4. Nonreligious symbols with negative emotional content, such as a gun.
5. Neutral symbols that were neither religious nor emotional, such as a square.

During the study, participants were shown images in each of the categories in a random order while undergoing brain imaging. One of the questions addressed in this study was whether or not certain symbols were more likely to affect the brain simply on the basis of their visual appearance. When evaluating the brain imaging data, we found that one of the differences in brain activity between viewing religious symbols and nonreligious symbols was (unsurprisingly) a change of activity in the primary visual cortex of the occipital lobe, where basic visual processing occurs. More interestingly, we also found that the beliefs that a person holds has an effect on how the brain responds to these symbols. Specifically, people who had a negative view on religion had more activation in response to religious symbols with negative emotional content. This finding suggests that a person's prevailing belief system measurably affects the way the brain processes primary incoming sensory stimuli, and hence, aesthetics are influenced by our existing beliefs.

In terms of awe, Dutch psychologist Michiel van Elk and colleagues (2019) published a study on the neural correlates of the awe experience. They found reduced activation of the default mode network (DMN)—a finding that we saw across a number of spiritual experiences (Figure 13.1). The DMN is a network that was discovered by examining what the brain tends to do when people are lying in a brain scanner, not doing anything in particular. Further research has shown that when one is idle, daydreaming about one's past and future tends to occur spontaneously (Raichle, 2015). The DMN appears to be inhibited during most spiritual experiences that have been studied in the scanner, such as under the influence of psychedelics (Speth et al., 2016), although it is not clear how specific this finding is to psychedelics or spiritual experience in general.

In the brain scans in Figure 13.1 from the van Elk et al. (2019) study, the brain scans on the left belong to participants who were passively watching a video meant to elicit awe (e.g., absorption condition), whereas those on the right are from participants who were asked to count the number of changes in the video (e.g., analytical condition). In the absorption condition, there was increased activation in the following brain areas: the superior frontal gyrus, the bilateral middle temporal gyri, the posterior cingulate cortex, the lateral occipital cortex and the temporal pole.

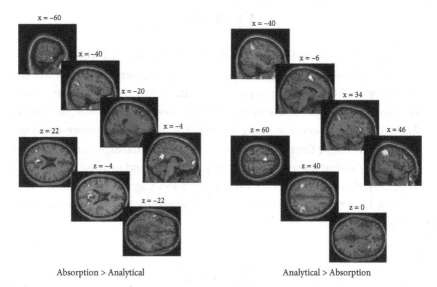

Absorption > Analytical   Analytical > Absorption

Figure 13.1 Reduced activity in the default mode network during awe.
Van Elk, M., Arciniegas Gomez, M. A., van der Zwaag, W., Van Schie, H. T.,
& Sauter, D. (2019). The neural correlates of the awe experience: Reduced
default mode network activity during feelings of awe. *Human Brain Mapping*,
40(12), 3561–3574. © 2019 The Authors. *Human Brain Mapping* published
by Wiley Periodicals, Inc. This is an open access article under the terms of the
Creative Commons Attribution License, which permits use, distribution and
reproduction in any medium, provided the original work is properly cited.

In addition to a reduction in DMN activity in active experiences of awe,
researchers have also looked at the neural differences between people who are high
in *dispositional* awe, or the tendency to have more awe experiences. A recent study
by Guan and colleagues (2018) found evidence for structural neural differences
in their 42 participants, with those high in dispositional awe having less regional
gray matter volume in the anterior cingulate cortex, the middle cingulate cortex,
the posterior cingulate cortex, and the middle temporal gyrus. These areas relate
to attention, conscious self-regulation, cognitive control and social emotion.

Given these preliminary results, it appears that the brain mechanisms necessary for experiencing awe, such as a reduction in DMN activity, are distinct from those that make a person more prone to having awe experiences.
As technologies for eliciting awe experiences become more effective, much
more research will be needed to discover exactly what is happening in the
brain during these experiences.

Conclusion

Aesthetic experiences describe mental states that usually involve a perception of deep beauty or the sublime. These experiences are best captured in the psychological literature by the emotion of awe. Most people will have some familiarity with these kinds of experiences, through art, music, or nature. Aesthetic experiences also share the most similarity with more common emotions. We hope the study of the varieties of spiritual experience becomes continuous with mainstream topics in psychology and neuroscience. In the same way that emotions were once judged too vague for scientific study, but now have thriving fields, we hope that the study of spiritual experience follows suit.

References

Algoe, S. B., & Haidt, J. (2009). Witnessing excellence in action: The "other-praising" emotions of elevation, gratitude, and admiration. *Journal of Positive Psychology*, *4*(2), 105–127.

American Psychiatric Association. (2013). *Diagnostic and statistical manual of mental disorders* (5th ed.).

Barrett, L. F. (2017). *How emotions are made: The secret life of the brain*. Houghton Mifflin Harcourt.

Burke, E. (1757/2019). From a philosophical enquiry into the origin of our ideas of the sublime and beautiful. In R. R. Clewis (Ed.), *The sublime reader* (pp. 79–89). Bloomsbury.

Chatterjee, A. (2014). *The aesthetic brain: How we evolved to desire beauty and enjoy art*. Oxford University Press.

Chen, S. (2012). *A documentary on Shenzhou-9. Hu-nan*. China: The Science and Technology Press of Hunan.

Clewis, R. R., Yaden, D. B., & Chirico, A. (2021). Intersections between awe and the sublime: A preliminary empirical study. *Empirical Studies of the Arts*. https://doi.org/ 0276237421994694

Darwin, C. (1872). *The expression of the emotions in man and animals*. Murray.

Darwin, C. (1892). *Charles Darwin: His life told in an autobiographical chapter, and in a selected series of his published letters*. J. Murray.

De Botton, A. (2012). *Religion for atheists: A non-believer's guide to the uses of religion*. Vintage.

Ekman, P. (1992). An argument for basic emotions. *Cognition & Emotion*, *6*(3–4), 169–200.

Ekman, P. (1993). Facial expression and emotion. *American Psychologist*, *48*(4), 384.

Fredrickson, B. L. (2013). Positive emotions broaden and build. In P. Devine & A. Plant (Eds.), *Advances in experimental social psychology* (Vol. 47, pp. 1–53). Academic Press.

Gordon, A. M., Stellar, J. E., Anderson, C. L., McNeil, G. D., Loew, D., & Keltner, D. (2017). The dark side of the sublime: Distinguishing a threat-based variant of awe. *Journal of Personality and Social Psychology, 113*(2), 310.

Graziosi, M., & Yaden, D. B. (2021). Interpersonal awe: Exploring the social domain of awe elicitors. *Journal of Positive Psychology, 16*(2), 263–271.

Gruber, J., Johnson, S. L., Oveis, C., & Keltner, D. (2008). Risk for mania and positive emotional responding: Too much of a good thing? *Emotion, 8*(1), 23.

Guan, F., Xiang, Y., Chen, O., Wang, W., & Chen, J. (2018). Neural basis of dispositional awe. *Frontiers in Behavioral Neuroscience, 12*, 209. https://doi.org/10.3389/fnbeh.2018.00209

Haidt, J. (2006). *The happiness hypothesis: Finding modern truth in ancient wisdom.* Basic Books.

Happold, F. C. (1970). *Mysticism: A Study and an Anthology.* Harmondsworth: Penguin.

Hassard, J., & Weisberg, J. (1999). *Environmental science on the Net: The global thinking project.* Parsippany, NY: Good Year Books.

Hegel, G. W. F. (1835/2019). Symbolism of the sublime. In R. R. Clewis (Ed.), *The sublime reader* (pp. 200–211). Bloomsbury.

Izard, C. E. (2013). *Human emotions.* Springer Science & Business Media.

Jaffe, R. (2011). *Anthropogenic relation to otherbiota: Connections to disorders and crises of ourtime.* Ashburn, VA: Health Studies Collegium.

James, W. (1902/2009). The varieties of religious experience: A study in human nature. *eBooks@Adelaide.* https://csrs.nd.edu/assets/59930/williams_1902.pdf

Joyce, J. (2008). *A portrait of the artist as a young man.* Oxford Paperbacks. (Original work published 1916)

Joye, Y., & Dewitte, S. (2016). Up speeds you down. Awe-evoking monumental buildings trigger behavioral and perceived freezing. *Journal of Environmental Psychology, 47*, 112–125.

Kant, I. (1789/2019). Analytic of the sublime. In R. R. Clewis (Ed.), *The sublime reader* (pp. 123–146). Bloomsbury.

Kawabata, H., & Zeki, S. (2004). Neural correlates of beauty. *Journal of Neurophysiology, 91*(4), 1699–1705.

Keltner, D., & Haidt, J. (2003). Approaching awe, a moral, spiritual, and aesthetic emotion. *Cognition & Emotion, 17*(2), 297–314.

Lobban, F., Taylor, K., Murray, C., & Jones, S. (2010). Bipolar disorder is a two-edged sword: A qualitative study to understand the positive edge. *Journal of Affective Disorders, 141*, 204–212.

Ouwehand, E., Wong, K., Boeije, H., & Braam, A. (2013). Revelation, delusion or disillusion: Subjective interpretation of religious and spiritual experiences in bipolar disorder. *Mental Health, Religion, & Culture, 17*(6), 615–628

Piff, P. K., Dietze, P., Feinberg, M., Stancato, D. M., & Keltner, D. (2015). Awe, the small self, and prosocial behavior. *Journal of Personality and Social Psychology, 108*(6), 883.

Pollan, M. (2019). *How to change your mind: What the new science of psychedelics teaches us about consciousness, dying, addiction, depression, and transcendence.* Penguin Books.

Puffer, E. D. (1906). *The psychology of beauty.* Houghton Mifflin.

Raichle, M. E. (2015). The brain's default mode network. *Annual Review of Neuroscience, 38*, 433–447.

Redfern, M. (1996, April 21). Science: A new view of home. Independent. https://www.independent.co.uk/arts-entertainment/science-a-new-view-of-home-1306095.html

Rudd, M., Vohs, K. D., & Aaker, J. (2012). Awe expands people's perception of time, alters decision making, and enhances well-being. *Psychological Science*, 23(10), 1130–1136.

Schneider, K. (2017). The resurgence of awe in psychology: Promise, hope, and perils. *Humanistic Psychologist*, 45(2), 103.

Schopenhauer, A. (1818/2019). World as will and representation. In R. R. Clewis (Ed.), *The sublime reader* (pp. 194–198). Bloomsbury.

Speth, J., Speth, C., Kaelen, M., Schloerscheidt, A. M., Feilding, A., Nutt, D. J., & Carhart-Harris, R. L. (2016). Decreased mental time travel to the past correlates with default-mode network disintegration under lysergic acid diethylamide. *Journal of Psychopharmacology*, 30(4), 344–353.

Sullivan, K. D. (1991). An Astronaut's view of earth. *Update (newsletter of the National Geographic Society's Geography Education Program)*, 1, 12–14.

Thayer, J. B. (1971). *A Western journey with Mr. Emerson*. Kennikat Press. (Original published 1884)

Valdesolo, P., & Graham, J. (2014). Awe, uncertainty, and agency detection. *Psychological Science*, 25(1), 170–178.

Van Cappellen, P., Saroglou, V., Iweins, C., Piovesana, M., & Fredrickson, B. L. (2013). Self-transcendent positive emotions increase spirituality through basic world assumptions. *Cognition & Emotion*, 27(8), 1378–1394.

Van Elk, M., Arciniegas Gomez, M. A., van der Zwaag, W., van Schie, H. T., & Sauter, D. (2019). The neural correlates of the awe experience: Reduced default mode network activity during feelings of awe. *Human Brain Mapping, 2019, 40(12), 3561–3574.* https://doi.org/10.1002/hbm.24616

White, F. (1998). *The overview effect: Space exploration and human evolution*. AIAA.

Whitley, D. S. (2009). *Cave paintings and the human spirit: The origin of creativity and belief*. Prometheus Books.

Wittmann, M. (2016). *Felt time: The psychology of how we perceive time*. MIT Press.

Yaden, D. B., Iwry, J., Slack, K. J., Eichstaedt, J. C., Zhao, Y., Vaillant, G. E., & Newberg, A. B. (2016). The overview effect: Awe and self-transcendent experience in space flight. *Psychology of Consciousness: Theory, Research, and Practice*, 3(1), 1.

Yaden, D. B., Kaufman, S. B., Hyde, E., Chirico, A., Gaggioli, A., Zhang, J. W., & Keltner, D. (2019). The development of the Awe Experience Scale (AWE-S): A multifactorial measure for a complex emotion. *Journal of Positive Psychology*, 14(4), 474–488.

Zickfeld, J. H., Schubert, T. W., Seibt, B., Blomster, J. K., Arriaga, P., Basabe, N., . . . Fiske, A. P. (2019). Kama muta: Conceptualizing and measuring the experience often labelled being moved across 19 nations and 15 languages. *Emotion*, 19(3), 402.

14

Paranormal Experiences

Ghosts, Angels, and Other Entities

The work of Swedish painter Hilma af Klint is having a revival. At the time of this writing her large, colorful, geometric paintings are hanging in the Guggenheim Museum of Art in New York City. The paintings themselves are stirring. University of Pennsylvania art professor Jackie Tileston related the words of one art critic, who said: "This isn't art criticism—this is awe. I'm not usually a weeper, but I could not stop the tears at this exhibit." While the paintings may cause some viewers to have aesthetic experiences, the process of creating them involved a different kind of experience—one that some in the art history community are not quite comfortable with.

The issue at stake is dating the birth of modernism in painting and abstract art. Usually, artists like Russian painter Wassily Kandinsky and Dutch painter Piet Mondrian are considered the founders of abstract art (note: perhaps coincidentally, spirituality played a major role in the work of both these artists as well), and the year 1911 is cited as its founding. Hilma af Klint's work, however, was completed almost 5 years earlier. This raises the interesting possibility that abstract modernism arrived earlier and was conceived by a woman. Even more fascinating, Klint described her work as the result of channeling a spirit that she called "Amaliel," who she said "commissioned" her to paint astral planes and the "immortal aspect of man." According to Tileston, many art critics who are enamored of and unwilling to complicate the idea of an earlier inventor of abstract modernist painting either choose to ignore or severely downplay this "paranormal" or spiritual aspect of Klint's creative process (personal communication). The problem with this neglect is that Klint left hundreds of notebooks attesting to her belief in the reality of her spiritual experiences in no uncertain terms (McNab, 2019). So, did Hilma af Klint invent abstract modernist paintings? Or, is Amaliel, the spirit that she experienced, responsible for the paintings?

The fields of psychology and neuroscience share a similar embarrassment about experiences involving spirits, heavenly entities, ghosts, and the

The Varieties of Spiritual Experience. David B. Yaden and Andrew B. Newberg, Oxford University Press. © David Yaden and Andrew Newberg 2022. DOI: 10.1093/oso/9780190665678.003.0014

like. While aesthetic and mystical experiences are just starting to be taken seriously in psychology, and there is a tradition in studying numinous experiences due to their connection with the study of religion, paranormal experiences involving a nonphysical entity have been relegated to the fringes of the field. We admit that we tend to hold this attitude as well. However, when we began collecting data on spiritual experiences, we were intrigued and surprised by the high number of responses reporting experiences of contact with spiritual beings of various kinds, ghosts, and the spirits of deceased family members. Here are the items related to paranormal experiences:

Known

I felt that I saw a recently deceased friend or relative.

I felt that I was visited by a dead friend or relative.

I felt that I encountered a ghost of someone I knew.

Unknown

I felt that I encountered a spiritual entity (other than God).

I felt a ghostly presence.

I did *not* feel that I saw a ghost. (this item is reverse scored)

Given the high prevalence of these responses, we believe it is important to explore these experiences.

James on Paranormal Experience

James's more famous brother, novelist Henry James, was enthusiastic about the possible reality of ghosts and occasionally spoke about this with William. Henry also wrote the most well-known literary ghost story in the English language, *The Turn of the Screw*, which has been described as "perhaps the most ambiguous and disturbing ghost story ever written" (H. James, 2008). The story involves a governess who sees ghosts in the presence of the children in her care. The children, however, refuse (as the governess views the situation) to admit to seeing the supposed ghosts—so she is left to wonder whether her own mind is sound.

Literary criticism of this story has focused largely on whether or not the "ghosts" in the story are real or a hallucination. Their reality has been left intentionally ambiguous. It is left to the reader to judge whether the governess is, in fact, seeing ghosts and trying to protect the children from a real supernatural threat, or whether she is hallucinating and putting the children in danger due to her erratic behavior. In other words, Henry wrote about ghosts in much the same way that his brother William wrote about the reality of spiritual experience in The *Varieties* (1902/2009)—he left the question of their reality suspended in mystery. An article on *The Turn of the Screw* in the *New Yorker* summarized how Henry James left the question open, and something similar could be said of *The Varieties*:

> Its profoundest pleasure lies in the beautifully fussed over way in which James refuses to come down on either side. In its twenty-four brief chapters, the book becomes a modest monument to the bold pursuit of ambiguity. It is rigorously committed to lack of commitment. At each rereading, you have to marvel anew at how adroitly and painstakingly James plays both sides. (Leithauser, 2012)

William James's wife Alice was also interested in mediums—people who claim they can communicate with the spirit world. William, Henry, and Alice all attended seances at various times. William James was hopeful that something new about the mind could be discovered from mediumship (searching for his "white crow" as described in Chapter 2). Some individual cases seemed particularly promising, particularly someone named Ms. Piper, who W. James expressed some guarded optimism about and the possibility of psychic phenomena in an article published by the Society of Psychical Research. James was generally disappointed in this line of research as these cases were generally revealed to be frauds (Richardson, 2006, p. 510).

In *The Varieties*, W. James included several experiences that involved the experience of a spirit, ghost, or otherwise nonphysical entity of some kind. He described such moments in the following way: "The person . . . will feel a 'presence' in the room, definitely localized, facing in one particular way, real in the most emphatic sense of the word, often coming suddenly, and as suddenly gone . . . " (W. James, 1902/2009, p. 47). To modern minds, James seems to be describing "ghost" experiences here.

William James's father's experience, which we described in Chapter 2, would likely be classed as paranormal because it involved a localized nonphysical entity in the room with him. The following example of a paranormal experience is taken from a friend of James's, who he called "one of the keenest intellects" that he knew and who apparently had multiple experiences of this kind:

On the previous night I had had, after getting into bed at my rooms in College, a vivid tactile hallucination of being grasped by the arm, which made me get up and search the room for an intruder; but the sense of presence properly so called came on the next night. After I had got into bed and blown out the candle, I lay awake awhile thinking on the previous night's experience, when suddenly I FELT something come into the room and stay close to my bed. It remained only a minute or two. I did not recognize it by any ordinary sense, and yet there was a horribly unpleasant "sensation" connected with it. It stirred something more at the roots of my being than any ordinary perception. (W. James, 1902/2009, p. 47)

While this example might read a little like the kind of "ghost story" one might invent to scare children, many people do report experiences like this—and sometimes take them quite seriously. There are a number of paranormal experiences that involve ghosts, angels, or demons, and responses to them can vary a great deal. There is a conceptual difference, though, between these kinds of experiences and the other varieties that we have reviewed, at least in part because they come in the form of a particular, discrete entity, rather than a diffuse, all-pervading presence as in numinous experiences.

Experiences involving the personage of Jesus Christ represent an interesting case, as experiences of Jesus Christ can sometimes involve a discrete bounded entity, but one in this case interpreted by Christians to be an omniscient, omnipotent, and benevolent God. For example, the following experience would be at the boundary between a numinous experience and a paranormal experience: "I thought I saw the Saviour, by faith, in human shape, for about one second in the room, with arms extended, appearing to say to me, Come" (W. James, 1902/2009, pp. 145–190). For Christians, the discrete figure of Jesus Christ *is* one and the same as the all-pervading God (Alston, 1993, p. 19), which makes a distinction between numinous and paranormal experiences difficult in such cases. Remember that our categories are not mutually exclusive and have fuzzy boundaries.

James was well aware that he was often treading on thin ice with his scientific audience by discussing these topics. He acknowledged this in a number of places, and when he did, he usually reverted back to providing more personal accounts, writing: "Lest the oddity of these phenomena should disconcert you, I will venture to read you a couple of similar narratives, much shorter, merely to show that we are dealing with a well-marked natural kind of fact" (W. James, 1902/2009, p. 48). So, as is the case throughout *The*

Varieties, he provided examples of people describing their experiences in their own words to impress on the audience of their subjective reality. Here, as in each of the previous experiences, his argument remained steadfast: That these experiences are demonstrably a part of human nature and are therefore worthy of scientific inquiry.

A contemporary of James's, Oxford philosophy professor Henry Sidgwick, was very interested in paranormal and psychic research. He cited James's work a number of times in his investigation of the subject. Sidgwick also sent out a survey asking about paranormal experiences, which is now referred to as the "Census of Hallucinations" (Society for Psychical Research, 2018). Here is one item from this survey:

> Have you ever, when believing yourself to be completely awake, had a vivid impression of seeing or being touched by a living being or inanimate object, or of hearing a voice; which impression, so far as you could discover, was not due to any external physical cause? (Luhrmann, 2012, p. 236)

About 10% of Sidgwick's sample affirmed that they had had an experience like this (which may touch on both revelatory and paranormal experiences). In most modern samples, this number is even higher. More modern phenomena that would also be classified under the heading of paranormal experiences are vivid UFO sightings or alien abduction-type experiences. Jung described UFO and alien experiences, which then were a very recent emerging phenomenon, as a modern manifestation of the same search for wholeness that he believed was apparent in other spiritual experiences (Jung, 1958/2020). Contemporary religious studies scholar Diana Walsh Pasulka made the case that modern UFO experiences/beliefs can be seen as a new religious movement (Pasulka, 2019). These experiences are beginning to be reported more frequently in studies asking for spiritual experiences (Appelle, 1996; Strassman, 2000).

Contemporary Research on Psi

The contemporary research into paranormal phenomena actually has its origins in two historical movements: *mesmerism* (i.e., promoting health through hypnotic or trance states) and *spiritualism* (i.e., the rise in interest in seances, mediumship, and spirit communication; Irwin & Watt, 2007). Recall

William James's interest in and work with the alleged psychic Ms. Piper—this was part of this spiritualism movement.

However, more recent attempts at experimental research into paranormal phenomena, often called *psi phenomena* or *paranormal processes*, owes its origins to J. B. Rhine at Duke University and his studies on extrasensory perception (ESP) beginning in 1927 (Irwin & Watt, 2007). In 1934, Rhine wrote a book called *Extrasensory Perception*, which detailed his experiments in ESP, which essentially tested phenomena such as telepathy (mind-to-mind communication), precognition (knowledge about the future inaccessible through ordinary senses), and retrocognition (knowledge about the past inaccessible through ordinary senses; Irwin & Watt, 2007). Perhaps the most famous cultural artifacts from these studies are what are known as *Zener cards* (Figure 14.1), developed by Karl Zener, which were used to test for ESP between subjects (Irwin & Watt, 2007).

The results from the use of these cards has been hotly debated. In 1938, a study by John L. Kennedy at Stanford found that the backs of the Zener cards gave cues to participants to guess correctly, and in 1936 a study by William Cox at Princeton University using playing cards instead of Zener cards to test for ESP found no statistically significant proof of psi phenomena. This indicates the matter was not only considered, but also empirically investigated at top-tier universities such as Duke and Princeton, despite the claims of many psi enthusiasts that these phenomena have never been scientifically studied.

Decades later, in the late 1970s and early1980s, several experiments in remote viewing were conducted at Stanford Research Institute; these experiments asked participants in one location who were blind to the location of the other participants to provide information about what the person

Figure 14.1 Zener Cards used in research on psychics. From https://commons. wikimedia.org/wiki/File:Cartas_Zener.svg

in the other location was seeing and to give details on the location of the other person (Tart et al., 1980). The results from such studies have been controversial. Meta-analyses of these studies did not show significant evidence of psi phenomena (Irwin & Watt, 2007). But there remain supporters of some evidence for these phenomena (e.g., see Bem et al., 2015).

Historically, governments have at times poured substantial resources into investigating these phenomena. Germany conducted parapsychology research as early as the 1870s (Wolframm, 2015). In the United States, the Central Intelligence Agency (CIA) became involved in testing the feasibility of these phenomena, at least in part to compete with research on this topic in the Soviet Union during the Cold War (Kress, 1999). In the late 1970s and early 1980s, the People's Republic of China (PRC) conducted research on "exceptional functions of the human body," which included things like mediumship and psychic ability (Zha & McConnell, 1991).

These investigations continue to the present day, although they are less common. For example, there are over 100 articles in the medical literature that have evaluated the effects of intercessory prayer on health, which could be seen as a kind of psi-type phenomenon as it involves the mind acting on the physical world (albeit usually through a supposed supernatural intermediary). While some individual studies have found that praying for others at a distance can lead to a beneficial health outcome, most studies do not show an effect of intercessory prayer (Roberts et al., 2007). For our purposes, we are exploring the varieties of spiritual experiences and thus are focusing on the nature of the experiences themselves rather than the status of their metaphysical reality. However, unlike most spiritual experiences, supporters of psi phenomena do posit falsifiable hypotheses, so the reality of these claims can be scientifically evaluated.

Perhaps the most recent well-known case of a scientist investigating psi phenomena was presented by Cornell psychologist Daryl Bem. Bem (2011) published an article in the *Journal of Personality and Social Psychology*, a prestigious psychology journal, called "Feeling the Future." In it, Bem purported to show positive results for ESP. Specifically, he allegedly showed that participants were able to anticipate whether positive or negative stimuli would be presented to them—in other words, that participants can see the future in some small way. While a handful researchers have taken Bem's findings as confirmatory (Bem et al., 2015), almost all other scientists take Bem's findings as a wakeup call that improvements in the methods of psychological science are needed (Ritchie, 2020).

Contemporary Ghost Research

Since researchers started including items about spiritual experience, many have noted that participants spontaneously report paranormal experiences. As leading researchers in the field have stated: "A controversial issue in the study of religious experience is the persistent finding that individuals who report various religious experiences also report various paranormal experiences" (Zollschan, Schumaker, & Walsh, 1995). Some scholars have explicitly excluded anything paranormal from the domain of religious or spiritual studies, as such phenomena are usually rejected by religious traditions (Baker et al., 2016). But, we have seen in our own research that these reports are simply too numerous to ignore.

The percentage of the U.S. population who believe that they have "had some degree of contact with a deceased person" is about 42% (Hood et al., 2009, p. 189). Other estimates are much higher, especially when it comes to bereavement. There are some factors that predispose individuals to having a paranormal experience. For example, religious individuals report paranormal experiences at a rate of about 48%, while nonreligious individuals report such encounters at about 32% (Hood et al., 2009, p. 190). Religious practices have also been shown to increase reports of paranormal experience. Of those who pray daily, about 42% report paranormal experiences, whereas those who pray less than once a week report paranormal experiences at about 29% (Hood et al., 2009, p. 190).

In the study by Lau et al. (2020), the authors coded spiritual excerpts for paranormal experience, which they referred to as *metaphysical phenomena*. The authors found that 51% of U.S. narratives, 39% of Indian narratives, and 56% of Chinese narratives made references to ESP (which includes telepathy, clairvoyance, precognition, realistic dreams, and intuitive impressions). Additionally, 7% of U.S. narratives, 7% of Indian narratives, and 4% of Chinese narratives contained references to *psychokinesis* (or mind–matter interaction). The following excerpts given by Chinese participants from the Lau et al. (2020) study illustrate some of these paranormal experiences:

When I was a child, I accidentally injured my knee once. My mom felt intense pain in the same place in her knee at the same time. Soon she got the phone call from school to ask her to go to the hospital ASAP. (p. 19)

Another category in the Lau et al., 2020, study, called "survival hypothesis," included near -death experience, out-of-body experience, and apparitional experience. References to these sorts of paranormal experience were made by 30% of U.S. narratives, 21% of Indian narratives, and 22% of Chinese narratives. The following is an example of paranormal experience of this apparitional type (Lau et al., 2020):

> I'm not sure if this counts, but after I came home from my grandmother's funeral, I sat on my bed. I don't recall ever falling asleep because I don't remember ever waking up. But I was sitting in my room and had a conversation with my grandmother. When it was over, I guess I woke up, but I wasn't really asleep. It's hard to describe. It was as if she took a moment to say bye." (p. 22)

Finally, the authors coded for *faith/energy healing*, which appeared in 18% of U.S. narratives, 29% of Indian narratives, and 21% of Chinese narratives. The exemplar of this type of paranormal experience that follows is from an Indian participant in the study:

> A professor, Sheikh and spiritual director in the Sufi tradition, shared with me his life-changing encounter with an angel. A couple of years ago he was in the hospital, at death's door due to a serious lung infection, feeling as if he were drowning. Finally he dozed, and saw an enormous Archangel place his hands on the left side of his chest and pull out "something." The Archangel communicated without words that all would be well, and that this was his initiation so that he could help others through the passageway to the Divine Light. (p. 23)

In a less scientific study, a Huffington Post poll found about the same range of people who believe in ghosts (about 45%) and, interestingly, found that about 43% of these people did not believe that ghosts can harm or interact with living beings (Spiegel, 2013). While it remains, in general, socially taboo to discuss whether one has had paranormal experiences, they appear rather common. In some cultural contexts, in England, for example, belief in ghosts is currently more prevalent than the belief in God (Dahlgreen, 2016).

In our research, we found that paranormal experiences were the least likely to relate to well-being than any of the other experiences. Unlike the other spiritual experiences discussed so far, paranormal experiences do not correlate positively with well-being. On the contrary, there is a slightly *negative* correlation between well-being and paranormal experiences. Additionally, paranormal experience is the only type of spiritual experience that is significantly related to mental illness. It may be the more frequent context of grief and bereavement related to these experiences that drives this finding (Table 14.1).

People reported a number of different kinds of paranormal experiences. Some of these involved supernatural entities: Participants mentioned guardian angels, spirits, and even (though rarely) demons. Other experiences included encounters with entities under the influence of psychedelic substances, particularly DMT (*N,N*-dimethyltryptamine). This aspect of psychedelic experiences is just beginning to be investigated by Roland Griffith's team at Johns Hopkins and offers a fascinating new direction in this research domain (Davis et al., 2021; Griffiths et al., 2019).

Ghost experiences are common across many cultures. In Thailand, there is a well-known ghost story that allegedly took place in the 1800s close to Bangkok. As religious studies professor Justin McDaniel (2011) related in *The Lovelorn Ghost and The Magical Monk*, the story centers on Mae Nak, a ghost who would reportedly kill anyone who tried to convince her still-living husband that she was a ghost. After a number of people had been murdered by

Table 14.1. Paranormal Experience With Well-Being, Mental Health, and Faculties of Consciousness

	Paranormal Unknown	Paranormal Known
Well-Being Outcomes		
More positive emotions	−.36**	−.16**
Better personal relationships	−.20**	−.10*
Greater sense of meaning in life	−.29**	−.10*
Mental Health Outcomes		
Depression	.24**	.19**
Anxiety	.33**	.18**
Faculties of Consciousness		
Sense of space changed	−.05	−.05
Noetic quality	−.12*	−.06
Sense of time changed	−.15**	−.18**

*p < .05. **p < .01.

the ghost, a Buddhist monk was called to chant sutras (Buddhist scriptures) in order to release the ghost from her attachments and rid the town of its killer ghost problem. To this day in Thailand, a ritual including a mock "funeral" for the ghost is carried out in honor of Mae Nak and features monks chanting sutras.

Buddhist monks are not the only religious representatives trained to handle ghosts and other paranormal phenomena; most religious traditions involve something like exorcism. In Hinduism, some descriptions of casting out demon-like beings is contained in the *Atharva Veda*, and in Islam *ruqya* describes a practice similar to exorcism. In Catholicism, Section 11 of the *Rituale Romanum* provides the guidelines for performing exorcisms, and the Vatican currently offers a course for priests on how to perform them (BBC, 2018). Mother Teresa, a modern Catholic saint, reportedly underwent an exorcism later in her life (Bindra, 2001).

One researcher has claimed that there is some cross-cultural support for at least one kind of paranormal experience that typically occurs during sleep. Researcher and University of Pennsylvania physician David Hufford described what he called the "Old Hag" experience, which involves a nightmare during which one feels paralyzed by the sight of what is often an older woman. Hufford wrote: "You are dreaming and you feel as if someone is holding you down. You can do nothing, only cry out. People believe that you will die if you are not awakened" (Hufford, 1982, p. 2). Hufford speculates that this experience likely results from a combination of hypnogogic imagery and sleep paralysis (SP), the latter of which affects about 8% of the population.

It appears somewhat similar experiences occur in many cultures. In their cross-cultural review of the dissociative state of SP, de Sá and Mota-Rolim (2016) summarized the different manifestations of SP hallucinations:

Interestingly, throughout human history, different peoples interpreted SP under a supernatural view. For example, Canadian Eskimos attribute SP to spells of shamans, who hinder the ability to move, and provoke hallucinations of a shapeless presence. In the Japanese tradition, SP is due to a vengeful spirit who suffocates his enemies while sleeping. In Nigerian culture, a female demon attacks during dreaming and provokes paralysis. A modern manifestation of SP is the report of "alien abductions", experienced as inability to move during awakening associated with visual hallucinations of aliens. In all, SP is a significant example of how a specific biological phenomenon can be interpreted and shaped by different cultural contexts. (p. 1)

Dream states impinging on one's awareness while in the process of waking appears to be one potential mechanism by which these experiences occur, though additional research is needed to identify more specific mechanisms.

Ghosts and the Machines

Coventry University lecturer Vic Tandy was working at night in a laboratory that was haunted, at least according to local legend. A cleaning worker had already quit because of a terrifying encounter with the supposed ghost that haunted the lab. On this particular night, Tandy suddenly had the sensation of being watched. His neck hair stood up, and he saw a floating gray entity out of the corner of his eye: "It seemed to be between me and the door, so the only thing I could do was turn and face it" (Arnot, 2000). This matched the description given by the cleaner.

On the following day, the same thing happened to Tandy. This time, though, he noticed that the metal blade of the fencing sword he was repairing was vibrating, providing a clue to solving this particular mystery. It turned out that a fan in the lab was creating a vibration below 20 Hz, which is considered an "infrasound" vibration and is outside the range of human hearing. This vibration, to be precise, was exactly 18.9 Hz, which is about the resonant frequency of the human eye. When a vibration matches that of the human eye, one can "see things that aren't there," as physicist Neil DeGrasse Tyson put it (Rogers, 2016). Tandy discovered this frequency in another supposedly "haunted" location. He wrote up his findings and published them under the title "The Ghost in the Machine" (Tandy & Lawrence, 1998) in the *Society for Psychical Research*, the same journal in which William James had also published in about 100 years earlier.

Another researcher, Olaf Blanke in Switzerland, investigated feelings of presence in the context of out-of-body experiences (Blanke et al., 2014). He was inspired, in part, by stories from high-altitude climbers who reported paranormal experiences. For example, Reinhold Messner described his experience of sensing a presence while climbing back down a mountain, which was "descending with us, keeping a regular distance, a little to my right and a few steps away from me, just outside my field of vision." In fact, this climber was a nonphysical entity that Messner believes he hallucinated.

Blanke and his team (2014) conducted brain scans on 12 patients who frequently had paranormal experiences. He found that these patients differed from controls in their frontoparietal regions, often associated with executive function. Then, in order to study feelings of presence in the laboratory, normal participants had sensors attached to their hands. When participants moved their hands, the motion would be replicated by a robotic hand that would touch participants on their back. Strangely, this created the illusion that participants were touching their own backs. When this feedback system was adjusted such that the participants' hand motions were uncoupled with the machine touching their back, some participants experienced feelings of a presence—as if there were other beings in the room. Several of the participants found the impression so unsettling that they asked for the experiment to stop.

How could this be? As the authors described, the motor system (which controls bodily movements) is highly connected to the sensory system. These parts of the brain make predictions about where one's body will be at a given moment and what it will feel. A mismatch between one's movements, one's sensations, and/or one's predictions can result in unusual perceptions. In this case, the mismatch between one's hand movement and a tactile sensation on one's back produced the feeling of a presence. Here, as in most or all of the other spiritual experiences, there was a temporary uncoupling of one's representation of one's body in space.

Ghosts and Chemistry

Some chemical causes for paranormal experiences have been identified. For example, in her TED talk, Carrie Poppy described her own personal experience with these phenomena (https://www.npr.org/templates/transcript/transcript.php?storyId=533791342). Over the course of several days, every evening in her apartment Poppy felt as if she was being watched. It was a vague sense of a presence coupled with a feeling of dread. She started to hear something move past her as well; she described it as a "whooshing" sound, almost like a wave crashing on a beach and whispering sounds. The feelings of dread increased to the point that she felt a pressure on her chest. The fear frequently drove her to tears.

Poppy began searching the internet for more information about ghosts, demons, and paranormal encounters. What she found may have saved her life. After googling a number of ghost hunters and paranormal groups, she eventually found her way to a skeptics website that works to debunk reports of the paranormal. A member told her that her symptoms were consistent with carbon monoxide poisoning. After calling her gas company, the utility worker found that there was indeed a carbon monoxide leak in her apartment—and told her that the levels were approaching the range that is considered deadly.

Other safe, nontoxic substances can also cause experiences of encounters with entities. Psychedelic researchers Alan Davis and Roland Griffiths of Johns Hopkins have begun to investigate whether individuals using these substances report experiences with particular nonphysical entities. They found that across all of the so-called classic hallucinogens (LSD, psilocybin, ayahuasca, and DMT) a substantial portion of users reported encountering a nonphysical "entity" (Davis et al., 2020). Furthermore, many users reported that they engaged in a two-way communication with the entity that they came into contact with. Most often, they described the entity as "intelligent" and "benevolent." While many researchers interpret this experience as an encounter with one's unconscious mind, many believe that these experiences are with a supernatural entity of some kind.

Kindred Spirits

Some supernatural entities are associated with local legends or religious doctrine, but others occur closer to home. The most frequent kind of paranormal experiences involve an apparition of a recently deceased family member or friend. The following experience was written by an individual who did not receive adequate anesthetic during surgery and who experienced excruciating pain but was comforted by a paranormal experience of a loved one:

> "The pain was fifteen on a scale of ten when the surgeon's hands were running over my bowels," she told me. "When my head was being massaged, I became aware of a faint light off to my left. When I noticed it, an incredible sense of love, comfort and caring washed over me. I then sensed the presence of my deceased mother, telling me it was not yet my time to die and

that she would help me. Then I was at peace and mercifully lost consciousness." (Nelson, 2010, p. 40)

Other experiences of this kind are more mundane, even domestic. Many people have experiences involving their recently deceased spouse. In one study, the majority of both men and women said they experienced their spouse in some way after their spouse had passed away (Luhrmann, 2012, p. 219). Many of these people felt a sense of a presence, while others would actually hear and/or talk with the deceased. However, most of those who had these experiences were too embarrassed to tell anyone about their experience for fear that they would be judged or their sanity would be questioned. In general, most of these individuals considered their experiences beneficial for the grieving process. Typically, these experiences peak a few weeks to a month after the death and then dissipate about a year later. This time course tracks with the reductions in negative mood, loneliness, crying, fatigue, and anxiety.

What underlying psychological and neurobiological systems may help to account for this process? We could draw inspiration from a Buddhist idea about ghosts, which is that they are mental projections related to one's attachments. Psychologically speaking, the attachment system certainly seems to be involved. A spouse is such a close attachment that some research even suggests that we begin to include our partners into our sense of self, as we have seen previously (Aron et al., 1992). It may be that we become so habituated to the physical and mental presence of a close other, like a spouse, that when their body is taken away we continue to habitually predict that the person will be present. Sometimes this prediction might be so strong that it intrudes into our actual perception of our environment, allowing us to see a projection of our own minds in our surroundings—as if our minds were projecting a hologram of an expected presence. On the other hand, it may be that in these moments we are truly perceiving a nonphysical presence, as believers would have it.

It is interesting that the most "far-out" seeming kind of spiritual experience, which is generally considered the strangest by the scientific establishment (and by our culture), is in some ways the closest to home. Paranormal experiences do not involve the sense of interconnectedness with all things, a vast and overwhelming God of all creation, or events conspiring in our favor—but rather involve an image of a yearned for loved one who is no longer with us.

Neuroscience

We have already considered some of the potential neurophysiological correlates of paranormal experiences. But there are a few other important possibilities. Experiences in sensory deprivation chambers are associated with a sensed presence and related hallucinatory experiences (Daniel & Mason, 2015), and there is some evidence that this is mediated by alpha brain wave activity in the visual areas of the brain (Hayashi et al., 1992). It could be that as sensory input is reduced, one's expectations begin to have more sway over one's perception. Such a process could also occur during various trance states in which sensory input is functionally reduced through the trance-inducing practice (Peres et al., 2012).

Our group (A. B. N.) collected neuroimaging data in a group of Brazilian mediums performing a practice called psychography (Peres et al., 2012). This practice involves entering a trance state and then writing whatever the "spirits" they perceive to have contacted ask them to write (for more information about this practice, see Krippner & Friedman, 2009). The brain scans demonstrated that highly proficient mediums had decreased activity in the frontal lobe and related language areas while purportedly communicating with the spirits. The implication is that the decreased activity allowed the mediums to release executive control and have this spiritual experience.

Figure 14.2 shows the scans from the Brazilian mediums performing psychography. The areas involved include the temporal lobe, anterior cingulate, and hippocampus. These areas are generally involved in language (temporal lobe), which is consistent with the process of writing in psychography; emotional responses (hippocampus); and concentration (anterior cingulate). The images show that the expert mediums had decreased activity (the

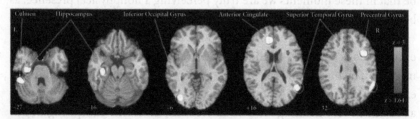

Figure 14.2 Brain scans of Brazillian mediums who felt that they were channeling spirits. From Andrew Newberg.

top lines) in these areas, while the less experienced mediums had increased activity (the bottom lines). This means that as people become more expert at entering the trance state and facilitating the experience of mediumship, their brain function changes. The decreased activity in the experts implies that the process becomes more "automatic" for them. It feels easier and feels as if the spirits flow through them. In addition, the experts feel as if the experience is happening to them rather than having them make it happen (which corresponds to James's criterion of passivity).

Of course, it is not clear whether this reduced brain activity directly caused the medium to have such an experience or if it allowed their brain to "quiet down" in order to actually perceive the spirits (James's methodological agnosticism suggests holding such questions in abeyance). One other finding from this study is that more novice mediums actually had the opposite pattern of brain activity during mediumistic trance. This finding suggests, perhaps, that there is a kind of "training" effect, and that people can theoretically learn how to have such experiences. This also may not be surprising since practices such as meditation and prayer are performed to heighten one's ability to have a spiritual experience over time.

Conclusion

Paranormal experiences refer to perceptions of discrete, nonphysical entities such as spirits, demons, and ghosts of deceased loved ones. People spontaneously provide accounts of these kinds of encounters when asked to describe spiritual experiences. There are a number of myths in religions about ghosts and angels as well as local legends; these cultural narratives undoubtedly play a role in these experiences. However, it may be that people who report these experiences are more likely to have had recent bereavement or other emotional trauma. Paranormal experiences during these highly emotional states are extremely common and may be helpful in that process, although this is not clear from the data. It is also possible that these experiences are more associated with mental illness than the other kinds of spiritual experience that we have reviewed throughout this part of the book. Regardless, paranormal experiences represent an important variety of spiritual experience and should be a target for future studies to explore their relationship with triggers, outcomes, and brain processes.

References

Alston William, P. (1993). *Perceiving God: The Epistemology of Religious Experience.* Chicago.

Appelle, S. (1996). The abduction experience: A critical evaluation of theory and evidence. *Journal of UFO Studies, 6,* 29–78.

Arnot, C. (2000, July 10). Ghost buster. *The Guardian.*

Aron, A., Aron, E. N., & Smollan, D. (1992). Inclusion of other in the self scale and the structure of interpersonal closeness. *Journal of Personality and Social Psychology, 63*(4), 596.

Baker, J. O., Bader, C., & Mencken, F. C. (2016). A bounded affinity theory of religion and the paranormal. *Sociology of Religion, 77*(4), 334–358. https://doi.org/10.1093/socrel/srw040

BBC. (2018). *Exorcism: Vatican course opens doors to 250 priests.* https://www.bbc.com/news/world-europe-43697573

Bem, D. J. (2011). Feeling the future: Experimental evidence for anomalous retroactive influences on cognition and affect. *Journal of Personality and Social Psychology, 100*(3), 407.

Bem, D. J., Tressoldi, P., Rabeyron, T., & Duggan, M. (2015). Feeling the future: A meta-analysis of 90 experiments on the anomalous anticipation of random future events. *F1000Research, 4,* 1188.

Bindra, S. (2001). *Archbishop: Mother Teresa underwent exorcism.* CNN. https://web.archive.org/web/20050917210156/http://archives.cnn.com/2001/WORLD/asiapcf/south/09/04/mother.theresa.exorcism/

Blanke, O., Pozeg, P., Hara, M., Heydrich, L., Serino, A., Yamamoto, A., . . . Arzy, S. (2014). Neurological and robot-controlled induction of an apparition. *Current Biology, 24*(22), 2681–2686.

Cox, W. S. (1936). An experiment on extra-sensory perception. *Journal of Experimental Psychology, 19*(4), 429–437.

Dahlgreen, W. (2016). *British people more likely to believe in ghosts than a creator.* YouGov. Retrieved January 31, 2019, from https://yougov.co.uk/topics/politics/articles-reports/2016/03/26/o-we-of-little-faith

Daniel, C., & Mason, O. J. (2015). Predicting psychotic-like experiences during sensory deprivation. *BioMed Research International, 2015,* 439379. https://doi.org/10.1155/2015/439379

Davis, A. K., Clifton, J. M., Weaver, E. G., Hurwitz, E. S., Johnson, M. W., & Griffiths, R. R. (2020). Survey of entity encounter experiences occasioned by inhaled *N,N*-dimethyltryptamine: Phenomenology, interpretation, and enduring effects. *Journal of Psychopharmacology, 34*(9), 1008–1020. https://doi.org/0269881120916143

de Sá, J. F. R., & Mota-Rolim, S. A. (2016). Sleep paralysis in Brazilian folklore and other cultures: A brief review. *Frontiers in Psychology, 7,* 1294.

Griffiths, R. R., Hurwitz, E. S., Davis, A. K., Johnson, M. W., & Jesse, R. (2019). Survey of subjective "God encounter experiences": Comparisons among naturally occurring experiences and those occasioned by the classic psychedelics psilocybin, LSD, ayahuasca, or DMT. *PloS One, 14*(4), e0214377.

Hayashi, M., Morikawa, T., & Hori, T. (1992). EEG alpha activity and hallucinatory experience during sensory deprivation. *Perceptual and Motor Skills, 75*(2), 403–412.

Hood, R. W., Hill, P. C., & Spilka, B. (2009). *The psychology of religion: An empirical approach.* New York, NY: Guilford.

Hufford, D. (1982). *The terror that comes in the night: An experience-centered study of supernatural assault traditions* (Vol. 7). University of Pennsylvania Press.

Irwin, H. J., & Watt, C. A. (2007). *An introduction to parapsychology.* McFarland.

James, W. (1902/2009). The varieties of religious experience: A study in human nature. *eBooks@Adelaide.* https://csrs.nd.edu/assets/59930/williams_1902.pdf

James, H. (2008). *Ghost stories.* Wordsworth Editions.

Jung, C. G. (1958/2020). *Flying saucers: A modern myth of things seen in the sky* (From Vols. 10 and 18, *Collected works*) (Vol. 2). Princeton University Press.

Kennedy, J. L. (1938). The visual cues from the backs of the *ESP* cards. *Journal of Psychology, 6,* 149–153.

Kress, K. A. (1999). Parapsychology in intelligence: A personal review and conclusions. *Journal of Scientific Exploration, 13*(1), 69–85.

Krippner, S., & Friedman, H. L. (Eds.). (2009). *Mysterious minds: The neurobiology of psychics, mediums, and other extraordinary people: The neurobiology of psychics, mediums, and other extraordinary people.* Praeger/ABC-CLIO.

Lau, E., McClintock, C., Graziosi, M., Nakkana, A., & Garcia, A. (2020). Content analysis of spiritual life in contemporary USA, India, and China. *Religions, 11,* 286.

Leithauser, B. L. (2012, October 29). *Ever scarier: On "The Turn of the Screw." New Yorker.*

Luhrmann, T. M. (2012). *When God talks back: Understanding the American evangelical relationship with God.* Knopf.

McDaniel, J. T. (2011). *The lovelorn ghost and the magical monk: Practicing Buddhism in modern Thailand.* Columbia University Press.

McNab, J. A. (2019). *The ghost artist: Tracing spectral embodiment as a figure of aesthetic resistance, in an unknown woman's eighteenth century paintings, and works by Hilma af Klint and Louise Bourgeois.* Doctoral Dissertation. https://dare.uva.nl/search?identifier=a22e4c86-df02-4943-a9d6-eeac9c7fc274

Nelson, K. (2010). *The spiritual doorway in the brain: A neurologist's search for the God experience.* Penguin.

Pasulka, D. W. (2019). *American cosmic: UFOs, religions, technology.* Oxford University Press.

Peres, J. F., Moreira-Almeida, A., Caixeta, L., Leao, F., & Newberg, A. (2012). Neuroimaging during trance state: A contribution to the study of dissociation. *PLoS One. 7*(11), e49360. https://doi.org/10.1371/journal.pone.0049360

Richardson, R. D. (2006). *William James: In the maelstrom of American modernism.* Houghton Mifflin.

Ritchie, S. (2020). *Science fictions: How fraud, bias, negligence, and hype undermine the search for truth.* Metropolitan Books.

Roberts, L., Ahmed, I., & Hall, S. (2007, January). Intercessory prayer for the alleviation of ill health. *Cochrane Database Systematic Review,* (1), CD000368. https://doi.org/10.1002/14651858.CD000368.pub2

Rogers, S. (2016). *Tuning in to the spooky "ghost frequency."* Interesting Engineering. https://interestingengineering.com/tuning-ghost-frequency

Society for Psychical Research. (2018). Our history. Retrieved June, 28, 2010.

Spiegel, L. (2013, February 2). *Spooky number of Americans believe in ghosts.* Huffington Post. https://www.huffpost.com/entry/real-ghosts-americans-poll_n_2049485

Strassman, R. (2000). *DMT: The spirit molecule: A doctor's revolutionary research into the biology of near-death and mystical experiences.* Simon & Schuster.

Tandy, V., & Lawrence, T. R. (1998). The ghost in the machine. *Journal-Society for Psychical Research, 62,* 360–364.

Tart, C. T., Puthoff, H. E., & Targ, R. (1980). Information transmission in remote viewing experiments. *Nature, 284*(13), 191.

Wolframm, H. (2015). *The stepchildren of science: Psychical research and parapsychology in Germany, c. 1870–1939.* Brill Online Books.

Zha, L., & McConnell, T. (1991). Parapsychology in the People's Republic of China: 1979–1989. *Journal of the American Society for Psychical Research, 85,* 119–143.

Zollschan, G. K., Schumaker, J. F., & Walsh, G. F. (1995). *Exploring the paranormal: Perspectives on belief and experience.* Prism Pr.

PART III

CONSIDERATIONS AND APPLICATIONS

As soon as a spiritual experience ends, the process of trying to understand and react to it begins. The final part of the book describes how people respond to their spiritual experiences, how clinicians can help people integrate these experiences, as well as how philosophers, theologians, and scientists have interpreted these experiences. At this point of the book, we hope that we have convinced you that people throughout history and up to today report spiritual experiences, and that they do so at surprisingly high rates, that a variety of kinds of experiences can be classed under this broad category, and that people can feel alternately haunted or elevated by them. But once the blinding flash of the illumination fades, what is one to make of one's memory of the experience? Indeed, what is one to make of reality itself after such an experience?

One answer to these questions is: *nothing*. In the same way that one may see strange images during a fever, one could merely attribute spiritual experiences to a neurophysiological oddity and say nothing more of the matter. Some people do exactly this. Another possible answer to these questions is: *everything*. Many people report a changed feeling about themselves and reality as a whole: Things seem new and fresh, as if they are seeing reality for the first time. Some people also change their fundamental beliefs about reality. Something about spiritual experiences seems to suggest to many people that our physical existence is only one part of a much larger reality. Even people who purport not to change their beliefs often seem tempted to make some adjustments to their levels of certainty regarding the nature of existence, self, and consciousness. Most peoples' response fits somewhere between unchanged and transformed, but the impact of these brief experiences is frequently striking nonetheless. These often profound changes raise challenges and opportunities for psychiatry, psychology, neuroscience, and spirituality in the 21st century.

15

Interpretations and Integration
of the Experience

When journalist Barbara Ehrenreich was a teenager, she found herself exhausted during a cross-country road trip. She had spent a couple of mostly sleepless nights in a car, and at some point, in the early morning, she left the car and began wandering through a small town. After walking aimlessly for a while, she described a sudden and dramatic experience she called "ineffable," "transcendent," and "mystical" in her book *Living With a Wild God: A Nonbeliever's Search for the Truth About Everything* (2014). She wrote:

> At some point in my predawn walk—not at the top of the hill or the exact moment of sunrise, but in its own good time—the world flamed into life. How else to describe it? There were no visions, no prophetic voices or visits by totemic animals, just this blazing everywhere. Something poured into me and I poured out into it. This was not the passive beatific merger with "the All," as promised by the Eastern mystics. It was a furious encounter with a living substance that was coming at me through all things at once. (Ehrenreich, 2014, p. 116)

This experience has similarities with a couple of the types of spiritual experiences described in the previous part of this book. Interestingly, the mention of the living substance could suggest a sense of presence, which would make this a numinous experience, yet it also seems to involve some degree of the self-loss and connectedness of a mystical experience. This is another example of how difficult it is to adequately classify many accounts of spiritual experience.

Spiritual experiences are often difficult to understand for those who have them. When Ehrenreich looked back on her experience later in life, she described her struggle to interpret and integrate her experience:

The Varieties of Spiritual Experience. David B. Yaden and Andrew B. Newberg, Oxford University Press. © David Yaden and Andrew Newberg 2022. DOI: 10.1093/oso/9780190665678.003.0015

It hadn't been until I reached my forties that I discovered what happened to me, or something very similar, has also happened to many other people, and that some of them had even found ways of talking about it, although usually in a vocabulary and framework foreign to me, if not actually re-pulsive. . . . So what do you do with something like this—an experience so anomalous, so disconnected from the normal life you share with other people, that you can't even figure out how to talk about it? I was also, I have to admit, afraid of sounding crazy. (Ehrenreich, 2014, p. xii)

Ehrenreich described her frustration with the lack of resources to learn about her experience as well as the social taboo around speaking about her expe-rience. She then mentioned *The Varieties of Religious Experience: A Study in Human Nature* (henceforth *The Varieties*; James, 1902/2009) explicitly and explained how it would have helped her to interpret and integrate her experience:

But for subjective accounts of . . . experiences, the most useful work remains the psychologist William James's chapter on "Mysticism" in *The Varieties of Religious Experience*, now more than a century old. I wish that I had found it many years ago. (Ehrenreich, 2014, p. 217)

The same lack of guidebooks and culture of silence around these experiences unfortunately largely remains today despite the pioneering work begun by James. We hope this book helps to fill this need.

James on the Sensation of Reality

James made clear that he included so many accounts in *The Varieties* (1902/2009) partly in order to convince his readers that spiritual experiences are a well-established fact of human subjectivity. That is, people really do have these experiences. Then, as now, some people who have not had such an experience will tend to doubt their reality when others report them. One view that can be safely confirmed is that reports of these experiences are *not* merely a matter of wishful thinking: People are not lying about having had such experiences. In James's view, and ours, there are simply far too many accounts from too many different kinds of people for this to be the case. Therefore, this doubt ought to be rejected once and for all. In the closing chapters of the *The Varieties*, James assumed that he had demonstrated the subjective reality of these experiences to his audience (as do we):

> Even the least mystical of you must by this time be convinced of the ex-
> istence of mystical moments as states of consciousness of an entirely spe-
> cific quality, and of the deep impression they have on those who have them.
> (James, 1902/2009, p. 302)

One of the lasting contributions of *The Varieties* is to help move the debate beyond whether or not people have such experiences and on to studying the experiences scientifically. We hope that the previous two parts of this book have similarly convinced readers that people really have these experiences.

It is important to note, though, that when James was discussing the re-
ality of these experiences, he was generally referring to something about the *content* of the experience. That is, the experience is usually felt to reveal something about the true nature of reality. He referred to this as their "noetic quality." James wrote about the noetic quality in different ways in different places. In one instance, he referred to knowledge being conferred, which would suggest that information has been gained from the experience:

> Although so similar to states of feeling, mystical states seem to those who
> experience them to be also states of knowledge. They are states of in-
> sight into depths of truth unplumbed by the discursive intellect. They are
> illuminations, revelations, full of significance and importance, all inarticu-
> late though they remain; and as a rule they carry with them a curious sense
> of authority for after-time. (James, 1902/2009, p. 287)

However, elsewhere he emphasized ineffability, which would seem to pre-
clude information being gained (at least the kind of information that can be put into words). He also wrote about how "the feeling of reality may be some-
thing more like a sensation than an intellectual operation so-called" (James, 1902/2009, p. 51). In this last statement, James appears to be claiming that one's sense of reality is more akin to a feeling of realness rather than any particular thoughts, beliefs, or knowledge *about* reality. Regardless of whether knowledge is conferred or not during spiritual experience, James is clear that many people report that their experiences *seem* very real. But what is it about these experiences that feels real?

James argued that one's relationship with the world often seems to change as a result of spiritual experiences. He wrote: "The outward face of nature need not alter, but the expressions of meaning in it alter. It was dead and is alive again. It is like the difference between looking on a person without love, or upon the same person with love" (James, 1902/2009, p. 357). This quotation describes a vague kind of emotional shift in one's relationship with reality.

One's beliefs can change in explicit ways as well. James discussed the tendency to take spiritual experiences as evidence for a supernatural dimension in existence. Despite James's inclination to downplay the role of beliefs whenever possible in *The Varieties* and to examine spiritual experience in terms of what can be addressed scientifically, he noted that the religious, spiritual, or otherwise supernatural interpretation of a spiritual experience is a rather reflexive response for many individuals. He wrote: "It is natural that those who personally have traversed such an experience should carry away a feeling of its being a miracle rather than a natural process" (James, 1902/2009, p. 174). That is, religious/spiritual experiences tend to increase one's religious/spiritual beliefs.

James also described other beliefs, besides those related to supernaturalism, that seem to arise from or are strengthened by spiritual experiences. James wrote:

> Mystical states in general assert a pretty distinct theoretic drift. It is possible to give the outcome of the majority of them in terms that point in definite philosophical directions. One of these directions is optimism, and the other is monism. (James, 1902/2009, p. 315)

Optimism consists of the belief that the future will be valuable or otherwise enjoyable in some way. Monism is the belief that existence is fundamentally one thing, and it is tied to the notion that all things are interconnected to one another. One might speculate that different types of spiritual experiences tend to result in different kinds of beliefs. Perhaps numinous experiences result in more supernatural explanations, whereas mystical experiences result in more monistic beliefs, though this has yet to be examined empirically.

Realer Than Real: Contemporary Research

We address research on the feeling of realness tied to James's "noetic quality" and then move on to James's comments about shifts in more specific beliefs.

In general, the feeling of realness associated with spiritual experiences has been empirically supported across a number of studies.

Several of the measures that operationalize James's concept of mystical experiences explicitly include the noetic quality in their items. Hood's (1975) Mysticism Scale (M-Scale) includes items related to the noetic quality, such as: "I have had an experience in which a new view of reality was revealed to me." The Mystical Experience Questionnaire (MEQ; Barrett et al., 2015) also includes items related to the noetic quality, such as: "You are convinced now, as you look back on your experience, that in it you encountered ultimate reality (i.e., that you 'knew' and 'saw' what was really real)."

We have conducted our own research on the noetic quality in spiritual experiences. We asked participants to reflect on "any variety of spiritual experience" and to rate how real they thought their experience felt at both the time of the experience and after some time had passed. Of course, both of these questions require an individual to look back in time, but it seems important to understand whether one's impression of realness was limited only during an experience or whether it persisted over time. For example, dreams generally feel quite real while they occur but immediately seem unreal upon waking.

The results (Figure 15.1; from Yaden, Le Nguyen, Kern, Wintering, et al., 2017) demonstrate that people rated their experience as *more* real than everyday life, both while the experience occurred ("During"), and though to a somewhat lesser extent, after the experience ended ("In Hindsight"). Notably, the scale goes from less real to more real—and spiritual experiences indeed felt, to a majority of individuals, "realer than real." It was especially surprising for us to see how few participants were willing to rate their experiences, given how unusual they are, as *less* real than ordinary life.

How can an experience feel "realer than real"? At first glance, this sounds like an error in basic logic. However, if one considers how we must differentiate dreams and daydreams from our actual sensory surroundings on a daily basis, we might better have a sense for why we might attribute a feeling of realness to different experiences. In the case of spiritual experiences, the question of realness becomes fundamental.

In previous work, we have considered a variety of states that might be called "epistemic states." Epistemic states refer to states of consciousness that influence our perceptions of what is real. For example, when dreaming, we do not typically recognize it as such, but rather feel that the dream is real. If we are being chased by a dinosaur in the dream, we run. We generally don't

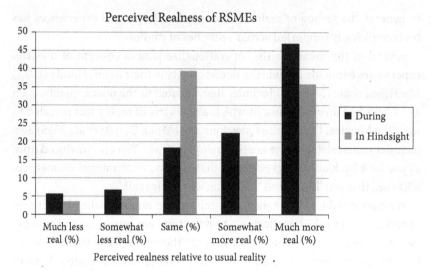

Figure 15.1 Feelings of realness during an experience and then in hindsight (Yaden et al., 2017). Copyright © 2017 by American Psychological Association. Reproduced with permission form American Psychological Association. Yaden, D. B., Le Nguyen, K. D., Kern, M. L., Wintering, N. A., Eichstaedt, J. C., Schwartz, H. A., Buffone, A.E., Smith, L.K., Waldman, M.R., Hood, R.W. & Newberg, A. B. (2017). The noetic quality: A multimethod exploratory study. *Psychology of Consciousness: Theory, Research, and Practice, 4*(1), 54.

realize that this might be a dream due to the fact that dinosaurs no longer exist. But the moment we wake up, we immediately feel that the dream is less than real, and our everyday sensory takes precedence.

But with spiritual experiences, the experience not only feels real during the experience but also *continues to feel real after the spiritual experience is over*. This seems to be a unique feature of spiritual experiences, as most of the time we immediately deem intensely altered states of consciousness as *less* real as soon as we leave them, as in waking from dreams. But the realness of spiritual experiences seems to transcend other epistemic states, including that of everyday reality.

It is interesting to speculate regarding what features we focus on when evaluating the relative degrees of realness of various experiences. Given how immediate and automatic these assessments are, it seems likely that there are brain processes that "tag" memories as more or less real. With dreams this seems to occur immediately on waking. Perhaps this occurs on the basis of the nature of the relationship between objects that one experiences during altered states. Regular relationships are what we typically perceive in everyday reality, whereas confusing and irregular relationships occur more often in dreams and in a negative way during psychotic states.

In reading the accounts of many participants in our surveys, people seem to see the visible world as changing and bound to time, whereas the "unseen order" or fundamental reality glimpsed in a spiritual experience is often seen as eternal and therefore more substantial (despite being presumably nonphysical). This intuition could be seen to stretch back to Plato's theory of the forms, and the notion of an underlying eternal essence has been apparent in most religious belief systems. One participant in our study wrote: "In these experiences, I feel the veil between myself and the rest of reality drop away." Several participants used the metaphor of the "veil":

> Whereas I would normally perceive of me being physically separate from others, I saw myself as being intertwined with them in an infinite dance of energy that was thinly veiled by physical existence.

Statements like these clearly point beyond appearances to the "unseen order" described by James and that we take as a definitional component for spiritual experience.

So What Is It Really?

Ultimately, most people who have had a spiritual experience spend time afterward trying to understand what it means to them. For most people, having a spiritual experience is the beginning of sometimes years-long processes of interpretation and integration. Typically, one must first decide what to believe about the experience. As with the example of Ehrenreich at the beginning of this chapter, some people think that the experience does not actually reflect a true reality but rather represents only some type of brain process, typically an abnormal one.

Princeton psychologist Tania Lombrozo has found that when people are presented with accounts of how normal brain function produces a belief in God, they are more likely to believe the neuroscientific account "corroborates" their belief in God. However, if belief in God is portrayed to *result from abnormal brain functioning*, then this fact is taken to undermine their belief in God (Plunkett et al., 2020).

Of course, brain function is an undeniable part of these experiences, though it is usually not clear what constitutes "normal" or "abnormal" functioning. One of the more obvious examples is psychedelic experiences. Everyone having a psychedelic experience knows that it starts by taking a psychoactive compound like LSD or psilocybin. In these cases, the drug (influenced by one's set and setting as well as the substance) causes an experience, and hence the experience is caused by a change in brain function. As we have seen in Part II, there are a number of reliable and observable changes in brain activity during spiritual experiences, and the brain changes associated with psychedelics are even more specifically characterized. Of course, if someone has an experience related to a near-death state or a seizure disorder, there is a reasonable presumption that the unusual brain state caused the experience, but in many cases the line between "normal" and "abnormal" is unclear.

Some people take the fact that there are measurable changes in brain function to be a sufficient explanation for what is perceived during spiritual experiences and infer that any things perceived are therefore necessarily delusions. However, the brain changes during *all* experiences—during dreams as well as waking life—so the fact that brain activity alters in predictable or measurable ways during spiritual experience tell us little if anything about perceptions during spiritual experiences.

For most people, the obvious interpretation of spiritual experiences is a religious/spiritual one (as most people hold religious and/or spiritual beliefs). According to this perspective, it may simply be that the brain enters a new and unusual state that has access to another realm of reality that humans do not typically have access to. According to this interpretation, spiritual experiences are literally real, and the supernatural or divine elements experienced reflect the true nature of mind and reality itself. There are extensive and well-developed approaches in many religions for how adherents ought to evaluate spiritual experiences. In some cases, these experiences are celebrated or even rewarded by religious traditions. In other cases, spiritual experiences are treated as heretical. This may be especially the case for women who report spiritual experiences, at least historically, as the typically patriarchally organized religious authorities may be even less willing to cede authority on the basis of a spiritual experience.

The interpretation process also occurs within nonreligious individuals, who might oscillate between naturalist and supernatural beliefs in some cases. Oxford philosopher A. J. Ayer was a well-known atheist who had a spiritual experience while near death (a near-death experience, NDE). He reportedly came to believe in supernaturalism for a very short while after his experience, but he then quickly returned to his view of naturalism and denied the possibility of anything supernatural. However, he was never again quite so certain about his atheism and apparently hedged just a tiny bit closer to agnosticism regarding the possibility of an afterlife. He also seemed emotionally changed by the experience, regardless of his brief flip-flop in beliefs. At a dinner party, Ayer's wife is said to have joked that he "has got so much nicer since he died" (Rogers, 2002, p. 349).

One's interpretation and integration of a spiritual experience will generally involve attempting to fit the experience within a preexisting mental framework. Keltner and Haidt described this process in the context of awe as a "need for accommodation," which refers to the process of creating new mental schemas (or how information is organized in the mind) to account for the experience. In our own research, we found that spiritual experiences did indeed tend to lead to more spiritual beliefs (Yaden, Le Nguyen, Kern, Belser, et al., 2017). Griffiths et al. (2019) also found that after spiritual experiences triggered by psychedelics people tended to endorse slightly more spiritual beliefs.

Beliefs About the World as a Whole

Interpretations of spiritual experiences involve not only beliefs about the supernatural, as mentioned, but also about how one feels about reality in general. In astronomer Carl Sagan's (1997) *Pale Blue Dot*, he quoted one of James's other (many) definitions of religion as "the feeling of being at home in the universe." This statement involves a feeling state in regard to reality. One can imagine that feeling at home in the universe is much different from feeling like one is living in a hostile and threatening place. These basic, broad changes in one's feelings and beliefs about everything appear to be positively shifted by spiritual experiences.

Contemporary psychologists have long measured these simple, unphilosophically sophisticated kinds of beliefs about how "the world" (or existence in general) seems to be to the people having these experiences. The cognitive triad is probably the best known case involving these basic kinds of beliefs. The cognitive triad, described by University of Pennsylvania psychiatrist Aaron Beck in the 1970s, consists of beliefs about (1) *one's self*, (2) *one's future*, and (3) *the world as a whole*. Beck is one of the cofounders of cognitive behavioral therapy (CBT; Beck et al., 1979), which is considered the gold standard in evidence-based psychotherapy (National Institute for Health and Clinical Excellence, 2011). One scale measuring the cognitive triad, called the Cognitive Triad Inventory (CTI; Beckham et al., 1986) includes items about one's general beliefs about the world, such as: "The world is a very hostile place."

In parallel with Beck's clinical work, so-called just world beliefs also received substantial research attention. Psychologist Melvin Lerner initiated this line of research in the 1960s with the just world hypothesis, arguing that many people see the world as operating in an intuitively karmic way wherein people "get what they deserve" (Lerner, 1980). In the decades since, just world beliefs have been compared with dozens of other variables (Furnham, 2003). One representative item on a common scale used to measure these beliefs, the Global Belief in a Just World Scale (Lipkus, 1991), is: "I basically feel that the world is a fair place."

Other beliefs focusing on the world as a whole have also been measured in the study of trauma. In the 1980s, psychologist Ronnie Janoff-Bulman described how beliefs about the world may change as a result of traumatic experiences. In particular, Bulman focused on how trauma survivors may change their views regarding the benevolence and meaningfulness of the world. In the World Assumptions Scale (WAS; 1989), Janoff-Bulman (1989) measured the benevolence, justice, randomness, and controllability of the world with subscales. This scale includes items such as: "The good things that happen in this world far outnumber the bad." Bulman described in her theoretical writing how one's "assumptive world" could become "shattered" after traumas.

Is it possible that beliefs about the world as a whole also change during spiritual experiences? Recently, psychologist Jeremy Clifton extended these lines of research on world beliefs by elaborating 26 additional beliefs, such as whether the world as a whole seems "safe," "enticing," and/or "alive." In a paper. "Primal World Beliefs," Clifton et al. (2019) found that participants reporting mystical experiences were more likely to see the world as a whole as good and as alive.

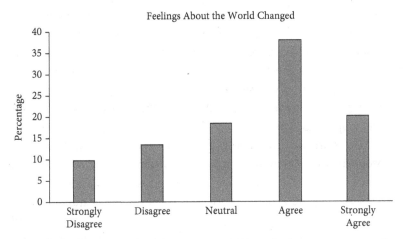

Figure 15.2 Feelings changing about "the world" or all of existence. Drawn by David Yaden.

In our Varieties Survey, we found that most participants indicated that their feelings about "the world" (i.e., all of existence) changed in some way as a result of their spiritual experience (Figure 15.2).

It may be that such shifts in beliefs are among the mechanisms through which people benefit from spiritual experiences. Although, as is the case with supernatural beliefs, there appear to be many cases in which people benefit from spiritual experiences without changing their beliefs—as was the case for Ehrenreich and Ayer.

Intentional States—The Content of Spiritual Experiences

Throughout this chapter we have seen that spiritual experiences feel real, and that one can change how they feel about existence as a result. So far, we have said that spiritual experiences must be substantially *altered states of consciousness* and are thereby differentiated from beliefs or thoughts as well as from emotions. Second, we have said that they refer to an *unseen order* of some kind. This criterion was included to differentiate spiritual experiences from just any unusual sensations that cannot quite be classified as beliefs or emotions.

Notice that the kinds of spiritual experiences referred to in Part II are differentiated on the basis of what it is that one perceives during the experience.

That is, accounts of experiences are differentiable because they refer to God (as in numinous experience), unity and/or self-loss (as in mystical experience), information from beyond the self (as in revelatory experience), a nonphysical entity like a ghost or an angel (as in paranormal experience – known or unknown), or beauty/sublimity (as in aesthetic experience – art or nature). Each of these types is differentiated on the basis of *what* is perceived during the spiritual experience.

Because spiritual experiences refer to something, they are what philosophers call "intentional states." Intentional states refer to mental states that represent, or are "about," something else. In the case of spiritual experiences, they are about an unseen order beyond appearances. Further, they can be subdivided based on particular kinds according to what kind of thing is perceived. Even spiritual experiences that seem to be about "everything," like mystical experiences, are referring to *some*thing—that thing just happens to be *every*thing.

The fact that spiritual experiences are intentional states means that beliefs inevitably reenter the discussion. As we have seen in this chapter, one must generally decide whether the subjective sensations that one has during spiritual experiences are of something real (revealing reality), something only in the mind (a hallucination), or remain undecided (agnostic). In the story at the beginning of this chapter, Ehrenreich decided to interpret the experience as a hallucination, albeit a mostly valuable one. In general, the content of spiritual experience usually demand some kind of interpretation and serious philosophical and/or theological reflection. The next chapter delves deeper into this issue.

Integration

Beyond interpreting the nature of one's experience, one must also generally psychologically integrate the experience into one's life narrative and sense of identity. Spiritual experiences are often powerfully disruptive events in one's life. As we have noted several times, the process of integrating spiritual experience can usually benefit from assistance from healthcare professionals— and in some cases such therapeutic support is essential.

A book called *Spiritual Emergency: When Personal Transformation Becomes a Crisis* (1989), edited by psychedelic researchers Stanislav and Christina Grof, includes chapters written by clinicians on how to handle patients struggling with their spiritual experiences. Describing the intention of their book, they wrote: "We feel that it is important to offer support to people undergoing crises of spiritual opening and to create circumstances in which the positive potential of these states can be fully realized" (Grof & Grof, 1989, p. xiii). As we have seen time and time again, there can be a fine line between positive spiritual experience and pathological states of dissociation and psychosis, but still more research is needed to better differentiate these states.

Providing further complexity, a number of individuals have had spiritual experiences that were initially difficult but deemed ultimately positive after successful integration. Clinicians can play an important role in integrating these experiences in a positive manner. There are organizations designed to provide education and clinical training in this process. For instance, in the United Kingdom, clinicians have pioneered the *Spiritual Crisis Network*, designed to help those suffering psychologically (usually from psychosis) to make meaning out of and integrate any spiritual content of their experiences that patients deem meaningful (Clarke, 2010).

In addition to the standard considerations that go into any clinical encounter, there are some further guidelines provided by Hastings (1983) and echoed by Lukoff et al. (2011) for clinicians attempting to help a patient to integrate an experience that may involve features that differ from the clinician's belief system (e.g., a patient describes feeling the presence of a god that the clinician does not believe in):

1. Ask the person to describe the experience or events.
2. Listen fully and carefully, without judging.
3. Reassure the person that the experience is not "crazy" or "insane," if this can be appropriately said.
4. Identify or label the type of event.
5. Give information about what is known about this kind of situation or process.
6. Where possible, develop reality tests to discover if the event is genuine. . . or if there are . . . alternative explanations.
7. Address the psychological reactions that result from the experience. . . (Hastings, 1983, p. 164).

Other guidelines to assist clinicians with helping patients to integrate their experiences have also been offered by David Lukoff, Francis Lu, and Paul Yang (p. 190). They are as follows:

In cases related to intensive religious and spiritual practices and experiences, therapy can make use of the following nine interventions:

- Normalize the experience.
- Create a therapeutic container.
- Help patient reduce environmental and interpersonal stimulation.
- Have patient temporarily discontinue spiritual practices.
- Use the therapy session to help ground the patient . . .
- Encourage the patient to become involved in simple, grounding, calming activities.
- Encourage the patient to express his or her inner world through drawing, journal writing, movement, and so on.
- Evaluate for medication,

In addition to healthcare professionals, religious leaders can sometimes help people to integrate spiritual experiences. For example, neurologist James Austin described a spontaneous spiritual experience in his book *Zen and the Brain* (1999). Austin was a practicing neurologist and a Zen meditation practitioner when he had the following spontaneous spiritual experience:

> It strikes unexpectedly at 9:00 AM, on the surface platform of the London subway system. . . . After the clatter of the departing train recedes, the empty platform is quiet. Waiting at leisure for the next train to Victoria Station, I turn and look away from the tracks, off to the south, in the general direction of the river Thames. . . . I idly survey this scene, unfocused, with no thought in mind. Instantly the entire view acquires three qualities: Absolute Reality, Intrinsic Rightness, Ultimate Perfection. (Austin, 1999, p. 537)

Austin goes on to describe how he sought guidance from his Zen meditation teacher. When Austin described his extraordinary experience to his teacher, she told him that she was happy for him, but that he should not "cling" to the experience. Instead, he should merely refocus his attention on his meditation practice. She told Austin, "Now move on. Leave the experience behind. . . . Others will come. Do not grasp them tightly" (Austin, 1999, p. 538). While spiritual experiences can be deeply personally meaningful, there is a long history in meditation traditions of deemphasizing their importance and refocusing individuals back to their practice, their community, and their responsibilities. The title of Buddhist teacher Jack Kornfield's book *After the*

Ecstasy, the Laundry (2001) illustrates well the need to integrate spiritual experiences into one's ordinary life.

Conclusion

Spiritual experiences are often monumental moments in one's life that require some kind of interpretation and integration within one's worldview. We have seen that spiritual experiences feel real, or even "realer than real," to those who have them. But one's interpretation of what it is that they encountered during their experience is likely an important factor in how the experience goes on to impact their life. We have seen broad ways in which one might interpret their experience, especially in regard to whether or not their experience was caused solely by brain processes or whether something supernatural was involved. We have also seen that one's beliefs about, or relationship with, reality in general can shift as a result of a spiritual experience, and that integrating these shifts can sometimes be aided by a healthcare professional. The next chapter moves beyond these broad interpretations to examine more specific philosophical beliefs regarding spiritual experiences.

References

Austin, J. H. (1999). *Zen and the brain: Toward an understanding of meditation and consciousness*. MIT Press.

Barrett, F. S., Johnson, M. W., & Griffiths, R. R. (2015). Validation of the revised Mystical Experience Questionnaire in experimental sessions with psilocybin. *Journal of Psychopharmacology, 29*(11), 1182–1190.

Beck, A. T., Rush, J. & Shaw, B. F. (1979). *Cognitive therapy of depression*. Guilford Press.

Beckham, E. E., Leber, W. R., Watkins, J. T., Boyer, J. L., & Cook, J. B. (1986). Development of an instrument to measure Beck's cognitive triad: The Cognitive Triad Inventory. *Journal of Consulting and Clinical Psychology, 54*, 566–567.

Clarke, I. (Ed.). (2010). *Psychosis and spirituality: Consolidating the new paradigm*. John Wiley & Sons.

Clifton, J. D., Baker, J. D., Park, C. L., Yaden, D. B., Clifton, A. B., Terni, P., . . . Seligman, M. E. (2019). Primal world beliefs. *Psychological Assessment, 31*(1), 82.

Ehrenreich, B. (2014). *Living with a wild God: A nonbeliever's search for the truth about everything*. Twelve.

Furnham, A. (2003). Belief in a just world: Research progress over the past decade. *Personality and Individual Differences, 34*(5), 795–817.

Griffiths, R. R., Hurwitz, E. S., Davis, A. K., Johnson, M. W., & Jesse, R. (2019). Survey of subjective "God encounter experiences": Comparisons among naturally occurring experiences and those occasioned by the classic psychedelics psilocybin, LSD, aya-huasca, or DMT. *PloS One, 14*(4), e0214377.

Grof, C., & Grof, S. (1986). Spiritual emergency: The understanding and treatment of transpersonal crises. *ReVISION, 8*(2), 7–20.

Grof, S., & Grof, C. (1989). *Spiritual emergency: When personal transformation becomes a crisis.* Tarcher.

Hastings, A. (1983). A counseling approach to parapsychological experience. *Journal of Transpersonal Psychology, 15*(2), 143–167.

Hood, R. W., Jr. (1975). The construction and preliminary validation of a measure of reported mystical experience. *Journal for the Scientific Study of Religion, 14*(1), 29–41.

James, W. (1902/2009). The varieties of religious experience: A study in human nature. *eBooks@Adelaide.* https://csrs.nd.edu/assets/59930/williams_1902.pdf

Janoff-Bulman, R. (1989). Assumptive worlds and the stress of traumatic events: Applications of the schema construct. *Social Cognition, 7,* 113–136.

Kornfield, J. (2001). *After the ecstasy, the laundry: How the heart grows wise on the spiritual path.* Bantam.

Lerner, M. (1980). *The belief in a just world: A fundamental delusion.* Plenum.

Lipkus, I. (1991). The construction and preliminary validation of a global belief in a just world scale and the exploratory analysis of the multidimensional belief in a just world scale. *Personality and Individual Differences, 12*(11), 1171–1178.

Lukoff, D., Lu, F. G., & Yang, C. P. (2011). DSM-IV religious and spiritual problems. *Religious and spiritual issues in psychiatric diagnosis: A research agenda for DSM V,* 171–198.

National Institute for Health and Clinical Excellence. (2011). *Common mental health disorders.* British Psychological Society and Royal College of Psychiatrists.

Plunkett, D., Buchak, L., & Lombrozo, T. (2020). When and why people think beliefs are "debunked" by scientific explanations of their origins. *Mind & Language, 35*(1), 3–28.

Rogers, B. (2002). *AJ Ayer: A life.* Grove Press.

Sagan, C. (1997). *Pale blue dot: A vision of the human future in space.* Random House Digital, Inc.

Yaden, D. B., Le Nguyen, K. D., Kern, M. L., Belser, A. B., Eichstaedt, J. C., Iwry, J., . . . Newberg, A. B. (2017). Of roots and fruits: A comparison of psychedelic and nonpsychedelic mystical experiences. *Journal of Humanistic Psychology, 57*(4), 338–353.

Yaden, D. B., Le Nguyen, K. D., Kern, M. L., Wintering, N. A., Eichstaedt, J. C., Schwartz, H. A., . . . Newberg, A. B. (2017). The noetic quality: A multimethod exploratory study. *Psychology of Consciousness: Theory, Research, and Practice, 4*(1), 54.

16

Beliefs Reprise

Philosophical Reflections

In the same way that it is easy to miss the overall arc of the argument in William James's *The Varieties* (1902/2009) due to all of the fascinating side roads into the various experiences that James included, some readers miss James's big reveal about his own beliefs about them toward the book's end. As mentioned throughout this book, we have followed James in holding off on describing James's philosophical perspective on the nature of spiritual experiences. In his Gifford Lectures, one can imagine that there was quite a bit of tension in the audience when he finally got around to revealing his beliefs on the topic. This chapter reveals James's philosophical beliefs about the ultimate metaphysical import of spiritual experience, but first it is worth understanding James's position in the field of philosophy to provide some context on his views.

From Cambridge to Cambridge

James's intellectual influence had, when *The Varieties* was published 1902, transcended psychology as he was by then also renowned as a philosopher. James was based in Cambridge, Massachusetts, at this time (at Harvard), but at the turn of the 20th century a philosophical renaissance was occurring in another Cambridge--namely, Cambridge University in England.

Bertrand Russell and his student Ludwig Wittgenstein were both at Cambridge University. Russell and Wittgenstein were (and remain) among the most iconic and important philosophers in the world. They were making what was widely seen as fundamental advances in logic, language, and mathematics, as well as a number of other subjects. Both Russell and Wittgenstein were aware of James's work in psychology as well as his philosophical writings. They both had good things to say about James's character. Wittgenstein once said of James: "That is what makes him a good philosopher; he was a real

The Varieties of Spiritual Experience. David B. Yaden and Andrew B. Newberg, Oxford University Press. © David Yaden and Andrew Newberg 2022. DOI: 10.1093/oso/9780190665678.003.0016

human being" (Monk, 1990, p. 478): Russell said of James that his "warm
heartedness and his delightful humour caused him to be almost universally
beloved" (Russell, 1946, p. 811). Their evaluation of James's writings, however, was much more variable.

Russell and Wittgenstein were both impacted by their reading of *The
Varieties*. In a letter to a friend, Russell described the profound impact
the book had on Wittgenstein: "I found that he has become a complete
mystic . . . and he seriously contemplates becoming a monk. It all started
from William James's *Varieties of Religious Experience*" (Myers, 2001, p. 461).
Some of Wittgenstein's students said that he frequently recommended *The
Varieties* to them and others (Monk, 1990). Russell also mentioned that
Wittgenstein thought *The Varieties* would "improve him in a way in which
he very much wanted to improve" (Monk, 1990, p. 112), referring here to his
moral character.

It is unclear whether Wittgenstein himself ever had a spiritual experience,
although he made somewhat oblique mention of them. Wittgenstein's philosophy of religion is complex and beyond the scope of what we can discuss
here—even the seemingly straightforward question of whether Wittgenstein
believed in God is deceptively difficult to answer. Wittgenstein appears to endorse a belief in God at times, although he also stated that *his belief does not
contain any content*. This is certainly not the typical kind of "belief in God"
that most people would endorse! Wittgenstein here described his paradoxi-
cally empty yet affirmative belief:

> I can well imagine a religion in which there are no doctrinal propositions,
> in which there is thus no talking. Obviously the essence of religion cannot
> have anything to do with the fact that there is talking, or rather: when
> people talk, then this itself is part of a religious act and not a theory. Thus
> it also does not matter at all if the words used are true or false or nonsense.
> (Monk, 1990, p. 305)

Again, endorsing a religion with no words appears to be a rather empty statement of "faith." One of Wittgenstein's students (note: Maurice O'Connor
Drury, who later became a psychiatrist) suggested to him that his religion
really consisted of the cultivation of a state of awe, combined with a strict silence regarding propositional statements of belief (Monk, 1990, p. 540). This
view can perhaps be best expressed by the statement for which Wittgenstein
is most famous: "Whereof one cannot speak, thereof one must be silent"

(1922, p. 7). While Wittgenstein believed religion was of the utmost importance, he believed nothing sensible could be said of it.

Russell's take on spiritual experience is different from Wittgenstein's. In his case, there is no question that he had had a spiritual experience. Russell's experience occurred in 1901, about a year before *The Varieties* was published. For context, he had just attended a poetry reading earlier that evening and shortly thereafter witnessed the suffering of someone close to him. He described a number of thoughts that seem to have come on as an epiphany (perhaps indicating a revelatory experience according to our rough categories). In his autobiography (Russell, 1951/2009), he described this epiphany as involving the importance of love above all and an abhorrence of violence. He wrote:

> At the end of those five minutes, I had become a completely different person. For a time, a sort of mystic illumination possessed me. I felt that I knew the inmost thoughts of everybody that I met in the street, and though this was, no doubt, a delusion, I did in actual fact find myself in far closer touch than previously with all my friends, and many of my acquaintances. (p. 149)

Russell described himself as transformed as a result of his "mystic illumination." This story may come as a surprise to some, as Russell is well known for his staunch atheism. Russell did clarify some points about this experience, though, essentially denying the parts that suggest that any true metaphysical knowledge was conveyed to him. However, he was adamant in endorsing the continued personal value of his experience. He wrote:

> The mystic insight which I then imagined myself to possess has largely faded, and the habit of analysis has reasserted itself. But something of what I thought I saw in that moment has remained always with me, causing my attitude during the first war, my interest in children, my indifference to minor misfortunes, and a certain emotional tone in all my human relations. (Russell, 1951/2009, p. 149)

Russell seems to have taken his personal experience into account when making his philosophical statements on such experiences. In an essay, "Mysticism and Logic," Russell put forth a nuanced perspective, writing 8 years after reading *The Varieties*: "The metaphysical creed, I shall maintain, is a mistaken outcome of this emotion, although this emotion, as colouring and informing all other thoughts and feelings, is the inspirer of whatever is best in Man" (Russell, 1910, p. 16). That is, Russell claimed that spiritual experiences can be psychologically valuable even if they do not provide accurate information about the nature of reality. According to Russell, spiritual experiences are likely delusions, yet they often have benefits.

Russell and Wittgenstein both had sophisticated perspectives when it came to interpreting spiritual experience from a philosophical perspective. This provides some context to Russell's summarizing statement, from his personal letters, on his view of *The Varieties*:

> We have all been reading with great pleasure James on Religious Experience—everything good about the book except the conclusions. (Russell, 1951/2009, p. 171)

What, then, are James's philosophical conclusions about which Russell and others in the Cambridge University group so objected?

James's "Professional" and "Personal" Conclusions

Perhaps this section should begin with a drumroll: James's perspective on the implications of spiritual experiences and whether they can be taken as evidence to support religious and spiritual beliefs. James's perspective on these questions was purposefully inscrutable throughout much of *The Varieties*. He argued consistently that spiritual experiences often have beneficial effects for those who have them (although of course also that they can be related to mental illness in some cases). But it has not been at all clear whether James himself believed these experiences should be considered entirely psychological (beneficial hallucinations) or whether they point to something about the nature of reality. In a move that the reader could now come to expect, and in a classically "Jamesian" manner, he provided contrasting perspectives.

James's views can be usefully subdivided into his "professional" and his "personal" conclusions.

In what could be considered James's *professional conclusion*, James doubled down on the methodological agnosticism that he maintained throughout *The Varieties* into a more general agnosticism. This agnosticism is particularly aimed at the knowledge about reality that can be taken from a spiritual experience. James was explicit that no indisputable evidence can be derived from spiritual experiences about any supernatural claims, yet at the same time he was equally explicit about the possible psychological value of such experiences. Here is a particularly clear statement of his position on both counts (by "infinitist" he meant something similar to a supernatural belief):

> Nevertheless, in the interests of intellectual clearness, I feel bound to say that religious experience, as we have studied it, cannot be cited as unequivocally supporting the infinitist belief. The only thing that it unequivocally testifies to is that we can experience union with SOMETHING larger than ourselves and in that union find our greatest peace. (James, 1902/2009, p. 397).

So far, this is rather uncontroversial and what one might predict James to claim, given his strict methodological agnosticism throughout *The Varieties*. It is a refreshingly explicit statement of this agnostic perspective. This is not a tentative agnosticism, either, which could be advanced on through future work. Instead, James claimed that this agnostic stance was not likely to change:

> In all sad sincerity I think we must conclude that the attempt to demonstrate by purely intellectual processes the truth of the deliverances of direct religious experience is absolutely hopeless. (James, 1902/2009, p. 344)

However, what we term James's *personal* conclusion is quite different from these statements. For this, some explanation of James's philosophical concept of "overbeliefs" is needed. Overbeliefs refer to beliefs for which one lacks sufficient evidence for or against, but which one is justified in adopting due to their beneficial effects. In order to understand the reasoning behind this kind of "belief on the basis of benefits," some understanding regarding the philosophical position that James is most known for, pragmatism, is required.

In *The Varieties*, James described pragmatism as an idea originating from his friend and colleague, philosopher Charles Sanders Peirce (although Peirce himself differentiated his own view of pragmatism from James's). In *The Varieties*, James summarized the philosophy of pragmatism as follows: "Beliefs, in short, are rules for action" (James, 1902/2009, p. 337). To expand a bit, for James, pragmatism generally meant that the consequences of a particular idea go beyond establishing not only its usefulness, but also its truth.

James's personal conclusion was derived from the notion of overbeliefs, which, for James, were justified by the philosophy of pragmatism. While, again, James admitted that spiritual experiences do not confer any special authority, he did indicate that they tend to give rise to "supernaturalism and optimism" (James, 1902/2009, p. 325). James was more explicit about the kind of supernaturalism he had in mind:

> The whole drift of my education goes to persuade me that the world of our present consciousness is only one out of many worlds of consciousness that exist, and that those other worlds contain experiences which have a meaning for our life also; and that although in the main their experiences and those of this world keep discrete, yet the two become continuous at certain points, and higher energies filter in. (James, 1902/ 2009, p. 392)

James then admitted that this personal overbelief kept him "more sane and true" (James, 1902/2009, p. 393). In other words, while James freely admitted that he has insufficient evidence for his personal supernaturalist belief, he chose to "believe" (i.e., as an overbelief) because he thought that this belief was psychologically beneficial for him. But James's overbelief as stated here is somewhat abstract, mentioning as it does continuous "worlds of consciousness." But elsewhere James was more explicit about what he meant—and the following quotation is the core of the momentous "reveal" that many readers of *The Varieties* miss. James—after long last and much delaying and hedging—described himself as a supernaturalist:

> If one should make a division of all thinkers into naturalists and supernaturalists, I should undoubtedly have to go, along with most philosophers, into the supernaturalist branch. (James, 1902/2009, p. 394)

He even went on to say that one could distinguish between what he termed "more refined" and "crasser" supernaturalism. He characterized the more refined kind as highly rationalistic and abstract systems which posit an eternal absolute. The crasser kind of supernaturalism, on the other hand, according to James, involves the possibility of incursions by a God into the laws of nature and is generally associated with the faith of, as he said, "uneducated people." James then admitted that his view fell closer to this crasser supernaturalism!

James's endorsement of supernatural beliefs may seem surprising to many readers (it was to us) and, one can imagine, may have been somewhat surprising to his audience. James's belief in supernaturalism appears to be something he came to later in his life, as he had made a number of statements supporting strict naturalism earlier in his life. But this belief appeared to be important to James and may have been a motivating component for much of the philosophical work that he would do over the next 8 years of his life after *The Varieties* was published. James essentially took evidence for the positive outcomes of spiritual experience and counted these consequences as evidence for the truth of spiritual beliefs. His argument was much broader than spiritual experience, however, and is worth briefly exploring in a bit more depth.

Pragmatism, as James described it, is primarily motivated by the observation that what is true is often what works best. For example, this can be easily observed in many areas of science and engineering. A particular theory of suspension bridges can be shown to be more or less true by demonstrating whether or not it bears weight. The difficulty, of course, is determining which belief works best outside the context of concrete engineering examples and in the vagueness and vicissitudes of life. Evaluating the usefulness of a belief is often not straightforward. A full-blown discussion of James's pragmatism is beyond the scope of this book, but its application to the question of the reality of spiritual experiences is crucial to understanding the last few chapters of *The Varieties*.

In *Cambridge Pragmatism: From Peirce and James to Ramsey and Wittgenstein* (2018), philosopher Cheryl Misak described how pragmatism was born in Cambridge, Massachusetts, with Peirce and James before it met with fierce resistance by Russell and Wittgenstein in Cambridge, England. Eventually, though, both Russell and Wittgenstein would come around to embrace some aspects of pragmatism through the influence of Frank Ramsey, a brilliant mathematician and philosopher who died tragically at age 26. Initially, though, Russell and Wittgenstein were adamantly opposed to James's pragmatic line of thinking in general—and they would remain opposed whenever it was applied to religious belief.

In the *History of Western Philosophy* (1946), Russell forcefully objected to James's pragmatism, especially as it pertained to religious belief. Here, Russell characterized James's philosophy of pragmatism as: "Roughly speaking, he [James] is prepared to advocate any doctrine which tends to make people virtuous and happy; if it does so, it is 'true' in the sense in which he uses that word" (Russell, 1946, p. 816). However, Russell described the "great intellectual difficulties" that he had with this view, as he noted that the consequences of a given belief may simply not be known in any given case.

Russell then pointed out that good consequences can flow from beliefs that we know are fantasy, and that this ought not make them "true." Russell poked fun at what can follow from the view when it is driven to an absurd extreme, writing: "I have always found that the hypothesis of Santa Claus 'works satisfactorily in the widest sense of the word'; therefore 'Santa Claus exists' is true, although Santa Claus does not exist" (Russell, 1946, p. 817).

Some of James's sloppier statements about pragmatism would seem to allow for such a belief, although he was generally more careful to specify that beliefs must work over longer periods of time, prove useful for other people, and also fit with one's other beliefs about reality. In general, Russell believed that James was motivated to adopt his pragmatic view of religious belief out of feelings of generosity rather than philosophical rigor:

> James is interested in religion as a human phenomenon, but shows little interest in the objects which religion contemplates. He wants people to be happy, and if belief in God makes them happy let them believe in Him. (Russell, 1946, p. 818)

Here, it seems that Russell was somewhat overstating the case about James's motivations being entirely beneficent to believers, as it seems that James himself was a believer—at least he was toward the end of his life. Elsewhere, Russell captured an aspect of James's often contradictory character that may motivate the distinction between what we have called his "professional" and "personal" conclusions:

> There were two sides to William James's philosophical interests, one scientific, the other religious. On the scientific side, the study of medicine had given his thoughts a tendency towards materialism, which, however, was held in check by his religious emotions. (Russell, 1946, p. 811)

With his professional and personal conclusions, James appears to have found a way to give voice to both aspects of his character in the closing chapters of *The Varieties*.

Contemporary Approaches to Beliefs
About Spiritual Experience

Pragmatism has entered mainstream philosophical discourse and has been applied to a number of topics, such as linguistics, ethics, aesthetics, and religious belief (for more technical treatments of pragmatism applied to religious beliefs, see Aikin, 2014, and Bishop, 2007). While James's pragmatic defense of religious belief has generally fallen by the wayside in philosophy, it may form the basis for faith among some in the general population.

There are a few responses to James's philosophical arguments that we can review briefly, albeit in a highly simplified form. In *36 Arguments for the Existence of God* (2010), philosopher Rebecca Goldstein provided a succinct summary of James's pragmatic argument and some common rebuttals to it. This book, as the name suggests, includes a number of other common arguments for, and against, the existence of God. Goldstein characterized James's argument as "the argument from Pragmatism (William James's Leap of Faith)." As an aside, according to Goldstein, the phrase "leap of faith" is yet another popular idiom coined by James (although it is often misattributed to Kierkegaard).

Goldstein's summary of James's argument is as follows (Goldstein, 2010, p. 494):

1. The consequences for a believer's life of believing should be considered as part of the evidence for the truth of the belief (just as the effectiveness of a scientific theory in its practical applications is considered evidence for the truth of the theory). Call this the pragmatic evidence for the belief.
2. Certain beliefs effect a change for the better in the believer's life—the necessary condition being that they are believed.
3. The belief in God is a belief that effects a change for the better in a person's life.
4. If one tries to decide whether or not to believe in God based on the evidence available, one will never get the chance to evaluate the pragmatic evidence for the beneficial consequences of believing in God (from 2 and 3).
5. One ought to make "the leap of faith" (the term is James's) and believe in God, and only then evaluate the evidence (from 1 and 4).

Goldstein then summarized four flaws with the premises of this argument. First, she questioned what a "change for the better" might mean. Such changes are not only often difficult to ascertain, but also highly sensitive to context. It might be better for a person, for example, to commit immoral actions if one is in an immoral society (i.e., in order to fit in), but this would not seem to make those actions right or true. Second, the various benefits from beliefs will likely differ from one person to the next depending on their life situation and psychological traits, but it seems absurd to believe that every person is entitled to their own "truth" based on the different idiosyncratic benefits that may come from various beliefs. Third, there are not only the benefits for one's self but also the benefits for other people to consider, and this would seem to make the calculation of a belief's benefit difficult or even impossible to attain. Fourth, it may not be possible to adopt beliefs on the basis of their benefits. Even if one found that a belief appears to have benefits, one is not typically able to adopt a belief by merely *choosing* to. These flaws often show that pragmatic approaches to truth usually ultimately rely on other approaches of truth, according to Goldstein. In any case, most contemporary philosophers do not take James's argument to be convincing.

There is another, somewhat related, argument that is perhaps closer to the one that most people adopt after having had a spiritual experience in order to justify their religious/spiritual beliefs. Goldstein called this "the argument from sublimity," and it begins with a premise drawn from perceiving an unseen reality in spiritual experiences. She explicitly related this argument to aesthetic experiences, but it would seem to apply equally to each of the kinds of spiritual experience described in Part II. It runs as follows (Goldstein, 2010, p. 498):

1. There are experiences that are windows into the wholeness of existence—its grandeur, beauty, symmetry, harmony, unity, even its goodness.
2. We glimpse a benign transcendence in these moments.
3. Only God could provide us with a glimpse of benign transcendence.
4. God exists.

The primary problem with this argument is that there are that there are other explanations for such experiences, which disputes Premise 3. According to Goldstein, the triggers for these kinds of experiences "are readily explicable from the evolutionary pressures that have shaped the perceptual systems of human beings" (Goldstein, 2010, p. 498). She referred to the tendency to see human qualities in the nature of reality (e.g., goodness, beauty), to anthropomorphize existence, as the "projection fallacy." The projection fallacy can be illustrated by a famous quote from philosopher David Hume, that "the mind has a great propensity to spread itself on external objects" (Hume, 1739, p. X). That is, we tend to see aspects of ourselves in the world, and we often fail to realize that our perceptions are conditioned by the kind of creatures that we are.

Note that both of these arguments and the summaries of their flaws are highly simplified versions of philosophical work on this topic. We point the reader elsewhere for more thorough examinations of these philosophical arguments.

In the next two sections, we examine two common contemporary approaches to analyzing the reality of spiritual experiences. The first is drawn from evolutionary considerations that assume spiritual experiences are psychological projections and attempt to explain how these delusions came to be part of our neurocognitive architecture. The second is drawn from an analogue to the philosophy of vision and assumes that spiritual experiences can be characterized as perceptions of a real supernatural being.

Assuming Illusion: Evolutionary Perspectives

The most common contemporary scientific interpretation of spiritual experience springs not from Jamesian pragmatism, but from evolutionary psychology. This view generally assumes these experiences are projections of the mind (hallucinations or delusions) and attempts to understand why humans would have them at all. The resulting explanations are then taken to be the most likely explanation for spiritual experience.

When taking an evolutionary lens, the capacity to have spiritual experiences can be seen as either a *spandrel* or an *adaptation*. In evolutionary theory, spandrels refer to accidental byproducts of evolution, or aspects of a species' biology that emerged due to *other* features that were in fact selected for. An adaptation, on the other hand, refers to a random mutation that was then selected for because it added to a species' fitness (ability to survive and reproduce).

Take first the notion of a spandrel. The capacity for spiritual experience could be a spandrel resulting from, for example, the human capacity to recognize mind in other people (i.e., mind perception). That is, humans have a cognitive module that allows us to attribute mind to other human beings, but this module may sometimes "misfire" and attribute mind to one's environment (we have called this a "social/spatial conflation"; Yaden et al., 2017). On this view, spiritual experiences do not directly result in any adaptive advantage, they are merely a "side effect" of another capacity that is adaptive.

Another theory that fits within the spandrel view is that spiritual experiences are merely confusing sensory experiences that make people more likely to take up a religious or spiritual belief from one's surrounding cultural milieu in an effort to explain what seems otherwise unexplainable (Barrett, 2000). This view, called "sensory pageantry," relies on the idea that religious/spiritual beliefs are "memes," or self-replicating ideas that spread through humans like a virus (Barrett, 2000; Boyer, 2003; Guthrie &Guthrie, 1995). Spiritual experiences, from this perspective, are merely moments of sensory confusion that make adopting these beliefs more likely to occur.

Alternately, the capacity for spiritual experiences might be an adaptation, making them a kind of benign or beneficial illusion. In this view, such experiences provide adaptive advantages to those who have them. Spiritual experiences might, for example, lift one's spirits and levels of motivation, which may provide a competitive advantage in survival or reproduction. One could well imagine the benefits of having a second wind of hope and vitality during times of despair. Darwin wrote about the need for an organism to desire life above death in order to try to survive and reproduce at all, and it seems that spiritual experiences can renew one's love of life like little else can.

However, given the complexity of brain processes that support spiritual experiences, it seems unlikely that spiritual experiences arose purely as the result of evolutionary adaptive advantages. Paleontologist Stephen J. Gould made the point that a "quarter of a wing doesn't fly," meaning that a wing could not have developed by starting out as a stubby wing and growing bigger over time into a better wing. A stubby wing is simply not a wing, and hence the wing, he argued, must have been for some other function, perhaps the ventilation of heat away from the body. As it grew bigger to be a better ventilator as a result of selection pressures, it eventually ended up having a different function—flying. Thus, if we consider the complexity of the brain processes involved in spiritual experiences, it seems more likely that it arose on the basis of being a spandrel. But, eventually, that spandrel may have ended up having an adaptive advantage and further developed into a more complex mechanism leading to some of the most powerful forms of human experience.

It is also possible that spiritual experiences don't benefit individuals directly, but rather benefit groups that have more individuals who have spiritual experiences. This possibility relies on the theory of "group selection." Group selection complements consideration of individuals with attention to groups in evolutionary thinking. It is a controversial theory because many theorists see it as redundant (claiming that a focus on individual competition is sufficient for explaining natural selection). But the evolutionary dynamics of spiritual experience can be illustrated somewhat more clearly when put in terms of group selection because the prosocial behavior and altruistic fellow-feeling that people report after spiritual experiences would have obvious benefits to group trust and cohesion (Graham & Haidt, 2010). David Sloan Wilson expanded this point to religions in general in *Darwin's Cathedral* (2002).

Psychologist Jonathan Haidt (2012) applied this line of argument to spiritual experiences with his "hive hypothesis." The hive hypothesis can be described metaphorically by the idea that humans are "90% ape, 10% bee" due to our overall tendency toward (advanced) ape-like behavior coupled with our capacity to come together into tight-knit, coordinated "hive-like" groups when threatened or when feeling elevated. According to Haidt, the "one for all, all for one" feeling that often arises from spiritual experience might be a key mechanism through which this enhanced group affiliation occurs.

Historically, these group-oriented views were inspired in part by French sociologist Emile Durkheim's *The Elementary Forms of the Religious Life* (Durkheim, 1912/1954), which prioritizes the establishment and maintenance of group social bonds above all else. Religion serves this bonding function, as would spiritual experiences. Durkheim engaged in a study of Australian Aboriginals and noted the "collective effervescence" that seemed to bring participants together during religious rituals. One way of understanding spiritual experience is through this lens of collective effervescence, which may have emerged as a way for groups to bond together.

In general, most evolutionary views begin with the premise that spiritual experiences are illusory and then attempt to understand why they occur through evolutionary reasoning. It is often employed as a form of "debunking" argument. Debunking arguments are based on the notion that once a more parsimonious explanation has been provided, then there is no rational reason to believe in the more complicated (and therefore less likely) supernatural interpretation (e.g., Kahane, 2011). The invocation of parsimony is based on Occam's razor, often translated as "plurality should not be posited without necessity." In practice, this rule generally posits that explanations that are the simplest, all else being equal, are usually the best ones. For some, the evolutionary explanation is sufficient to "explain away" spiritual experience.

Assuming Divinity: Perception-Based Perspectives

One can also approach spiritual experience under the assumption that it is evidence for a religious or spiritual reality. Of course, this is the route taken by religions and spiritual traditions. In terms of contemporary work that takes spiritual experiences to be caused by something supernatural, there is far less to draw from as this assumption is very rare in contemporary science and scholarship.

One exception to this is philosopher William Alston, who articulated a perception-based view in his book *Perceiving God* (1993). Alston began by providing a number of accounts of spiritual experiences (many taken from *The Varieties*), with a special emphasis on numinous experiences in which people claimed to encounter God directly. For example, he included the following experience from *The Varieties*:

All at once I . . . felt the presence of God—I tell of the thing just as I was conscious of it—as if his goodness and his power were penetrating me altogether. . . . I think it well to add that in this ecstasy of mine God had neither form, color, odor, nor taste; moreover, that the feeling of his presence was accompanied by no determinate localization. . . . At bottom the expression most apt to render what I felt is this: God was present, though invisible; he fell under no one of my senses, yet my consciousness perceived him. (Alston, 1993, p. 12)

For Alston, the most important part of this and other spiritual experiences is that the experiencer reports that God is perceived as a particular "object" of experience. He drew on philosophical work on vision science to support his arguments on this point. He illustrated what he meant by comparing perceiving God to perceiving a chair: "I sometimes see some item of furniture for the first time, and thereby learn of its existence as well as some of its properties. And more than one person has passed from unbelief to belief through (putatively) experientially encountering God" (Alston, 1993, p. 3). Of course, it is rare that experiences of God are as unambiguous as seeing a chair, but Alton proceeded on the basis of this premise.

Alston then asked a provocative question regarding whether there is, in principle, a difference between one reporting seeing a chair in a room and seeing God in a room. Usually, perceptions of objects like chairs appear in our awareness and are then supported by a consensus from other people (one sees a chair, other people agree about seeing a chair, so we believe that there is a chair). While perceiving a chair seems, at first glance, very different from perceiving God, on the other hand we have seen time and again that many people report perceiving God, often with similar kinds of qualities—thus making it a kind of consensus perception. That is, many people have reported experiencing God, so it could actually be considered to have consensus support. Alston essentially argued that when people have spiritual experiences, they can reasonably assume that a perception of God has occurred.

While this style of argument will likely appeal to some more than others, Alston also included an important critique of James's approach that is worth considering. Alston viewed his perception-based argument as distinct from James's. Alston saw his view as

... dissenting from the numerous theorists who construe experiences of the sort we are discussing as purely subjective feelings or sensations to which is superadded an explanation according to which they are due to God, the Holy Spirit, or some other agent recognized by the theology of the subject's tradition. (Alston, 1993, p. 16)

Alston remarked that James (note: as well as earlier theologians like Schleiermacher and later psychologists like Wayne Proudfoot) seemed to conceptualize spiritual experiences as mostly feeling states, or altered states of consciousness (as we do), but then *also* referred to what is perceived during the experience itself (the "object" of perception during the experience). Alston wrote: "In particular there is a confusion between what is involved in identifying an experience as of a certain sort and what the experience *is* or consists of" (Alston, 1993, p. 40). That is, Alston noticed (as we have) that such experiences are often defined by what is perceived during the experience.

This point raises serious concerns about our definition of spiritual experience. We have argued throughout this book that while spiritual experiences can be categorized in certain ways, most often based on the *content* of the experience, consisting of, for example, God or unity. However, it is possible that there are other, perhaps underlying, dimensions to these experiences that we have touched on throughout. These underlying dimensions, which may carry more universality to them, include changes in faculties of consciousness, a sense of experiential intensity, or mind perception. These more universal elements may ultimately be expressed in very specific terms, or labels (e.g., "God"), which are focused on the content of the experience.

Some further explanation is in order here. To back up, we agree with James that spiritual experiences are substantially *altered states of consciousness*, first and foremost, and that their content is often somewhat ambiguous and therefore some interpretation is usually required. However, we also agree with Alston that experiences have recognizable content and seem to involve a perception *of something*, like God or unity. As we have seen in Part II, most people refer to what they seem to have perceived when they label their experience (we have also discussed that these are intentional states).

Contemporary philosopher Dean Zimmerman and linguist Mark Baker of Rutgers University have attempted to bridge Alston's argument with ongoing work in cognitive science. (Note: Cognitive science is an umbrella term capturing psychology, neuroscience, philosophy, computer science, and linguistics.) In *On perceiving God: Prospects for a cognitive science of religious experience* (Baker & Zimmerman, 2019) they discuss the hypersensitive agency detection device (HADD), which is generally associated with evolutionary debunking arguments. In this article, they summarized the views of psychologist Justin Barrett, a believer in a combination of the evolutionary account and the perception-based account. Barrett holds that there really is a God, and we have evolved in a way that allows us to perceive and form true beliefs about God.

> (H)ADD . . . is probably an evolutionary "spandrel"—selected for survival-enhancing features that had nothing to do with production of beliefs about supernatural beings. However, they claim that . . . the development of the god-faculty through evolutionary processes prepares one for the acquisition of true religious beliefs when one has genuine religious experiences. (p. 188)

Zimmerman and Baker go even further, claiming that the ability to perceive God evolved because it is adaptive due to the fact that (they believe) God really exists. They put the issue plainly, "A God module could have evolved because it was useful for interacting with God" (Baker & Zimmerman, 2019, p. 22). Obviously, this view of spiritual experience proceeds from the premise that God actually exists. There are, of course, many objections to this view. In books like psychologist Julien Musolino's *The Soul Fallacy* (2015) and philosopher Daniel Dennett's *Breaking the Spell* (2006), many argue that supernatural beliefs are so far-fetched and have so little evidence to support their possibility, that such beliefs amount to being antiscientific. Others, of course, see ways to integrate scientific and supernatural perspectives.

Still, proceeding from the premise that God exists is rare in contemporary science and philosophy. As we see in the next section, supernatural beliefs are a minority view.

The Psychology of Philosophy

Scientists and philosophers are among the least likely people on the planet to endorse a belief in God. While over 85% of the U.S. population report a belief in God, belief in God among scientists is almost half that amount (https://www.pewforum.org/2009/11/05/scientists-and-belief/). Among distinguished scientists (those belonging to the National Academy) the number is far lower, with only about 8% endorsing supernatural beliefs (Larson & Witham, 1998). Some evidence suggests that psychologists are among the most atheistic of all scientists (Argyle & Beit-Hallahmi, 2013). This may be, at least in part, due to the fact that their work requires more contemplation of the issue of how nonphysical causes (i.e., a mind) could possibly affect a physical brain.

Among professors of philosophy at top universities, the number of believers is also quite low. Philosophers David Bourget and David Chalmers (who we are discussed further in Chapter 19 on consciousness) created a survey that is well known among contemporary philosophers. This survey, called the PhilPapers Survey, asked philosophers to choose the views that they subscribe to across a number of philosophical questions. They found that about 73% of philosophers in top departments endorsed "atheism," while only 15% endorsed "theism."

What is the relationship between spiritual experiences and beliefs among contemporary professional philosophers? One of James's biographers, William Richardson, said that James was always interested in a "philosophy of psychology and a psychology of philosophy." For example, in *Pragmatism* (1908), James created two clusters of philosophical views and psychological traits that he believed would cluster together (Table 16.1).

One of us (D. B. Y.) conducted a survey of professional philosophers to test this idea in collaboration with philosopher Derek Anderson (Yaden & Anderson, 2021). The aim of this survey was to measure relationships between philosophical views and psychological traits, including life experiences. As part of this survey, we asked philosophers if they had ever had various experiences, and some of these questions were directly relevant to spiritual experience:

- "I have had a profound religious experience or awakening that changed the direction of my life"
- "I have had a transformative experience of feeling closely connected to everything"
- "I have had a transformative experience of some kind, after which I felt like a different person"

We then correlated these questions with their philosophical views. We found that each of these experiences was significantly correlated with the belief in God. Additionally, we found that the religious experience question was

Table 16.1 William James's Distinction Between Philosophical Types

The Tender-Minded	The Tough-Minded
rationalistic (going by "principles")	empiricist (going by "facts")
intellectualistic	sensationalistic
idealistic	materialistic
optimistic	pessimistic
religious	irreligious
free-willist	fatalistic
monistic	pluralistic
dogmatical	skeptical

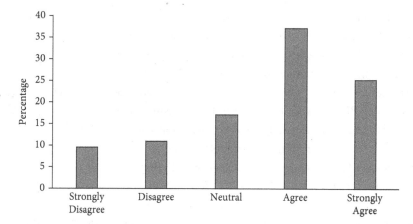

Figure 16.1 Beliefs changed from experience. Drawn by David Yaden.

associated with the belief that the mind is nonphysical, that free will exists, and that there is more to the world than the physical (i.e., nonphysicalism).

Remember, correlation does not equal causation, so care must be taken when interpreting these findings. One might be tempted to think that philosophers who had one of these experiences were led to adopt these views as a result. But it is also possible that holding certain beliefs leads one to have (or possibly to interpret) more experiences as religious/spiritual. Last, as in all cases of correlation, remember that it is possible for a third variable to explain the relation. For example, a personality trait could predict both spiritual beliefs and experiences. Taken together, these findings show that some contemporary philosophers are having spiritual experiences, and that it is at least possible that they are using them as evidence for their beliefs.

While more research needs to be done on this topic, it is clear that people do report that their beliefs do often change after spiritual experience. In our Varieties Survey, we asked our participants whether their "religious, spiritual, or philosophical beliefs changed in some way after their experience," and the majority reported that they did (Figure 16.1).

Conclusion

Throughout this book, following James, we have focused on the causes, correlates, and consequences of spiritual experiences and tried to set aside the question of whether they are "real" in the metaphysical sense. But how should one treat the kind of knowledge that sometimes seems to come from these experiences about the nature of reality? Wittgenstein might suggest that one stays silent about their interpretation of their experience. For Russell, one can acknowledge and appreciate the psychological value of the experiences while treating any apparent knowledge as delusional. For James, professionally, one simply cannot not know whether the experience points to any further reality. In his personal conclusion, though, James claimed that one can make a leap of faith by adopting a belief that spiritual experiences provide evidence for supernaturalism due to their good effects.

Contemporary science generally proceeds from the assumption that spiritual experiences are evolutionarily conditioned illusions, though some take seriously the possibility that such experiences are perceptions of a supernatural being or dimension of reality. The field of neurotheology, which one of us is a founder of and proponent of (A. B. N.), takes a hybrid approach that seeks to integrate and study each of these perspectives. Whatever one's beliefs, we try to tread carefully when it comes to deciphering what is really real and remain open to the many perspectives that lay claim to understanding reality. Overall, we are proponents of adopting a methodological agnosticism in the study of spiritual experiences.

References

Aikin, S. (2014). *Evidentialism and the will to believe*. Bloomsbury.

Alston, W. P. (1993). *Perceiving God: The epistemology of religious experience*. Cornell University Press.

Argyle, M., & Beit-Hallahmi, B. (2013). *The social psychology of religion (psychology revivals)*. Routledge.

Baker, M., & Zimmerman, D. (2019). *On perceiving God: Prospects for a cognitive science of religious experience*. Oxford Scholarship Online.

Barrett, J. L. (2000). Exploring the natural foundations of religion. Trends in cognitive sciences, 4(1), 29–34.

Bishop, J., 2007. *Believing by faith: An essay in the epistemology and ethics of religious belief*. Oxford University Press.

Boyer, P. (2003). Religious thought and behaviour as by-products of brain function. *Trends in Cognitive Sciences*, 7(3), 119–124.

Dennett, D. C. (2006). *Breaking the spell: Religion as a natural phenomenon* (Vol. 14). Penguin.

Durkheim, E. (1954). *The elementary forms of religious life* (J. W. Swain, Trans.). New York: Free Press of Glencoe. (Original work published 1912)

Goldstein, R. (2010). *36 arguments for the existence of God: A work of fiction*. Pantheon.

Graham, J., & Haidt, J. (2010). Beyond beliefs: Religions bind individuals into moral communities. *Personality and Social Psychology Review, 14*(1), 140–150.

Guthrie, S. E., & Guthrie, S. (1995). *Faces in the clouds: A new theory of religion*. Oxford University Press.

Haidt, J. (2012). *The righteous mind: Why good people are divided by politics and religion*. Vintage.

Hume, D. (1739). *A treatise of human nature*. Courier.

James, W. (1907/2003). *Pragmatism: A new name for some old ways of thinking*. Barnes & Noble.

James, W. (1902/2009). The varieties of religious experience: A study in human nature. *eBooks@Adelaide*. https://csrs.nd.edu/assets/59930/williams_1902.pdf

James, W. (1908). *Pragmatism* (Vol. 1). Harvard University Press.

Kahane, G. (2011). Evolutionary debunking arguments. *Noûs, 45*(1), 103–125.

Larson, E. J., & Witham, L. (1998). Leading scientists still reject God. *Nature, 394*(6691), 313–314.

Misak, C. (2018). *Cambridge Pragmatism: From Peirce and James to Ramsey and Wittgenstein*. Oxford University Press.

Monk, R. (1990). *Wittgenstein: The duty of genius*. Cape.

Musolino, J. (2015). *The soul fallacy: What science shows we gain from letting go of our soul beliefs*. Prometheus Books.

Myers, G. E. (2001). *William James: His life and thought*. Yale University Press.

Russell, B. (1910). *Mysticism and logic*. Courier.

Russell, B. (1946). *History of Western philosophy*. Routledge.

Russell, B. (1951/2009). *Autobiography*. Routledge. (Original work published 1951)

Wilson, D. S. (2002). *Darwin's cathedral: Evolution, religion, and the nature of society*. University of Chicago Press.

Wittgenstein, L. (1922). *Tractatus logico-philosophicus*. Routledge & Kegan Paul.

Yaden, D. B., & Anderson, D. A, (2020). The psychology of philosophy: Associating philosophical views with psychological traits in professional philosophers. *Philosophical Psychology, 34*(5), 721–755.

Yaden, D. B., Haidt, J., Hood, R. W., Jr., Vago, D. R., & Newberg, A. B. (2017). The varieties of self-transcendent experience. *Review of General Psychology, 21*(2), 143–160.

17

Transformations

Most of the outcomes from spiritual experiences reviewed so far have been evidence of short-term changes—usually in the range of days, weeks, or sometimes months. These changes have involved mostly positive and some pathological outcomes, as well as some shifts in beliefs. There are less empirical findings to support long-term changes, but some personal accounts suggest that the effects can last years, decades, or even entire lifetimes. Spiritual experiences are thus notable not only for their intensity in the moment, but also for the transformative changes they can exert on people over long periods of time.

From the perspectives of psychology and neuroscience, it is remarkable that such brief altered states of consciousness can sometimes have long-lasting impacts on beliefs, mood, and behavior. One of the only other comparable dynamics in human experience is severe trauma. Intuitively, we know that suffering a great tragedy can leave an individual dramatically changed, but we rarely consider beneficial instances of this—that positive experiences can have lasting results, too. It appears that the impact of some spiritual experiences is so great that the individual becomes an altogether new self—that is, some spiritual experiences can be transformative.

Marsha Linehan is now known mostly as a world-renowned clinical psychologist, but she had substantial firsthand experience with being under the care of psychiatrists and psychologists as a patient. As she described in her autobiography, *Building a Life Worth Living* (2020), Marsha Linehan had spent much of her late adolescence in psychiatric hospitals. She had suffered tremendously, and sometimes by her own hand, as she had attempted suicide numerous times. This is sadly quite common in cases of borderline personality disorder, which was Linehan's diagnosis.

However, Linehan's life changed one evening in January 1967 when she was an undergraduate in college. During one of the periods between hospitalizations, when she was spending time living in a Catholic convent, she had what she calls an "enlightenment experience." She wrote:

The Varieties of Spiritual Experience. David B. Yaden and Andrew B. Newberg, Oxford University Press. © David Yaden and Andrew Newberg 2022. DOI: 10.1093/oso/9780190665678.003.0017

Then I went into the chapel, knelt at a pew, and gazed at the cross behind the altar. I don't recall what I was saying to God at the time, if anything, but as I gazed at the large crucifix, all of a sudden the whole of the chapel became suffused with a bright golden light, shimmering all over. . . And I immediately, joyfully knew with complete certainty that God loved me. That I was not alone. God was within me. I was within God. (Linehan, 2020, p. 102)

Linehan described having the sense that her spiritual experience, which appears to have been a numinous experience, was transformative. Like we have seen in many of those who described their spiritual experiences, she was also initially hesitant to describe it to anyone else. She wrote:

I told very few people of my experience. Partly because it was a private experience, but also because I didn't know how to describe it. I knew most people would not be able to understand it completely, either. What I understood was that something transformative had happened. (Linehan, 2020, p. 104)

Linehan's transformation changed her life immediately and dramatically. Her suicidal thoughts vanished, and she became better able to interact with her friends and family. Linehan's transformation eventually changed not only her own life but also that of many others. After finishing her PhD in psychology, she created a new form of psychotherapy called dialectical behavior therapy (DBT; Linehan, 2014). DBT is routinely used to treat people suffering from suicidal ideation and borderline personality disorder, as it has been shown to be one of the few psychotherapies to be effective for this patient population. It is likely that Linehan's DBT has saved many lives, and we can trace its development, at least in some small way, back to Linehan's transformative moment. Why do spiritual experiences sometimes result in lasting changes and the conviction that one has been transformed?

James on Transformation

James discussed transformation in several places throughout *The Varieties* 1902/2009). For example, he mentioned the lasting impacts that can come from spiritual experiences: "A changed attitude towards life, which is fairly constant and permanent, although the feelings fluctuate" (James, 1902/2009,

p. 196). James went beyond simply describing their long-term impact; he also claimed that spiritual experiences can change the individual themselves. He wrote: "The great thing which the higher excitabilities give is COURAGE; and the addition or subtraction of a certain amount of this quality makes a different man, a different life" (James, 1902/2009, p. 201). That is, spiritual experiences can result in persisting positive effects as well as the sense that one has become a new self, which can sometimes even last a lifetime.

These changes in some individuals are not merely differences in degree but also differences in kind. James referred to Saint Paul's case to illustrate this point:

> Considering at first those striking instantaneous instances of which Saint Paul's is the most eminent, and in which, often amid tremendous emotional excitement or perturbation of the sense, a complete division is established in the twinkling of an eye between the old life and the new. (James, 1902/2009, p. 166)

In order to examine further the nature of these changes, James focused on saints. For James, saints were individuals who go well beyond the duty of citizenry and achieve true moral excellence. James called such people "spiritual geniuses." He explained how spiritual geniuses are those special few who are able to continue to live from their higher moral self after their spiritual experiences. James went on to describe saints in some detail, providing a description of what it feels like to be a saint (James, 1902/2009, pp. 206–207):

1. A feeling of being in a wider life than that of this world's selfish little interests; and a conviction, not merely intellectual, but as it were sensible, of the existence of an Ideal Power. In Christian saintliness this power is always personified as God; but abstract moral ideals, civic or patriotic utopias, or inner visions of holiness or right may also be felt as the true lords and enlargers of our life . . .
2. A sense of the friendly continuity of the ideal power with our own life, and a willing self-surrender to its control.
3. An immense elation and freedom, as the outlines of the confining selfhood melt down.
4. A shifting of the emotional centre towards loving and harmonious affections, towards "yes, yes," and away from "no," where the claims of the non-ego are concerned . . .

These saintly characteristics, James claimed, are often associated with behavioral consequences. First, there is a tendency for asceticism, or marked reduction in consuming physical pleasures. Second is increased willpower to achieve one's aims. Third, there is an urge to "purify" one's self and sublimate one's goals. Fourth, increased charity exists toward everyone, especially including the poor and suffering, as well as, in some cases, one's enemies. James included some personal accounts of the feelings and actions that spring from these moral shifts (drawn from Starbuck's survey; James, 1902/2009, p. 213):

- "I began to work for others..."
- "I spoke at once to a person with whom I had been angry..."
- "I felt for every one, and loved my friends better..."

James, ever looking to outcomes, proposed examining the effects of saintliness. Are saints worthy of our admiration? James wrote: "What I then propose to do is, briefly stated, to test saintliness by common sense" (James, 1902/2009, p. 252). He began with high praise, that "saints, with their extravagance of human tenderness, are the great torch-bearers of this belief, the tip of the wedge, the clearers of the darkness" (James, 1902/2009, p. 271). Here, James argued that society makes progress due to the actions of morally pioneering saints.

However, in a thoroughly Jamesian move that should by now be hardly surprising—he immediately introduced a contrasting perspective. James suggested examining the excesses and impracticalities of the saintly impulse. Referencing philosopher Immanuel Kant's *Critique of Pure Reason*, James wrote: "Were I to parody Kant, I should say that a 'Critique of pure Saintliness' must be our theme" (James, 1902/2009, p. 249). James proceeded to enumerate various excesses of historical saints. In particular, he focused on ascetic practices—providing numerous examples of self-mortifications undertaken in the excessive desire to prove one's piety. He concluded that the practices of saints can sometimes become pathological, writing: "That the scrupulosity of purity may be carried to a fantastic extreme must be admitted" (James, 1902/2009, p. 225). That is, sometimes the ascetic practices of saintly individuals can look like mental illness.

James addressed philosopher Friedrich Nietzsche's views on saintliness as well. For James, Nietzsche represented an extreme position against the value of saintliness. Nietzsche's ideal person did not conform to religious values, but rather sought personal power above all. James, using uncharacteristically harsh language, compared Nietzsche's views to the "sick shriekings" of a dying rat (James, 1902/2009, p. 32). James then backtracked a little by showing some (perhaps facetious) empathy for Nietzsche before taking up the task of refuting his argument (James, 1902/2009, p. 282):

> Poor Nietzsche's antipathy is itself sickly enough, but we all know what he means, and he expresses well the clash between the two ideals. The carnivorous-minded "strong man," the adult male and cannibal, can see nothing but mouldiness and morbidness in the saint's gentleness and self-severity, and regards him with pure loathing. The whole feud revolves essentially upon two pivots: Shall the seen world or the unseen world be our chief sphere of adaptation? and must our means of adaptation in this seen world be aggressiveness or non-resistance? The debate is serious.

James met Nietzsche's criticism of saints by taking issue with the idea that there need be merely one type of person that we agree is ideal. He asked his readers to consider horses. It would seem absurd to claim that there is a single best type of horse when they fulfill various functions, such as riding, plowing, racing, and so on. So, too, with society, he argued, different types of people may be more or less ideal for different functions. The contemporary way of putting this issue is to value "neurodiversity" or the inherent worth of people with different kinds of brains.

James then imagined a world in which all people were like Nietzsche's Übermensch. This world, he suggested, would likely become one of "bullies, robbers, and swindlers" (James, 1902/2009, p. 283) in which few people would like to live. A world in which all people were like saints, on the other hand, would be marked more by sympathy and fairness of the kind people enjoy to have among their friends. James reached a qualified conclusion that while both types of people are inevitable, and a mix is probably desirable, we should champion saints as they work to better the world for us all, often at their own expense.

Notably, James's notion of saints was not limited to the religious sphere. James found contemporary manifestations of the saintly psychology (both positive and pathological) in those who tirelessly fight for social justice and higher moral ideals (James, 1902/2009, p. 273):

In this respect the Utopian dreams of social justice . . . are, in spite of their impracticability and non-adaptation to present environmental conditions, analogous to the saint's belief in an existent kingdom of heaven. They help to break the edge of the general reign of hardness, and are slow leavens of a better order.

In the end, James concluded his account of saintliness with an endorsement and an encouragement to follow these moral exemplars to the extent to which we are able. In general, despite the contrasting perspectives that he provided, James supported saintliness. He suggested that saintliness, as a constellation of characteristics, can serve as a kind of beacon for people to navigate toward. The tremendous charitable works of contemporary saints, bodhistavas, walis, and gurus, as well as their secular counterparts, testified to the value of this view, as do some contemporary civil rights and social justice advocates. Concluding his thoughts on the topic, he stated: "Let us be saints, then, if we can, whether or not we succeed visibly and temporally" (James, 1902/2009, p. 284).

While James drews a clear connection between spiritual experience and moral transformations resulting in saintliness, he acknowledged that these are the minority of cases. Most spiritual experiences result in a much smaller and shorter impact. He drew on empirical research to support this point. "The only statistics I know of, on the subject of the duration of conversions, are those collected for Professor Starbuck. . . . According to the statement of the subjects themselves, there had been backsliding of some sort in nearly all the cases" (James, 1902/2009, p. 196). James thus acknowledged that lasting and dramatic transformations, though they are far more interesting from a psychological standpoint, are the exception and not the rule.

Contemporary Research on Transformation

We begin our examination of transformations from a contemporary perspective with some philosophical clarification. Yale philosopher L. A. Paul's book, *Transformative experience* (2014) provided an analytical account of transformative experience that brings specificity to this otherwise vague and amorphous concept.

According to Paul, an experience is considered transformative when it satisfies two subdimensions that she called "epistemic transformation" and "personal transformation" (Paul, 2014). *Epistemic transformation* refers to experiences that are impossible to imagine from the standpoint of one who has not actually had one. Paul drew on the famous thought experiment from philosopher Frank Jackson, called "Mary the color scientist" to illustrate this point. In this illustrative story, a scientist named Mary has lived her entire life in a colorless room but has spent her time studying the color red, such that she knows most of the scientific facts about how the color is perceived by the human eye (note: some versions require that she knows "all of the physical facts" but Paul lessened the strictness of this point). However, Mary had never actually seen the color red. According to Paul, when Mary saw the color red for the first time, she had an epistemic transformation.

Personal transformation refers to experiences that change one's preferences, perspective, desires, or values. Paul gave the examples of reading powerful fiction or taking a college course as examples that can change one's core preferences. One can imagine learning new facts about, say, the meat industry, in a class that might change one's preferences and desires in regard to eating meat. In such a case, one's preclass self could not imagine themselves changing their preferences about steaks, but the information conveyed in the class does just that.

In many cases, epistemic and personal transformation occur simultaneously, and such cases are referred to simply as "transformative experiences." Paul's paradigmatic example of a transformative experience is becoming a parent. This decision, she claimed, involves aspects that are unknowable until they have been experienced—such as holding your child in your arms for the first time. It can also change one's core preferences. It is difficult for most people to imagine sacrificing one's life (or even the majority of one's time and energy) for another person who they have never met, but this is in fact exactly what most people do when they become a parent.

Paul mentioned spiritual experience as an instance of transformative experience: "There are many other kinds of experience that qualify: one that needs special mention, and deserves more extensive discussion, is the case of religious experience" (Paul, 2014, p. 104). We agree with her call for more philosophically rigorous work regarding the nature of the changes that occur due to spiritual experience.

Transformative experience in Paul's sense is therefore a descriptor for experiences that are difficult or impossible to imagine and that change one's motivations—some spiritual experiences certainly fit these criteria. While spiritual experiences involve substantially altered states of consciousness, transformative experiences can consist of a broad range of major life events, so spiritual experiences would be a subtype of transformative experience. Last, many spiritual experiences probably do not result in lasting changes to one's motivations, although some clearly do.

Lasting Changes

"Quantum change" is one way of characterizing brief experiences that exert a long-term impact, as argued by a book with this title (Miller & C'de Baca, 2001). The authors argued that some experiences result in long-lasting and sometimes permanent changes. Miller and C'de Baca (2001) described experiences that are similar to what we have called spiritual experiences, although they leave much of their definition implicit. These authors described their subject in the following way: "Quantum change is a vivid, surprising, benevolent, and enduring personal transformation" (Miller & C'de Baca, 2001, p. 4). They take the moral transformation of Ebenezer Scrooge, a character in Charles Dickens's *A Christmas Carol*, as their prototypical case. In this story, Scrooge went from being a miserly, critical, and angry man to a generous and kind person after a night of dreams and visions of ghosts and spirits.

Authors Miller and C'de Baca (2001) described two types of quantum change experiences: the "insightful type" and the "mystical type." The *insightful type* relies primarily on a belief change of some kind, usually coming in the form of an epiphany. This type fits most closely with what we have called revelatory experiences. The *mystical type* involves a vaguer shift in one's feeling about one's relationship with the world and other people, involving feelings of connection and a noetic quality. This type fits with what we have called mystical experiences. The authors closed *Quantum Change* with the question of whether personality can really change as a result of either type of experience. Empirical research can now address that topic.

Personality is generally stable over time and across many years of life (Epstein, 1979). In the *Principles of Psychology*, James wrote: "In most of us, by the age of thirty, the character has set like plaster, and will never soften again" (James, 1980, p. 124). The evidence largely supports James's statement: Empirically, personality generally remains mostly unchanged when people retake personality tests (Big 5), even after many years have passed (McCrae & Costa, 1994).

It appears, though, that personality can also change in certain circumstances. In some cases, people can change their personality through deliberate effort. One study found that college students who made it a goal to change certain aspects of their personalities were able to do so, as long as they were assisted by reminders throughout the semester (Hudson & Fraley, 2015). Participants in this study were able to increase their extraversion and conscientiousness and to decrease their neuroticism over a period of months. However, these changes were rather small in size, and it is not known how long these changes persisted.

Personality change has also been observed in the context of spiritual experience. In psilocybin research at Johns Hopkins, researcher Katherine MacLean found that the personality trait "openness to experience," which, like all personality traits, is presumed to remain stable over one's life, tended to increase after psilocybin experiences (MacLean et al., 2011). This research finding has been replicated in subsequent psychedelic research (Madsen et al., 2020), although additional replications should be made before this finding is considered robust.

It is also possible that other aspects of psilocybin experiences last a lifetime, although this has not been examined in truly longitudinal research. One illustrative study, however, involved recontacting participants in the Good Friday experiment 25 years later (Doblin, 1991). (Recall this is the study, conducted by Walter Pahnke, that involved administering psilocybin to divinity students during a Good Friday service.) The follow-up study found that the majority of the participants reportedly continued to benefit from their experience. The author summarized the findings in the following way: "Despite the difficult moments several of the psilocybin subjects passed through, the subjects who participated in the long-term follow-up reported a substantial amount of persisting positive effects and no significant long-term negative effects" (Doblin, 1991, p. 24). This finding should, however, be interpreted carefully as it relies on the long-term memory of participants and longitudinal research needs to be conducted to confirm these observations.

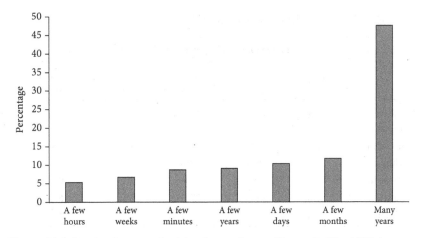

Figure 17.1 Lasting impact of spiritual experiences. Drawn by David Yaden.

In our own research, we asked participants both how long an average spiritual experience lasts and how long it impacted their life. We found that spiritual experiences lasted an average of about 18 minutes, and that most participants reported feeling their effects for many years (Figure 17.1).

The research from our survey of spiritual experiences further confirmed the positive transformative nature of these experiences (Newberg & Waldman, 2016). Over 90% of people reported improvement in their spiritual and religious lives as a result of having the spiritual experience. People also reported improvements in their health and well-being, meaning and purpose in life, and their fear of death. Less than 5% of the respondents reported any kind of negative result from an intense spiritual experience in any particular domain (Table 17.1).

Even in cases of lasting positive change, that is not to say that one's transformation makes them immune to all of the many imperfections that come from being human. Far from it. James noted the inevitable tendency to lapse and generally return to baseline. Linehan addressed this point when she found herself struggling with mental illness later in her life. In her autobiography she wrote about her thoughts while in the midst of a depression:

> What about the spiritual experience that had transformed me? It is true that I had been transformed, but knowing that I would never walk back over the line to the seeming insanity of my previous life didn't mean that I wouldn't still suffer moments of depression. (Linehan, 2020, p. 113)

Even dramatically positive transformations don't mean "happily ever after."

Table 17.1 Benefits of Spiritual Experience[a]

	How Has This Experience Changed the Following				
	Much Better	Somewhat Better	No Change	Somewhat Worse	Much Worse
Family relationships	33%	27%	33%	5%	1%
Fear of death	55%	20%	23%	1%	0%
Health	28%	28%	42%	2%	1%
Purpose in life	55%	25%	17%	2%	0%
Religiousness	27%	25%	37%	5%	6%
Spirituality	71%	18%	9%	1%	1%

[a]From Newberg and Waldman, 2016.

The "True" Self

Colloquial use of the term "transformative experience" refers simply to any event that changes a person in a long-lasting way. But people are changing all the time and most of these changes don't seem to particularly matter because they are so gradual. We constantly change in terms of how we dress, the phrases that we use, and the people that we associate with most, and each moment our brains are adapting and forming new connections, but these are not seen as transformations. What is it about cases like Marsha Linehan's or Ebenezer Scrooge's that lead us to use the term "transformative"?

One line of research that is relevant to the kinds of changes that might be dubbed transformative is focused on the "true self." University of Pennsylvania psychologist Nina Strohminger and her colleagues showed that it is specifically *moral* traits that people rate as consistently being the true self. In a series of studies, Strohminger and colleagues presented participants with stories of people changing or losing aspects of their personality (e.g., being shy), memories (e.g., remembering time spent with parents), desires and preferences (e.g., favorite food), perceptual capacities (e.g., nearsightedness), and morality (e.g., virtuousness). Of these mental faculties, morality was by far the most important element when judging one's true self.

These findings make intuitive sense. People who become less moral are seen as straying farther from their true self, whereas those who become more moral are seen as becoming their true selves. This maps with how people often say that they feel more "themselves" after spiritual experiences. Conversely, people suffering psychosis are often described as "not themselves" in common parlance. Thus, *moral* changes may be a key marker for transformation. As Strohminger and colleagues wrote: "Moral traits are considered more important to personal identity than any other part of the mind" (Strohminger & Nichols, 2014). This finding suggests that the reason for why people often consider spiritual experiences to be transformative have to do with the resulting changes in one's moral character.

This raises the question: Why do spiritual experiences often result in moral changes? One possibility for the change in moral character has to do with connecting with a specific religious perspective that requires one to pursue a higher moral standard. Most religious traditions encourage charity, compassion, and love of fellow human beings. Thus, a numinous experience, for example, might seem to connect the experiencer with God and subsequently a religious tradition that would require greater moral character. The individual might find it obligatory to pursue a higher moral life in the face of the experience of God's presence. However, not all spiritual experiences lead to such conversions, as we have seen that atheists seem to benefit from these experiences as well. Also, there is no evidence that religious individuals are more moral on average than nonreligious individuals.

Another possibility is that if there is a powerful state of connectedness or unity that arises as part of many spiritual experiences. If one feels intimately connected to all of humanity, one might act with a much greater compassion toward everyone who is felt to be a part of that larger whole. In any case, in our data, we do see that most participants indicated that their sense of identity changed as a result of their spiritual experience (Figure 17.2).

Enlightenment and the Brain

Most and perhaps all leaders of major religions described having transformative spiritual experiences. One of James's more controversial suggestions is that spiritual experiences are the source of religions themselves. This would position spiritual experiences as incredibly impactful on society and human

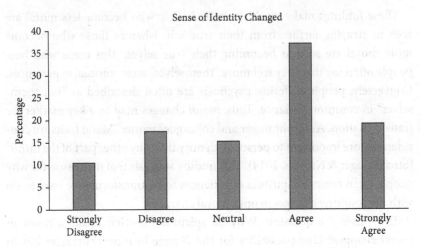

Figure 17.2 Identity changed from experience. Drawn by David Yaden.

history. Accordingly, there is a rich tradition of debate in the field of religious studies on this point.

Regardless of whether spiritual experiences are the *source* of religions, it is uncontroversial that the founders of most of the world's religions reported spiritual experiences. Jesus spent 40 days in the desert, communicating with God and Satan. Moses had the 10 commandments revealed to him on Mt. Sinai. Muhammed received the words of the Koran in a cave. Another spiritual experience from a founder of a major world religion came from Buddha's experience of enlightenment. Born as a wealthy prince, he had access to many worldly pleasures. While walking one day, he witnessed an older person, a sick person, and a dying person. These distressing sights of the reality of life led him to abandon his family and royal status to become a monk. After many years of practice, he had a spiritual experience under a tree, which he felt transformed him—instilling in him peace with the inevitable changes of life and a commitment to compassion.

Buddhism is based around the insights of this spiritual experience and the teachings that the Buddha gave for the rest of his life. What kinds of changes in one's brain might help to make such long-lasting change in attitude and behavior possible? As Rick Hanson wrote about in *The Buddha's Brain* (2009) and *Neurodharma* (2020), there are a number of suppositions that one can make about the kind of brain changes that might be associated with lasting enlightenment.

Enlightenment, in the Buddhist context and beyond, generally refers to not only the experience itself, but also to the persistent change in the character and nature of the transformed individual. Of course, *all* changes in attitude and behavior are likely associated with changes in the brain at some level, but are there any measurable changes that provide additional insights? The results of a growing number of neuroscientific studies point to persistent changes in the brains of people who have had spiritual experiences or perform spiritual practices such as meditation or prayer for prolonged periods of time.

Our team performed one of the first longitudinal single-photon emission computed tomography (SPECT) imaging studies of a meditation practice, Kirtan Kriya, in older people. The results of that study showed that even when not meditating, the people who went through the 8-week program had significant increases in frontal lobe activity (Newberg et al., 2010). Since the frontal lobe is involved in focus and concentration, as well as the regulation of emotions, it is no surprise that these people also experienced improvements in these cognitive domains. This study is also consistent with several magnetic resonance imaging (MRI) studies (which we have mentioned previously) showing that long-term meditators, particularly Buddhist monks, have thicker frontal lobes (Lazar et al., 2005). Just like exercising makes a muscle that makes it thicker and stronger, meditation and other spiritual practices can make the brain function more effectively.

But these studies looked more at the long-term effects of spiritual practices rather than the direct result of a transformative spiritual experience. Part of the problem is methodological. Since we don't know who is going to have a spiritual experience or when it will happen, we don't know who to study and when (although in the next chapter we show that psychedelics are now making this kind of research possible).

In another study that we conducted, people underwent a 7-day retreat based on the spiritual exercises of St. Ignatius. This Christian contemplative tradition involves a period of deep reflection and meditation. We scanned participants before and after they participated in their spiritual retreat. We found significant differences in dopamine and serotonin receptor binding (Newberg et al., 2018).

There is a big question remaining when it comes to the transformations that can result from intense spiritual experiences: How do long-lasting changes occur from such a short experience? Since these experiences can occur over a time period of mere minutes, how does the brain undergo such a radical and long-lasting shift so quickly? The brain typically does not substantially alter its long-term functioning on such a short timescale. It also appears that a critical period may be opened from a spiritual experience that allows for plasticity, and thus changes in brain function occur within this period of time. A number of open questions require additional research on how spiritual experiences sometimes make lasting transformations possible.

Conclusion

Change happens on different timescales; it can occur gradually or suddenly. This has been called change by "creeps" or "jerks"—our focus throughout this book has been on "jerks," or the more sudden changes. But similarly, the impact of these changes can last different lengths of time: The impact of most experiences fades quickly, yet others can last a lifetime. This chapter has focused on long-lasting transformations arising from brief spiritual experiences. In cases where these changes are positive, understanding how such brief moments exert such long-lasting changes could potentially benefit people who are suffering, if this process could be somehow harnessed.

References

Doblin, R. (1991). Pahnke's "Good Friday experiment": A long-term follow-up and methodological critique. *Journal of Transpersonal Psychology, 23*(1), 1–28.

Epstein, S. (1979). The stability of behavior: I. On predicting most of the people much of the time. *Journal of Personality and Social Psychology, 37*(7), 1097.

Hanson, R. (2009). *Buddha's brain: The practical neuroscience of happiness, love, and wisdom.* New Harbinger.

Hanson, R. (2020). *Neurodharma: New science, ancient wisdom, and seven practices of the highest happiness.* Harmony.

Hudson, N. W., & Fraley, R. C. (2015). Volitional personality trait change: Can people choose to change their personality traits? *Journal of Personality and Social Psychology, 109*(3), 490.

James, W. (1890). *The principles of psychology.* Harvard University Press.

James, W. (1902/2009). *The varieties of religious experience: A study in human nature. eBooks@Adelaide.* https://csrs.nd.edu/assets/59930/williams_1902.pdf

Kant, I. (1781/1908). Critique of pure reason. 1781. *Modern Classical Philosophers.* Cambridge, MA: Houghton Mifflin, 370–456.

Lazar, S. W., Kerr, C. E., Wasserman, R. H., Gray, J. R., Greve, D. N., Treadway, M. T., . . . & Fischl, B. (2005). Meditation experience is associated with increased cortical thickness. *Neuroreport, 16*(17), 1893–1897.

Linehan, M. (2014). *DBT Skills training manual.* Guilford.

Linehan, M. (2020). *Building a life worth living: A memoir.* Random House.

McCrae, R. R., & Costa, P. T., Jr. (1994). The stability of personality: Observations and evaluations. *Current Directions in Psychological Science, 3*(6), 173–175.

MacLean, K. A., Johnson, M. W., & Griffiths, R. R. (2011). Mystical experiences occasioned by the hallucinogen psilocybin lead to increases in the personality domain of openness. *Journal of Psychopharmacology, 25*(11), 1453–1461.

Madsen, M. K., Fisher, P. M., Stenbæk, D. S., Kristiansen, S., Burmester, D., Lehel, S., . . . Knudsen, G. M. (2020). A single psilocybin dose is associated with long-term increased mindfulness, preceded by a proportional change in neocortical 5-HT2A receptor binding. *European Neuropsychopharmacology, 33,* 71–80.

Miller, W. R., & C'de Baca, J. (2001). *Quantum change: When epiphanies and sudden insights transform ordinary lives.* Guilford Press.

Newberg, A. B., & Waldman, M. R. (2016). *How enlightenment changes your brain: The new science of transformation.* Penguin Random House.

Newberg, A. B., Wintering, N., Khalsa, D. S., Roggenkamp, H., & Waldman, M. R. (2010). Meditation effects on cognitive function and cerebral blood flow in subjects with memory loss: A preliminary study. *Journal of Alzheimer's Disease, 20*(2), 517–526.

Newberg, A. B., Wintering, N., Yaden, D. B., Zhong, L., Bowen, B., Averick, N., & Monti. D. A. (2018). Effect of a one-week spiritual retreat on dopamine and serotonin transporter binding: A preliminary study. *Religion, Brain & Behavior, 8*(3), 265–278.https://doi.org/10.1080/2153599X.2016.1267035,

Paul, L. A. (2014). *Transformative experience.* Oxford University Press.

Strohminger, N., & Nichols, S. (2014). The essential moral self. *Cognition, 131*(1), 159–171.

18

Clinical Applications

The amount of suffering caused by mental illness is almost unimaginable. Of course, life isn't easy for anyone, but mental illness can take the enjoyment out of otherwise adequate physical and social conditions. (Note: There are, of course, systemic reasons that provide additional obstacles for some people on the basis of their race, class, gender, sexual orientation, disability or illness, religion, or other reasons.) While some people are able to manage their mental illness quite well, these disorders can, in some cases, make life a living hell for those afflicted. As a result of this suffering, many people seek healthcare professionals to help manage their mental illnesses. Effective psychotherapies and pharmacotherapies are indeed available, so seeking help is a good idea. However, there have been few breakthroughs in the field of mental health for several decades and mental illness remains on the rise worldwide. Thankfully, this dire situation may be about to change—at least in some small way—due to exciting new developments on the mental health treatment horizon.

Treatments involving psychedelics are among the most recent and most promising of a new class of mental health interventions (Yaden et al., 2021). It should also be mentioned that a number of studies over the past 25 years supported the use of religious/spiritual practices, such as meditation, to assist with mental health problems (Rosmarin & Koenig, 1998), though the effect sizes are quite modest. But psychedelic substances—as well as the spiritual-type experiences they seem to trigger—offer a novel treatment option with potentially more meaningful clinical effects. Psychedelic substances have now been shown to be effective for several mood and substance use disorders in numerous clinical trials that we describe in this chapter. British psychiatrist Ben Sessa puts this possibility rather provocatively: "Psychedelics are the newest thing we have in pharmacology for the past seventy-five years. Everything else is old hat compared to this" (cited in Earp and Savulescu's *Love Drugs*, 2020, p. 270).

As previously mentioned, people have used psychedelics for centuries in religious and spiritual contexts, by numerous indigenous peoples, and they

The Varieties of Spiritual Experience. David B. Yaden and Andrew B. Newberg, Oxford University Press. © David Yaden and Andrew Newberg 2022. DOI: 10.1093/oso/9780190665678.003.0018

were studied scientifically in the 1950s and 1960s. However, the quantity and quality of new clinical research using these substances led Sessa (2012) and others to proclaim the current period of research a "psychedelic renaissance." The emerging psychedelic treatment paradigm is bringing spiritual experiences into the center of research and clinical discussion. It appears that psychedelics—and the spiritual experiences that they elicit—are poised to transform psychiatry.

The Psychedelic Roots of Twelve-Step Programs

We have already heard a bit about Bill Wilson, the founder of AA, who struggled tremendously with alcoholism. As mentioned, Wilson could not maintain his job or family obligations due to his constant drinking. He eventually sought treatment in 1934 from a physician who was employing an experimental technique using a substance called scopolamine (which is sometimes classified as a psychedelic-like substance). Scopolamine is an antagonist at acetylcholine receptors (different from how most of the psychedelics that we review interact with the brain), which causes feelings of euphoria and hallucinations at certain doses (Julien, 2013). (Note: It is found in the plant *Atropa belladonna* and is sometimes called "belladonna" or "deadly nightshade" due to its toxicity at higher doses.)

Wilson underwent scopolamine therapy three times, but relapsed after each of these treatments. Before his fourth attempt, he met with a friend and former drinking buddy who then came to be a member of the "Oxford Group," which advocated sobriety through a felt sense of acceptance of God in one's life. This time, the psychedelic treatment resulted in a transformative spiritual experience. Wilson wrote of his experience:

> Slowly the ecstasy subsided. I lay on the bed, but now for a time I was in another world, a new world of consciousness. All about me and through me was a wonderful feeling of Presence. A great peace stole over me and I thought, "No matter how wrong things seem to be, they are all right." (cited in Kurtz, 1988, p. 20)

Wilson became, and this time remained, sober. Wilson went on to found Alcoholics Anonymous (AA), on which all 12-step programs are based, which includes support groups for all manner of substance and behavioral addictions. As we already mentioned, this system places "spiritual experience" at its pinnacle (it is the 12th step). The 12-step programs advocate an abstinence-only approach to addiction that involves attending group meetings, sharing stories, providing service, and fostering social bonds. Twelve-step programs, used by many millions of people across the world, appear to be effective for the treatment of addiction, as demonstrated in a recent Cochrane report (which evaluated the strength of evidence of medical treatments; Kelly et al., 2020).

Controversially, some 12-step programs are opposed to other evidence-based treatments, like medication-assisted treatments (MATs). MATs involve a class of medications for individuals with substance use disorders that either block the subjective sensations (the "high") associated with a drug of abuse, diminish cravings to continue ongoing use, or protect against overdose. The most well-known application of MAT is perhaps methadone, which is for individuals with opioid use disorder, but there are a growing number of increasingly targeted pharmacological treatments available for other substance use disorders. Despite the substantial evidence for the effectiveness of MAT in reducing mortality associated with overdose (Strain, 2015), 12-step programs sometimes view these treatments as merely "swapping one drug for another." The abstinence-only policy in 12-step programs is controversial among medical professionals because it sometimes can block people from getting effective and potentially life-saving treatments. With the advent of psychedelic therapies, the use of psilocybin to induce spiritual experiences presents a new form of MAT that seems to align better with the emphasis of 12-step programs on spiritual experiences (Yaden et al., 2021).

Wilson's initial experience was not the only time that he used psychedelics. As he wrote in his autobiography, in the 1950s Wilson later used LSD under the care of British psychiatrist Humphry Osmond. Osmond was at the forefront of psychedelic treatments at the time, even coining the term "psychedelic." (Note: Osmond coined the term in a letter to writer and psychedelic advocate Aldous Huxley, writing: "To fathom hell or soar angelic, Just take pinch of psychedelic"). Wilson wrote that using psychedelics could be helpful to some people struggling with addictions (now referred to as substance use disorders in the *Diagnostic and Statistical Manual of Mental Disorders*, *DSM*). Wilson's reasoning was that he believed that spiritual experience to be the key to sobriety, but many AA members had difficulty achieving this state without assistance. Wilson wrote:

It is a generally acknowledged fact in spiritual development that ego reduction makes the influx of God's grace possible. If, therefore, under LSD we can have a temporary reduction, so that we can better see what we are and where we are going—well, that might be of some help. The goal might become clearer. So I consider LSD to be of some value to some people, and practically no damage to anyone. (Alcoholics Anonymous, 1984, p. 370)

Wilson's use of, and advocacy for, psychedelics as a means to achieve spiritual experiences to treat addictions was actively suppressed by some influential members of AA (J. Miller, 2019). It remains to be seen whether psychedelic-assisted psychotherapy for substance use disorders forms an exception to the abstinence-only policy of 12-step programs in the future (Yaden et al., 2021). But for the millions of people suffering from mood or substance use disorders, many may choose to take Wilson's advice and avail themselves to this treatment when it becomes available. Among these people, many of them can expect to have a spiritual experience.

James on Psychoactive Substances

James had a number of experiences with psychoactive substances. He allegedly tried peyote (the psychedelic component is mescaline), which was sent to him by a colleague. But recall that there appears to have been something wrong with the dose that he had been sent because it only made him ill. He wrote about this in a letter to his brother, Henry James: "I took one bud three days ago, was violently sick for twenty-four hours, and had no other symptom whatever. . . I will take visions on trust!" (James, 1920, p. 37). If James had had a psychedelic experience, it is likely that the history of psychedelic research and application would be substantially different and, we believe, far more developed by now.

James had also read about another psychoactive substance, nitrous oxide, in a pamphlet written by Benjamin Blood, "The Anesthetic Revelation and the Gist of Philosophy." In it, Blood described the revelatory effects of using this drug. James wrote of Blood's thought that it "fascinated me so 'weirdly' that I am conscious of its having been one of the stepping-stones of my thinking ever since." James reviewed this small book in an article in *The Atlantic*, and he later wrote an article on the topic in the prestigious psychology journal *Psychological Review*, which elaborated his thinking on using psychoactive substances.

When James tried nitrous oxide, he was so impressed that he claimed that it caused the "the strongest emotion" of his life. While on the drug, he wrote a number of paradoxical statements that read almost like absurdist poetry, like: "thought deeper than speech!" In *The Varieties*, 1902/2009), he described his experience in more detail:

> Looking back on my own experiences [with nitrous oxide], they all converge towards a kind of insight to which I cannot help ascribing some metaphysical significance. The keynote of it is invariably a reconciliation. It is as if the opposites of the world, whose contradictoriness and conflict make all our difficulties and troubles, were melted into unity. Those who have ears to hear, let them hear; to me the living sense of its reality only comes in the artificial mystic state of mind. (James, 1902/2009, p. 293)

James thus came down decidedly in support of the idea that psychoactive substances can provide experiences of insight and genuine personal significance.

The Psychedelic Renaissance

Psychoactive substances have been used for millennia, usually in combination with religious and spiritual rituals (Schultes, 1969). Indigenous peoples across multiple continents have used several different forms of psychedelics at least for centuries, and possibly for thousands of years, according to evidence from cave paintings and from traces of psychedelic alkaloids in tools and skeletal remains (for a review, see Johnson et al., 2019; Muraresku, 2020). In ancient Greece, it is possible that a ritual called the Eleusinian Mystery Rites involved the use of a psychedelic substance in which many Greek citizens reportedly took part, including Plato and Cicero (Webster, 2000). Some scholars have also pointed to the Rig-Veda, a centuries-old book in the Hindu tradition, which mentions a psychoactive substance called "soma," which some believe may have consisted of mushrooms containing psilocybin. The use of ayahuasca in South America has been dated to at least 1,000 years ago after a recent archeological discovery (M. J. Miller et al., 2019), and the peyote cactus (containing mescaline) has been used in Mexico and by Native Americans for at least 5,000 years (El-Seedi et al., 2005).

In more recent history, psilocybin mushrooms came under scientific investigation after mycologist and banker Gordon Wasson and his wife, pediatrician Valentina Pavlovna Guercken, brought them back from Mexico in 1955, where they had used them in a religious ritual. Recall that the mushrooms were provided by a Mazatec healer (called a curandera) named Maria Sabina. As mentioned previously, Sabina's community was subsequently massively disrupted by tourists from the United States and Europe who came to take part in her psilocybin ceremonies, for which she was never properly remunerated.

In 1938, Swiss chemist Albert Hoffman synthesized LSD. His first LSD experience from accidental ingestion in 1943, celebrated yearly by psychedelic enthusiasts on "bicycle day" (April 19th), memorializes his ride home from the lab as he experienced the world's first LSD experience. The discovery of LSD, which is structurally similar to the neurotransmitter serotonin, considerably advanced scientific research on serotonin. This research led (albeit indirectly) to the development of selective serotonin reuptake inhibitors (SSRIs), which are currently the most common form of antidepressant medications.

Hoffman's LSD experience is notable because he did not have the same kind of expectations that one would likely have if they participated in a religious ritual or had otherwise been told about the potential effects of psychedelics. Hoffman first described his experience as "a remarkable restlessness, combined with a slight dizziness" and "a not unpleasant intoxicated-like condition, characterized by an extremely stimulated imagination." He then wrote: "I perceived an uninterrupted stream of fantastic pictures, extraordinary shapes with intense, kaleidoscopic play of colors." While Hoffman did not mention any explicit religious or spiritual content, he did describe the furniture seeming to come alive for a time, which may indicate a degree of mind perception. He reported that some of the experience was frightening, but that this gave way to a "feeling of good fortune and gratitude." When he stepped outside into his garden later that evening, Hoffman reported: "Everything glistened and sparkled in a fresh new light. The world was as if newly created" (cited in Horgan, 2010).

Many psychedelic experiences appear indistinguishable from spiritual experiences. We therefore take psychedelics to be a trigger that often, but not always, elicits spiritual experiences for our purposes. Many people find it difficult or impossible to differentiate between personal accounts of psychedelic and nonpsychedelically triggered spiritual experiences. For example, Huston Smith, in his classic article, "Do Drugs Have Religious Import?" (1964), reported asking a class at Princeton to identify which of the following experiences was psychedelically induced and which was spontaneous:

I

Suddenly I burst into a vast, new, indescribably wonderful universe. Although I am writing this over a year later, the thrill of the surprise and amazement, the awesomeness of the revelation, the engulfment in an overwhelming feeling-wave of gratitude and blessed wonderment, are as fresh, and the memory of the experience is as vivid, as if it had happened five minutes ago. And yet to concoct anything by way of description that would even hint at the magnitude, the sense of ultimate reality . . . this seems such an impossible task. The knowledge which has infused and affected every aspect of my life came instantaneously and with such complete force of certainty that it was impossible, then or since, to doubt its validity.

II

All at once, without warning of any kind, I found myself wrapped in a flame-colored cloud. For an instant I thought of fire . . . the next, I knew that the fire was within myself. Directly afterward there came upon me a sense of exultation, of immense joyousness accompanied or immediately followed by an intellectual illumination impossible to describe. Among other things, I did not merely come to believe, but I saw that the universe is not composed of dead matter, but is, on the contrary, a living Presence; I became conscious in myself of eternal life. . . . I saw that all men are immortal: that the cosmic order is such that without any peradventure all things work together for the good of each and all; that the foundation principle of the world . . . is what we call love, and that the happiness of each and all is in the long run absolutely certain.

The class was unable to correctly identify the drug-induced experience, guessing at no better than chance. The answer, by the way, is that the first one was drug induced, and the second was spontaneous (it is a report from R. M. Bucke that James included in *The Varieties*). Research has also confirmed that psychedelically triggered and spontaneously occurring spiritual experiences are often remarkably similar (Davis et al., 2020; Griffiths et al., 2019; Yaden et al., 2017).

We saw (in Chapter 6 on triggers) how psychedelics became a topic of scientific research in the 1950s and 1960s, resulting in a wave of research at major research institutions and with government funding. Some of these studies showed psychedelics are nontoxic, are largely nonaddictive, and have the potential to treat depression and addiction, which has been confirmed in more recent research (Nichols, 2016). A more recent meta-analysis of this early research on alcoholism found that participants in these studies who were given psychedelics reduced their drinking substantially more than controls (Krebs & Johansen, 2012).

The Harvard Psilocybin Project, headed by Timothy Leary and Richard Alpert (who later became known as Ram Dass after studying with a guru in India), contributed to understanding the importance of "set and setting" (a phrase Leary coined) in research articles and well-known books like *The Psychedelic Experience* (Alpert, Leary, & Metzner, 1964/2008). But they also contributed to the era of prohibition brought on by prohibitive government mandates and regulations through their sweeping revolutionary pronouncements and somewhat lax research ethics (Alpert had given some psychedelics to Harvard undergraduates despite being instructed not to by the university).

After years of abandonment, researchers at Johns Hopkins School of Medicine started, in the year 2000, to navigate the difficult process of gaining approval to restart research on psychedelics in the United States. The team, led by psychopharmacologist Roland Griffiths, was intrigued by the research findings from the 1960s, but Griffiths personal interest was driven largely by a curiosity about how altered states of consciousness from psychedelics relate to those produced by meditation. This research program has now expanded to a large lab, the Center of Psychedelic and Consciousness Research (CPCR) at Johns Hopkins with other faculty, such as Matthew Johnson, Frederick Barrett, and Al Garcia-Romeu, as well as one of us (D. B. Y.). In addition to Johns Hopkins, at the time of this writing a number of other psychedelic research labs are opening in the United States at University of California, Berkeley; University of California San Francisco; Yale; and Harvard. There are also major existing labs in Zurich, Dublin, Melbourne, and London. The ongoing swell of research on psychedelics may mark a new era for psychiatric research and treatments.

Resurrecting the Good Friday Experiment

The first study conducted by Griffiths and his team at Johns Hopkins was a more rigorous replication of the Good Friday experiment. Recall (from Chapters 6 and 17) that the Good Friday experiment involved administering psilocybin to divinity school students during a church service. Griffiths identified several methodological problems with the Good Friday experiment that motivated replicating the study. First, the original study was basically unblinded because it was in a group setting. This meant that participants could quickly tell who was on psilocybin and who was not. The group setting also meant that participants could easily influence one another's experiences. Also, the placebo substance was niacin (vitamin B), which has no psychoactive qualities, so participants could easily guess whether they were in the experimental or control condition.

Griffiths's team at Johns Hopkins corrected these issues with an updated experimental design (Griffiths et al., 2006). Participants at Hopkins would receive either psilocybin or a control substance in a room with no other participants (other than two trained guides), so there would be no influence from other participants. Additionally, rather than niacin, participants were given an "active" placebo that would cause psychoactive effects—a high dose of Ritalin (methylphenidate). Last, the session guides were also blinded, meaning they did not know whether any particular participant had been given psilocybin or methylphenidate, so they could not even inadvertently influence the experience of the participants.

The results of this study have been described several times in this book because this study marked the beginning of a new era in the investigation of psychedelic-associated spiritual experiences. The results demonstrate that spiritual experiences can now be induced in controlled laboratory settings. Specifically, the results show that most participants administered psilocybin reported a full mystical experience; about 61% in the psychedelic condition and almost no participants (7%) in the control condition reported a mystical experience. Mystical experience was measured using the Mystical Experience Questionnaire (MEQ; designed by Hopkins researchers Fred Barrett, Matthew Johnson, Katherine MacLean, Bill Richards, and Roland Griffiths—also described in Chapter 12 on mystical experiences). This measure includes items related to unity, the noetic quality, sacredness, positive mood, transcendence of time and space, and ineffability. The scale was explicitly designed based on James's thinking on mystical experience (note: along with further developments from Stace and Pahnke, as mentioned previously).

Compared to placebo, participants who were given psilocybin reported elevated mood and sense of meaning 2 months later. Participants in the psilocybin condition also demonstrated altered prosocial attitudes, which were measured using observer report (participants chose someone close to them who researchers could call to ask if the participants seemed more prosocial after their psilocybin and placebo sessions). Participants in the psilocybin condition were rated as significantly more prosocial according to these observer reports.

After about a year had passed, researchers followed up with the participants, asking how meaningful the experience remained. Even after about 14 months, participants ranked their experience with psilocybin among the top five most meaningful (58%) and spiritually significant (67%) moments of their entire lives. This is a remarkable finding. As Griffiths said: "As a scientific phenomenon, if you can create a condition in which 70 percent of people will say they have had one of the most meaningful experiences of their lives . . . well, as a scientist that's just incredible" (Pollan, 2019, p. 77).

Other psychedelic studies have followed up on this spiritual component of psychedelic experiences. Griffiths and his team at Hopkins (2018) conducted a psilocybin study pairing psychedelics with spiritual practices such as meditation, prayer, and journaling. The researchers found that the participants who incorporated spiritual practices into their lives after their psilocybin experience benefited more from the experience. Another psychedelic research group in Zurich, Switzerland, headed by Franz Vollenweider, has found that psychedelics enhance the experience and practice of mindfulness meditation in a retreat setting (Smigielski et al., 2019). Together, these findings provide support for the claim that psychedelics enhance spiritual practices and rituals and may help to explain why they have been used in such settings for centuries.

Therapeutic Applications of Psychedelics

Beyond the benefits to well-being, prosociality, and meaning in life, psychedelics have been shown to be effective in treating a range of mental illnesses. Here, we focus on some studies using psychedelics to treat substance use and mood disorders, but research is ongoing and the literature is quickly expanding.

Supporting findings from early psychedelic research, and underscoring Bill Wilson's personal appraisal, it appears that psychedelics have antiaddictive effects. Psilocybin has been shown to be effective in treating several different substance use disorders, including those of alcohol (Bogenschutz et al., 2015) and nicotine (Johnson et al., 2014). This is unusual, as most forms of MAT for addiction are targeted to treating addictions to specific substances, whereas psychedelics appear effective across a range of substance use disorders. This may suggest that psychedelics target a common underlying mechanism in these disorders.

In terms of alcohol, Bogenschutz and colleagues (2015) conducted a study on alcohol dependence and showed that drinking days dropped about 32% in the month following the psychedelic session, with effects from the session lasting over 20 months. In terms of nicotine, Johns Hopkins professor Matthew Johnson and colleagues showed that when psilocybin was paired with cognitive behavioral therapy (CBT), 80% of the participants remained smoke-free 6 months later (Johnson et al., 2014). Hopkins researcher Albert Garcia-Romeu and colleagues then showed that one's score on the MEQ predicted one's odds of successfully quitting (Garcia-Romeu et al., 2014). However, a limitation to these studies is that they are "open label" or unblinded. Researchers at Johns Hopkins are conducting several more rigorous follow-ups. Barrett is conducting a blinded study on comorbid depression and alcohol use. Johnson is conducting a blinded study in opioid addictions. University of Alabama researcher Peter Hendricks is also conducting an ongoing study on treating cocaine addiction with psilocybin.

Part of the efficacy of psychedelics may be due to their capacity to alter mood, as psychedelics have also been shown to be effective treatments for mood disorders like depression and anxiety. One study from a psychedelic research team at Imperial College London, headed by David Nutt and Robin Carhart-Harris, found that psychedelics effectively reduced treatment-resistant depression (Carhart-Harris et al., 2016). This was followed by a more rigorous trial conducted by Alan Davis and the Johns Hopkins team, showing that depression was effectively reduced following psilocybin (Davis et al., 2021).

End-of-life care is another compelling area of application for psychedelics (Yaden et al., 2021). Currently, healthcare providers only have painkillers and antidepressants to provide comfort during this difficult period. Psychedelic treatments could allow for people to transcend the emotional difficulties in order to reconnect with their loved ones. Two studies, one at Johns Hopkins and the other at New York University, showed that this is just what occurred when patients with a life-threatening cancer diagnosis were given psilocybin (Griffiths et al., 2016; Ross et al., 2016).

Thus, psychedelics and the spiritual experiences they give rise to have shown remarkable effectiveness in treating several different mood and substance use disorders and may even provide some benefit for those near death.

Potential Mediators

These therapeutic successes raise the issue of *why* psychedelics work, which is a question we have considered throughout this book with regard to spiritual experiences in general.

Expectation likely plays an important role in psychedelic experiences and treatment applications. Recall that Wilson only had his spiritual experience from his psychedelic treatment after the visit from the Oxford Group. Was his success related more to the fact that he needed multiple sessions of the drug, or was it due to the change in his mindset resulting from the conversation that he had with the members of the Oxford Group? Or some combination of both? The mindset and overall social context undoubtedly influence psychedelic experiences and their outcomes, but the extent and bounds of this influence is not yet known with any specificity.

Expectations and psychological factors are partially experimentally controlled by the use of placebos, so that at least both the experimental and control groups have the same expectations. But it is still possible for one's expectations to influence one's experience. One's expectations may come from the surrounding culture, but they can also be more intentionally shaped. For example, at Johns Hopkins, subjects are provided with "flight instructions," which are designed to help people navigate their experiences. These suggestions for how to handle the experience effectively include aphorisms and other advice that anecdotally seem to help people manage their fears and derive benefit from their experiences. For example, the guide includes the lyrics written by John Lennon: "Turn off your mind, relax, and float downstream" (Pollan, 2019, p. 63). It is quite possible that the preparations for these sessions impact the experiences themselves, though this has not yet been systematically investigated.

Additionally, a number of psychotherapeutic paradigms, such as CBT, are being combined with psychedelic treatments. Another psychotherapeutic approach that seems well suited is acceptance and commitment therapy (ACT). This therapy is evidence based and involves mindfully embracing the present moment. One study by Johns Hopkins researcher Alan Davis shows that mental flexibility, a key concept in ACT, may be an important moderator in positive treatment outcomes (Davis et al., 2020). It is likely that the particular type of psychotherapy combined with psychedelic treatment will impact the experience, and psychedelic treatments will likely benefit from using evidence-based rather than eclectic approaches.

Of course, of most interest to us is the possibility that the altered state of consciousness itself is a mediator of the therapeutic outcomes. Does the degree to which one reports having had a spiritual experience predict one's beneficial outcomes? The answer appears to be yes. Across a number of studies, scores on the MEQ is predictive of therapeutic success (Yaden & Griffiths, 2020). This suggests that the subjective experience of a psychedelic state may be key to treatment outcomes—and this brings the study of spiritual experience to center stage in the study of psychedelics in general.

Additional evidence regarding the features of the mental state that people experience during psychedelics comes from a field study conducted at Burning Man. Yale psychologist Molly Crockett and her team, including Matthias Forstmann, Daniel Yudkin, and Annayah Prosser, attended so-called transformational festivals like Burning Man and asked people there if they had had a "transformative experience" and what psychoactive substances they had tried. Among people who had used psychedelics, those who indicated that they had a transformative experience and felt "connected to other people" indicated substantially enhanced positive mood that lasted for days after their experience (Forstmann et al., 2020). So feelings of connectedness to others seems to be an important factor of these experienes.

However, it is still unknown whether subjective experiences are needed at all for treatment success. Would psilocybin be just as beneficial if it were administered to participants while they were under general anesthesia (and therefore unconscious)? This "trip-free" psychedelics hypothesis is provocative and should be tested, although evidence showing that features of the subjective experience predicted positive outcomes appears contrary to this hypothesis (for a debate, see Olson, 2020; Yaden & Griffiths, 2020). This point brings the underlying neural mechanisms involved in psychedelic experiences into focus.

Pharmacology and Neuroscience of Psychedelics

One of the many benefits, scientifically speaking, of psychedelics is that they provide a laboratory model of spiritual experience. In this case, the chemical properties of the trigger are extremely well defined. One of the problems with studying religious rituals and practices is that they involve so many different components, including their particular words, physical movements, and symbols that engage beliefs, emotions, autonomic arousal, and attention in complex ways. They also only rarely result in intense spiritual experiences. With psychedelics, on the other hand, there is a consistent chemical trigger, and a relatively reliable effect, even though the subjective experience that arises is itself highly complex and is impacted by beliefs as well as one's clinical and cultural context.

As mentioned, psychedelics such as psilocybin or LSD have a chemical structure that is very similar to serotonin (Figure 18.1). Studies have shown that one particular subtype of serotonin receptor appears to mediate the subjective effects of these psychedelics: the serotonin 2a receptor. If the serotonin 2a receptor is blocked by another drug first, the psychoactive effects are also blocked. Serotonin is the neurotransmitter that is targeted by many depression treatments, such as fluoxetine (Prozac). These antidepressants are known as selective SSRIs due to their capacity to block the process by which neurons recycle serotonin from the synapse (the space between neurons) into the neuron itself after it has been released. Hypothetically, this results in more serotonin availability in the brain. However, it speaks to the complexity of the brain that it is still not known exactly how SSRIs exert their antidepressant effects.

Some recent theories on how psychedelics result in beneficial outcomes point to a protein that is also affected by serotonin, called brain-derived neurotrophic factor (BDNF). BDNF is important for neurogenesis, or the growth of new neurons. This substance is released during exercise, and some have argued that it accounts for some of exercise's antidepressant effects. BDNF may also play an important role in psychedelics. In one study in mice (Ly et al., 2018), when BDNF was blocked, so were the beneficial effects of psychedelics. This BDNF neurogenesis process from psychedelics may increase brain plasticity for a period of time. These neurochemical observations have yet to be systematically connected to other levels of analysis, though, such as changes to subjective experience measured with self-report.

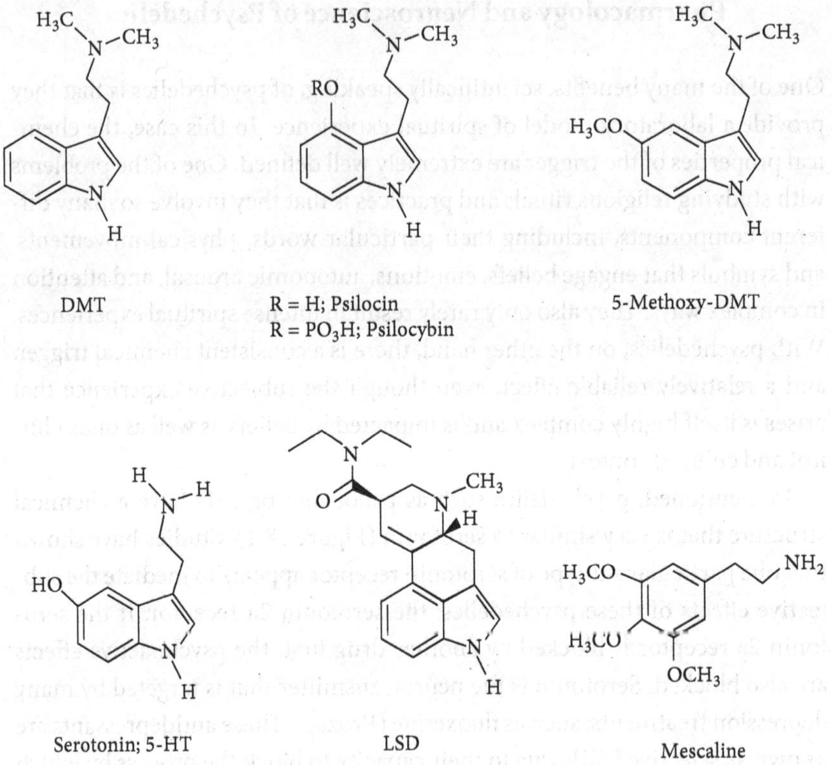

Figure 18.1 Similar chemical structures of serotonin and several psychedelics. DMT, *N,N*-dimethyltryptamine. Drawn by David Yaden. Reprinted from Pharmacology & Therapeutics, 101(2), p. 131–181, Copyright 2004, with permission from Elsevier.

Some neuroimaging findings may provide clues regarding the mechanism through which psychedelics exert their effects. The Imperial College London team led by Carhart-Harris and David Nutt has produced some intriguing neuroimaging findings in the default mode network (DMN). The DMN, recall, was discovered from the observation that when participants in neuroimaging studies lie in brain scanners and are told to "do nothing," a particular network becomes activated. This brain network is generally associated with memories and imagining future possibilities involving one's self. Using functional magnetic resonance imaging (fMRI), Carhart-Harris evaluated functional connectivity in the brain of people given either LSD or placebo and found an inhibition of the DMN structures under the influence of LSD. Furthermore, activity in the angular gyrus and insula correlated with the dissolution of the ego self (see Carhart-Harris et al., 2014; Tagliazucchi et al., 2016). Carhart-Harris claimed that these findings supported the relationship between Freudian concepts such as the unconscious and how these can be altered under certain circumstances, such as the use of psychedelics (Carhart-Harris & Friston, 2010). But this research is still in its early stages, and it is unclear how the sense of self-loss is impacted by psychedelics or what the brain-based findings really tell us (remember the previously mentioned issues with reverse inference about brain findings). Additionally, it is unclear how specific this DMN finding is to psychedelics, as this finding has been observed as resulting from other substances as well (e.g., Doss et al., 2020).

While the impact of psychedelics on the DMN is intriguing, it is likely a very preliminary step in the enormous scientific task of understanding how psychedelics impact brain function. To be sure, we are still very far from getting a complete picture of the underlying neuroscience of psychedelic experiences. Yet understanding the mechanisms through which benefits are conferred is essential to making progress in using psychedelic-assisted psychotherapy. Evidence-based medicine proceeds through not only knowing that a particular intervention works, but also *how* it works. This is the great next task of research on psychedelic treatments. Understanding these mechanisms of psychedelic treatment will also likely shed light on some of the mechanisms of a broad range of spiritual experience.

Discovering how psychedelics convey their beneficial effects and how to minimize their risks is an area in which a great deal of careful scientific research is still required. We believe that it is essential not to repeat the mistakes of earlier eras by rushing this research or by overly enthusiastic or wishful thinking about their benefits—these substances are no panacea (Yaden et al., 2021). Yet, it's also important to recognize their genuine potential. In *Love Drugs*, Earp and Savulescu (2020, p. 269) put this issue regarding psychedelic research plainly:

> Let's bring this work into the light and subject it to the same scientific standards as any other therapeutic intervention involving the use of a chemical substance. There is little to be gained remaining in the dark.

Nonpharmacological Applications

While much recent work has been focused on psychedelics, there are already a number of studies that have explored the impact of religious and spiritual practices on mental health. These rituals and practices represent behavioral rather than pharmacological ways of triggering spiritual experiences.

We have mentioned a number of different forms of meditation and prayer practices from religious traditions throughout this book. Meditation has been incorporated into healthcare and psychotherapeutic settings, with largely great success as these techniques generally reduce anxiety and chronic pain, while increasing well-being (Goyal et al., 2014). Various forms of meditation and prayer have all been effective in certain conditions and populations (Goldberg et al., 2018; Gonçalves et al., 2015; González-Valero et al., 2019; Spinelli et al., 2019).

Another study we performed found that practicing the rosary, a Catholic prayer practice, was associated with reduced anxiety (Anastasi & Newberg, 2008). These practices also produce changes in particular brain regions that can be seen in neuroimaging studies and that may provide clues about why these practices are beneficial. For example, our study of Kirtan Kriya meditation revealed brain changes in areas, such as the frontal lobes and limbic system, that regulate emotions (Moss et al., 2012).

A number of studies have shown that over long periods of time meditation practices that increase frontal lobe size and function may help modulate emotions such as depression or anxiety (Hölzel et al., 2011). Studies have also implicated the cingulate gyrus and also reductions of activity in the DMN (Brewer et al., 2011; Brewer & Garrison, 2014; Garrison et al., 2015). Another study examined people who practiced a lot of prayer; it showed the orbito-frontal cortex might be involved, which might lead to better regulation of the flow of incoming information (Kober et al., 2017). However, these are merely speculations based on the general functions of brain regions that are active during these practices (we reiterate our caution about reverse inference from brain-based findings).

In addition to the positive effects of spiritual practices, we have seen that sometimes these practices can give rise to difficult experiences as catalogued by the Dark Night project (recall that this is the group gathering accounts of negative meditation experiences). However, practices like meditation and prayer much more often result in positive results, and they can also elicit spiritual experiences (recall the figure from Chapter 6 on triggers). However, the extent to which spiritual experiences are elicited by these meditation practices in secular healthcare settings is not currently known. Other problems in this context are also possible; for example, some individuals become uncomfortable when certain spiritually related interventions interfere with their belief system. In our experience with implementing the Buddhist-inspired mindfulness meditation program, we have occasionally had highly religious individuals who felt that meditation was not allowed by their religion. In such cases, it is often advisable to point interested patients to a practice from their own religious or secular tradition (Yaden et al., 2020).

Large portions of the world's population regularly engage in some religious rituals and practices, yet they are generally not mentioned by healthcare professionals due to the lack of evidence for their effectiveness. On the other hand, there is extensive research documenting that those individuals who are more religious or spiritual have reduced amounts of depression, anxiety, substance abuse, suicide, and other mental health problems (Rosmarin & Koenig, 2020). Whether it is the practices or the experiences, or both, that confer benefit is not known. In *Rituals and Practices in World Religions* (Yaden, Zhao, et al., 2020), we catalogued a large number of rituals and practices across religions and argued that perhaps it is worth examining the effectiveness of these rituals and practices in order to discover applications that fit within patients' preexisting religious or spiritual traditions.

One additional technology that might eventually be relevant regarding therapeutic applications of spiritual experiences has to do with the direct stimulation of the brain using magnetic fields. Transcranial magnetic stimulation (TMS) works by applying magnetic fields to different parts of the brain to activate or inhibit neurons in certain patches of the cortex. One interesting study showed that by using TMS to reduce activity in the inferior parietal lobe, subjects slightly increased in implicit measures of religiosity and spirituality (Crescentini et al., 2014). In a related study, increasing activity in the inferior parietal lobe slightly reduced participants religiosity and spirituality according to implicit measures (Crescentini et al., 2015). There have also been a growing number of studies exploring the effectiveness of TMS in patients with various psychological problems, such as depression or anxiety (Cirillo et al., 2019; Sonmez et al., 2019). We will have to wait for more studies as well as substantial advances in the technology before we can determine whether direct brain stimulation can induce spiritual experiences.

Challenges for Application

Unsurprisingly, some important philosophical and ethical issues are raised when considering the application of spiritual experiences in contemporary healthcare treatments. We have seen that psychedelic experiences can indeed result in long-lasting and dramatic changes. Philosopher L. A. Paul (who we described in Chapter 17 on transformations) argued that fully informed consent may be difficult or impossible for some transformative experiences. How, Paul (2014) asked, can one consent to an experience that may change them into a new self?

To illustrate, when the Beatles began to experiment with psychedelics, both John Lennon and George Harrison had already had psychedelic experiences after having been dosed at a party without their knowledge. They both described how important and "life changing" the experience had been for them. However, Paul McCartney wasn't sure that he wanted his life changed. He said, "We heard that you were never the same after you took it—it alters your life, and you can never think in the same way again. I think John was rather excited by this prospect but I was rather frightened by it" (Beatles, 2002, p. 255). For McCartney, these fears were dispelled after trying it, and the Beatles went on to study meditation due, at least in part, to their psychedelic experiences. But how can clinicians provide information and respond to fears such as those voiced by McCartney?

There are guidelines that can help with thinking through these issues raised by applications involving spiritual experience. Some readily available principles are those that every researcher must know in order to get certified to do research on humans by institutional review boards (IRBs). These principles are autonomy, beneficence, and justice. Autonomy has to do with respecting one's capacity to make decisions for themselves, without undue influence, and is especially relevant to providing full information about the study. Beneficence refers to the intention to benefit people's lives through research. Justice refers to how the results of research are distributed among people and whether or not this is done fairly.

In terms of autonomy, McCartney was likely not the only person made nervous by the prospect of taking a psychedelic substance, even if it was in order to treat substantial suffering from mental illness. For this reason, "enhanced consent" may be required to undergo psychedelic treatments. In an article, "Ethics and Ego Dissolution: The Case of Psilocybin," authors Smith and Sisti (2020) argued that certain features of psychedelic experiences, such as the possible shifts in values and personality as well as the challenging content of many experiences, mean that special care must be taken throughout the consent process. Similarly, intense meditation or prayer retreats could have similar effects. These changes are generally for the better, but one can imagine reasons why one might be reticent to have an intense spiritual experience. In general, potential participants and patients should be fully informed about what they are about to experience.

In terms of beneficence, one interesting consideration is the harm done by *not* applying a treatment that is known to reduce suffering. It is worth remembering that when pain medication and anesthesia for surgery became available, there were people (many of them clergy) who objected to the "unnaturalness" of such interventions (Dormandy, 2006). While this seems ridiculous now, some may currently hold this attitude toward psychedelic treatments. If this attitude results in obstructing treatment, it may run afoul of the principle of beneficence. As philosopher Derek Anderson argued: "If we can do research that has the potential to greatly benefit individuals and society and which poses a sufficiently minimal risk of causing harm to individuals and society, then (so long as the research itself can be conducted in a morally acceptable way) we have a moral obligation to pursue that research" (Yaden et al., 2015, p. 227). A similar line of reasoning can be applied to the clinical application of psychedelics, as there is a need to attend to both the potential risks *and* benefits.

There is also a question of who receives these treatments, and this is covered by considerations of justice and equity. Typically, at least in the United States, wealthy people have access to the newest and best treatments while poorer people do not, which is clearly an instance of inequity. Psychedelic treatments, TMS, as well as meditation programs, involve many hours of time from healthcare providers and costs to patients. During psychedelic treatments in particular, people must be monitored by mental health professionals, usually clinical psychologists or psychiatrists. Therefore, there is a substantial risk that such treatments may become widely available only to those able to afford it. Psychedelic researcher Peter Hendricks is well aware of this issue and is conducting psychedelic research in samples with lower socioeconomic status for this reason and we hope others follow suit. Policymakers and healthcare leaders will need to confront the danger that access to psychedelic treatment is limited only to the wealthy.

These issues are easier to deal with when considering treating those who are suffering, but what about applications involving the already well, also called "enhancement" (or the betterment of well people)? The use of psychedelics for the purpose of increasing well-being, for self-improvement, or for spiritual reasons would fall under the category of enhancement. In general, people are more willing to "repair" than "enhance" because it is harder to weigh the risks when there is no immediate suffering to alleviate. People are also less willing to endorse enhancements that impact core aspects of one's self (e.g., one's values and personality) (Medaglia et al., 2019; Riis et al., 2008). According to psychologist John Medaglia, these attitudes about enhancement are widespread and present some possible obstacles to the application of psychedelics for the purposes of enhancement (Yaden et al., 2018).

Beyond these ethical considerations, the largest concern for applying spiritual experiences as a kind of intervention is the prospect of having a negative or even terrifying experience. Much attention has been paid to "bad trips," or negative psychedelic experiences, and while much of this was generally misleading or false propaganda promoted during the era of government prohibition, bad trips do occur. Even meditation practices can go awry. While careful attention has been given to reduce the chances of bad trips under professional supervision, this remains probably the single largest challenge in applying psychedelics, and spiritual experiences in general, to treatment domains.

It is also important to consider potential medically relevant side effects. Meditation or prayer can sometimes reduce blood pressure and heart rate, which could be problematic for certain people with heart disease or autonomic nervous system dysfunction. TMS can result in headaches and can cause scalp discomfort and muscle spasms. Psychedelics modestly raise heart rate and blood pressure during the time of drug action, but the physical effects are negligible, and, as mentioned, toxicity and the possibility of addiction are relatively low. The main risks for treatments involving psychedelics are the levels of fear and anxiety that some people can experience (Johnson et al., 2008). The risks of adverse effects are highest when psychedelics are taken outside of the laboratory. (note: For this reason, in addition to the fact that psychedelics remain illegal in most places, we are not advocating the recreational use of psychedelics here.)

In a survey of people who had taken psychedelic experiences outside of the laboratory, the Johns Hopkins team found that 11% of survey participants reported that they considered their psychedelic experience to have posed a risk of some kind (Carbonaro et al., 2016). Of the respondents, 2.6% behaved in a physically aggressive or violent manner, and 2.7% received medical help. Of those whose experience occurred more than 1 year before, 7.6% sought treatment for enduring psychological symptoms. While a study that compared the harm to self and others across all recreational substances found that *psychedelics were among the least harmful* (alcohol, tobacco, heroin, and cocaine are among the most harmful; Nutt et al., 2010), the findings related to the risks of psychedelic substances are still sobering and point to some real risks with recreational use.

However, inside the laboratory, there have so far been very few adverse events or signs of lasting negative effects. As Pollan (2019) summarized: "Since the revival of sanctioned psychedelic research beginning in the 1990s, nearly a thousand volunteers have been dosed, and not a single serious adverse event has been reported" (p. 14). This is despite the fact that many participants reported that their experiences were extremely psychologically challenging.

These findings point to the complexities of the psychedelic experience—people report both positive feelings and engaging with difficult psychological material. Psychedelic treatments require substantial psychological integration, ideally with trained mental health professionals. Here Pollan described his interpretation and integration of his experience on psychedelics:

> I honestly don't know what to make of this experience. In a certain light at certain moments, I feel as though I had had some kind of spiritual experience. I had felt the personhood of other beings in a way I hadn't before; whatever it is that keeps us from feeling our full implication in nature had been temporarily in abeyance. There had also been, I felt, an opening of the heart. (Pollan, 2019, p. 135)

The risks of psychedelics, both inside and (especially) outside the laboratory, increase for those with preexisting or latent psychiatric conditions. One study found a fourfold increase in the risks of developing delusional thought patterns after psychedelic experiences in psychiatric patients (Abraham et al., 1996), although safety guidelines are dramatically reducing such risks in clinical settings (Johnson et al., 2008). Overall it remains the case that for some individuals, particularly those with preexisting psychiatric conditions, psychedelic approaches to triggering intense spiritual experiences may not be appropriate, or at least need to be carefully considered.

Conclusion

The use of various approaches such as meditation, prayer, retreats, and psychedelics in treatment contexts may represent an important avenue for helping people with mental health problems. Mindfulness and other meditation practices have become widespread, and psychedelic compounds may be poised to make a breakthrough in psychiatry and psychotherapy. These approaches would bring spiritual experiences to the center of mainstream medical and academic discourse. Such treatments require systematization, additional randomized clinical trials, and ongoing ethical analysis to ensure that participants and patients are well informed about the experience. But the potential upside of these approaches for the treatment of mental health and enhancement of well-being may be on a worldwide scale that James could have scarcely imagined.

References

Abraham, H. D., Aldridge, A. M., & Gogia, P. (1996). The psychopharmacology of hallucinogens. *Neuropsychopharmacology, 14*(4), 285–298.

Alcoholics Anonymous (1984). *Pass it on: The story of Bill Wilson and how the AA message reached the world.* New York: Alcoholics Anonymous World Services.

Alpert, R., Leary, T., & Metzner, R. (1964/2008). *The Psychedelic Experience.* Penguin.

American Psychiatric Association. (2013). *Diagnostic and statistical manual of mental disorders (DSM-5®).* American Psychiatric Pub.

Anastasi, M. W., & Newberg, A. B. (2008). A preliminary study of the acute effects of religious ritual on anxiety. *Journal of Alternative and Complementary Medicine, 14*(2), 163–165.

Beatles (2000). *The Beatles Anthology.* Chronicle Books.

Bogenschutz, M. P., Forcehimes, A. A., Pommy, J. A., Wilcox, C. E., Barbosa, P. C. R., & Strassman, R. J. (2015). Psilocybin-assisted treatment for alcohol dependence: A proof-of-concept study. *Journal of Psychopharmacology, 29*(3), 289–299.

Brewer, J. A., & Garrison, K. A. (2014). The posterior cingulate cortex as a plausible mechanistic target of meditation: Findings from neuroimaging. *Annals of the New York Academy of Science,1307,* 19–27. https://doi.org/10.1111/nyas.12246

Brewer, J. A., Worhunsky, P. D., Gray, J. R., Tang, Y. Y., Weber, J., & Kober, H. (2011). Meditation experience is associated with differences in default mode network activity and connectivity. *Proceedings of the National Academy of Sciences of the United States of America, 108*(50), 20254–20259.

Carbonaro, T. M., Bradstreet, M. P., Barrett, F. S., MacLean, K. A., Jesse, R., Johnson, M. W., & Griffiths, R. R. (2016). Survey study of challenging experiences after ingesting psilocybin mushrooms: Acute and enduring positive and negative consequences. *Journal of Psychopharmacology, 30*(12), 1268–1278.

Carhart-Harris, R. L., Bolstridge, M., Rucker, J., Day, C. M., Erritzoe, D., Kaelen, M., . . . Taylor, D. (2016). Psilocybin with psychological support for treatment-resistant depression: An open-label feasibility study. *Lancet Psychiatry, 3*(7), 619–627.

Carhart-Harris, R. L., & Friston, K. J. (2010). The default-mode, ego-functions and free-energy: A neurobiological account of Freudian ideas. *Brain, 133*(4), 1265–1283.

Carhart-Harris, R. L., Leech, R., Hellyer, P. J., Shanahan, M., Feilding, A., Tagliazucchi, E., . . . Nutt, D. (2014). The entropic brain: A theory of conscious states informed by neuroimaging research with psychedelic drugs. *Frontiers in Human Neuroscience, 8*, 20.

Cirillo, P., Gold, A. K., Nardi, A. E., Ornelas, A. C., Nierenberg, A. A., Camprodon, J., & Kinrys, G. (2019). Transcranial magnetic stimulation in anxiety and trauma-related disorders: a systematic review and meta-analysis. *Brain and Behavior, 9*(6), e01284. https://doi.org/10.1002/brb3.1284

Crescentini, C., Aglioti, S. M., Fabbro, F., & Urgesi, C. (2014). Virtual lesions of the inferior parietal cortex induce fast changes of implicit religiousness/spirituality. *Cortex, 54*, 1–15. https://doi.org/10.1016/j.cortex.2014.01.023

Crescentini, C., Di Bucchianico, M., Fabbro, F., & Urgesi, C. (2015). Excitatory stimulation of the right inferior parietal cortex lessens implicit religiousness/spirituality. *Neuropsychologia, 70*, 71–79. https://doi.org/10.1016/j.neuropsychologia.2015.02.016

Davis, A. K., Barrett, F. S., & Griffiths, R. R. (2020). Psychological flexibility mediates the relations between acute psychedelic effects and subjective decreases in depression and anxiety. *Journal of Contextual Behavioral Science, 15*, 39–45.

Davis, A. K., Barrett, F. S., May, D. G., Cosimano, M. P., Sepeda, N. D., Johnson, M. W., . . . Griffiths, R. R. (2021). Effects of psilocybin-assisted therapy on major depressive disorder: A randomized clinical trial. *JAMA Psychiatry, 78*(5), 481–489.

Dormandy, T. (2006). *The worst of evils: The fight against pain.* Yale University Press.

Doss, M. K., May, D. G., Johnson, M. W., Clifton, J. M., Hedrick, S. L., Prisinzano, T. E., . . . Barrett, F. S. (2020). The acute effects of the atypical dissociative hallucinogen salvinorin A on functional connectivity in the human brain. *Scientific Reports, 10*(1), 1–12.

Earp, B. D., & Savulescu, J. (2020). *Love Drugs: The Chemical Future of Relationships.* Stanford University Press.

El-Seedi, H. R., De Smet, P. A., Beck, O., Possnert, G., & Bruhn, J. G. (2005). Prehistoric peyote use: Alkaloid analysis and radiocarbon dating of archaeological specimens of *Lophophora* from Texas. *Journal of Ethnopharmacology, 101*(1–3), 238–242.

Forstmann, M., Yudkin, D. A., Prosser, A. M., Heller, S. M., & Crockett, M. J. (2020). Transformative experience and social connectedness mediate the mood-enhancing effects of psychedelic use in naturalistic settings. *Proceedings of the National Academy of Sciences of the United States of America, 117*(5), 2338–2346.

Garcia-Romeu, A., Griffiths, R. R., & Johnson, M. W. (2014). Psilocybin-occasioned mystical experiences in the treatment of tobacco addiction. *Current Drug Abuse Reviews, 7*(3), 157–164.

Garrison, K. A., Zeffiro, T. A., Scheinost, D., Constable, R. T., & Brewer, J. A. (2015). Meditation leads to reduced default mode network activity beyond an active task. *Cognitive, Affective & Behavioral Neuroscience, 15*(3), 712–720. https://doi.org/10.3758/s13415-015-0358-3

Goldberg, S. B., Tucker, R. P., Greene, P. A., Davidson, R. J., Wampold, B. E., Kearney, D. J., & Simpson, T. L. (2018). Mindfulness-based interventions for psychiatric disorders: A systematic review and meta-analysis. *Clinical Psychology Review, 59*, 52–60. https://doi.org/10.1016/j.cpr.2017.10.011

Gonçalves, J. P., Lucchetti, G., Menezes, P. R., & Vallada, H. (2015). Religious and spiritual interventions in mental health care: A systematic review and meta-analysis of randomized controlled clinical trials. *Psychological Medicine, 45*(14), 2937–2949. https://doi.org/10.1017/S0033291715001166

González-Valero, G., Zurita-Ortega, F., Ubago-Jiménez, J. L., & Puertas-Molero, P. (2019). Use of meditation and cognitive behavioral therapies for the treatment of stress, depression and anxiety in students. A systematic review and meta-analysis. *International Journal of Environmental Research and Public Health*, *16*(22), 4394. https://doi.org/ 10.3390/ijerph16224394

Goyal, M., Singh, S., Sibinga, E. M., Gould, N. F., Rowland-Seymour, A., Sharma, R., . . . Haythornthwaite, J. A. (2014). Meditation programs for psychological stress and well-being: A systematic review and meta-analysis. *JAMA Internal Medicine*, *174*(3), 357–368.

Griffiths, R. R., Hurwitz, E. S., Davis, A. K., Johnson, M. W., & Jesse, R. (2019). Survey of subjective "God encounter experiences": Comparisons among naturally occurring experiences and those occasioned by the classic psychedelics psilocybin, LSD, ayahuasca, or DMT. *PloS One*, *14*(4), e0214377.

Griffiths, R. R., Johnson, M. W., Carducci, M. A., Umbricht, A., Richards, W. A., Richards, B. D., . . . Klinedinst, M. A. (2016). Psilocybin produces substantial and sustained decreases in depression and anxiety in patients with life-threatening cancer: A randomized double-blind trial. *Journal of Psychopharmacology*, *30*(12), 1181–1197.

Griffiths, R. R., Johnson, M. W., Richards, W. A., Richards, B. D., Jesse, R., MacLean, K. A., . . . Klinedinst, M. A. (2018). Psilocybin-occasioned mystical-type experience in combination with meditation and other spiritual practices produces enduring positive changes in psychological functioning and in trait measures of prosocial attitudes and behaviors. *Journal of Psychopharmacology*, *32*(1), 49–69.

Griffiths, R. R., Richards, W. A., McCann, U., & Jesse, R. (2006). Psilocybin can occasion mystical-type experiences having substantial and sustained personal meaning and spiritual significance. *Psychopharmacology*, *187*(3), 268–283.

Hölzel, B. K., Carmody, J., Vangel, M., Congleton, C., Yerramsetti, S. M., Gard, T., & Lazar, S. W. (2011). Mindfulness practice leads to increases in regional brain gray matter density. *Psychiatry Research: Neuroimaging*, *191*(1), 36–43.

Horgan, J. (2010). *Doubts about psychedelics from Albert Hofmann, LSD's discoverer*. *Scientific American*. https://blogs.scientificamerican.com/cross-check/ doubts-about-psychedelics-from-albert-hofmann-lsds-discoverer/

James, W. (1902/2009). *The varieties of religious experience: A study in human nature*. *eBooks@Adelaide*. https://csrs.nd.edu/assets/59930/williams_1902.pdf

James, W. (1920). *The Letters of William James* (Vol. 2). Little, Brown.

Johnson, M. W., Garcia-Romeu, A., Cosimano, M. P., & Griffiths, R. R. (2014). Pilot study of the 5-HT2AR agonist psilocybin in the treatment of tobacco addiction. *Journal of Psychopharmacology*, *28*(11), 983–992.

Johnson, M. W., Hendricks, P. S., Barrett, F. S., & Griffiths, R. R. (2019). Classic psychedelics: An integrative review of epidemiology, therapeutics, mystical experience, and brain network function. *Pharmacology & Therapeutics*, *197*, 83–102.

Johnson, M. W., Richards, W. A., & Griffiths, R. R. (2008). Human hallucinogen research: Guidelines for safety. *Journal of Psychopharmacology*, *22*(6), 603–620.

Julien, R. M. (2013). *A primer of drug action: A concise nontechnical guide to the actions, uses, and side effects of psychoactive drugs, revised and updated*. Holt Paperbacks.

Kelly, J. F., Abry, A., Ferri, M., & Humphreys, K. (2020). Alcoholics anonymous and 12-step facilitation treatments for alcohol use disorder: A distillation of a 2020 Cochrane review for clinicians and policy makers. *Alcohol and Alcoholism*, *55*(6), 641–651.

Kober, S. E., Witte, M., Ninaus, M., et al. (2017). Ability to gain control over one's own brain activity and its relation to spiritual practice: A multimodal imaging study. *Frontiers in Human Neuroscience, 11,* 271. https://doi.org/10.3389/fnhum.2017.00271

Krebs, T. S., & Johansen, P. Ø. (2012). Lysergic acid diethylamide (LSD) for alcoholism: Meta-analysis of randomized controlled trials. *Journal of Psychopharmacology, 26*(7), 994–1002.

Kurtz, E. (1988). *AA: The story.* Harpercollins.

Ly, C., Greb, A. C., Cameron, L. P., Wong, J. M., Barragan, E. V., Wilson, P. C., . . . Duim, W. C. (2018). Psychedelics promote structural and functional neural plasticity. *Cell Reports, 23*(11), 3170–3182.

Medaglia, J. D., Yaden, D. B., Helion, C., & Haslam, M. (2019). Moral attitudes and willingness to enhance and repair cognition with brain stimulation. *Brain Stimulation, 12*(1), 44–53.

Miller, J. (2019). *US of AA: How the twelve steps hijacked the science of alcoholism.* Chicago Review Press.

Miller, M. J., Albarracin-Jordan, J., Moore, C., & Capriles, J. M. (2019). Chemical evidence for the use of multiple psychotropic plants in a 1,000-year-old ritual bundle from South America. *Proceedings of the National Academy of Sciences of the United States of America, 116*(23), 11207–11212.

Moss, A. S., Wintering, N., Roggenkamp, H., Khalsa, D. S., Waldman, M. R., Monti, D. A., & Newberg, A. B. (2012). Effects of an eight week meditation program on mood and anxiety in patients with memory loss. *Journal of Complementary and Alternative Medicine, 18*(1):48–53.

Muraresku, B. C. (2020). *The immortality key: The secret history of the religion with no name.* St. Martin's Press.

Nichols, D. E. (2016). Psychedelics. *Pharmacological Reviews, 68*(2), 264–355.

Nutt, D. J., King, L. A., & Phillips, L. D. (2010). Drug harms in the UK: A multicriteria decision analysis. *Lancet, 376*(9752), 1558–1565.

Olson, D. E. (2020). The subjective effects of psychedelics may not be necessary for their enduring therapeutic effects. *ACS Pharmacology & Translational Science, 4*(2), 563–567.

Paul, L. A. (2014). *Transformative Experience.* OUP Oxford.

Pollan, M. (2019). *How to change your mind: What the new science of psychedelics teaches us about consciousness, dying, addiction, depression, and transcendence.* Penguin.

Richards, W. A. (2015). *Sacred knowledge: Psychedelics and religious experiences.* Columbia University Press.

Riis, J., Simmons, J. P., & Goodwin, G. P. (2008). Preferences for enhancement pharmaceuticals: The reluctance to enhance fundamental traits. *Journal of Consumer Research, 35*(3), 495–508.

Rosmarin, D. H., & Koenig, H. G. (Eds.). (2020). *Handbook of spirituality, religion and mental health.* Academic Press.

Ross, S., Bossis, A., Guss, J., Agin-Liebes, G., Malone, T., Cohen, B., . . . Su, Z. (2016). Rapid and sustained symptom reduction following psilocybin treatment for anxiety and depression in patients with life-threatening cancer: A randomized controlled trial. *Journal of Psychopharmacology, 30*(12), 1165–1180.

Schultes, R. E. (1969, January). *Hallucinogens of plant origin.* American Association for the Advancement of Science.

Sessa, B. (2012). *The psychedelic renaissance: Reassessing the role of psychedelic drugs in 21st century psychiatry and society.* Muswell Hill Press.

Smigielski, L., Kometer, M., Scheidegger, M., Krähenmann, R., Huber, T., & Vollenweider, F. X. (2019). Characterization and prediction of acute and sustained response to psychedelic psilocybin in a mindfulness group retreat. *Scientific Reports, 9*(1), 1–13.

Smith, H. (1964). Do drugs have religious import? *Journal of Philosophy, 61*(18), 517–530.

Smith, W. R., & Sisti, D. (2021). Ethics and ego dissolution: The case of psilocybin. *Journal of Medical Ethics, 47*(12), 807–814.

Sonmez, A. I., Camsari, D. D., Nandakumar, A. L., et al. (2019). Accelerated TMS for depression: A systematic review and meta-analysis. *Psychiatry Research, 273,* 770–781. https://doi.org/10.1016/j.psychres.2018.12.041

Spinelli, C., Wisener, M., & Khoury, B. (2019). Mindfulness training for healthcare professionals and trainees: A meta-analysis of randomized controlled trials [published correction appears in *Journal of Psychosomatic Research,* 2019, *123,* 109733]. *Journal of Psychosomatic Research, 120,* 29–38. https://doi.org/10.1016/j.jpsychores.2019.03.003

Strain, E. (2015). Pharmacotherapy for opioid use disorder. UpToDate. Retrieved April 6, 2018, from https://www.uptodate.com

Tagliazucchi, E., Roseman, L., Kaelen, M., Orban, C., Muthukumaraswamy, S. D., Murphy, K., . . . Carhart-Harris, R. (2016). Increased global functional connectivity correlates with LSD-induced ego dissolution. *Current Biology, 26*(8), 1043–1050.

Webster, P. (2000). Mixing the Kykeon, part 1. *ELEUSIS: Journal of Psychoactive Plants and Compounds, 4,* 1–8.

Yaden, D. B., Anderson, D. E., Mattar, M. G., & Newberg, A. B. (2015). Psychoactive stimulation and psychoactive substances: Conceptual and ethical considerations. In J. H. Ellens & T. B. Roberts (Eds.), The Psychedelic Policy Quagmire: Health, Law, Freedom, and Society (pp. 219–236). Praeger.

Yaden, D. B., Berghella, A. P., Regier, P. S., Garcia-Romeu, A., Johnson, M. W., & Hendricks, P. S. (2021). Classic psychedelics in the treatment of substance use disorder: Potential synergies with twelve-step programs. *International Journal of Drug Policy, 98,* 103380.

Yaden, D. B., Eichstaedt, J. C., & Medaglia, J. D. (2018). The future of technology in positive psychology: Methodological advances in the science of well-being. *Frontiers in Psychology, 9,* 962.

Yaden, D. B., & Griffiths, R. R. (2020). The subjective effects of psychedelics are necessary for their enduring therapeutic effects. *ACS Pharmacology & Translational Science, 4*(2), 568–572.

Yaden, D. B., Le Nguyen, K. D., Kern, M. L., Belser, A. B., Eichstaedt, J. C., Iwry, J., . . . Newberg, A. B. (2017). Of roots and fruits: A comparison of psychedelic and nonpsychedelic mystical experiences. *Journal of Humanistic Psychology, 57*(4), 338–353.

Yaden, D. B., Nayak, S. M., Gukasyan, N., Anderson, B. T., & Griffiths, R. R. (2021). The Potential of Psychedelics for End of Life and Palliative Care.

Yaden, D. B., Yaden, M. E., & Griffiths, R. R. (2021). Psychedelics in psychiatry—keeping the renaissance from going off the rails. *JAMA Psychiatry, 78*(5), 469–470.

Yaden, D. B., Zhao, Y., Peng, K., & Newberg, A. B. (2020). *Rituals and Practices in World Religions.* Springer International Publishing.

19

Consciousness and Altered States

Among life's biggest questions, up there with the origins of the universe, is: Why and how are we conscious at all? We are like the proverbial fish swimming in the water of our consciousness, only rarely taking the time to acknowledge the mystery that is with us every waking moment. Our sense of being aware at all, or what is commonly called "phenomenal consciousness," or just consciousness, is not currently understood by scientists. Scientists do, of course, understand many of the *contents of consciousness* (e.g., our various mental processes like perceptions, thoughts, and emotions) and a bit about "altered states of consciousness" as we have seen throughout this book. But the container in which all of these mental processes occur, phenomenal consciousness itself, remains a hotly debated scientific and philosophical subject. The study of spiritual experiences intersects with the topic of consciousness in several places, and this chapter examines spiritual experience in regard to two broad aspects of consciousness: (1) altered states of consciousness and (2) beliefs about the nature of consciousness itself.

Typically, scientists distinguish between the so-called "easy problems" of consciousness and the "hard problem" of consciousness, categories that were introduced by philosopher David Chalmers (who we met in Chapter 16 for his survey of philosophers). The *easy problems of consciousness* refer to mapping changes in brain function with changes in subjective sensations (Chalmers, 1995). Subjects like perceptions, thoughts, emotions, and altered states of consciousness all fall under the easy problems of consciousness—because we understand how science can go about addressing these topics and, eventually (it is hoped), provide some answers. Further complicating the terminology, there is also the label of altered states of consciousness, which is fundamental to defining spiritual experience (and, again, falls under the easy problems).

The *hard problem of consciousness* refers to understanding the nature of awareness itself. In other words, how does the physical brain give rise

The Varieties of Spiritual Experience. David B. Yaden and Andrew B. Newberg, Oxford University Press. © David Yaden and Andrew Newberg 2022. DOI: 10.1093/oso/9780190665678.003.0019

to subjective awareness? This issue is also sometimes referred to as the "explanatory gap" because we are currently unable to scientifically explain the leap from brain function to subjective experience. The hard problem represents the deep and fundamental question: How and why are we aware at all?

Scientists are often uneasy about discussing the concept of consciousness because in many cases it is unclear whether one is referring to the so-called easy problems of consciousness or the hard problem. For example, when the psychedelic research group at Johns Hopkins (described in the previous chapter) was awarded a grant by a group of philanthropists (Tim Ferriss, Matt Mullenweg, Blake Mycoskie, Craig Nerenberg, and the Steven and Alexandra Cohen Foundation) to become the world's first psychedelic research center, the question of what to name it was raised. Roland Griffiths, the director of the program, wanted to include the term "consciousness" in the title, but many of the other faculty took issue with the term. Griffiths argued that the field of psychopharmacology is concerned with both the behavioral and *subjective* effects of psychoactive substances, so consciousness fits within the purview of their study. Plus, psychedelics clearly result in altered states of consciousness. Both of these meanings fall under the easy problems of consciousness, and it seems likely that psychedelics will indeed illuminate some of these subjects (Yaden et al., 2021).

But Griffiths also thought that psychedelics could perhaps be helpful in understanding the nature of consciousness itself and could even possibly somehow bear on the hard problem of consciousness. The other faculty at the center argued that this latter sense of consciousness is not amenable to scientific research. In the end, Griffiths got his way, and the Johns Hopkins lab is called the Center of Psychedelic and Consciousness Research (CPCR). Griffiths is, of course, aware of the difficulties inherent in studying the nature of consciousness and therefore calls the term in the center's title "aspirational."

Contemporary science as a whole is in a similar position. The easy problems of consciousness encompass all of the studies that psychologists and neuroscientists do when they attempt to understand the relationships between subjective experience, the brain, and behavior. The hard problem of consciousness, on the other hand, generally falls in the domain of philosophy. Some believe that science may be able to eventually provide information relevant to, or even solve, the hard problem of consciousness. But others believe that the problem is scientifically intractable and will forever remain a great mystery.

The Easy Problems of Consciousness

James coined the term "stream of consciousness" (note: this term is generally attributed to James, though others had used it previously in other, somewhat obscure, publications), which refers to the sense that parts of our sensory experience (e.g., sights, sounds, tastes) as well as our mental life (e.g., thoughts, emotions, memories) flow through our consciousness. This term was later invoked to describe the style of a number of modernist writers, such as Virginia Woolf and James Joyce, due to their emphasis on introspection and associative leaps between the thoughts of their characters (Jin, 2011). Of course, being aware of the contents in one's stream of consciousness depends on being conscious at all.

The kind of consciousness that is absent when under anesthesia is sometimes referred to as phenomenal consciousness (Block, 1995). Phenomenal consciousness is the "what it feels like." Philosopher Thomas Nagel illustrated the nature of phenomenal consciousness in an article, "What Is It Like to Be a Bat?" (1974), which described the importance of acknowledging the inner subjective life of the mind (and how it varies across people and animals). Phenomenal consciousness is often contrasted with "access consciousness" (Block, 1995). Access consciousness is a more limited concept that refers to mental content that is available for rational thought and decision-making. Many researchers believe that a self is a necessary precondition for access consciousness. Defining the self is another very difficult issue; recall that James called the self "the most puzzling puzzle with which psychology has to deal" (James, 1890, p. 298). But our focus here is on the broader phenomenal consciousness—or the "what it feels like" to have a first-person subjective perspective.

When various contents of consciousness such as sensation, cognition, and emotions are altered by spiritual experiences, the study of such elements would all fall under the easy problems of consciousness. It has become a standard joke among scientists and philosophers when discussing the easy problems of consciousness to remark that understanding these mental processes is far from easy! Of course, the scientific study of perception, cognition, and emotions is enormously difficult, and psychology and neuroscience have only just begun to provide reliable information on these subjects.

Altered States of Consciousness

Throughout this book, we have referred to substantially altered states of consciousness and even included them as a defining component of spiritual experience. The phrase "altered states of consciousness" was popularized in the 1960s and became an umbrella term for a wide variety of mental states (Hood et al., 2018, p. 263). By this term, we have meant something that we believe is somewhat self-evident and is difficult to define. Just try to describe the feeling of being drunk without referring to the substance itself; most find it quite difficult to provide a precise verbal description. Sometimes referring to certain physical sensations or an increased tendency for certain behaviors or emotions can help, but these will vary across people in their specifics. Others have also observed this self-evident or intuitively obvious aspect when attempting a definition of substantially altered states of consciousness. As philosopher Susan Blackmore wrote:

> Like much to do with consciousness, the notion of states of consciousness and altered states of consciousness (ASCs) seems superficially obvious. For example, we all know that it feels to be different from normal to be drunk or delirious with fever, and we may guess, even without experiencing it, that it feels different again to be high on drugs, or to be in a mystical state. So we can call these ASCs. (Blackmore, 2017, p. 100)

Of course, this is not a definition but rather a list of additional examples. Blackmore continued to note some additional difficulties in defining this term. For example, many people have the intuition that physiological measures, like brain scans or even drug dosages, provide an adequate "objective" definition. But this actually provides little help, as people can respond to similar stimuli very differently. For example, we have all seen how different people we know can respond in dramatically different ways to a few drinks, so counting the number of drinks as an indicator of an altered state would tell us too little. Similarly, it is obvious people can have much different internal experiences even though they are behaving in the same way, so behavior is often also uninformative. Conversely, people can feel similarly during some kinds of experiences despite different triggers (recall the difficulty in distinguishing reports of spiritual experiences triggered by psychedelics and those triggered through other means). In the end, one must generally assess altered states of consciousness by *asking people how they feel*. The realization that sometimes self-report is the best measure available was discovered long ago in medicine when it comes to pain, to take just one example. Rather than complex physiological measures, the best way for nurses and physicians to assess pain levels is to simply ask.

Setting aside the various problems with self-report (of which there are many), this discussion also raises the question of how one can know whether or not they are in an altered state of consciousness. Ultimately, some kind of description, if not precise definition, is necessary. Psychologist Charles Tart attempted a definition of altered states of consciousness: "a qualitative alteration in the overall pattern of mental functioning, such that the experiencer feels his consciousness is radically different from the way it functions ordinarily" (Tart, 1972, p. 1203). Of course, this description relies crucially on the concept of how one feels "ordinarily." This has led some researchers to prefer the umbrella terms "nonordinary states of consciousness" (e.g., Grof, 2006) or "anomalous experiences" (Cardeña et al., 2000) to explicitly reference how *altered states are a deviation from normality.*

One must generally rely on the notions of normal and abnormal when specifying mental states that we call altered states of consciousness. Of course, abnormal does not necessarily mean pathological. The *Diagnostic and Statistical Manual of Mental Disorders* (*DSM*; American Psychiatric Association, 2013) refers to altered states of consciousness when describing some forms of mental illness and describes them using an appeal to a deviation from normality. For example, dissociative disorders are characterized as "a disruption of and/or discontinuity in the normal integration of consciousness, memory, identity, emotion, perception, body representation, motor control, and behavior" (American Psychiatric Association, 2013, p. 291). Here we see an explicit mention of a shift from "normal" in an altered state, but because dissociative disorders are a mental illness, such a shift in state must also be combined with suffering and dysfunction.

As we have seen again and again, a pathological framing does not often work for spiritual experiences, as they are much more frequently positive in their outcomes. Some researchers have attempted to get around this issue by inverting these mental health categories. For example, Grob et al. (2011) used the terms "positive derealization" and "positive depersonalization." This approach allows the terms to cover positive instances, but still—it seems somewhat inappropriate to use a pathological term for positive experiences that occur far more often than the pathological instances. Conversely, entirely positive terms like "peak experience" don't seem to work either, as sometimes these states do have negative outcomes. James seemed to acknowledge this issue. (Note: James titled one lecture series that he gave in 1998 "Exceptional Mental States." "Exceptional" has a somewhat more neutral connotation.)

In order to advance beyond characterizing altered states of consciousness in terms of deviations from normality, we must get more specific about what particular features of one's normal state of consciousness seem to change. For example, our thoughts and perceptions are changing all the time (without resulting in substantially altered states of consciousness), so it must be particular elements of our consciousness that are especially related to what we call altered states of consciousness. The next section explores what these particular aspects of consciousness are that seem to change during altered states.

Underlying Dimensions and Constructed Labels

The typology in Part II of this book provided categories with which to group major types of spiritual experiences that people tend to report. These categories do indeed encompass the way that many people tend to describe their experiences. If the reader were to ask any group of people in the United States whether they have had a spiritual experience, anywhere from one fourth to one third of the group will likely say they have. Of these experiences, most of them can be grouped into the categories we provided.

However, we do not think of these categories as fixed and immutable categories. Indeed, we have already mentioned that many specific spiritual experiences can be placed in multiple categories. In other words, we do not essentialize these categories. That is, we do not believe that these categories successfully "carve nature at its joints" to use a well-worn phrase from Plato. These categories are not even close to as precise or mutually exclusive as something like the periodic table of the elements (nothing in psychology or neuroscience approaches this level of precision). Besides the fact that any given spiritual experience can involve multiple categories, we also believe that the categories themselves could change substantially across different cultures as well as over time.

These qualifying statements may make it seem like we are conceding entirely to the constructivist view, as we acknowledge the role of culture and beliefs in the experience of and report of spiritual experiences. But we also believe that there are underlying dimensions to spiritual experiences that are close to being human universals, which is closer to the perennialist account.

Our common clusters model, as we have mentioned, is a kind of compromise between these two views in that it posits that some set of clusters of subjective qualities appears in most spiritual experiences across cultures, but not necessarily the same set, and they are certainly not described in exactly the same way. But this model does not really address the cultural variation or provide a coherent scientific model with any specificity. In the midst of this remaining ambiguity, we believe that we can borrow from some contemporary models in emotion research to move the discourse in the study of spiritual experience forward.

This tension between underlying dimensions and culturally specific labels can be best illustrated by the emotion research literature. In Chapter 13, we introduced the basic emotion theory advocated by psychological researchers like Paul Ekman and Carol Izard. According to this theory, emotions like fear, anger, joy, sadness, disgust, and surprise are distinct categories that arise from particular kinds of circumstances and are associated with distinct facial expressions and unique patterns of changes in the brain and one's physiology. However, in Lisa Feldman Barrett's book *How Emotions Are Made* (2017), she argued that the evidence does not support the distinctiveness of these emotion categories, and that we should therefore not essentialize these categories. William James actually shared some of this concern, writing the following in his *Principles of Psychology* (1890):

> The trouble with the emotions in psychology . . . is that they are regarded too much as absolutely individual things. So long as they are set down as so many eternal and sacred psychic entities, like the old immutable species in natural history, so long all that can be done with them is reverently to catalogue their separate characters, points, and effects. (James, 1890, p. 449)

Instead of thinking of particular emotions as specific entities, psychologist James Russell (1980) argued that all emotions can be broken down according to how they vary across just two dimensions: *valence* and *arousal*. Valence refers to how pleasant or unpleasant an emotion feels (e.g., pleasant would be high valence, unpleasant low valence). Arousal refers to the general level of alertness or energy associated with the emotion (joy would be high arousal, contentment would be low arousal) (see Figure 19.1).

Various emotions can then be plotted onto the two dimensions as axes (usually referred to as the emotion circumplex). Barrett argued that the underlying dimensions of the emotion circumplex (valence and arousal) are

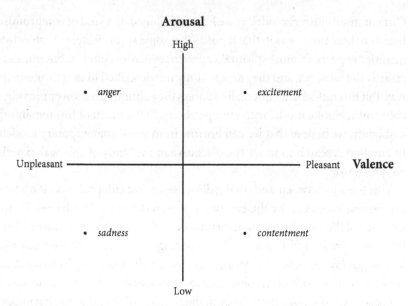

Figure 19.1 The emotion circumplex. Drawn by David Yaden.

potentially cross-culturally universal, whereas the particular emotions are culturally constructed labels for particular points on the plot (e.g., excitement, contentment) that will change across cultures and over time as the precise meaning of the words changes. In other words, this perspective is a middle ground between the view that there are both universal aspects of emotions and cultural variation. It is possible that the situation is similar with spiritual experiences.

We have seen that spiritual experiences are capable of altering fundamental aspects of the contents of consciousness. For example, the senses of time, space, self, and mind perception, as well as its intensity, vividness, and valence, are all altered in various ways during spiritual experiences. These, or some set of these kinds of changes, could potentially form the underlying dimensions of spiritual experience in the same way that valence and arousal make up the underlying dimensions of emotions. We are not the first to make this observation, as some researchers have argued for two dimensions underlying spiritual experience, such as arousal and attribution (Beit-Hallahmi & Argyle, 1997, p. 95), but we believe that more dimensions are necessary.

In the case of spiritual experience, we believe that the underlying dimensions can be visualized in a multidimensional space. Ultimately, while we do not know how many dimensions will be required—we call this an *n*-dimensional space (note: where *n* is simply a variable that can stand for any number)—we suggest that there are most likely about 5–10 dimensions that are relevant. Specifically, we believe that the degree of mind perception, sense of unity/connectedness, change in the sense of time, emotional valence, overall arousal, and the noetic quality are some likely candidates. Of course, this is a bit more difficult to depict than a two-dimensional plot like the emotion circumplex (see Figure 19.2 with just three dimensions). But one could imagine plotting the various categories of spiritual experience that we introduced in this *n*-dimensional space. For example, numinous experience may have high mind perception and medium alteration to faculties of consciousness like an altered sense of time, space, and self. A mystical experience, on

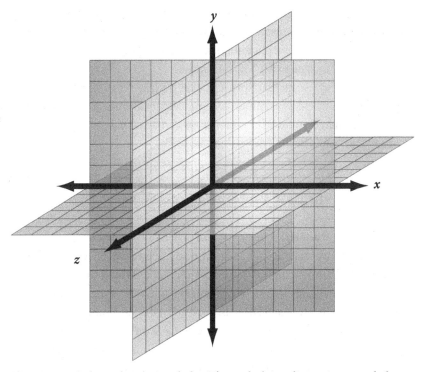

Figure 19.2 A three-dimensional plot. The underlying dimensions needed to depict spiritual experiences would likely be many more than three, but this becomes difficult to visualize. Permission is granted to copy, distribute and/or modify this document under the terms of the GNU Free Documentation License, Version 1.2.

the other hand, may have low mind perception and high alteration to the senses of time, space, and self.

Importantly, we do not believe that popularly used labels like "spiritual experience" can be dispensed with now or anytime in the near future. While we think that in order to advance scientifically it may be necessary to drop terminology that carries a great deal of baggage regarding culturally based metaphysical beliefs, we acknowledge that most people will continue to use these terms to describe their experiences. Indeed, it is almost impossible for most people to refer to them in any other way. Imagine if those Gallup questions asking if people had what they consider to be a "spiritual experience," instead asked whether they had "an altered state of consciousness involving changes to the following underlying dimensions of consciousness." We think that most people would have no idea how to answer such a strange question, whereas most people readily understand terms like "spiritual experience." Additionally, more abstract characterizations, while perhaps most appropriate for scientific research going forward, do not adequately acknowledge the fact that most people understand these experiences as providing a glimpse into an "unseen order" of some kind.

We have already seen that spiritual experiences often involve changed beliefs about the world as a whole, God, and supernaturalism in general. But substantially altered states of consciousness can also change people's beliefs about consciousness itself.

The Hard Problem of Consciousness

We have seen that altered states of consciousness, like most subjects in psychology and neuroscience, fall under the so-called easy problems of consciousness. But do spiritual experiences tell us anything about the hard problem of consciousness? At this point, no scientific evidence has come close to addressing this question because any of the brain or subjective changes that occur during spiritual experience would consist of still more iterations of the easy problem (Yaden et al., 2021). Indeed, it is not clear what kind of scientific evidence could possibly bear on the hard problem of consciousness. Spiritual experiences do, however, seem to change our *beliefs about* the nature of consciousness.

The 21st century has seen a shift from debates focusing on the existence or nonexistence of an omniscient, omnipotent, and benevolent creator (i.e.,

God) to debates about the nature of consciousness. This is especially the case among scientists and philosophers. One of the overall issues in this discourse is whether consciousness is physical or nonphysical. Therefore, debates between the existence of God and the nature of consciousness remain linked, but there has been a shift in emphasis.

Scientists and philosophers have proposed a number of different possible relationships between the brain and the mind (i.e., consciousness). Perhaps the most famous, and maybe most intuitive, is that proposed by philosopher Rene Descartes. Descartes described a view called substance dualism, in which mind and matter are two distinct kinds of things, one physical and one nonphysical. While many people erroneously think that Descartes's view is responsible for widespread dualistic views, psychologist Paul Bloom argued in *Descartes' Baby* (2005) that the idea of dualism regarding the mind and body is innate, and evidence for it even can be observed in young children. Most people therefore are "intuitive dualists" and only change their minds after learning more about psychology and neuroscience.

The objections to this dualistic view usually emphasize the problem of interaction. How would the nonphysical mind affect the physical brain and vice versa? Descartes suggested that the pineal gland, a structure close to center of the brain, might be the site at which this interaction takes place. This seems entirely implausible to contemporary neuroscientists, and there is no evidence to support this pineal gland–based hypothesis.

Philosopher David Chalmers provided a typology of various contemporary views of consciousness in an article, "Consciousness and Its Place in Nature" (Chalmers, 2003). These arguments are organized according to type, proceeding from Types A through F. These types include three different forms of materialism (A–C), which generally claim that the mind and matter are the same, and the mind is entirely reducible to matter. Some philosophers, such as Daniel Dennett, even argue that there is no such thing as consciousness to explain and that its appearance to us is just an illusion. Then, there are two different forms of dualism (D and E) that state that mind and matter are distinct. Lastly, Chalmers described a type of monism (i.e., mind and matter are somehow different aspects of the same stuff), Type F. This article provided a typology of contemporary views on the hard problem of consciousness that is accessible to the general reader.

Incidentally, Type F monism describes a view that James helped to pioneer. While Bertrand Russell was critical of James's pragmatism, he admired some of James's views on consciousness. Russell wrote:

James's doctrine of radical empiricism was first published in 1904, in an
essay called "Does Consciousness Exist?" The main purpose of this essay
was to deny that the subject-object relation is fundamental.... For my part,
I am convinced that James was right on this matter, and would, on this
ground alone, deserve high praise among philosophers. (B. Russell, 1945/
2004, p. 812)

James's view, sometimes called "neutral monism," was that reality does
not consist of either mind or matter exclusively (or both separately),
but rather that these are two aspects of the same fundamental "stuff"
of reality. James argued against the notion that consciousness consists
of a particular entity—emphasizing that it is not so much a particular thing inside one's head, as an ongoing complex *process*. James
wrote: "Consciousness ... is the name of a nonentity, and has no right to
be among first principles. Those who still cling to it are clinging to a mere
echo, the faint rumor left behind by the disappearing 'soul' upon the air
of philosophy" (James, 1904, p. 477).

However, James also provided a contrasting view on consciousness. In his
writings in the last years of his life, James seemed to conceive of consciousness quite differently. Rather than the more reductive take that he provided
in his 1904 article "Does Consciousness Exist?" he instead provided a view of
consciousness that seems less aligned with Bertrand Russell's thinking and
shares more in common with Carl Jung's semispiritual notion of the "collective unconscious." The collective unconscious is generally conceived of as a
kind of reservoir of consciousness to which we are all in some way connected.
(We have previously mentioned that Jung was far more influenced by James
than Freud in the second half of his life, a fact obscured by the posthumous
editing of his autobiography, and it appears possible that Jung took his idea of
the collective unconscious from James.)

In The Varieties of Religious Experience: A Study in Human Nature
(1902; *The Varieties* for short), James provided the outline of a view by which
human consciousness might transcend one's physical body and material
circumstances. Here James described how one might interact with such a
realm of consciousness during spiritual experience:

He becomes conscious that this higher part is coterminous and continuous
with a MORE of the same quality, which is operative in the universe outside
of him, and which he can keep in working touch with, and in a fashion get

on board of and save himself when all his lower being has gone to pieces in the wreck. (James, 1902/2009, p. 385)

What is this "MORE" that James referred to here, which one can come into contact with during spiritual experiences according to James? In the last year of his life, James appeared to refer to an understanding of consciousness whereby our own individual consciousness may merge with some greater consciousness, in the way that single rivers flow into the ocean.

> Out of my experience, such as it is (and it is limited enough) one fixed con-
> clusion dogmatically emerges, and that is this, that we with our lives are like
> islands in the sea . . . and the islands also hang together through the ocean's
> bottom. Just so there is a continuum of cosmic consciousness, against
> which our individuality builds but accidental fences, and into which our
> several minds plunge as into a mother-sea or reservoir. (James, 1909/1986,
> p. 374)

So, in the final year of his life, James appeared to have embraced a supernatural view of reality and a view of consciousness that is quite different from his naturalistic formulations earlier in his life. However, James remained true to a kind of professional agnosticism, as he called this view only a "dramatic probability," or a hypothesis. He did not advance the belief as an article of faith, but it does appear that James's mystical side held more sway toward the end of his life. (Note: It is possible to understand James's evolution on the issue of naturalism and supernaturalism as "early James" in which he embraced naturalism and "late James" in which he embraced supernaturalism, although he continued to insist that there were no certainties to be had in this domain.)

A Shift in the Fundamental Questions

Turning back to contemporary beliefs about the nature of consciousness, it is notable that among the committed atheists who described their spiritual experiences in popular books, such as Sam Harris, Barbara Ehrenreich, and Michael Pollan, each of them end their books with discussions of consciousness. Specifically, these authors mentioned how they have slightly changed their views on the nature of consciousness as a result of their spiritual experiences. Harris, Ehrenreich, and Pollan repeatedly renounced theistic or supernatural beliefs, yet they each explored the question of whether consciousness is entirely physical or whether it could exist beyond the brain.

Harris reiterated his position in many places that he did not hold supernatural beliefs. He also made clear that he believed that the mind is dependent on the brain. But Harris rejected some forms of materialism, such as the position held by Dennett that consciousness does not exist. Harris wrote: "And yet the deflationary attitude toward consciousness taken by many scientists—wherein reality is considered only from the outside, in third-person terms—is also unwarranted. A middle path exists between making religion out of spiritual life and having no spiritual life at all" (Harris, 2014, p. 204).

Pollan, when reflecting on what he learned from his psychedelic experiences, left room for more possibilities about the nature of consciousness. He remarked how he was less certain in his understanding than before his experiences (which, as we have seen, he sometimes referred to as "spiritual"):

> I still tend to think that consciousness must be confined to brains, but I am less certain of this belief now than I was before I embarked on this journey. . . . Mysteries abide. But this I can say with certainty: the mind is vaster, and the world ever much more alive, than I knew when I began. (Pollan, 2019, p. 414)

Ehrenreich, while rejecting the notion of God "along with theism of any kind" (Ehrenreich, 2014, p. 236), seemed to leave open some wiggle room regarding the nature of consciousness. While she kept the point ambiguous, she described how physical processes of sufficient complexity, such as those that seem to occur in our brain, may give rise to consciousness in the world. This consciousness, which she referred to as "the Other," is something that she appeared to believe may be perceived during certain substantially altered states of consciousness. She ended her book with the line, referring to her notion of a possibly conscious "Other": "I have the impression, growing out of the experiences chronicled here, that it may be seeking us out" (Ehrenreich, 2014, p. 236).

Thus, we see that even atheists who reject the possibility of God as described in traditional religions will sometimes invoke the mystery of consciousness in order to gesture at possibilities beyond strict materialism. In our survey of philosophers, we observed a high but not completely overlapping relationship between belief in God and the belief that consciousness is non-physical (Yaden & Anderson, 2021). Therefore, as these examples and data make clear, it is possible to believe that (1) consciousness is not confined to the brain, while rejecting (2) supernatural beliefs (though these two views do tend to co-occur).

How might a materialist find the possibility of consciousness that exists beyond the brain as a plausible possibility? There are several accounts that try to make the case for this possibility. For example, neurologist Kevin Nelson, yet another atheist who reported having a spiritual experience that he interpreted in naturalistic terms, described a provocative argument by analogue (2010). He referred to an idea famously popularized by astronomer Carl Sagan called the "Drake equation." The Drake equation was intended to estimate the probability that there is extraterrestrial life in the universe. The most recent formulation of this equation is

$$A = N_a st * f_{bt}$$

In this equation, A stands for the number of "technological species" (life forms who would be able to communicate with us) that have ever existed. $N_a st$ stands for number of planets deemed potentially habitable by intelligent life in the universe, and f_{bt} represents the possibility for intelligence to emerge on any one of these planets. The result is an extremely rough approximation of how to estimate the possibility that an intelligent species like us has existed elsewhere in the universe.

Nelson argued that one could apply this kind of approach described in the Drake equation to the question of consciousness, swapping [intelligent extraterrestrial species] with [consciousness] and [planets similar to Earth] with [physical substrates similar to the brain]. Such an equation would provide an extremely rough estimate of the possibility that consciousness exists beyond human brains. This application, though, is possibly even more speculative than finding other intelligent life forms, as less is known about the conditions required to give rise to consciousness.

Speculative attempts like this aside, the fact remains that we are not sure *what* consciousness is or *where* it resides. We have mentioned previously the so-called problem of other minds, which shows us that we cannot even be certain that other people are aware. The reader knows that she or he is aware, *but cannot be sure who or what else is aware.* Of course, practically speaking, we extrapolate from our own subjective experience in order to believe mind is in other people, but this mind can only be inferred through other's actions (though it cannot be proven). During spiritual experiences, however, people tend to report perceiving consciousness or mind directly, often as somehow pervading all of one's surroundings or in the form of nonphysical divinity or entities. Such experiences can change the way people think about the nature of consciousness.

What conclusions can then be drawn regarding the nature of consciousness from spiritual experiences? Many people have firm beliefs regarding the nature of consciousness, such as (1) that the mind is identical to the brain (physicalism); (2) that mind is everywhere and "in all things" (panpsychism or neutral monism); (3) that mind is a nonphysical substance that interacts with physical reality (dualism); and/or (4) that there is an ultimate mind controlling everything (theism). But, interestingly, despite all of this uncertainty, we have only rarely seen people frankly admit that they do not know what the fact of the matter is regarding consciousness—though we admit that we find such instances of existential honesty refreshing when they occur.

Ultimately, we adopt this agnostic perspective regarding the nature of consciousness. We hold rough probabilities regarding the likelihood of the various options regarding the nature of consciousness (which differ between the two authors). This approach strikes us as most in keeping with what we know about the nature of consciousness—which is very little. Incidentally, we find this epistemic humility is conducive to an ongoing experience of awe and wonder at these mysteries. We call this agnostic view, when combined with an appreciation for the value of spiritual experience, "mystical agnosticism." (Note: Others have also used this phrase. For example, Robert Anton Wilson referred to himself as a "mystical agnostic.")

Conclusion

Altered states of consciousness, along with most of the subjects of psychology and neuroscience, fit within the easy problem of consciousness and are therefore well within the normal domains of scientific inquiry (Yaden et al., 2021). However, the hard problem of consciousness is currently (and perhaps forever) beyond the reach of science, despite the aspirations of scientists to provide relevant data. We have seen that spiritual experiences are altered states of consciousness involving a perception of an unseen order could perhaps be described in future research by plotting statistical clusters of subjective qualities across multiple underlying dimensions. Last, it appears that people often (though by no means always) shift their beliefs about consciousness after having spiritual experiences.

References

American Psychiatric Association. (2013). *Diagnostic and statistical manual of mental disorders (5th ed.).*

Barrett, L. F. (2017). *How emotions are made: The secret life of the brain.* Houghton Mifflin Harcourt.

Beit-Hallahmi, B., & Argyle, M. (1997). *The psychology of religious behaviour, belief and experience.* Taylor & Francis.

Blackmore, S. (2017). *Consciousness: A very short introduction.* Oxford University Press.

Block, N. (1995). On a confusion about a function of consciousness. *Behavioral and Brain Sciences, 18*(2), 227–247.

Bloom, P. (2005). *Descartes' baby: How the science of child development explains what makes us human.* Random House.

Cardeña, E. E., Lynn, S. J. E., & Krippner, S. E. (2000). *Varieties of anomalous experience: Examining the scientific evidence.* American Psychological Association.

Chalmers, D. J. (1995). Facing up to the problem of consciousness. *Journal of Consciousness Studies, 2*(3), 200–219.

Chalmers, D. J. (2003). Consciousness and its place in nature. *Blackwell Guide to the Philosophy of Mind,* 102–142.

Ehrenreich, B. (2014). *Living with a wild God: A nonbeliever's search for the truth about everything.* Hachette UK.

Grob, C. S., Danforth, A. L., Chopra, G. S., Hagerty, M., McKay, C. R., Halberstadt, A. L., & Greer, G. R. (2011). Pilot study of psilocybin treatment for anxiety in patients with advanced-stage cancer. *Archives of General Psychiatry, 68*(1), 71–78.

Grof, S. (2006). *When the impossible happens: Adventures in non-ordinary realities.* Sounds True.

Harris, S. (2014). *Waking up: A guide to spirituality without religion.* Simon & Schuster.

Hood, R. W., Jr., Hill, P. C., & Spilka, B. (2018). *The psychology of religion: An empirical approach.* Guilford Press.

James, W. (1890). *The principles of psychology.* New York, NY: Holt.

James, W. (1902/2009). The varieties of religious experience: A study in human nature. *eBooks@Adelaide.* https://csrs.nd.edu/assets/59930/williams_1902.pdf

James, W. (1904). Does consciousness' exist? *Journal of Philosophy, Psychology and Scientific Methods, 1*(18), 477–491.

James, W. (1909). "Confidences of a psychical researcher". In *Essays in Psychical Research,* p. 361-375. Harvard University Press.

Jin, M. A. (2011). James Joyce's epiphany and Virginia Woolf's "moment of importance." *Studies in Literature and Language, 2*(1), 114–118.

Nagel, T. (1974). What is it like to be a bat? *Philosophical Review, 83*(4), 435–450.

Nelson, K. (2010). *The spiritual doorway in the brain: A neurologist's search for the God experience.* Penguin.

Pollan, M. (2019). *How to change your mind: What the new science of psychedelics teaches us about consciousness, dying, addiction, depression, and transcendence.* Penguin Books.

Russell, B. (2004). *History of Western philosophy.* Routledge. (Original work published 1945)

Russell, J. A. (1980). A circumplex model of affect. *Journal of Personality and Social Psychology, 39*(6), 1161.

Tart, C. T. (1972). States of consciousness and state-specific sciences. *Science, 176*(4040), 1203–1210.

Yaden, D. B., & Anderson, D. E. (2021). The psychology of philosophy: Associating philosophical views with psychological traits in professional philosophers. *Philosophical Psychology, 34*(5), 721–755.

Yaden, D. B., Johnson, M. W., Griffiths, R. R., Doss, M., Garcia-Romeu, A., Nayak, S., Gukasyan, N., Mathur, B. N., Barrett, F. S. (2021). Psychedelics and consciousness: Distinctions, demarcations, and opportunities. *International Journal of Neuropsychopharmacology, 24*(8), 615–623.

20

Conclusion

Ever not Quite

In James's discarded first draft of The *Varieties* (1902/2009) the opening line read: "There is something in life, as one feels its presence, that seems to defy all possible resources of phraseology" (Perry, 1948, p. 258). The supposed ineffability of spiritual experiences has been widely discussed, and some have suggested that it is impossible to understand these experiences unless you have had one. Yet we have seen that quite a bit can be said about these experiences. Further, through analyzing personal accounts and by conducting scientific research on spiritual experiences, parts of them can be understood. As we have seen, it is possible to make progress in understanding spiritual experiences, or, in other words, to make progress in "effing" the "ineffable."

In this closing chapter, let us return to James's (1902/2009) quotation that we used to introduce our topic in the opening chapter:

> One conclusion was forced upon my mind at that time, and my impression of its truth has ever since remained unshaken. It is that our normal waking consciousness, rational consciousness as we call it, is but one special type of consciousness, whilst all about it, parted from it by the filmiest of screens, there lie potential forms of consciousness entirely different. We may go through life without suspecting their existence; but apply the requisite stimulus, and at a touch they are there in all their completeness, definite types of mentality which probably somewhere have their field of application and adaptation. No account of the universe in its totality can be final which leaves these other forms of consciousness quite disregarded. How to regard them is the question. (James, 1902/2009, p. 293)

We have come a long way in terms of exploring the question of "how to regard" these experiences. We began with James's influences and the key ideas in *The Varieties*, especially James's focus on experience rather than belief

The Varieties of Spiritual Experience. David B. Yaden and Andrew B. Newberg, Oxford University Press. © David Yaden and Andrew Newberg 2022. DOI: 10.1093/oso/9780190665678.003.0020

as well as his methodological agnosticism. We reviewed the last century of advances in how psychology and neuroscience study of spiritual experience. In Part II, we saw that we need to consider different types of spiritual experience rather than treating them as singular, and we reviewed contemporary research on several different major types of spiritual experiences. We saw, contra Freud, that the vast majority of spiritual experiences are profoundly positive, and that they are surprisingly prevalent in the normal population, although of course they can arise in mental illness as well. In Part III, we considered responses to, interpretations of, and beliefs about spiritual experiences, as well as how they may be applied in mainstream psychiatry and psychotherapy. We also mentioned some ideas and frameworks for their future study.

In this final chapter, we conclude by suggesting that we need to bring forward the lessons from James and *The Varieties* as well as from the last century of research, while stepping boldly beyond 20th-century paradigms and into a fully 21st-century understanding of spiritual experiences.

Multifaceted to the End

Throughout this book, we have described James's thought and character as frequently contradictory. But perhaps "contradictory" is not quite the right word, and maybe a more charitable way to describe the variety of perspectives he offered would be "multifaceted." These multifaceted perspectives transcend traditional disciplinary boundaries, and perhaps it is for this reason that his thought has inspired so many fields and subfields. James been cited favorably as a precursor to so many subfields in psychology that sometimes he is simply referred to as the "father of modern psychology" as a whole. As we have seen, his influence also extends well beyond psychology. He is seen as a founding influence on the field of religious studies. In philosophy, he is a cofounder of the well-known view of pragmatism and was cited by Husserl as indirectly inspiring phenomenology. James advanced several unique philosophical views concerning consciousness, the self, emotions, and several others. Many of the terms he introduced are still used, and a number of his philosophical views continue to be discussed. James also deeply influenced psychiatry through his views related to pragmatism. (Note: This influence occurred through James's impact on Adolf Meyer, the Johns Hopkins psychiatrist who is considered the founder of modern psychiatry; Lamb, 2014.)

Of course, of most relevance to us, James founded the scientific study of spiritual experience. He brought the subject closer to the academic mainstream, provided a foundation for its ongoing scientific study, and offered an array of hypotheses to pursue. We and many others have benefited tremendously from his foundational work. To be sure, his "science of religions" has been realized and is thriving in the 21st century.

James's character could also be considered multifaceted. James seemed always willing to consider new ideas and give them their due, even when they were in opposition to claims he had just made. We see this throughout his work on spiritual experience. For example, recall that James provided what we call his professional conclusion that methodological agnosticism ought to remain the rule when studying spiritual experience, but then immediately offered his personal conclusion in which he came down on the side of faith in a supernatural interpretation.

In order to better understand James's personal conclusion, it is helpful to return to James's personal life. In particular, his notion of overbeliefs, developed philosophically later in his life, may have sprung from an episode in his young adulthood. During a period of deep depression, James inwardly wrestled with the idea of determinism, the idea that all of our actions are dictated entirely by the causal flow of the physical universe. This would mean that there is no possibility of free will (most scientific worldviews do indeed entail determinism). James knew this, and the thought apparently distressed him a great deal. He changed his mind, however, after reading the work of French philosopher Charles Renouvier. James wrote:

> I think that yesterday was a crisis in my life. I finished the first part of Renouvier's second Essais and see no reason why his definition of free will ... need be the definition of an illusion. At any rate, I will assume for the present—until next year—that it is no illusion. My first act of free will shall be to believe in free will. (Perry, 1935, p. 323).

James appeared to have adopted what he would later call an "overbelief" about the reality of free will, and this may have contributed to his recovery from this period of depression. (Note: Interestingly, in our survey of philosophers, we actually found that belief in determinism was associated with depression; Yaden & Anderson, 2021.) James was also modeling here his view that one can choose to adopt a belief, and that one can justify doing so on the basis of its expected benefits. Later on, as he described at the end of *The Varieties*, James similarly adopted a spiritual belief on the basis of the benefits that spiritual experiences seem to bring.

James may have been the kind of person who is particularly in need of these benefits. In *The Varieties*, James contrasted what he called the "healthy-minded" type, a kind of person who remains naturally optimistic and pays special attention to the goodness and beauty in human life, from the "morbid-minded" type (or the "sick soul") who cannot ignore the suffering and tragic circumstances of life. Like most people, James likely embodied a mix of both of these tendencies. But his biographers (e.g., Myers, Perry, Richardson, Simon) mostly agree that he never entirely shook off the depressive tendencies of his youth, and that James may have seen himself as mostly a member of the morbid-minded category. At one point in *The Varieties*, James illustrated the morbid-minded view by painting a rather bleak picture of human existence:

> Mankind is in a position similar to that of a set of people living on a frozen lake, surrounded by cliffs over which there is no escape, yet knowing that little by little the ice is melting, and the inevitable day drawing near when the last film of it will disappear, and to be drowned ignominiously will be the human creature's portion. The merrier the skating, the warmer and more sparkling the sun by day, and the ruddier the bonfires at night, the more poignant the sadness with which one must take in the meaning of the total situation. (James, 1902/2009, p. 109)

James believed that spiritual experiences were especially important for the morbid-minded type of person, those who cannot help but see our existential situation as akin to living on thin ice that will inevitably melt. In spiritual experiences, though, one feels morally elevated, filled with joy, and a "veil" separating the physical world from an unseen order appears to be raised. In such moments, one feels lifted from our precarious circumstances and delivered to the safety of firm, eternal, ground. Of course the question remains whether such perceptions of salvation are real or an illusion.

On the basis of his pragmatism, James adopted an overbelief regarding the reality of the eternal realm beyond this physical existence: "By being faithful in my poor measure to this over-belief, I seem to keep myself more sane and true" (James, 1902/2009, p. 393). That is, he endorsed these beliefs on the basis of their medicinal effects on his life. In last paragraph of *The Varieties*, James wrote that such overbeliefs can make the difference "between a life of which the keynote is resignation and a life of which the keynote is hope" (James, 1902, p. 398).

Of course, we can expect a contrasting (or multifaceted) perspective from James, and he indeed delivered it in numerous places. Most of his earlier work, for example, appeared to flatly refute the possibility of supernaturalism or consciousness beyond the brain. Indeed, he advocated a materialistic and naturalistic worldview through much of his life. Even after changing his views, he still insisted that supernaturalism remained only a possibility—a hypothesis—and never presumed its certainty. Throughout his life, James would tell his students to temper faith with skepticism, saying "after taking a bath in religion, come out and take another bout with philosophy" (Perry, 1948, p. 266). Last, despite his personal overbeliefs, he continued to insist on an agnostic approach to the study of spiritual experiences to the end.

As for the end of Jamse's life, he died of heart failure in his wife Alice's arms on August 20, 1910, at his summer home in New Hampshire. He was buried in his family's plot in Cambridge, Massachusetts. During the last year of his life, he had continued to work on philosophical topics and was writing a book that would be a response to his critics, and it was especially aimed at those who pointed to the many contradictions in his work. He hoped to, as he put it, "round out his system of philosophy," but he never finished the work. This kind of work is probably not the kind one can ever really finish, after all.

James was mourned by his loved ones and celebrated by his colleagues. A number of the most renowned scientists and philosophers of his time testified to James's influence in their remembrances of him. Bertrand Russell, for example, wrote a postscript to a recently published article that was sharply critical of James's pragmatism that testified to Russell's sincere respect for James as a thinker and a human being.

Some memorializations of James's legacy no doubt extended into exaggeration, but nonetheless showed the admiration James garnered from his contemporaries. Philosopher Alfred North Whitehead said: "In western literature there are four great thinkers. . . . These men are Plato, Aristotle, Liebnz, and William James." Later, James scholar John McDermott said of his legacy: "William James is to classic American philosophy as Plato was to Greek and Roman philosophy, an originating and inspirational fountainhead" (Richardson, 2007, p. xiv).

James's last publication was called "A Pluralistic Mystic" (1910). (Note: This was the last publication in his lifetime, but there were other posthumous publications based on his unfinished work.) Throughout this essay, he described the views of Benjamin Blood, who recall had written a pamphlet called *The Anesthetic Revolution*, which described the ways in which various psychoactive substances could alter consciousness. James was an admirer of this work, and in typical James-ian generosity, James gave the last words that he published to Blood by quoting him:

> Let *my* last word, then . . . be *his* word:—"There is no conclusion. What has concluded, that we might conclude in regard to it? There are no fortunes to be told, and there is no advice to be given."—Farewell! (James, 1910, p. 759).

Multilevel Interdisciplinary Research

James's multifaceted perspectives live on in the psychology and neuroscience of spiritual experience. Contemporary psychologists Ray Paloutzian and Crystal Park have called for a "multilevel interdisciplinary paradigm" (2014) when studying topics related to religion and spirituality and it applies to the study of spiritual experience. The term "multilevel" refers to different levels of analysis, spanning social-cultural aspects, cognitive processes, emotions, and neuroscience. Attempts to build explanatory bridges between levels of analysis requires interdisciplinary cooperation. For spiritual experience, these disciplines include psychology, neuroscience, pharmacology, religious studies, philosophy, anthropology, and psychiatry—among others. In fact, in one of our (A. B. N.'s) books, *Principles of Neurotheology* (Newberg, 2010), it is stressed that the only way to truly understand the nature of religious and spiritual experiences is by incorporating these different fields under one framework. We have attempted to draw from these disparate fields throughout this book. This is an approach that James would no doubt have endorsed.

Different fields tend to emphasize different aspects of spiritual experiences, and we have attempted to synthesize these views throughout. For example, scholarly fields like religious studies, as well as other fields that emphasize social forces, like anthropology, tend to endorse cultural constructivist views of spiritual experience. We have shown that the cultural norms and the beliefs of particular religions undoubtedly influence the phenomenological features and interpretations of spiritual experiences. We can see this clearly in the fact that people in India tend to see visions of Vishnu, whereas people in the United States tend to see visions of Christ. On a deeper level, too, culture influences our expectations in ways that are so pervasive they are difficult to make explicit. These cultural expectations likely impact spiritual experiences in all manner of ways. Scientists themselves are often not aware of the culturally derived expectations they bring into their own research (as we acknowledge of ourselves).

On the other hand, more scientifically oriented fields, such as neuroscience, psychology, psychiatry, and pharmacology, tend to emphasize more perennialist views of spiritual experience on the basis that we all share the same basic nervous system. In the same way that we can expect to see specific changes to one's physiology, behavior, and subjective report in all humans from several glasses of alcohol or caffeine, we can expect to see some similarities across people when they take psychedelics. Of course, there are different cultural meanings that must be acknowledged, and these undoubtedly change one's subjective experience, but in the same way, there are also unchanging facts of biology that impact—and make possible—spiritual experience.

Overall, the subjective qualities of spiritual experiences appear to be influenced by one's underlying biology, mental processes, as well as cultural influences. In psychiatry, the *Diagnostic and Statistical Manual of Mental Disorders* (*DSM*) of the American Psychiatric Association advocates what is called a "biopsychosocial" perspective to mental illness. We suggest that a biopsychosocial understanding inform a 21st-century science of spiritual experience.

Beyond 20th-Century Paradigms

The findings from a number of contemporary research fields support several of James's suppositions regarding spiritual experiences. Most important, James's mostly positive perspective on spiritual experiences has been largely vindicated. As we have seen, again and again, James insisted on examining the outcomes rather than speculating about the metaphysical origins of spiritual experience. In other words, what are the results? In answer, we can say that spiritual experiences, on the whole and in the long run (note: as James would often say in regard to pragmatism), are pervasive, positive, and profound.

We have seen that many current approaches to the topic of spiritual experiences introduce problems due to the baggage that they bring along with them. The two main paradigms through which spiritual experiences are seen in terms of (1) their metaphysical import and (2) their positive or pathological outcomes. This is often obvious in the terms used to describe them.

James used the term "religious experience," although recall that he wrote that he would be happy with almost any label (he also used "conversion experience" and "mystical experience"). We have used the term "spiritual experience" due to the recommendations of scholars and from our data showing that this is the most commonly endorsed term. "Mystical experience," used by psychologist Ralph Hood, is also becoming common again, especially in academic settings related to psychedelic research, such as by Roland Griffiths's group at Johns Hopkins (Griffiths et al., 2006; Hood, 1975). Some have proposed a combination of terms for scholarly settings: religious, spiritual, and mystical experiences (RSMEs), but the problem with each of these terms is that they contain clear metaphysical assumptions about supernaturalism.

Some researchers have instead used terms that emphasize the self-loss that is sometimes observed in these states in order to avoid these metaphysical issues and implications. Psychologist Mark Leary coined "hypoegoic states" (Leary & Guadagno, 2011), and psychedelic researcher Robin Carhart-Harris used "ego dissolution" (Nour et al., 2016). We have used the term "self-transcendent experiences" as an umbrella term (Yaden et al., 2017). But, as we have seen, self-loss does not accompany all spiritual experiences and appears not to be the key mediator of their benefits. Therefore, this self-loss–based approach may be a too limited label.

Still other researchers have drawn from the literature on psychopathology and the *DSM*. Dissociative, manic, or psychotic states bear some similarities to spiritual experiences insofar as they are altered states of consciousness that can sometimes have religious or spiritual content. However, as we have seen, psychopathology is defined in terms of negative outcomes, and spiritual experiences do not usually involve impairment in functioning. A few researchers have acknowledged this problem of outcome by retrofitting the word "positive." For example, some use terms such as "positive depersonalization" (Grob et al., 2011). A similar problem arises with purely positive labels, such as "ecstatic" experience or even Maslow's (1964) "peak experiences." The problem with both psychopathological and positive labels is that they involve a degree of circular reasoning insofar as experiences are categorized according to how they are also evaluated; this practice makes the outcomes from such experiences a foregone conclusion.

While these considerations may seem like a return to the semantic issues that we addressed in previous chapters, they are increasingly important to confront for the field. We have argued that we might borrow from contemporary emotion research in order to provide an updated theoretical model for understanding spiritual experience. We proposed that we can imagine some set of underlying dimensions that change during substantially altered states of consciousness (e.g., time, space, self, mind perception, valence, intensity), and particular experiences or categories of experiences can then be plotted onto this n-dimensional space. This allows us to acknowledge the influence of changing cultural labels as well as consistent subjective features that tend to occur across cultures.

However, we acknowledge that a return to the term "altered states of consciousness" is a little disappointing as well. After all, everything alters consciousness to some extent (even a cup of tea due to the caffeine), so it becomes difficult to say when an experience passes into an altered state of consciousness. Despite proposing a more minimal conceptualization of spiritual experience that may be more scientifically useful, that is not to say that we imagine or expect that people begin using terms like this to describe their experiences. Indeed, terms like spiritual experience or self-transcendent experience are often the only way most people know how to refer to these moments. As with the title of one of the our (A. B. N.'s) previous books, *Why God Won't Go Away*, we don't expect to see labels like spiritual experience going away anytime soon for most people.

Of Ultimate Concern

Spiritual experiences are, for some people, the most important moments in their life. For such people, spiritual experiences are what theologian Paul Tillich called an issue of "ultimate concern" (1965). From an existential perspective, these experiences can sometimes even seem to justify life itself for those who have them.

Recall that Dostoevsky said that he would be willing to trade *all* of the joys of his life for just a moment of spiritual experience (which occurred during his seizures). He also wrote of these moments: "During these five seconds I live a whole human existence, and for that I would give my whole life and not think that I was paying too dearly" (cited in Salzman, 2000, p. 120). Can we take him seriously? Is it possible that for some, these brief moments can make life as a whole worth living?

Of course, there are other considerations when weighing the relative importance of spiritual experience for one's life. In the novel *Lying Awake*, author Mark Salzman described a nun named Sister John who had spiritual experiences, like Dostoevsky, during her seizures. The protagonist takes great joy and comfort in these spiritual raptures. She described her experiences (what we might recognize as numinous experiences) in the following way:

> an invisible sun
> a shock wave of pure Being
> swept my pain away, swept everything away
> until all that was left was God (Salzman, 2000, p. 6)

When Sister John attempted to describe her experience to a neurologist, she was sure he would not understand. She told him: "I have the feeling of transcending my body completely. It's a wonderful experience, but it's spiritual, not physical (Salzman, 2000, p. 47). When the neurologist told her that these experiences are the result of a tumor growing in her temporal lobe and that she should have it removed for her health, she must decide whether to remove the tumor and lose her visions—or keep having spiritual experiences but jeopardize her health.

Ultimately, she decided to have the tumor removed. But her reason for doing so involved her community. She decided that because being able to serve her community was more important to her than her spiritual experiences, she would agree to the surgery. While Dostoevsky may have been willing to trade his entire life for such experiences, Sister John choose her health and her community.

The tension between these two perspectives often plays itself out in the integration of spiritual experiences. For some, spiritual experiences demand drastic action, becoming for a time the center of attention in one's life. In some cases, like we saw in Bill Wilson's and Marsha Linehan's stories, this can result in a miraculous return to healthy functioning. In other cases, like we saw in David Lukoff's story, this can result in the need for temporary hospitalization before a full return to health. In the case of the Buddha, it resulted in leaving his family and becoming a wandering religious teacher. As in all spiritual experiences, great or small, their value in any given case seems to inevitably lie in their effects on individuals and the people around them. Such considerations are an important part of integration.

Description and Application

When we began writing this book, we imagined it as a largely descriptive endeavor, in conscious contrast to the many current books in psychology that are presented as evidence-based self-help books. We hoped to articulate James's perspective and show its continued relevance, provide a number of personal accounts of spiritual experience, and then review relevant contemporary research in psychology and neuroscience. We did not imagine there would be much in the way of potential clinical applications of spiritual experiences, other than attempting to normalize the experiences that people are already having.

However, the emerging research on meditation practices and psychedelics has raised the stakes involved with the scientific study of spiritual experiences. It is remarkable that spiritual experiences are on the cusp of being applied en masse in psychiatry through the systematic use of psychedelics, the latter of which is a remarkable shift that occurred largely over the years that we wrote this book (Yaden, Yaden, & Griffiths). A transformation of modern psychiatry may be on the horizon specifically with regard to psychedelic-assisted psychotherapy. While there are undoubtedly challenges in applying these treatments, the tremendous suffering caused by mental illness demands that we follow where the data lead. It is hoped this shift, if it occurs, will bring the study of spiritual experiences, long relegated to the periphery of psychological research into the center of important and viable research subjects.

As psychedelics enter mainstream research and application in secular healthcare settings, metaphysically loaded, supernatural framings of the topic will likely become increasingly problematic. Indeed, in such healthcare settings we must inevitably strive to demystify the mystical and secularize the spiritual. While patients and study participants are always welcome to bring their own beliefs into such settings, clinicians and researchers must be vigilant in not pushing their own beliefs onto patients and study participants (Yaden, Yaden, & Griffiths, 2021). In much the same way, the massively popular programs of yoga and meditation have often been secularized in order to make them more applicable to people of any/all belief systems. At the same time, we must recognize and honor the personal beliefs and cultural perspectives that every individual brings to these experiences. We believe that a new clinical subfield will likely be required in order to work through the many complexities these experiences raise. Last, we think it is essential to maintain the utmost respect for every individual's unique process of interpretation and integration, as James would have no doubt advocated.

Conclusion

Going forward, we believe that for the sake of making progress in both scientifically understanding spiritual experiences and applying them clinically, we need to do three things that—in thoroughly Jamesian fashion—may initially seem somewhat contradictory.

First, we need to remember the many lessons that the last century or so of science and scholarship, from *The Varieties* onward, has taught us. We need to bring forward the best of these insights to future research and clinical work. We believe that methodological agnosticism is an essential prerequisite in scientific and clinical work on spiritual experiences. Additionally, we saw that in the intervening century after *The Varieties* was published, research emerged from a number of different fields. We need to acknowledge the role that a number of disciplines of science and scholarship will play in this research, including psychology, neuroscience (including neurotheology), religious studies, philosophy, pharmacology, and psychiatry. Consilience refers to the idea that evidence across different disciplines and levels of analysis, across the sciences and the humanities, can be synthesized in order to strengthen understanding. We will certainly need consilience in the study of spiritual experience.

Second, we need to boldly step beyond 20th-century paradigms to embrace a truly 21st-century scientific study of spiritual experience to emerge. We have seen the problems with terms that connote metaphysical assumptions as well as those that draw from definitionally pathological or positive perspectives. While acknowledging the different ways in which people describe their experiences, scientific and clinical approaches will likely need to rely on a clearer conceptualization based on altered states of consciousness combined with a variety of descriptors of subjective qualities.

Last, we must retain a sense of epistemic humility regarding spiritual experiences. While we can explain parts of spiritual experiences—especially regarding some of their causes, correlates, and consequences—it may be impossible to ever fully explain them. These experiences touch on life's biggest mysteries, our most heartfelt feelings, and our most profound sense of reality itself.

James wrote that almost nothing can be explained *completely*. As we have seen, spiritual experiences intersect with beliefs regarding the existence of God, supernaturalism, and about the nature of consciousness. Despite incredible success in elucidating the physical world, science may not be able to fully adjudicate the metaphysical and epistemic issues surrounding spiritual experience—at least at present, and possibly not ever. We expect to see tremendous strides in our scientific understanding of spiritual experience in the next century, but we must acknowledge the limits on what we can claim to know. James used a phrase to describe the inevitable incompleteness of our scientific knowledge in general, writing "'Ever not quite!' . . . There is no complete generalization, no total point of view, no all-pervasive unity, but everywhere some residual resistance to verbalization, formulation, and discursification, some genius of reality that escapes from the pressure of the logical finger, that says 'hands off,' and claims its privacy, and means to be left to its own life." (James, 1909, p. 776). While we encourage on-going and future scientific and scholarly efforts to understand spiritual experience, we conclude by giving James the last word on the prospects for a *complete* scientific explanation of spiritual experience:

Ever not quite!

References

Griffiths, R. R., Richards, W. A., McCann, U., & Jesse, R. (2006). Psilocybin can occasion mystical-type experiences having substantial and sustained personal meaning and spiritual significance. *Psychopharmacology, 187*(3), 268–283.

Grob, C. S., Danforth, A. L., Chopra, G. S., Hagerty, M., McKay, C. R., Halberstadt, A. L., & Greer, G. R. (2011). Pilot study of psilocybin treatment for anxiety in patients with advanced-stage cancer. *Archives of General Psychiatry, 68*(1), 71–78.

Hood, R. W., Jr. (1975). The construction and preliminary validation of a measure of reported mystical experience. *Journal for the Scientific Study of Religion, 14*(1), 29–41.

James, W. (1909). *A pluralistic mystic*. Hibbert Journal, 8, p. 739-759.

James, W. (1910). A pluralistic mystic. *Hibbert Journal, 8,* 739–759.

James, W. (1902/2009). *The varieties of religious experience: A study in human nature. eBooks@Adelaide.* https://csrs.nd.edu/assets/59930/williams_1902.pdf

Lamb, S. D. (2014). *Pathologist of the mind: Adolf Meyer and the origins of American psychiatry*. JHU Press.

Leary, M. R., & Guadagno, J. (2011). The role of hypo-egoic selfprocesses in optimal functioning and subjective well-being. In K. M. Sheldon, T. B. Kashdan, & M. F. Steger (Eds.), *Designing positive psychology: Taking stock and moving forward* (pp. 135–146). Oxford University Press.

Maslow, A. H. (1964). *Religions, values, and peak-experiences* (Vol. 35). Ohio State University Press.

Newberg, A. B. (2010). *Principles of neurotheology*. Ashgate.

Nour, M. M., Evans, L., Nutt, D., & Carhart-Harris, R. L. (2016). Ego-dissolution and psychedelics: validation of the ego-dissolution inventory (EDI). *Frontiers in Human Neuroscience, 10*, 269.

Paloutzian, R. F., & Park, C. L. (Eds.). (2014). *Handbook of the psychology of religion and spirituality*. Guilford Press.

Perry, R. B. (1935). *The Thought and Character of William James*. Boston: Little, Brown & Co.

Perry, R. B. (1948). *The thought and character of William James*. Briefer version.

Richardson, R. D. (2007). *William James: In the maelstrom of American modernism*. HMH.

Salzman, M. (2000). *Lying awake*. Knopf.

Tillich, P. (1965). *Ultimate concern*. Harper & Row.

Yaden, D. B., & Anderson, D. E. (2021). The psychology of philosophy: Associating philosophical views with psychological traits in professional philosophers. *Philosophical Psychology, 34*(5), 721–755.

Yaden, D. B., Haidt, J., Hood, R. W., Jr., Vago, D. R., & Newberg, A. B. (2017). The varieties of self-transcendent experience. *Review of General Psychology, 21*(2), 143–160.

Yaden, D. B., Yaden, M. E., & Griffiths, R. R. (2021). Psychedelics in psychiatry—keeping the renaissance from going off the rails. *JAMA Psychiatry, 78*(5), 469–470.

Index

peripheral nervous system, 80
Perry, Richard, 29
Persinger, Michael, 114–15
personality
    changes in, 335–36
    stability of, James on, 335–36
personality psychology, 97
personality research, 64
personality traits
    Big 5, 97–98
    not related to spiritual experiences, 98
    and spiritual experiences, 97–98
personality types, and spiritual
        experiences, 96–115
peyote, 347, 348–49
phenomenologically sensitive analysis, 8
phenomenology, 8, 390
philosophers
    atheism among, 323
    spiritual experiences of, and
        beliefs, 324–25
    types (psychological traits) of, James on,
        324, 324t
philosophically sensible analysis, 8–9
philosophy
    James's influence on, 390
    James's study of, 15, 23
    and psychology, interactions of, 14
    psychology of, 323–25
    religious, James on, 33–34
    sublime and, 257, 258t
PhilPapers Survey, 323
photisms, 193–94
physiology, 9
    German work on, 20–21
    James's study of, 32, 37, 73
    and psychology, research on,
        Starbuck on, 36
    of spiritual experiences, James
        on, 73–75
    and subjective experience, James on, 25
pineal gland, 381
Pinker, Steven
    The Better Angels of Our Nature: Why
        Violence Has Declined, 107
    on James, 6
Piper, Ms., 271, 273–74
Planck, Max, 215

Plato, 37
Pollan, Michael, 383–84
    How to Change Your Mind, 114, 231–
        32, 256
    on psychedelic experience, 365
Poppy, Carrie, 281–82
positron emission tomography (PET),
        87, 88–89
Power Through Repose (Call), 28
practices, 45–46. See also meditation;
        prayer; spiritual practices
    and spiritual experiences, 109–12
pragmatism, 8–9, 121–25, 313–14,
        390, 392–93
    founders of, 121–22
    Goldstein on, 315–17
    overbeliefs and, 311–12
    psychiatry and, 129
Pragmatism: A New Name for Some Old
        Ways of Thinking (James), 121, 324
PRAISE-Be acronym, 45–46
prayer
    brain activity during, 110, 360
    centering, effects on brain, 180–81, 181f
    contemplative, 109, 110
    conversational, 110
    effects on nervous system, 80–81, 83
    intercessory, 275
    liturgical, 109
    material, 110
    medical side effects of, 364
    and meditation, comparison of, 111
    neuroimaging during, 88
    and paranormal experiences, 276
    petitionary, 110
    practices, 109–10
    prevalence of, 109
    psychedelics and, 353
    and spiritual experiences, 112
    therapeutic applications, 360
precognition, 274, 276
prefrontal cortex, in centering
        prayer, 180–81
prefrontal lobe, in creative thinking, 204–5
Principles of Psychology, The (James), 14–
        15, 24, 26, 377
problem of other minds, 385–86
projection fallacy, 316–17

psychometrics, 63–64. *See also* Starbuck,
	Edwin; survey(s), of spiritual
	experiences
	contemporary, in study of spiritual
		experiences, 66–69
psychopathology, 396. *See also* mental
	illness
	apophenia and, 214
	spiritual experiences and, 123–25
	spiritual experiences associated with,
		James on, 131, 166
psychopathy, and mind perception, 175–
	76, 176*f*
psychopharmacology, 112–14
psychosis/psychotic disorders, 129–30
	apophenia in, 215
	and depression, 216–17
	neuroscience of, 219–20
	and religious delusions or
		hallucinations, 123, 172
	and religious preoccupation, 123–24
psychotherapy, combined with
		psychedelics, 356
psychotic communication
		breakdown, 219–20
Puffer, Ethel D., 250–51
	The Psychology of Beauty, 251
purity, of saints, 331

quantum change, 335
	insightful type, 335
	mystical type, 335

raclopride, 88–89
Ramsey, Frank, 313
randomness, meaning in, 213–16
rationality, James and, 24–25
reality
	beyond appearances, spiritual
		experiences and, 146–47
	of spiritual experiences, James
		on, 292–94
	unseen, James's concept of, 40, 146–47
realness, feelings of, during an experience
	and in hindsight, 295, 296, 296*f*
Red Book, The (Jung), 56
relaxation response, 80
Relaxation Response, The (Benson), 28

relaxation techniques
	James's interest in, 26–27, 28
	and spiritual experiences, 168
religion. *See also* science of religion(s)
	belief-based definition of, James's, 40
	definition of, 41–43, 44–47
	Durkheim on, 38–39
	Henry James Sr.'s interest in, 16, 23
	institutional versus personal, James
		on, 39–40
	James's definition of, 38–41, 146–
		47, 299
	and moral motivation, James on, 126
	as multidimensional construct, 44–47
	psychological study of, Starbuck on, 36
	relationship-based definition of,
		James's, 40–41
	Schleiermacher on, 38–39
	spiritual experiences as source
		of, 339–40
	spirituality and, 41–44
	substantive definition of, 44
	Tillich on, 38–39
	William James's interest in, 23, 33, 34
Religion, Values, and Peak Experiences
		(Maslow), 58
Religion for Atheists (de Botton), 46–47
religiosity
	measurement of, 43–44
	and spiritual experiences, 101–2
religious aestheticism, 259–60
*Religious and Spiritual Issues in Psychiatric
		Diagnosis*, 172
religious experience (term), 396
religious experience(s), 3–4. *See also*
		spiritual experience
	and beliefs, reciprocal relationship of, 38
	versus beliefs, 33–34
	definition of, 7
	of Henry James Sr., 17–18
	James's hope for future work on, 6–7, 9
	James's selective attention to, 38
	and paranormal experiences, 276
	as preferred term, 41, 42*f*
Religious Experience Research Center, 67
religious figures, and possible neurological
		diagnoses, 73, 76, 77*t*
religious or spiritual problem, 129–30, 185